LEOPOLD
MUSEUM

EGON SCHIELE

Masterpieces from the Leopold Museum

Verlag der Buchhandlung Walther König

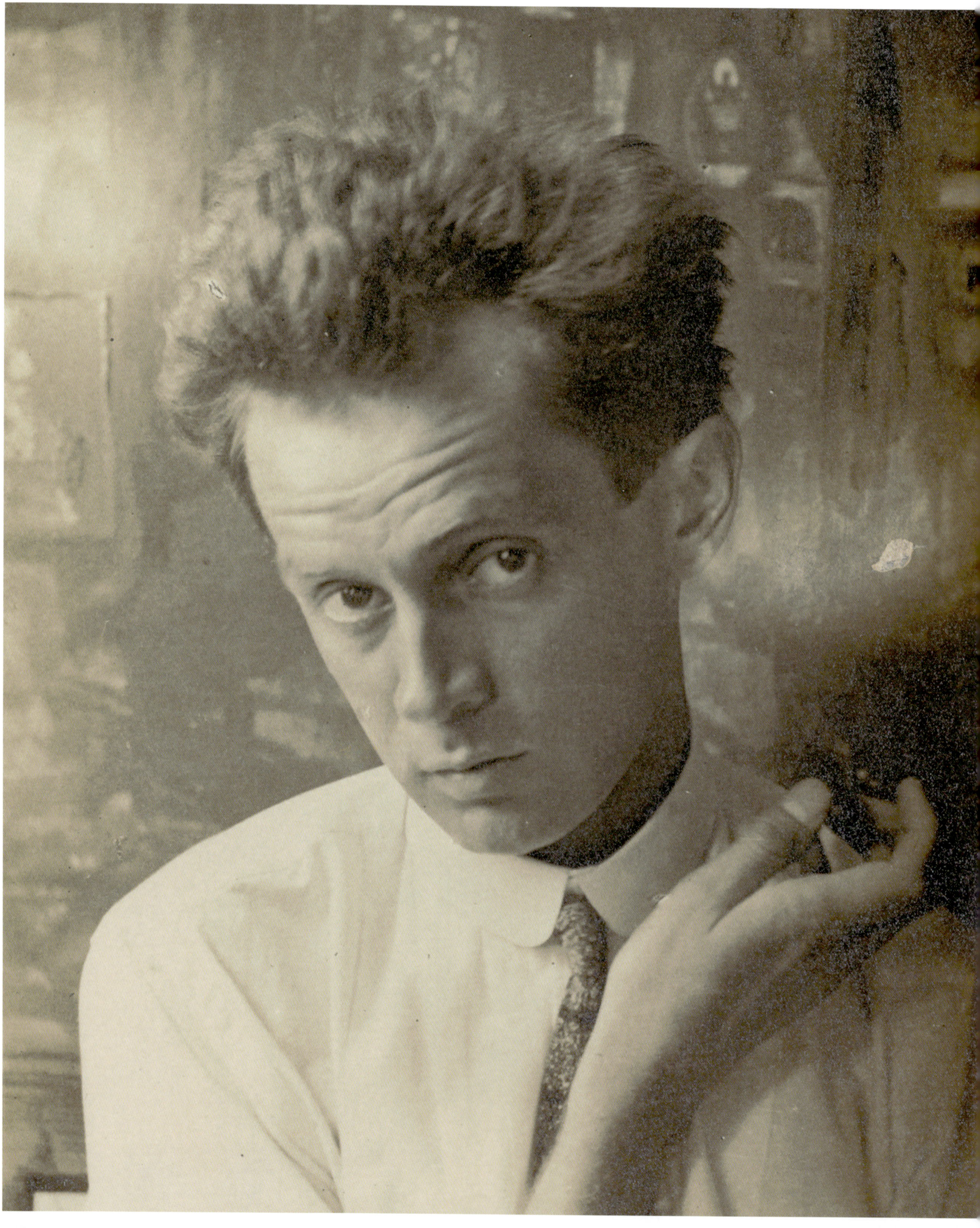

PROLOGUE

Hans-Peter Wipplinger

The Leopold Museum houses the largest and most eminent collection of works by the artist Egon Schiele (1890–1918), comprising 42 paintings, 184 drawings, gouaches and graphic works, 66 autographs and nine photographs. Nowhere else can the development of this ground-breaking artist of the early 20th century be traced through such a multifaceted selection of works, which includes examples of his earliest creations, of his world-renowned Expressionist period, and of his late oeuvre created shortly before Schiele's untimely death.

With Egon Schiele as the collection's figurehead, the Leopold Museum has established itself as a leading institution for Austrian art of the second half of the 19th and the early 20th century. Masterpieces by numerous exponents of this period of *Vienna around 1900* provide visitors with an art historical frame of reference. These include works by Gustav Klimt, Oskar Kokoschka, Koloman Moser, Richard Gerstl, Alfred Kubin, Herbert Boeckl, Anton Kolig and Albin Egger-Lienz.

The collection further comprises eminent arts-and-crafts objects as well as items of fin-de-siècle (furniture) design, including valuable creations executed by the *Wiener Werkstätte* surrounding Josef Hoffmann and Koloman Moser. The 19th century, meanwhile, is amply represented with important works by Friedrich Gauermann, Ferdinand Georg Waldmüller, Emil Jakob Schindler and Anton Romako, to name but a few.

While the Leopold Museum, which opened in 2001, is a relatively young institution, the success story of its collection, which is enjoyed each year by some 350,000 art enthusiasts from all over the world, dates back as far as the early 1950s, when Rudolf Leopold (1925–2010) discovered his passion for art.

The world of visual arts became an essential part of his life and an important pursuit for more than six decades. Spurred on by his unbridled enthusiasm, he went on to become one of the most internationally renowned art collectors. Rudolf Leopold, who earned his doctorate in medicine from Vienna University in 1953, attended art history classes alongside his main studies and started collecting art during this time. Even back then, his focus was on works by Egon Schiele, who at the time had largely faded into obscurity and was perceived merely as a national art phenomenon.

Owing to his fascination with Egon Schiele, Rudolf Leopold embarked on a road of the artist's rediscovery – something which seems hardly imaginable nowadays considering Schiele's current status on the art market. The highly gifted collector Leopold was interested neither in fashions nor in trends, but concentrated only on individual, eminent works by artists who mesmerized him – above all Egon Schiele. Thus, the joy of seeking out and discovering unknown or forgotten works was a characteristic, or indeed a criterium, of the collector Rudolf Leopold. While the library he bequeathed to the Egon Schiele Documentation Center at the Leopold Museum is testament to his in-depth study of art literature, he believed that it was only possible to develop the necessary feeling for the quality of an artwork through its critical and comprehensive contemplation. Rudolf Leopold's subtle interpretations of individual works by Schiele, which can be found in the present publication, illustrate an intimate dialogue with and understanding of "his" artworks.

Acknowledging the lifetime achievements of this art enthusiast, we must mention his commitment to initiating and organizing numerous exhibitions in Austria and abroad that helped Egon Schiele's oeuvre win international recognition. Already in 1955 Rudolf Leopold compiled a selection of works by Schiele for a presentation of Austrian Modernism at the Stedelijk Museum in Amsterdam, which earned the artist his

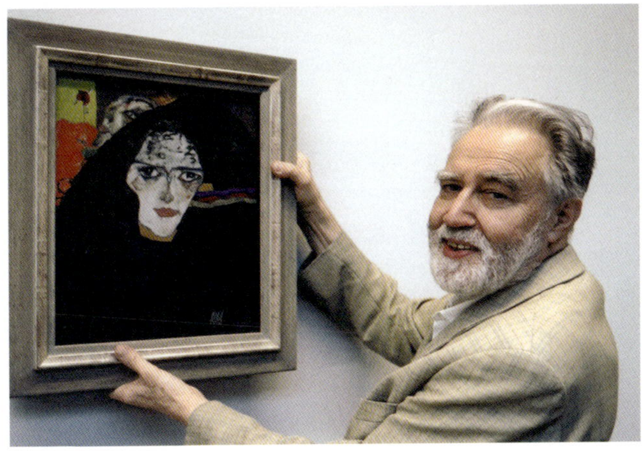

Rudolf Leopold | 2001

first international success after his death. Further important exhibitions of Schiele works from Rudolf Leopold's collection took place in London (1964), in New York (1965) together with works by Klimt, in Munich (1975), Japan (1979), Venice (1984), and as part of the legendary Viennese presentation *Dream and Reality* (1985). The series of exhibitions entitled *Schiele and His Time*, which shone the spotlight on Egon Schiele's oeuvre and its context and were shown from 1988 in Zurich, Munich, Wuppertal and London, reflected the seriousness and interests of the eminent collector Rudolf Leopold. Additional Schiele presentations took place in Tübingen, Düsseldorf, Hamburg, Tokyo, Oslo, Rome, Athens, Paris, Barcelona, as well as at the Museum of Modern Art in New York. Rudolf Leopold's comprehensive Schiele monograph published in 1972 with the Salzburg publishing house Residenz as well as with Phaidon publishers in London, which includes a catalogue raisonné of the artist's paintings, is considered a milestone in Schiele research and continues to represent an important reference work today.

The formation of this collection, which grew in size and importance in Leopold's home until it reached universal significance and garnered public interest through international exhibitions and accompanying publications – culminating in a foundation set up in 1994 with the intention of keeping the collection intact – is simply exceptional. The collectors Rudolf and Elisabeth Leopold generously transferred their collection comprising some 6,000 exhibits into a non-profit private foundation together with the Republic of Austria and the Austrian National Bank which, in turn, undertook to build a museum to house the collection and to help finance the institution. The museum building, planned and executed by the architects (Laurids) Ortner & (Manfred) Ortner, was erected in the Vienna MuseumsQuartier, where it has provided a suitable framework for the collection both in functional and aesthetic terms ever since. This alliance of the civic commitment shown by Rudolf and Elisabeth Leopold and the visionary conduct of cultural-political decision makers acting as advocates on behalf of the public, made it possible for this outstanding collection to be secured for Austria.

The success story of the Vienna Leopold Museum continues. Alongside its primary function of preserving its internationally unique collection and of making this cultural heritage accessible to the public through museum presentations, the Leopold Museum constitutes not only a lively hub and art venue but also acts as an important education, mediation and research center. Indispensable to today's Viennese art scene, the Leopold Museum contributes significantly to the cultural identity of this city, which radiates across the globe.

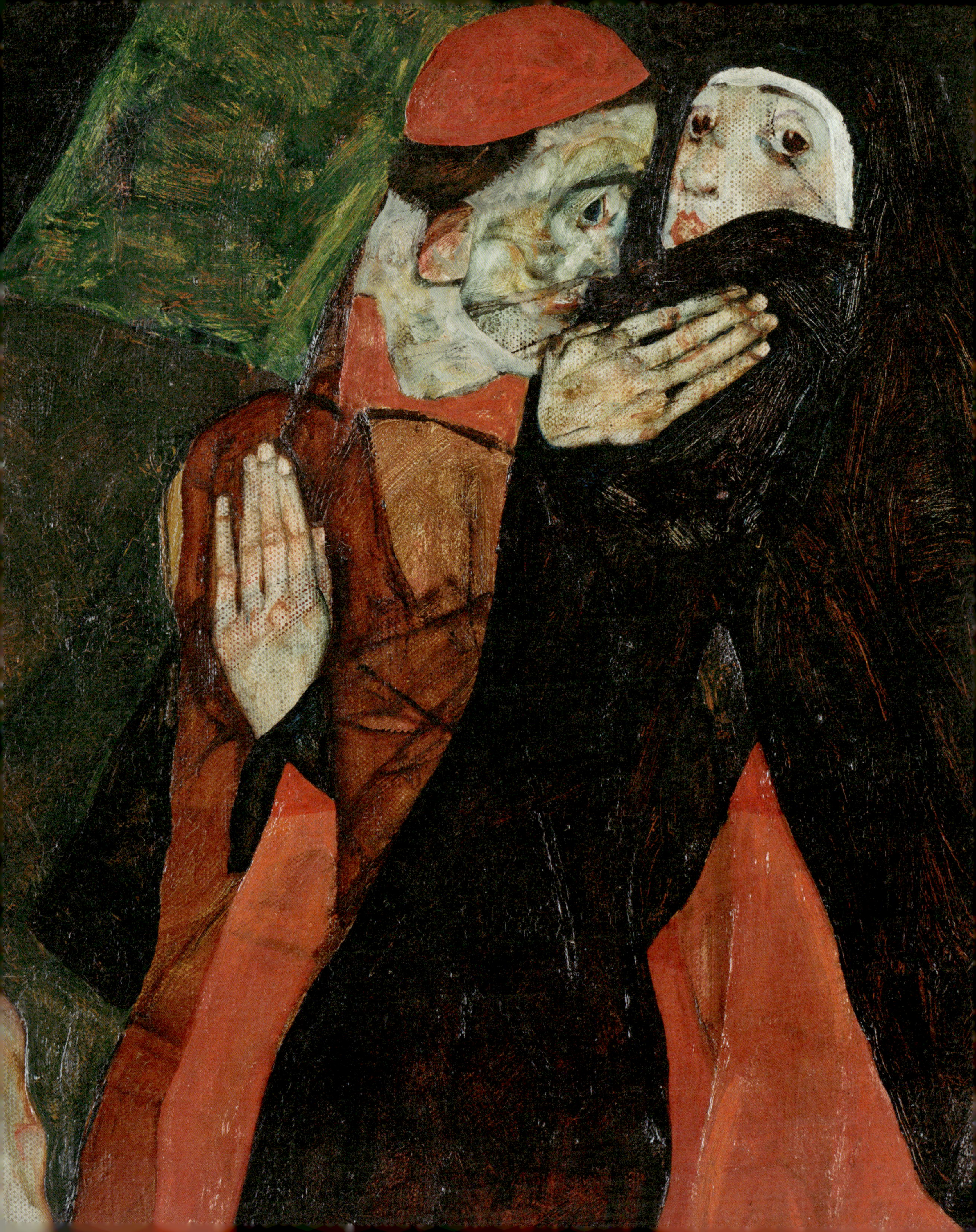

A SKETCH OF THE ERA

Elisabeth Leopold

*Art cannot be modern;
art is eternal.*

Egon Schiele, who was born in 1890, grew up in a time of radical upheaval, in an era of decline and renewal. He began drawing at an early age. The drawings that have survived primarily depict trains that the child saw at the station in Tulln, a small city on the Danube near Vienna, where his father was the stationmaster. Later, in Klosterneuburg, he painted houses and landscapes; from the window of his school there he had a good view of parts of the city. At age 16 he passed the entrance examination at the Vienna Academy of Fine Arts. From this time onward, and after a few short years of seeking and discovering his own identity, Vienna would be the backdrop against which the young and highly talented Schiele developed into one of the greatest artists of the 20th century.

Otto Breicha chose the words *Finale und Auftakt* [Finale and Prelude] for his book on Vienna between 1898 and 1914. One cannot find more fitting words to describe this era. In the second half of the 19th century the city had risen to become the opulent and luxurious metropolis of the great Austro-Hungarian Empire. The palaces of the Ringstrasse were erected, and life in Vienna was dominated by operas, operettas and the intoxicating waltzes of Johann Strauss. In the visual arts the celebrated painter Hans Makart (1840–1884) reigned unchallenged with his pompous oversized historicist canvases. Yet the grandiose culture of the monarchy was overshadowed by a silent foreboding of things coming to an end, as its exuberant *joie de vivre* gradually gave way to the melancholy of approaching decline. Nowhere was the dramatic last flourishing of this epoch as palpable as in Vienna, the sprawling capital of the vast Hapsburg Empire.

It was against this complex background of a vast multinational empire on the verge of collapse that the "prelude" of the new century occurred. It burst forth boldly with a flourishing of intellectual life and fantastic artistic creativity in all fields. A new style developed in the architecture of Otto Wagner (1841–1918), Josef Hoffmann (1870–1956) und Adolf Loos (1870–1933). The symphonies of Gustav Mahler seemed to herald a new spirit: as the director of the Court Opera, he conducted the operas of Richard Wagner in the stagings of Alfred Roller (1864–1935). Arnold Schoenberg was a radical reviver of composition, postulating that he had "broken through all of the boundaries of a bygone aesthetic". Anton von Webern and Alban Berg became his students. With his work entitled *The Interpretation of Dreams* published precisely at the turn of the century, the genius psychiatrist Sigmund Freud found a new path to the human unconscious. Around the same time, the Austrian artist Alfred Kubin (1877–1959) was creating his demonic images, which emanate from the realm of dream and fantasy. Ernst Mach was working toward his envisioned reorientation in human thinking. The highly controversial book *Sex and Character* by Otto Weininger exaggerated the differences in values to an extreme that can be likened to a declaration of war between the sexes. Literature was dominated by authors such as Arthur Schnitzler, Hugo von Hofmannsthal, Robert Musil and Karl Kraus. In Salzburg, the poet Georg Trakl's expressive verse combined imagery rich in beauty with premonitions of death. It seems as if the poet Georg Trakl and the artist Egon Schiele were kindred spirits: Schiele too incorporated the image of death into his artistic oeuvre.

In the visual arts, the first sign of artistic renewal was the founding of the Vienna Secession in 1897. In the ensuing years the Secession presented the European avant-garde in numerous exhibitions that introduced the art of the French Impressionists, Auguste Rodin (1840–1917), Vincent van Gogh (1853–1890), as well as Ferdinand Hodler (1853–1918) and the Belgian Symbolists to the Viennese public.

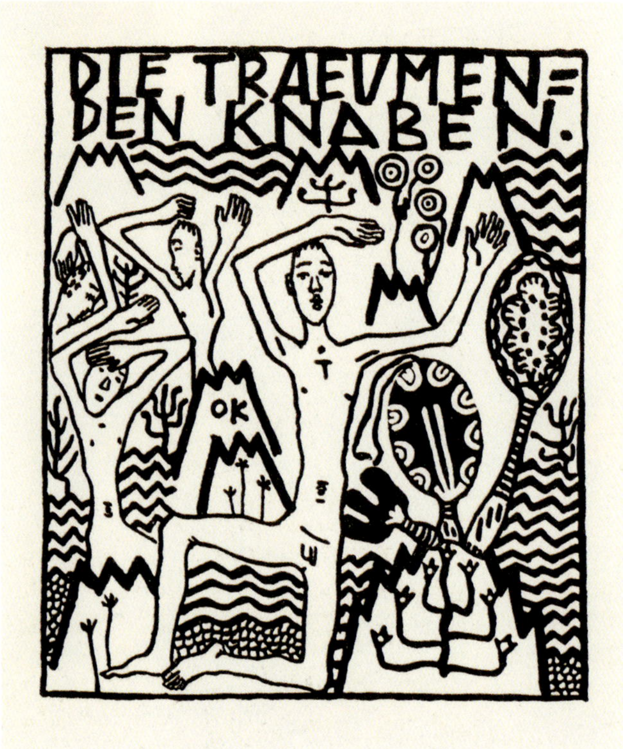

OSKAR KOKOSCHKA
Nude Boys in Island Landscape.
Title vignette for *The Dreaming Boys* | 1909
Leopold, Private Collection

In the Wiener Werkstätte, the artists Koloman Moser (1868–1918) and Josef Hoffmann worked with Fritz Waerndorfer toward their vision of a "Gesamtkunstwerk", or total work of art, bringing aesthetic design to everyday life.

Gustav Klimt (1862–1918), the first president of the Secession, had begun his career as a historicist painter in the Makart tradition and was now seeking new directions. His first dramatic steps toward Modernism were taken from 1894 with his *Faculty Paintings*[1] created for Vienna University. The pessimistic tenor, the grandiose composition and the allegorical interpretation profoundly shook public sensibilities, igniting a dispute that lasted for years. Another of his innovations was the linear approach taken in the *Beethoven Frieze*[2] (1901/02), an approach that would later be developed by the Expressionist artists.

Oskar Kokoschka (1886–1980) and Egon Schiele (1890–1918) numbered among the next generation of this artistic renewal and were the key exponents of Austrian Expressionism. Oskar Kokoschka began with the poetic fairytale *The Dreaming Boys*[3] and continued to develop his extreme view of the world in his flamboyant drama *Murderer, Hope of Women,* for which he also designed the poster[4]. Egon Schiele, who was Kokoschka's junior by four years, rose like a meteor on the firmament of the art world in 1910 and went on to create an inspired oeuvre over the course of relatively few years. He broke radically with old traditions, creating his very own brand of Expressionism in theme, composition and depth of expression. His initially provocative renderings were followed by painterly, sensitive canvases in which he sought to depict spiritual content through expressive, often surreal oneiric images. Throughout a varied career, Schiele maintained his excellent draftsmanship with his expressive curved line to the end. He died at the youthful age of 28.

1918 was not only the year of Egon Schiele's death, but also of the deaths of Gustav Klimt, Koloman Moser and Otto Wagner. The same year saw the end of World War I and thus the final collapse of the "Old World" with the Habsburg Empire dissolving into several states. A new era of economic decline and political unrest began. Art also embarked on new paths. After World War II the significance of the departures that marked the fin de siècle in Vienna began to be appreciated at last. It is thanks to the tireless efforts of Rudolf Leopold and the significance of his collection that the long underappreciated artist Egon Schiele has risen to be renowned around the world today.

1 | See Tobias G. Natter: "Catalogue of Paintings", in: idem (ed.): *Gustav Klimt. The Complete Paintings*, Cologne 2012, nos. 126, 127, 157.

2 | See Natter 2012 (see fn 1), no. 141.

3 | See Alfred Weidinger/Alice Strobl: *Oskar Kokoschka. Die Zeichnungen und Aquarelle 1897–1916*, Salzburg 2008, no. 192–199.

4 | See Weidinger/Strobl 2008 (see fn 3), no. 299.

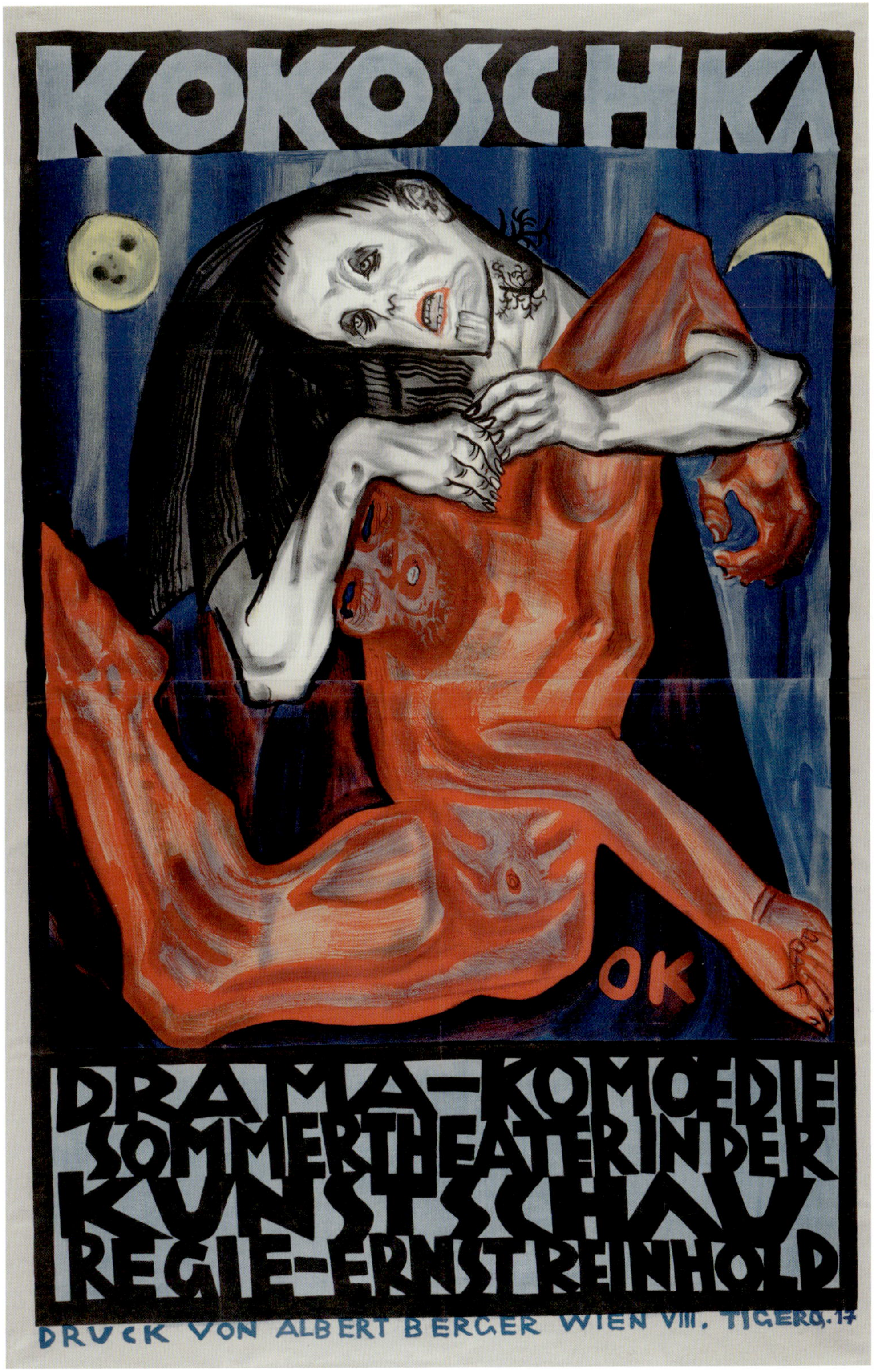

OSKAR KOKOSCHKA
Pietà. Poster for the play *Murderer, Hope of Women*
at the *Internationale Kunstschau* | 1909
Leopold Museum, Vienna, Inv. 2673

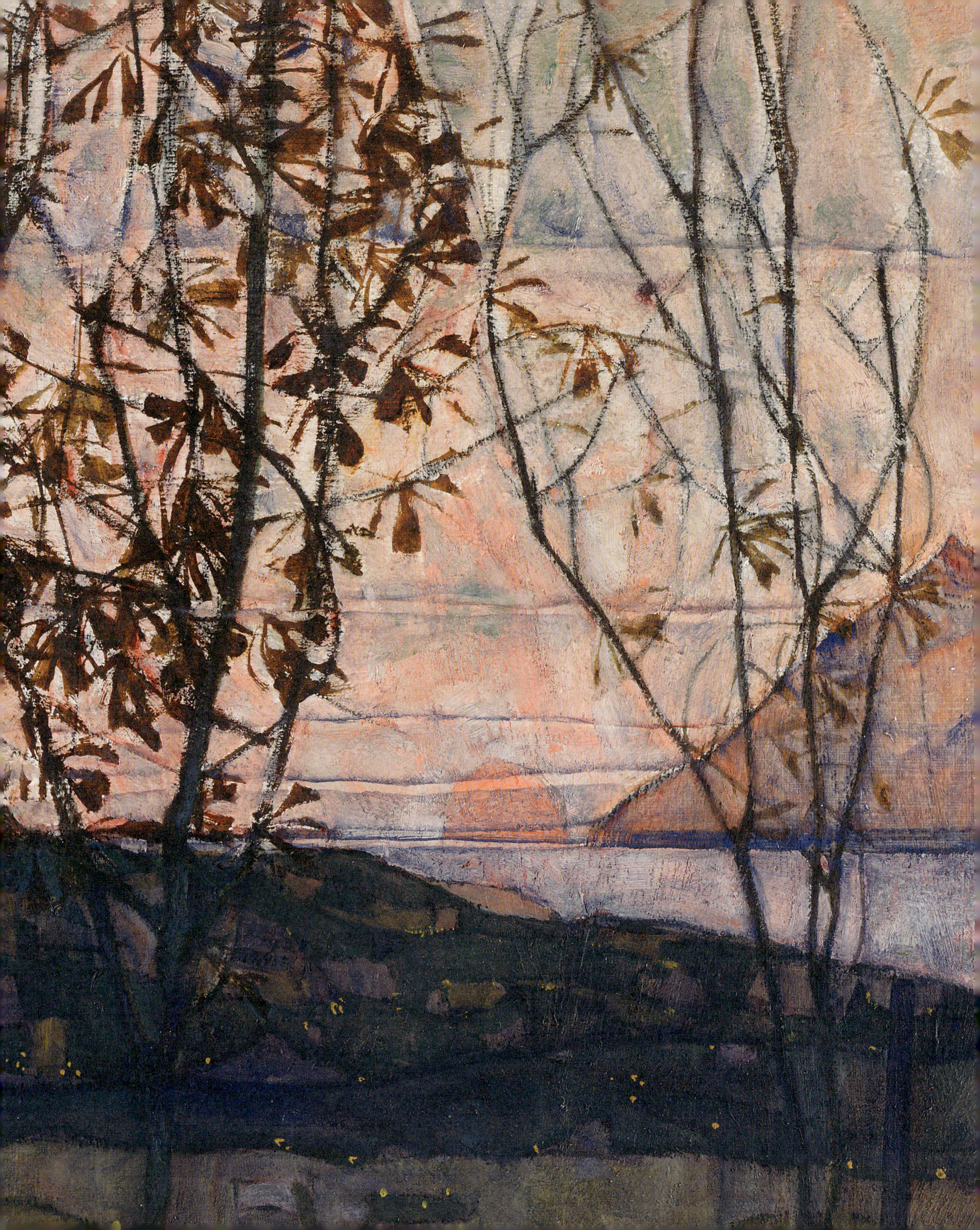

AN INTRODUCTION TO EGON SCHIELE'S WORK

Rudolf Leopold *

In time you will find it absolutely convincing, once you begin to look not simply at it but into it.

In addition to his work as an artist, the young Egon Schiele also produced a number of poems, most of which he then transformed into visual art, into carefully lettered graphic statements like the two reproduced here. The closing words of his poem *Fir Woods* (see p. 12) have an almost programmatic meaning for Schiele and his oeuvre: "Everything is living dead". To him death was a constant presence, part of being alive – like Eros. Schiele also wrote at this time of his "passion to experience all there is". And unquestionably he did experience – and *create* – with passion.

In the poem *A Self-Portrait* (see p. 13), conventional syntax has been almost wholly abandoned; the words and phrases are like molten fragments thrust up into consciousness under great pressure from below. Schiele was as much an Expressionist in his writing as in his art.[1]

In his work from 1910 Schiele managed to break free of the prevailing Viennese style and invent his own Expressionism – a term first applied to art only in 1911. But, in fact, Schiele explored such a wide variety of styles that he cannot properly be identified with any particular movement or school. In his remarks at the opening of the Schiele exhibition at the Albertina in 1990, Konrad Oberhuber rightly noted that it is no exaggeration to say that Schiele occupied a place as unique in the art of his time as that of Michelangelo in the Renaissance.

Though Schiele suffered from a lack of understanding of his art in Vienna especially in his early career, he was aware of his own importance from an equally early stage. In September 1911, he wrote to Dr. Oskar Reichel: "I have it in me to record [...] to want to explore, to invent, to discover, with all the means at my disposal, which already threaten to ignite and consume themselves [...] and to shed light on the darkest eternities of our little world [...] So I am constantly creating more, seemingly endless new works out of myself [...] I am so rich that I must give myself away".

At the beginning of that year, Schiele had sent Reichel a picture "from my very latest series"[2] – either *Deliriums*[3] or *Prophets (Double Self-Portrait)*[4] – one that then continued with *The Lyricist* (see p. 93), the *Self-Seer II (Death and Man)* (see p. 95), the *House and Wall in a Hilly Landscape* (see p. 101), and *Vision and Destiny (Self-Portrait)*[5]. In his letter accompanying the painting, he wrote to the Viennese collector: "In time you will find it absolutely convincing, once you begin to look not simply at it but into it. This is the picture about which G. Klimt remarked that he would be happy to have such visions. It is definitely, just now, the finest work painted in Vienna."[6]

From our own vantage point it is clear that Schiele was altogether correct in his high opinion of himself. There are only a few works by Gustav Klimt (1862–1918) from this time that can compare with his. In terms of genuine artistry – and that includes the conquest of new territory – his only serious competitors among the Viennese painters of the day were Klimt and Oskar Kokoschka (1886–1980), and at that time Kokoschka was living in Berlin.

Both Kokoschka and Schiele saw Gustav Klimt as the most important stylistic force in Viennese painting at the time. Yet it was certainly not only Klimt's art but also Klimt's personality that encouraged them to find their own artistic style. It is important to note that later even Klimt found inspiration in Schiele. The pose of Schiele's 1909 *Danae*[7] appears to have influenced his *Leda*[8] from 1917. In addition, Schiele's extremely sensitive *Autumn Tree in Stirred Air (Winter Tree)* (see p. 153), from 1912, clearly had an effect on Klimt's *Apple Tree II*[9], painted four years later. The monk-like bridegroom in Klimt's

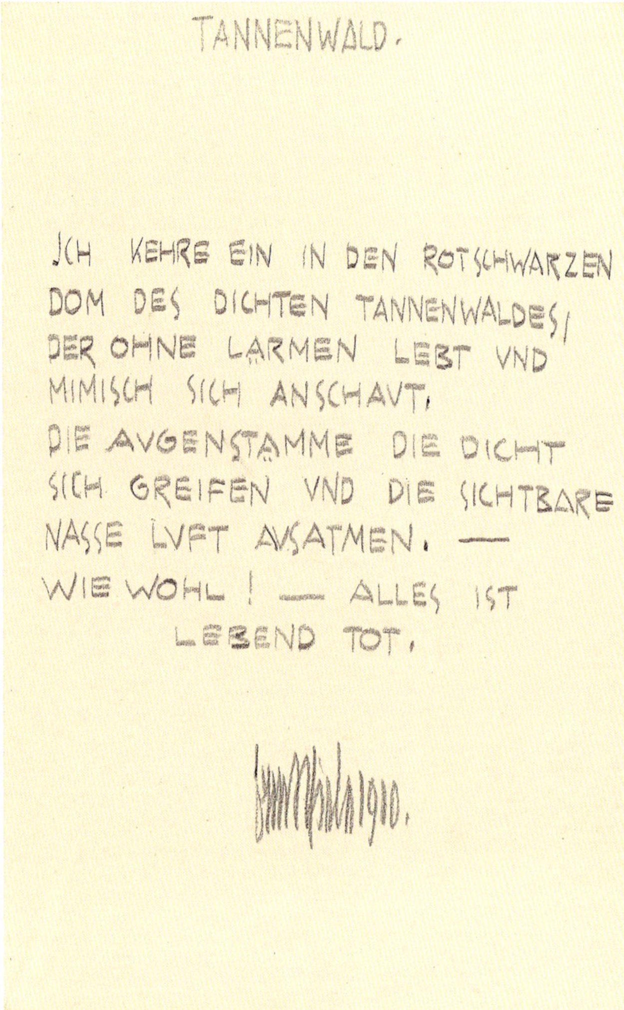

TANNENWALD.

ICH KEHRE EIN IN DEN ROTSCHWARZEN
DOM DES DICHTEN TANNENWALDES,
DER OHNE LARMEN LEBT VND
MIMISCH SICH ANSCHAVT,
DIE AVGENSTAMME DIE DICHT
SICH GREIFEN VND DIE SICHTBARE
NASSE LVFT AVSATMEN. —
WIE WOHL! — ALLES IST
LEBEND TOT.

EGON SCHIELE
Poem *Fir Woods* | 1910
Leopold, Private Collection

unfinished painting *The Bride*[10], from 1917/18, is essentially the figure of the dying monk, reversed, from Schiele's 1912 work *Agony*[11]. One has only to look at the combination of the one shoulder hunched, the other one dropped, and the angled head. Schiele had exploited such elements in his compositions from the beginning.

With this brief excursus on Klimt's indebtedness to Schiele, I certainly do not mean to detract from Schiele's far greater indebtedness to the older painter. In his search for his own style Schiele borrowed not only from Klimt but also from Kokoschka, who was four years his senior. Both Schiele and Kokoschka were inspired by the clean contours of Klimt's *Beethoven Frieze*[12]. Kokoschka was also fascinated by Mycenaean art, and in some instances incorporated direct borrowings from it in his work. It must also be noted that Kokoschka borrowed from Schiele; his nude studies of a Savoyard boy from 1912 have the decisive outlines typical of Schiele's nudes from 1910, and his *Self-Portrait with Brush*[13] and the preliminary drawing for it – both from 1914 – in which the head is shown in half profile with the eyes looking in the opposite direction, are obviously patterned after some of Schiele's compositions, notably his 1912 painting *Self-Portrait with Chinese Lantern Plant* (see p. 145). All in all, however, reciprocal borrowings between the two most important Austrian Expressionists were neither frequent nor of particular significance.

Like every great artist, Schiele was rooted in a definite tradition. He never denied his indebtedness to Viennese Secessionism in general or Klimt in particular, despite his commitment to "New Art." He nevertheless transformed everything he received from that tradition into something uniquely his own. Its importance in his early development seems insignificant compared to the contributions he himself made to the art of his time.

Like Klimt, he had a gift for creating compositions of such formal perfection that one cannot imagine them otherwise. But unlike the older painter, whose approach was primarily decorative, Schiele's works reveal a greater concern for structure. The differences between the two artists are apparent in other aspects as well. Whereas Klimt sought to create excitement in his images by combining unlike elements, juxtaposing abstract and ornamental "painted mosaics", for example, with highly realistic sections, Schiele achieved this with his carefully calculated arrangements alone. The intellectual content in Klimt's figural compositions is presented in greatly embellished ceremonial allegories and symbols, few of which strike us today as convincing and meaningful. Klimt's obstinate nature and love of sensual excess were simply inadequate for the representation of anything more profound or tragic. This is perfectly apparent if one compares his *Mother with Two Children (Family)*[14], painted in 1909/10, with Schiele's *Dead Mother I* (see p. 87), created in late 1910. Schiele was more successful at plumbing such depths because he identified with his subject matter.

Unprettified depictions of the darker side of human existence were naturally foreign to the highly decorative "Jugendstil", certainly to its Viennese variant. The Expressionists Kokoschka and Schiele were the first to incorporate the tragic and ugly into their work as a way of evoking stronger emotions; one might even say that they invented the use of ugliness as an element of pictorial composition and introduced its potential to the art of the 20th century. The images they created in their determination to express the depths of experience are as compelling and valid today as they were then. The current widespread interest in the two artists and frequently lavish praise accorded them are proof that our present-day tastes in art are in agreement with those of the Expressionist avant-garde of the early 20th century.

Only after careful study of his entire oeuvre and stylistic analysis of all of its essential details can one determine Schiele's place in the art of his time. In numerous ways he is very different from other Expressionists, such as those of the group known as *Brücke*. To appreciate his individuality and achievement it is necessary to see them in the light of Viennese painting and its chief representatives. He is radically different from the young Kokoschka, for example; his approach clearly emphasized structure, whereas Kokoschka's was more improvisational, more painterly. Kokoschka concentrated mainly on the portrait, whereas Schiele created any number of expressive landscapes whose artistic quality is in no way inferior to that of his figural compositions. And while Kokoschka was to develop in his painting a spectacular, almost Baroque flamboyance, Schiele in the depth of his being remained attuned to the Gothic, at once a dreamer and a realist.

There are a number of features common to both, of course, and these are what set Viennese Expressionism apart from similar movements elsewhere. In his early years, his most crucial period in this regard, Schiele, like Kokoschka, preferred unusual subjects, and he painted them in somber, subtly nuanced tones that have little to do with the often deliberately garish colors of the German Expressionists. The Expressionism of the two Viennese painters – and of those who followed in their footsteps – favored psychological penetration. Their revealing portraits and atmospheric landscapes reflect an intuitive, questioning dialogue with their chosen subject matter. The early Expressionists in Germany, by contrast, tended to favor violence and provocation, presenting them in highly exaggerated colors and crude contours (the large patches of color in the earliest works of the Brücke painters clearly reveal the influence of French Fauvism). Unlike the Brücke artists, Kokoschka and Schiele based their work on an art style whose leading masters were Gustav Klimt, Ferdinand Hodler (1853–1918), and Edvard Munch (1863–1944). (In his draftsmanship, Schiele was also influenced in many respects by Toulouse-Lautrec, 1864–1901.) The two were indebted to Klimt and Hodler in questions of form, but in their subject matter they borrowed from Munch. Schiele cannot but have been intrigued by the novel way in which Munch interpreted human drives without obtrusive symbolism and also addressed the dark side of life in his art, making loneliness, sorrow, despair and death dominating themes in his works. His own depictions of such subjects are nevertheless quite unlike those of the Norwegian master. The fact that Schiele was one generation younger than Munch is apparent especially in his unique concept of the erotic. In Schiele's works there is nothing reminiscent of Munch's battle of the sexes or the menace of his "demon woman."

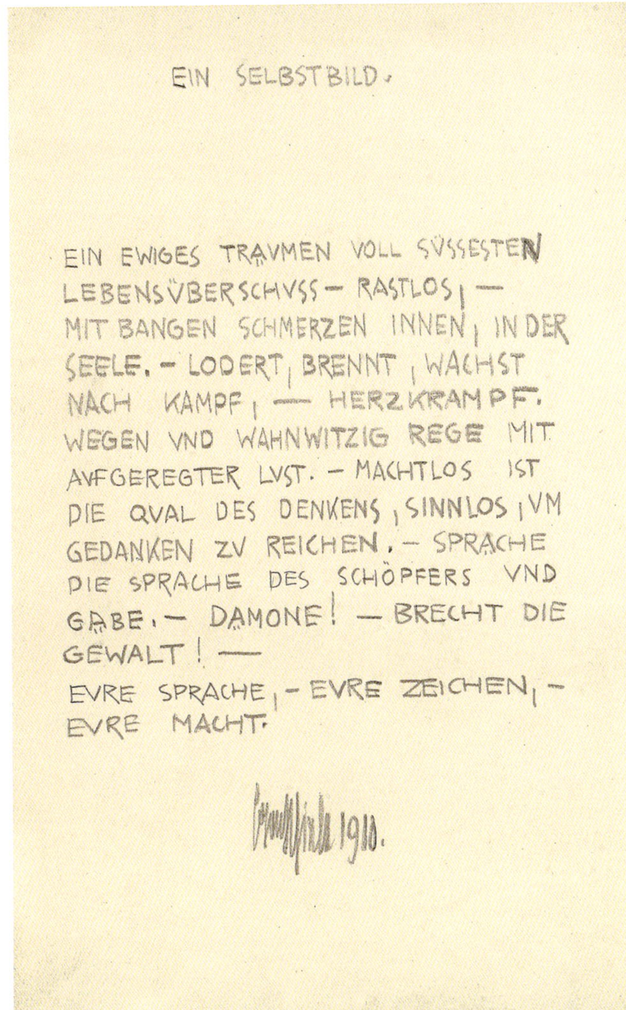

EIN SELBSTBILD.

EIN EWIGES TRAVMEN VOLL SVSSESTEN
LEBENSVBERSCHVSS — RASTLOS, —
MIT BANGEN SCHMERZEN INNEN, IN DER
SEELE. — LODERT, BRENNT, WACHST
NACH KAMPF, — HERZKRAMPF.
WEGEN VND WAHNWITZIG REGE MIT
AVFGEREGTER LVST. — MACHTLOS IST
DIE QVAL DES DENKENS, SINNLOS, VM
GEDANKEN ZV REICHEN. — SPRACHE
DIE SPRACHE DES SCHÖPFERS VND
GABE. — DAMONE! — BRECHT DIE
GEWALT! —
EVRE SPRACHE, — EVRE ZEICHEN, —
EVRE MACHT.

1910.

EGON SCHIELE
Poem *A Self-Portrait* | 1910
Leopold, Private Collection

The two artists were very different psychologically, of course, but they also lived in very different worlds. Turn-of-the-century Vienna in no way resembled the society that was portrayed by Henrik Ibsen and August Strindberg and that shaped Munch's thinking and emotional life to the end. The decadence that was Vienna in the years around 1900 and afterward was excitable and impulsive, sex-driven and obsessed with death. It was the time and place that brought forth Hugo von Hofmannsthal and Arthur Schnitzler, Otto Weininger and Sigmund Freud. In this Vienna at the turn-of-the-century, life was not simply a matter of flamboyant fashions and superficial pleasures. Despite all the aestheticism and tolerance – the latter considered a Viennese specialty – there was a yearning for fundamentals, for essential correlations, for a certain something hidden beneath the pretty surfaces and behind the imposing facades. The pompous self-confidence of the late 19th century in Vienna is overshadowed in art and in literature by the thought of its impending end. This is true in the work of Anton Romako (1832–1889), for example, which was later to be of importance for the young Kokoschka. Its dissolution into tragicomic meaninglessness, into an orgy of sinister decay and grotesque absurdity, is the subject of Alfred Kubin's (1877–1959) 1907 novel *The Other Side*, or of the *Tubutsch* story by Albert Ehrenstein, which Kokoschka would illustrate four years later. Life appeared to be a "sickness unto death". Revelation in the midst of decay and the fascination of the process of dying were subjects that also occupied Georg Trakl all his life; a study of the parallels between his poetry and the art of Schiele would be well worthwhile.

Very early in the work of the young Schiele, one comes to expect his rigorous rejection of the non-committal and superficial. Instead, one sees him struggling to express the deepest human emotions. His paintings speak of the torment of the loner, the distress of the seeker beset by visions, the pain and despair of the sick, and the sorrow of the hopeless. Schiele manages to elevate subjective emotion to the level of universal truth. For him autumn functions as a symbol of all that is fleeting in human existence. Even inanimate nature is filled with spirit. In his figural compositions, his landscapes with trees or houses, and even in his cityscapes, the actual forms are replaced by his own highly idiosyncratic perceptions of them; his moods and feelings are transformed into visionary symbols of human experience that speak directly to the receptive viewer. Schiele managed to grace even the most ordinary objects with new meaning. Expressionism was more concerned with actual human experience than any other artistic trend in our century – and of its proponents virtually no one was so obsessively focused on it as the young Schiele. For that reason he devoted as much attention to his own feelings as he did to his mission as an artist. He turned his own suffering into images of men with a calling, men who see what others do not, who create what others cannot.

Schiele was an Expressionist, but it is a mistake to let oneself get caught up in the confessional, animistic, visionary and ecstatic aspects of his work and in so doing to lose sight of his extreme preoccupation with form. It is also a mistake – one committed often enough – to dismiss Schiele's formal solutions as merely decorative. To be sure, his very earliest works reflect Jugendstil's preoccupation with superficial effects, but he soon succeeded in completely subordinating that interest to his own purposes. He did not cut himself off from his origins in Jugendstil as thoughtlessly as did others who arrived at Expressionism by way of similar paths. It is precisely his seamless transformation of Jugendstil – specifically its Viennese version – into Expressionism that makes Schiele so important in art history.

Otto Benesch, who learned to appreciate the artist's work at his father's knee, called Schiele one of the most gifted draftsmen of all time. And he was right: the first medium Schiele perfected, and the one in which he first demonstrated his artistry, even mastery, was a line distinctively his own. At the same time he developed an astonishing ability to emphasize with line what was important and ignore what was not. Few have managed to communicate so vividly not only forms but emotions with line alone – often only with outlines – as did Schiele. His superb draftsmanship alone sets him apart from other Expressionists. None of them commanded such subtlety of line: from incisive to caressing, from tensile to delicate, demure, nervous, scribbled, extended, interrupted or suddenly veering off in a new direction. His repertoire was so comprehensive that he might have done without color altogether and no one would have missed it.

Nevertheless, Schiele was also an important colorist, a painter who by no means simply filled in the spaces between his lines and exploited colors for their ability to evoke emotional responses. Their latter function was essential to him, to be sure, but it is also important to notice how Schiele used color to help give structure to his compositions. In his paintings and watercolors the drawing usually functions as a sensitive framework into which colors are introduced in such a way as to be of equal importance. It is the combination of the two that communicates such varied human emotions and states of mind. A brief ten years elapsed between Schiele's first public appearance, when he took part in an exhibition of local artists in the monastery at Klosterneuburg, and his triumph in the spring exhibition of the Vienna Secession in 1918, six months before his death – time enough for him to prove himself a pathbreaking master of Expressionism, and not only the Viennese permutation of that movement.

But those who interpret Schiele solely in terms of his importance for Expressionism – great as it is – fail to appreciate other features of this highly complex artist. In 1916, earlier than many of the other Expressionist pioneers, Schiele turned away from the programmatic concerns of that movement and adopted a new, much more realistic style, but one often suffused with mannerism. Early in 1918, however, he began to develop yet another approach in his paintings, one at first having more to do with form – in *The Family (Squatting Couple)*[15] and *Two Squatting Women* (see p. 275) – and only later with painting itself – in *Three Standing Women (fragment)* (see p. 279) and *Lovers III (Man and Woman II)*[16]. These compositions have virtually nothing to do with Expressionism. Their figures are more three-dimensional and are presented in a more painterly manner.

Five years after Pablo Picasso (1881–1973) and Georges Braque's (1882–1963) pioneering invention, Schiele introduced geometry into his work and began to think "cubistically", and even then his Cubism was very different from theirs. But with this new concern for the depiction of three-dimensional volumes in space he was years ahead of Picasso – even though his early death prevented him from completing a number of the paintings that prove it.

These references to his later development are not meant to detract from Schiele's stature as an Expressionist. On the contrary, I am convinced that, with the exception of this new breakthrough in his painting on the eve of his death, his greatest work was produced in the years between 1910 and 1915. Even then he resisted committing himself to a specific approach and thereby limiting his options. He was mercurial; one sees him deciding on one style one day and on another one the next, and this is what makes the study of his artistic development so fascinating. His art is anything but predictable; it is organic, open to all possibilities. His commitment was not to any particular group but to art itself. Hence the inscription on one of his watercolors: "Art cannot be modern; art is eternal"[17].

1 | Otto Breicha is probably correct in his insistence that with these poems Schiele, doubly gifted like Kokoschka, Gütersloh and Kubin, anticipated Expressionist writing in Austria (see *Finale und Auftakt,* written with Gerhard Fritsch, Salzburg, 1964).

2 | Letter card from Egon Schiele to Oskar Reichel, 31st January 1911 (postmark), private collection; Egon Schiele Autograph Database, ESAD, ID: 113.

3 | See Rudolf Leopold: *Egon Schiele. Gemälde, Aquarelle, Zeichnungen,* Salzburg 1972, no. 170; and Jane Kallir: *Egon Schiele. The Complete Works,* New York 1998, no. P.190.

4 | See Leopold 1972 (see fn 3), no. 171; and Kallir 1998 (see fn 3), no. P.191.

5 | See Leopold 1972 (see fn 3), no. 175; and Kallir 1998 (see fn 3), no. P.194.

6 | See fn 2.

7 | See Leopold 1972 (see fn 3), no. 130; and Kallir 1998 (see fn 3), no. P.148.

8 | See Tobias G. Natter: "Catalogue of Paintings", in: idem (ed.): *Gustav Klimt. The Complete Paintings,* Cologne 2012, no. 231.

9 | See Natter 2012 (see fn 8), no. 219.

10 | See Natter 2012 (see fn 8), no. 244.

11 | See Leopold 1972 (see fn 3), no. 218; and Kallir 1998 (see fn 3), no. P.230.

12 | See Natter 2012 (see fn 8), no. 141.

13 | See Johann Winkler/Katharina Erling: *Oskar Kokoschka. Die Gemälde 1906–1929,* Salzburg 1995, no. 112.

14 | See Natter 2012 (see fn 8), no. 188.

15 | See Leopold 1972 (see fn 3), no. 289; and Kallir 1998 (see fn 3), no. P.326.

16 | See Leopold 1972 (see fn 3), no. 299; and Kallir 1998 (see fn 3), no. P.329.

17 | See Kallir 1998 (see fn 3), no. D.1185.

* Rudolf Leopold (1925–2010) first published this essay in 1972; a previous version of it was published in 1995.

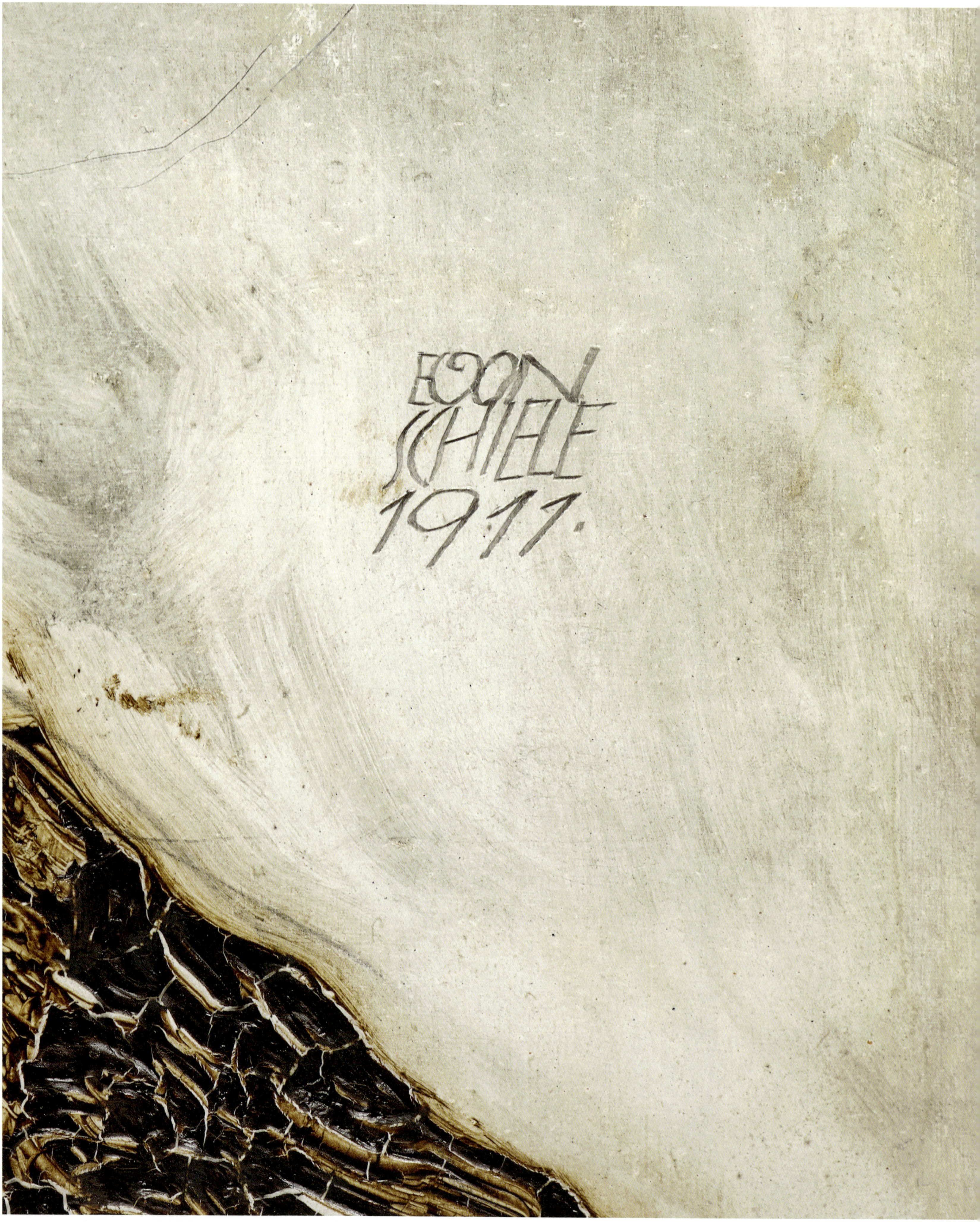
EGON
SCHIELE
1911.

PLATES AND CATALOGUE

Texts by Elisabeth Leopold, Rudolf Leopold, Franz Smola, Birgit Summerauer

ABBREVIATIONS

Titles in inverted commas are those that Egon Schiele himself gave his works. These titles are either inscribed on the front or reverse side of the works or mentioned in Schiele autographs.

L	Rudolf Leopold: *Egon Schiele. Gemälde, Aquarelle, Zeichnungen,* Salzburg 1972.
K	Jane Kallir: *Egon Schiele. The Complete Works,* New York 1998.
N	Tobias G. Natter (ed.): *Gustav Klimt. The Complete Paintings,* Cologne 2012.
ESAD	Egon Schiele Autograph Database. All autographs cited here can be accessed online at: http://www.egonschiele.at.
EL, RL, FS, BS	Initials of the authors Elisabeth Leopold, Rudolf Leopold, Franz Smola, Birgit Summerauer

1906

PORTRAIT OF A YOUNG GIRL

Family tradition has it that this is the portrait of a Bohemian servant girl.
The rendering of the head, especially, demonstrates how successful Schiele had become at academic drawing. (RL)

Black chalk, charcoal on paper
39.6 × 30.6 cm
Leopold Museum, Vienna, Inv. 1465
K D.11

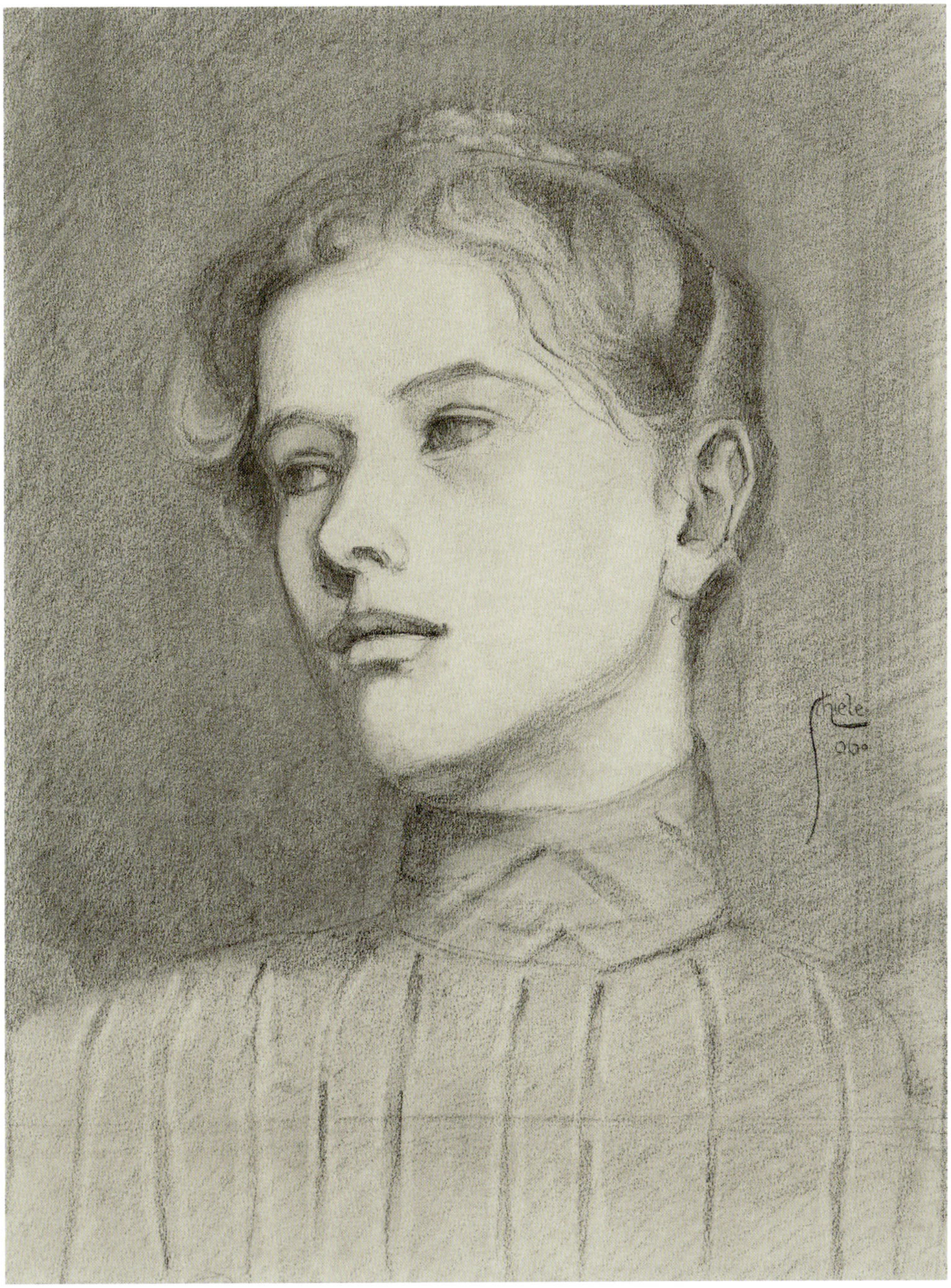

1907

PORTRAIT OF THE ARTIST'S MOTHER (MARIE SCHIELE) WITH FUR COLLAR

In this very finished work it is obvious that the 17-year-old artist has learned from the Vienna Secessionists. When presenting a figure from the side they always favored a strict profile view. Yet the young Schiele tried to soften the profile somewhat and add life to this portrait of his mother through the fur collar of the jacket, the area above the upper lip, the forehead with eyebrows, and by having his subject look to the side. The placement of this portrait on the page is already masterful. (RL)

Pencil, watercolor, gouache, opaque white on paper
32.1 × 22.5 cm
Leopold Museum, Vienna, Inv. 2309
L 28; K P.10

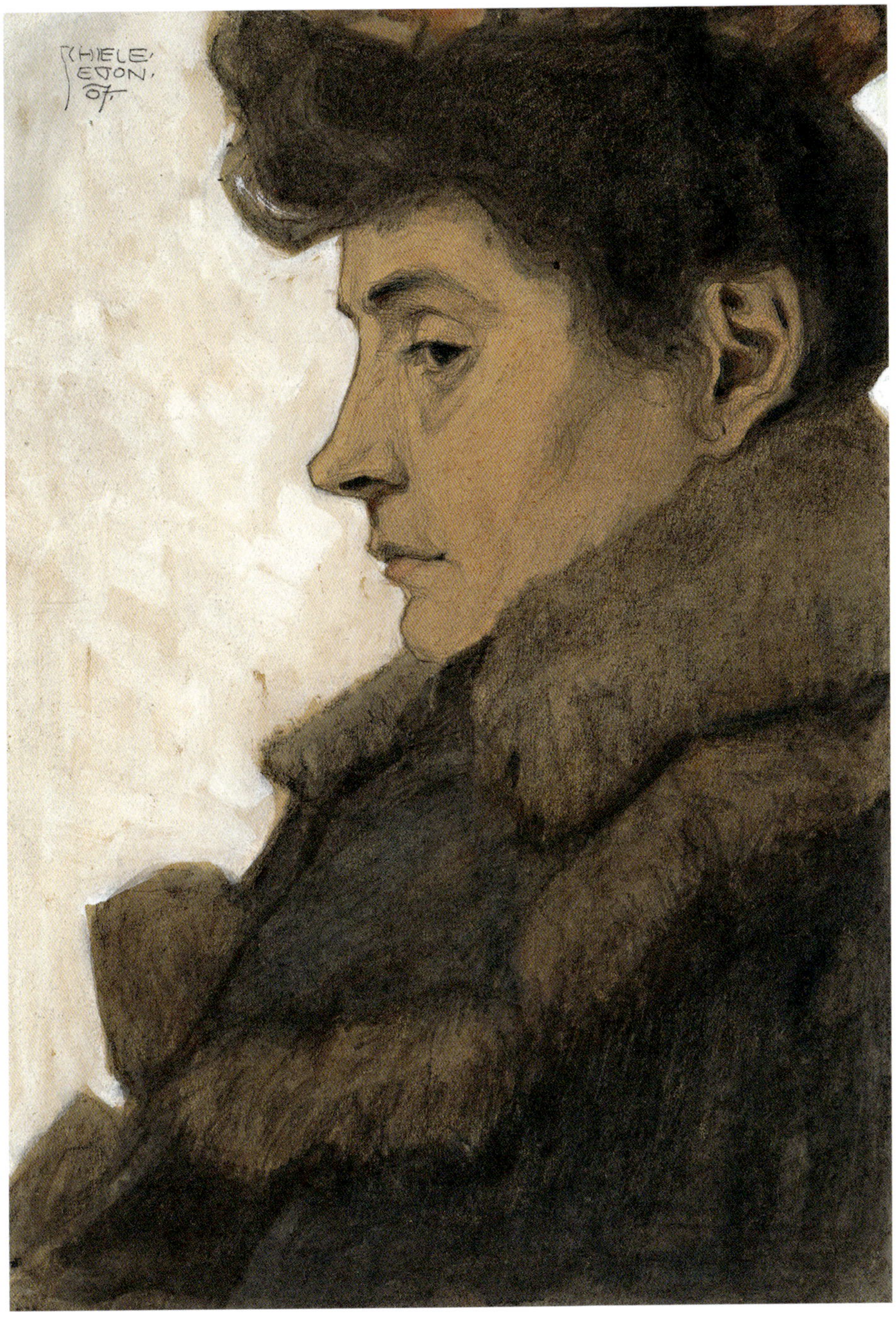
SCHIELE
EGON
07

1907

ITALIAN FARMER

Most of the drawings Schiele completed in 1907 were created during his studies at the Vienna Academy of Fine Arts. The painting department's curriculum included "painting and drawing in the style of antiquity", "painting of the head and the human form" and "evening nude drawing", among other classes. Owing to Schiele's constant drawing training and extraordinary talent, he executed compositional studies, landscapes and portrait drawings of remarkable quality and quantity already during those early years. For many of his portraits he used family members, friends and acquaintances as his sitters. The present bust portrait shows a smartly dressed young man wearing a hat, gazing rigidly into the distance. What is striking about the rendering is Schiele's confident employment of foreshortening and hatching in order to convey depth and volume in a believable manner.
Schiele signed the drawing with the precise date of its creation – March 2, 1907 – as he did with many of his works from these early years. (BS)

Charcoal on paper
39.9 × 30 cm
Leopold Museum, Vienna, Inv. 5949

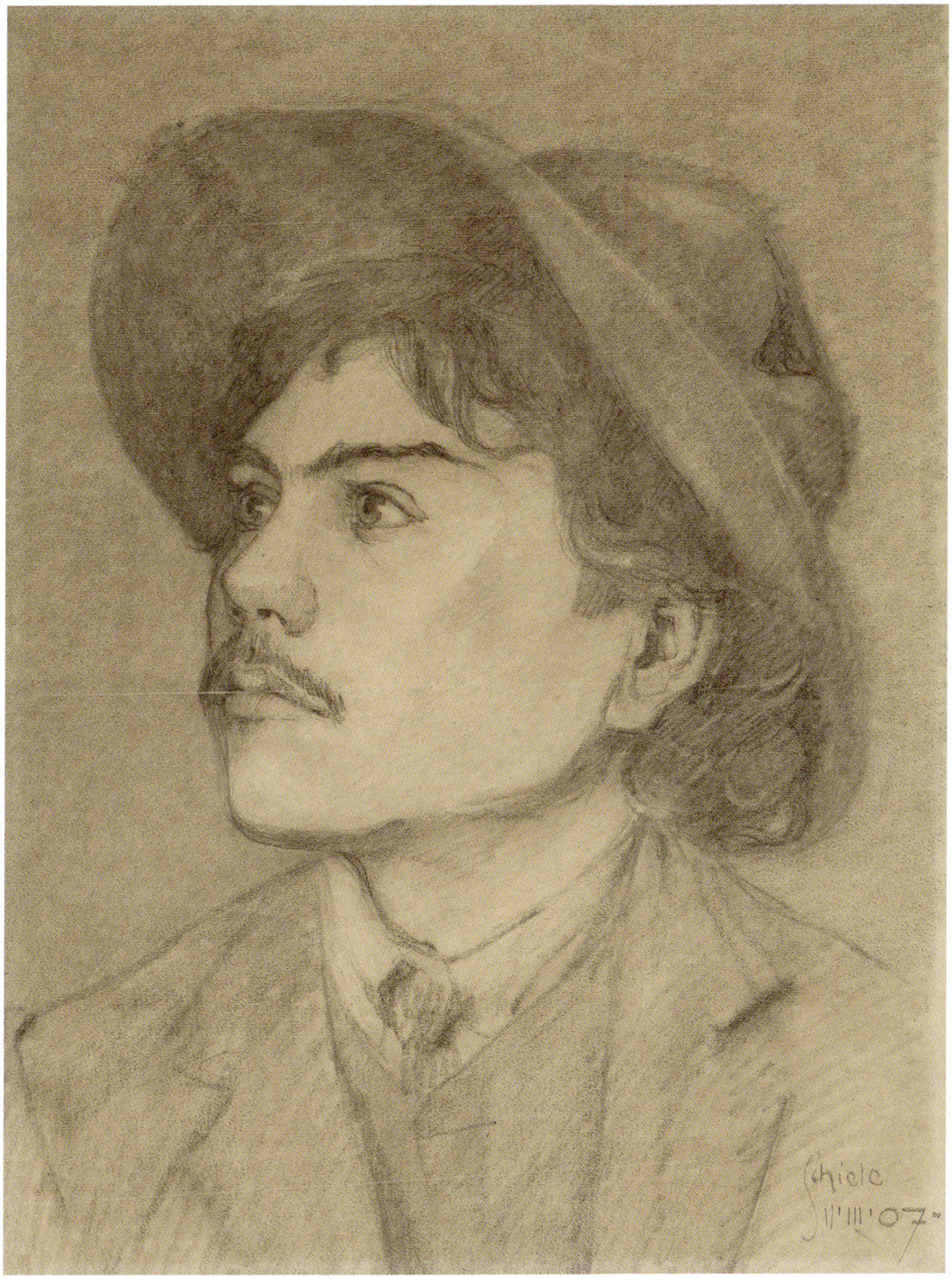
Schiele
11·III·07·

1907

VILLAGE AT THE FOOT OF A HILL

This view across a meadow shows houses and autumnal trees in a hollow, with sloping fields and meadows behind and a mountain at the very top.

For all its seeming naturalism, Schiele's subject has been composed with great care. One notes how the angle of the gently undulating boundary at the bottom of the foreground meadow opposes that of the two shrub-lined paths on the opposite slope. That rise seems to be an appropriate distance away, but it also appears to lift vertically, as though it were a separate plane, while the mountain above has been cut off by the top edge of the picture. Both of these features are wholly consistent with the compositional style of the Secessionists. (RL)

Oil on cardboard, mounted on wood
25 × 17.9 cm
Leopold Museum, Vienna, Inv. 471
L 60; K P.65

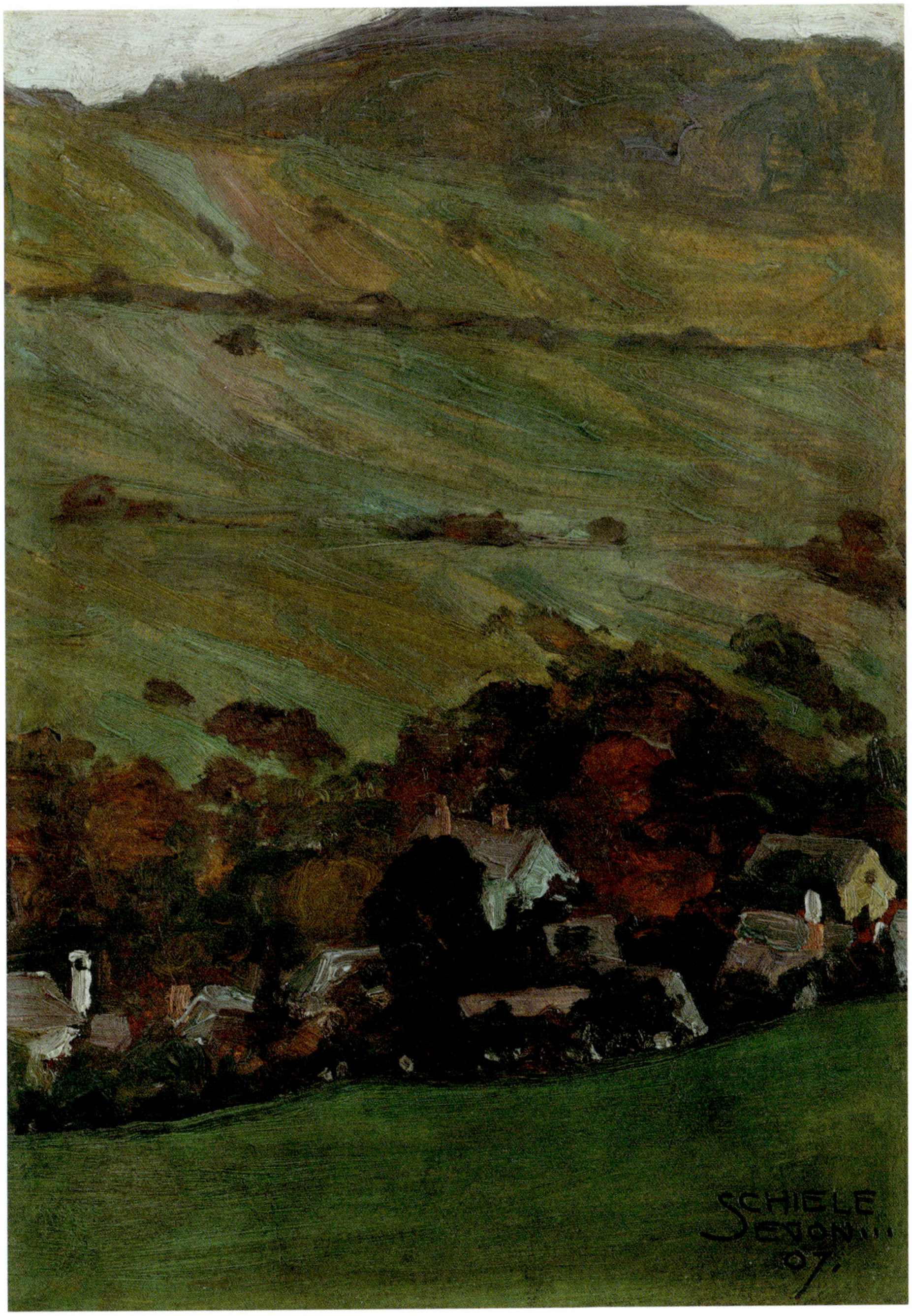
SCHIELE
EGON
07

1907

BARE TREES, HOUSES AND SHRINE (KLOSTERNEUBURG)

Schiele was 17 and a half years old at the time he created this painting. I found it especially interesting to search for the subject that had inspired his composition. Unfortunately, it was not easy to find, for none of these Klosterneuburg houses are still standing. There is only a wayside shrine with an iron hand protruding from the top section, and Schiele did not even include the hand in his painting. Luckily, a photograph of a painting from about 1910 by Franz Horst (1862–1950) enabled me to identifiy the spot where Schiele stood.

Horst's painting presents a more conventional view, with the shrine roughly in the center of the picture. Schiele, by contrast, placed it on the far right, and moved it up so close to the viewer that it is cut off by the top and bottom edges. And, unlike Horst, Schiele omitted the iron hand, as it would have had no meaning in his picture. In this, as in every other way, Schiele appears to have forced his own sense of composition on the reality before him.

With the unusual twilight colors of this cluster of houses, the contrasting light sky, and the vehement strokes of dark graphite in the still-wet pigment, the young Schiele managed to evoke a distinct mood. (RL)

Oil, pencil on cardboard
15.3 × 25.3 cm
Leopold Museum, Vienna, Inv. 473
L 75; K P.87

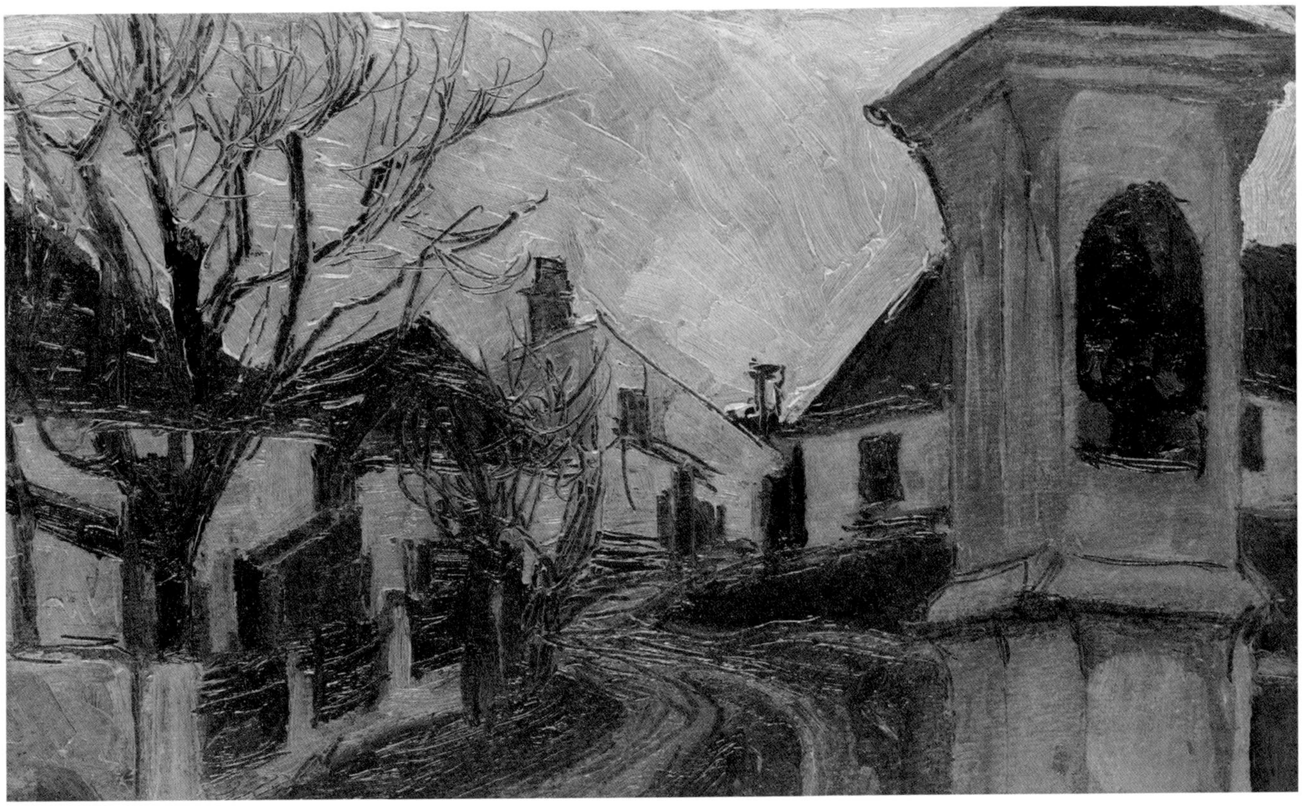

1908

NUDE BOY LYING ON A PATTERNED BLANKET

Here Schiele has fully adopted Jugendstil, not only its characteristic ornamentation on the fabric but also its fondness for ink and gold-bronze pigment. For the background he used this color unmixed, creating a vivid contrast to the dark coverlet below and the delicate green of the boy's hair.
More important for the development of his own signature style is Schiele's rendering of the body. With the exception of a few faint traces of green, the color of the paper itself was left untouched. It is the outline of the body that becomes important, with a distinct angularity developed at the knees and elbows. By the end of 1908 (see p. 31), this angular outline style would be fully perfected. (RL)

Pencil, gouache, gold paint, India ink on paper
23.8 × 31.5 cm
Leopold Museum, Vienna, Inv. 1466
L 121; K D.106

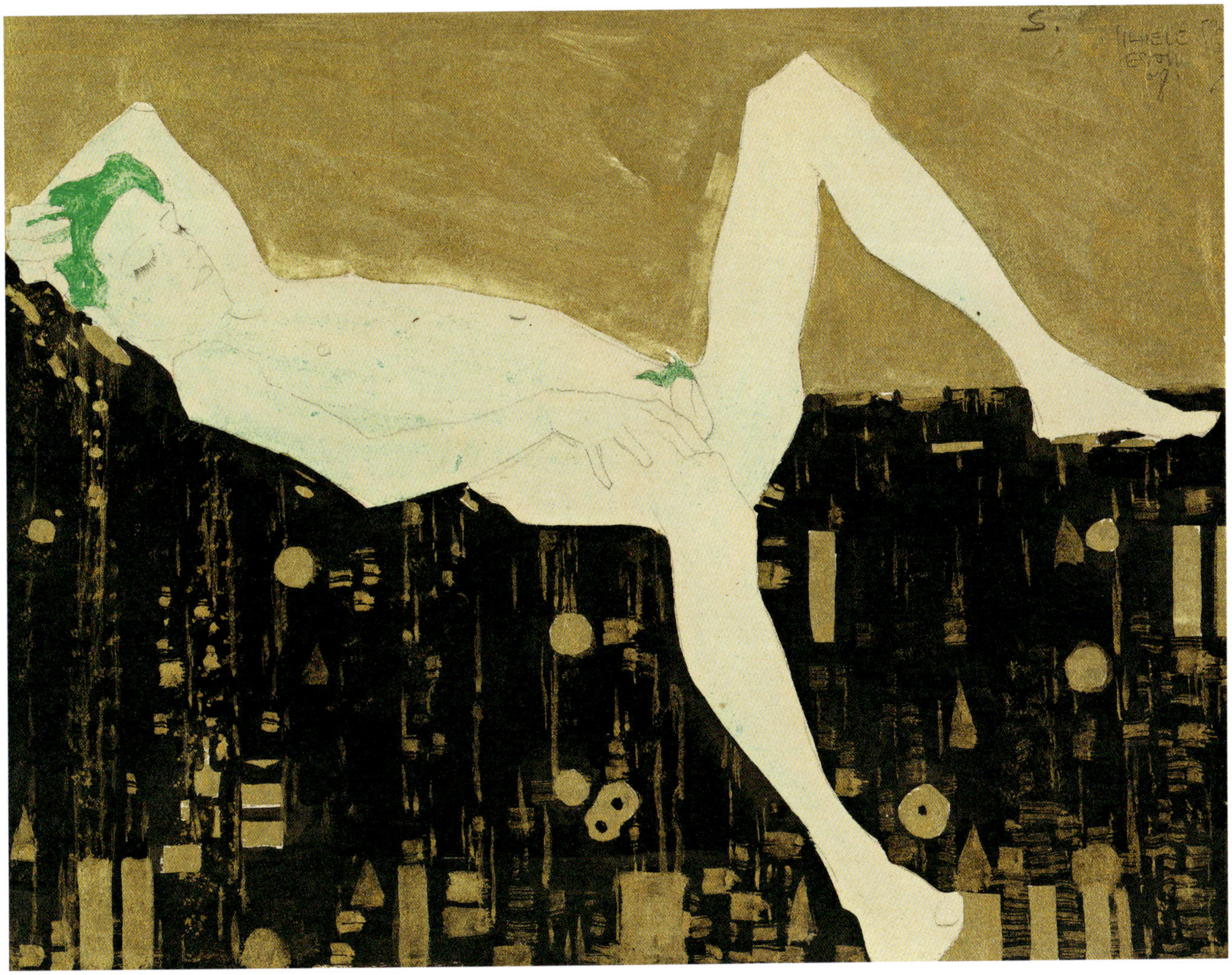

1908

STYLIZED FLOWERS IN FRONT OF DECORATIVE BACKGROUND

In this painting the gold background, unlike the one shown on p. 29, has been patterned. With its alternating brushstrokes, it almost appears to be hammered bronze. The juxtaposition of contrasting shades of gold further enriches the composition. It would be difficult to imagine a greater contrast to this background than the plant Schiele places in front of it, its leaves in utterly unnatural shades of violet and its decoratively shaped blossoms a yellow-orange. What is most striking, however, is the way Schiele structured the outlines of these leaves; in many respects these outline forms, created in late 1908, already anticipate the ones of the great nudes on canvas that he would execute in 1910. (RL)

Oil, silver and gold bronze on canvas
65.5 × 65.5 cm
Leopold Museum, Vienna, Inv. 474
L 127; K P.146

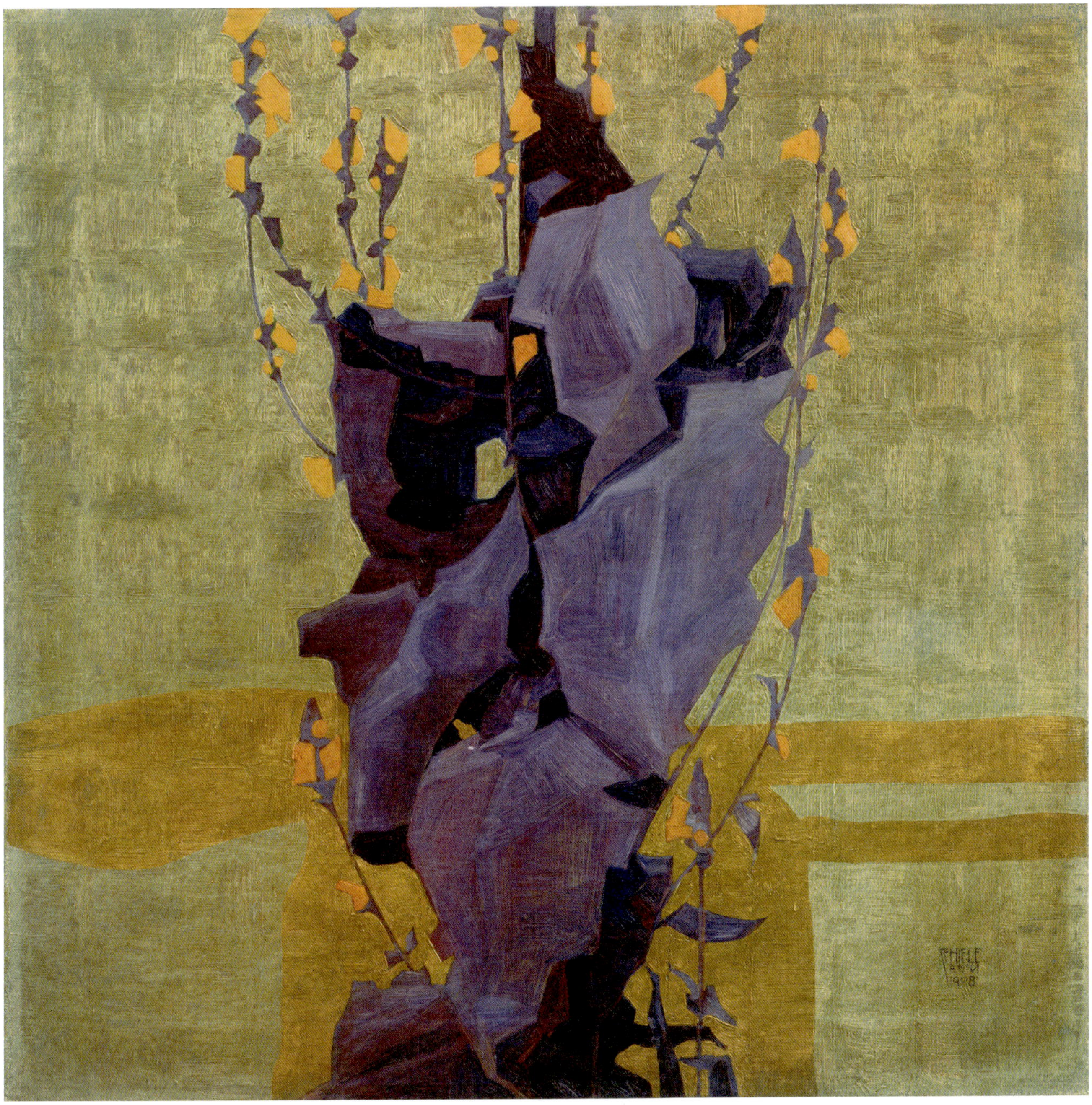

1910

CHRYSANTHEMUMS

According to the records of Arthur Roessler, Schiele met Gustav Klimt, who was a generation older than him, in 1907. Klimt soon became a fatherly friend and early inspiration to the young Schiele. Alongside his academic works, Schiele already executed creations inspired by Klimt and Viennese Jugendstil during this period. However, from late 1909 Schiele increasingly freed himself from the aesthetic-decorative conventions of Jugendstil in favor of his very own Expressionism. In the years 1910 to 1915 especially, Schiele went against the aestheticizing traditions of art nouveau by expressing tragedy and ugliness as a dimension of his pictorial design.

While the decorative floral painting *Chrysanthemums*, like many works created in 1910, still displays some hallmarks of Viennese Jugendstil, it already clearly anticipates Schiele's later compositional and expressionistic characteristics. Schiele dispensed with a realistic rendering of the flowers and abstracted the buds and stems growing directly upwards into the black surface of the canvas in a columnar manner. The three watercolors of a white, red and yellow chrysanthemum (K D.745–747), kept today at the Albertina in Vienna, represent immediate preliminary studies for the eponymous painting. According to Klaus Albrecht Schröder, these studies express the effect of the flowers as expressive lineaments more distinctly.[1] (BS)

1 | *Egon Schiele*, ed. by Klaus Albrecht Schröder, Munich 2005 (exh. cat. Albertina, Vienna, 6th December 2005–19th March 2006), p. 128.

Oil on canvas
61 × 91.9 cm
Leopold Museum, Vienna, Inv. 478
L 142; K P.180

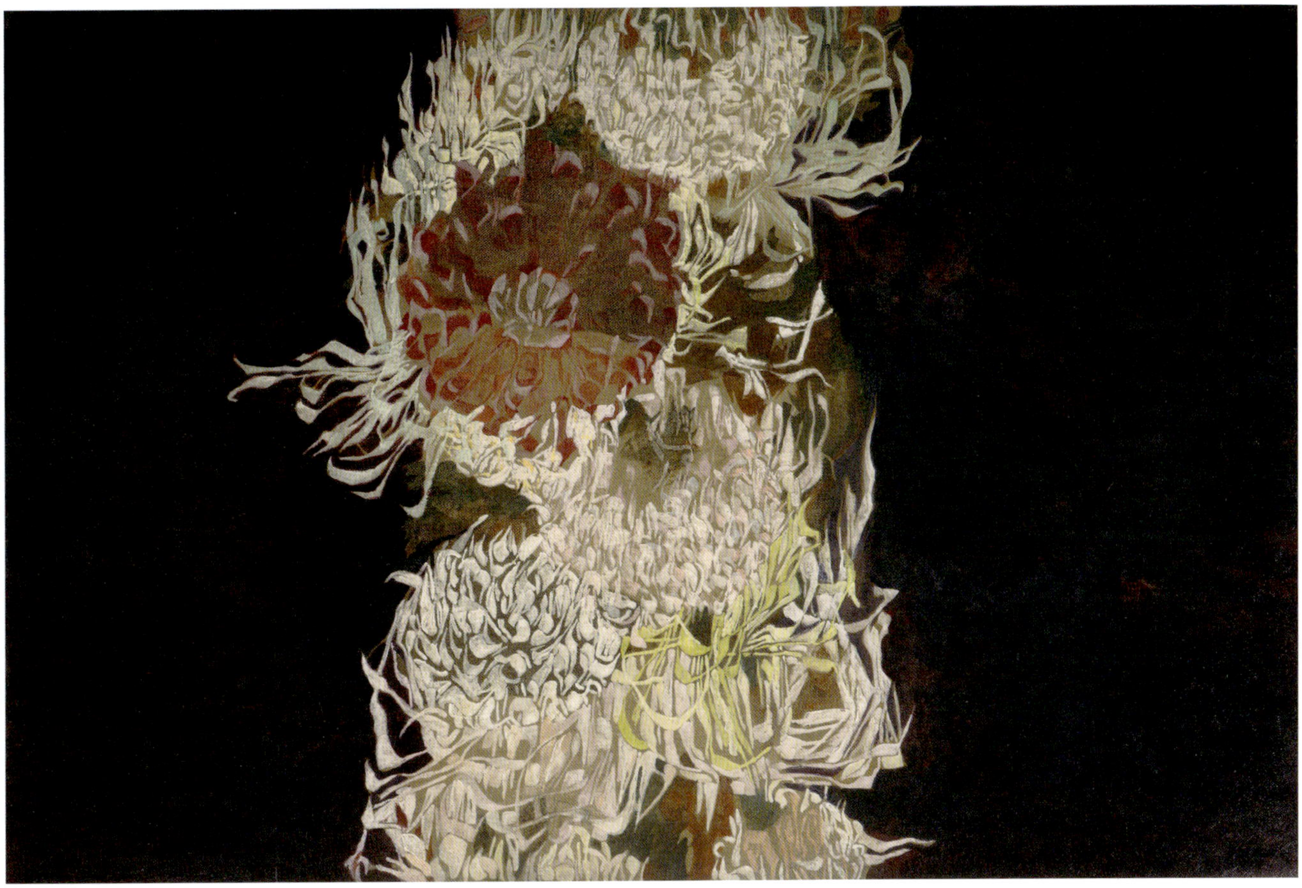

1909

BLACK-HAIRED MAN, SITTING

This work is a beautiful example of the fluid, secure drawing of the 19-year-old Schiele, in a style wholly divorced from academicism. One marvels not only at the outline of the body but also at the form of the hand resting on the right shoulder. Schiele deliberately painted the flesh tones an almost uniform light reddish brown, contrasting it with the solid black of the head, rendered in ink. (RL)

Pencil, India ink, watercolor on brown paper
31.7 × 31.5 cm
Leopold Museum, Vienna, Inv. 1385
K D.326

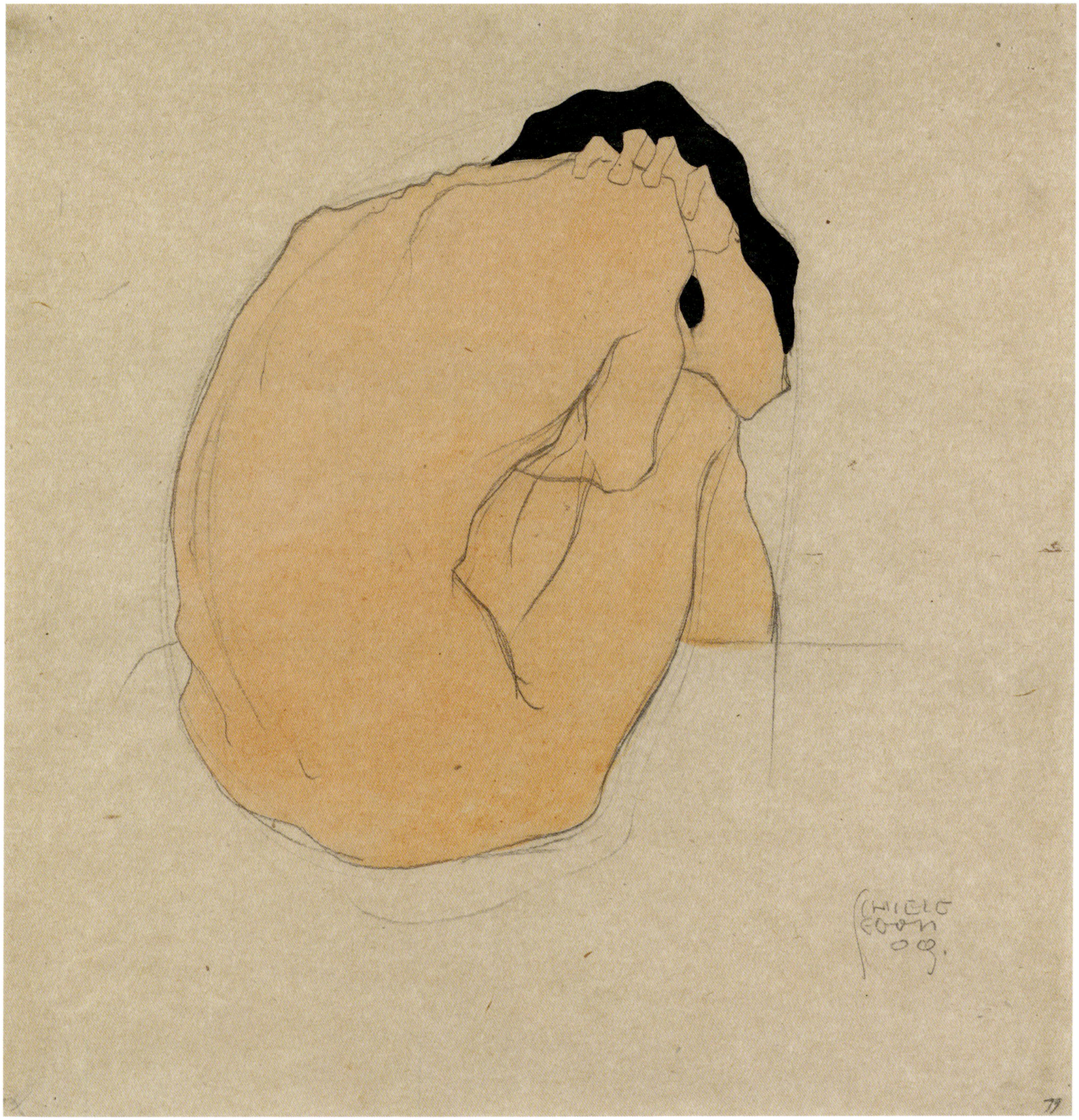

1909

NUDE SELF-PORTRAIT WITH RED HEAD BAND

This work on paper represents a direct preparatory drawing for the painting *Nude Self-Portrait with Ornamental Drapery* created in 1909 (L 135; K P.154). The way Schiele managed in this study to incorporate his nude into the tall, narrow rectangle in a well-balanced manner, the way he – in detail – aligned parts of the outline of the right upper arm to be parallel with the slanting line of the back, the way he used the shoulder turned towards the beholder to interrupt the line between neck and chest – all this reveals a great deal of artistic autonomy, even though the posture does echo that of the pregnant woman in Gustav Klimt's 1903/04 work *Hope I* (N 162), which Schiele had borrowed and inverted.

Schiele went beyond Klimt and the attitudes of Secessionism and Jugendstil by striving towards a forced expressiveness through the depicted's emaciation and slightness of build as well as the emphasis on the pubic hair. Admittedly, he had not yet found the adequate means to achieve this: the relatively soft lines and the contrasting of individual, ornamental patches of color are still very much aligned with the pictorial traditions of Jugendstil. The courage to portray ugliness, rendered exciting and fascinating through formal solutions, is more clearly apparent in this preparatory drawing and other known studies than in the painting. The headband visible in this depiction also features in Schiele's *Self-Portrait with Headband* (K D.344). (RL)

Pencil, colored crayon, colored chalk on paper
39.6 × 29.5 cm
Leopold Museum, Vienna, Inv. 2369
K D.343

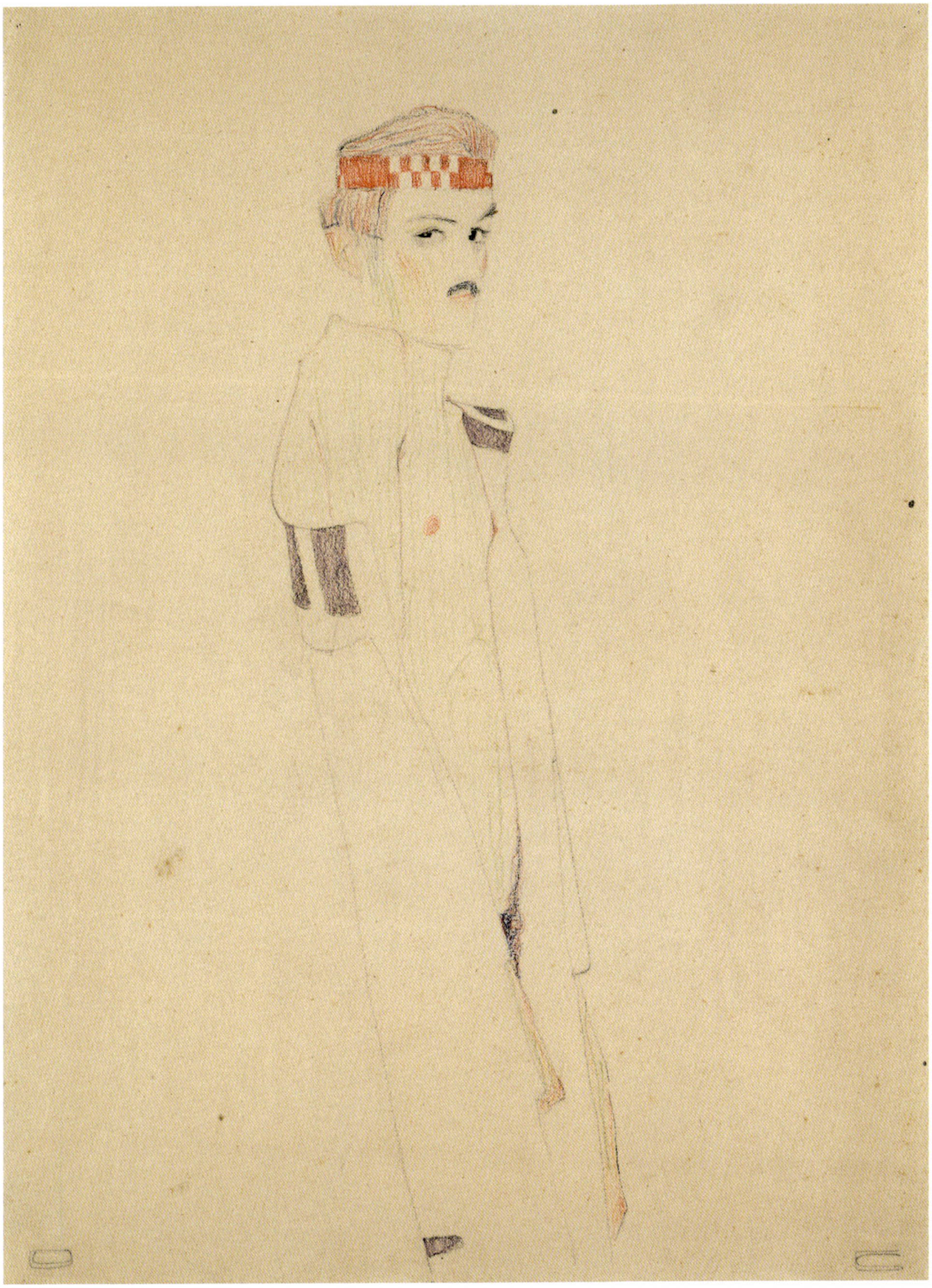

1910

GIRL CROUCHING IN A FLOWER MEADOW

Kokoschka's color lithograph *Pietà. Poster for the play "Murderer, Hope of Women" at the "Internationale Kunstschau"* (see p. 9) greatly influenced this work by Schiele, who was four years younger than Kokoschka. In contrast to the almost amorphous figure of the dead Christ in Kokoschka's lithograph, however, the pose of Schiele's figure, the arrangement of the girl's head, arms and body already anticipate Schiele's own sense of anatomical structure.

Schiele wrote the word "March" on the back of his picture. According to Otto Benesch, the work may have been a design for spring in a proposed cycle of the seasons. (RL)

India ink, pen, gouache on paper
27.8 × 18.3 cm
Leopold Museum, Vienna, Inv. 1463
K D.721

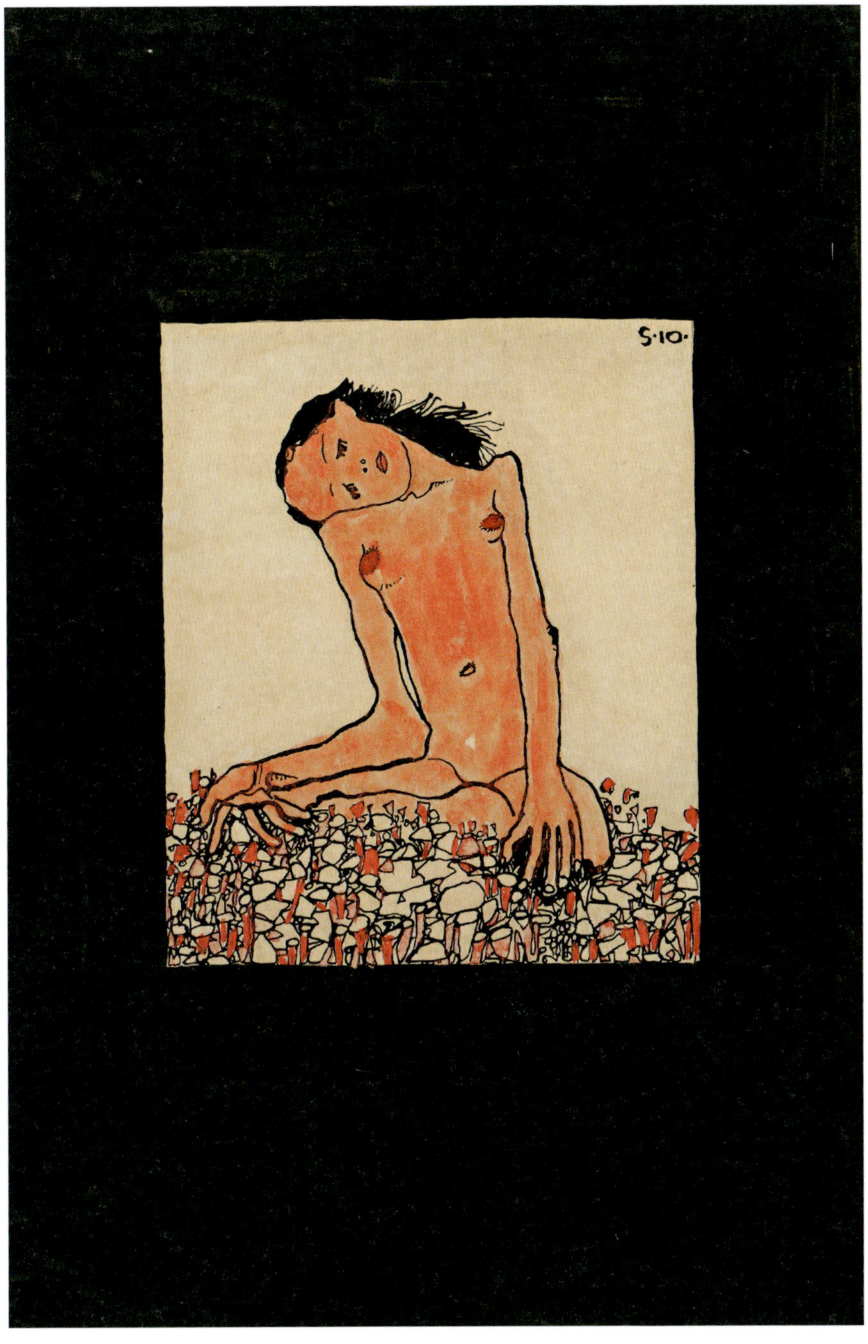

FEMALE NUDE WITH RAISED ARMS

This drawing is a seemingly spontaneous arrangement of head, hands, and body, but with the line of the chin omitted so as not to detract from the diagonals of the forearms. Schiele's talent for omitting the non-essential and emphasizing what was important is already unmistakably apparent in this drawing. The lids of the closed eye are two simple arcs touching in the center, the upper one echoing the curve of the brow. That line is continued, in turn, by the lines at the base of the hand. Everything is in some way related to everything else.

Whereas Schiele's earlier works were intended to be mainly decorative, we now see him focusing on structure. The outlines of the arms and torso clearly reflect this concern more than they do the anatomical realities. Note the continuation of the line of the right breast and the auxiliary line leading to the right elbow. This articulation of the form has nothing to do with the rendering of this particular body; it is strictly a matter of artistic structure.

The similiarities with the great nudes on canvas from this same year (see p. 47; L 140, 141, 143a–145; K P.168–172) and the corresponding works on paper are obvious. (RL)

Black chalk on paper
41.6 × 24 cm
Leopold Museum, Vienna, Inv. 1461
L 32; K D.514

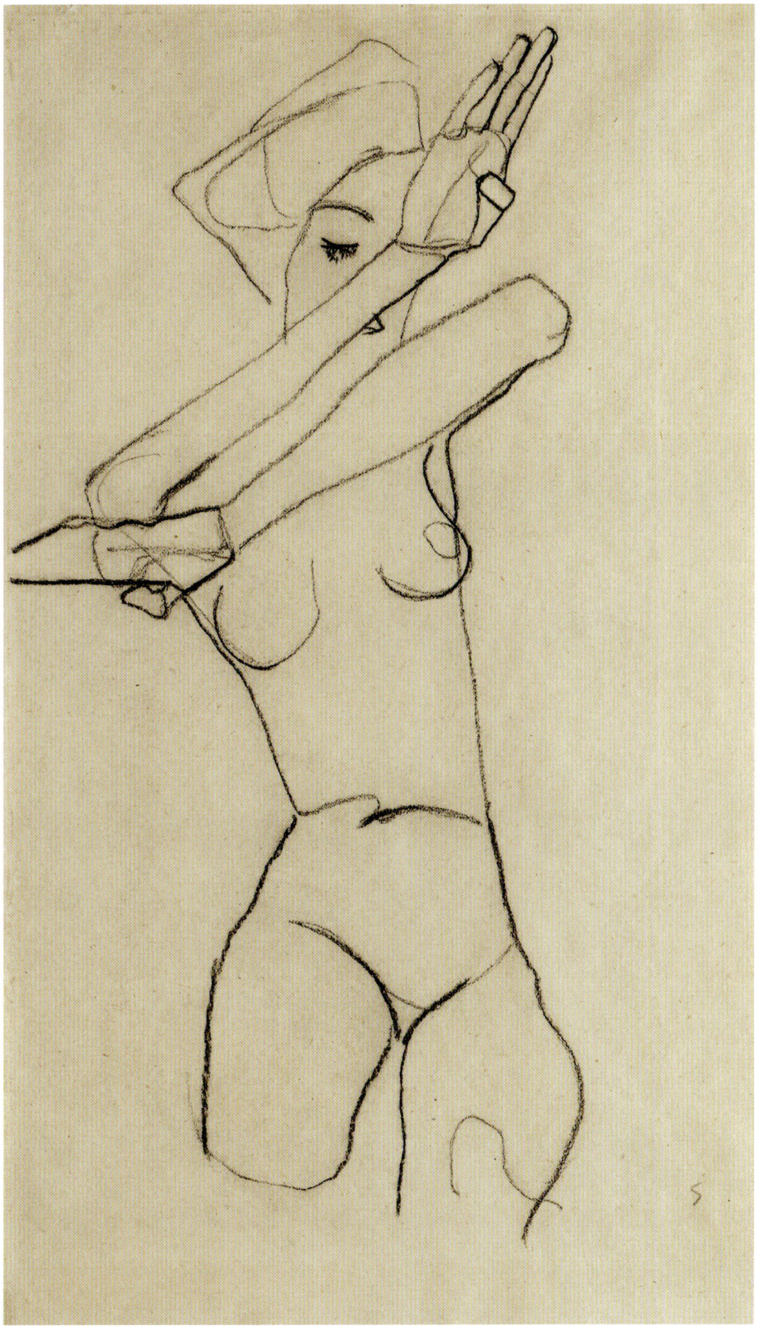

1910

SELF-PORTRAIT AS KNEELING NUDE

In his title vignette for *The Dreaming Boys* (see p. 8), Kokoschka was strongly influenced by Mycenaean works of art.[2] Kokoschka's emaciated figures not only reflect those in the depiction of a siege on a Mycenaean funnel-shaped silver rhyton, but he also borrowed the second woman on the tower, complete with the position of her arms, for the central figure in his composition.

That figure, in turn, was clearly what inspired Schiele to create the self-portrait reproduced here. However, he made a number of important changes: the lower part of the kneeling leg is allowed to point to the back, the gestures and the position of the head have been rethought, and the rather casual outline of the original has given way to one that is emphatic and controlled. (The less successful right hand is the only form Schiele reworked before producing the painted version, L 140; K P.168.) The compositional correspondences between the various parts of the body are even more evident in the painting. In that work it is also obvious that Schiele succumbed to a degree of formalism. In the *Seated Male Nude (Self-Portrait)* (see p. 47), the artist would soon achieve a perfect blending of gesture, structure, and expressiveness. (RL)

2 | Cf. Jaroslav Leshko: "The Influence of the Mycenaen Discoveries on Modern Art", in: *Mitteilungen der Österreichischen Galerie*, year 13, no. 57, 1969.

Black chalk, gouache on brown paper
63 × 45 cm
Leopold Museum, Vienna, Inv. 1380
K D.692

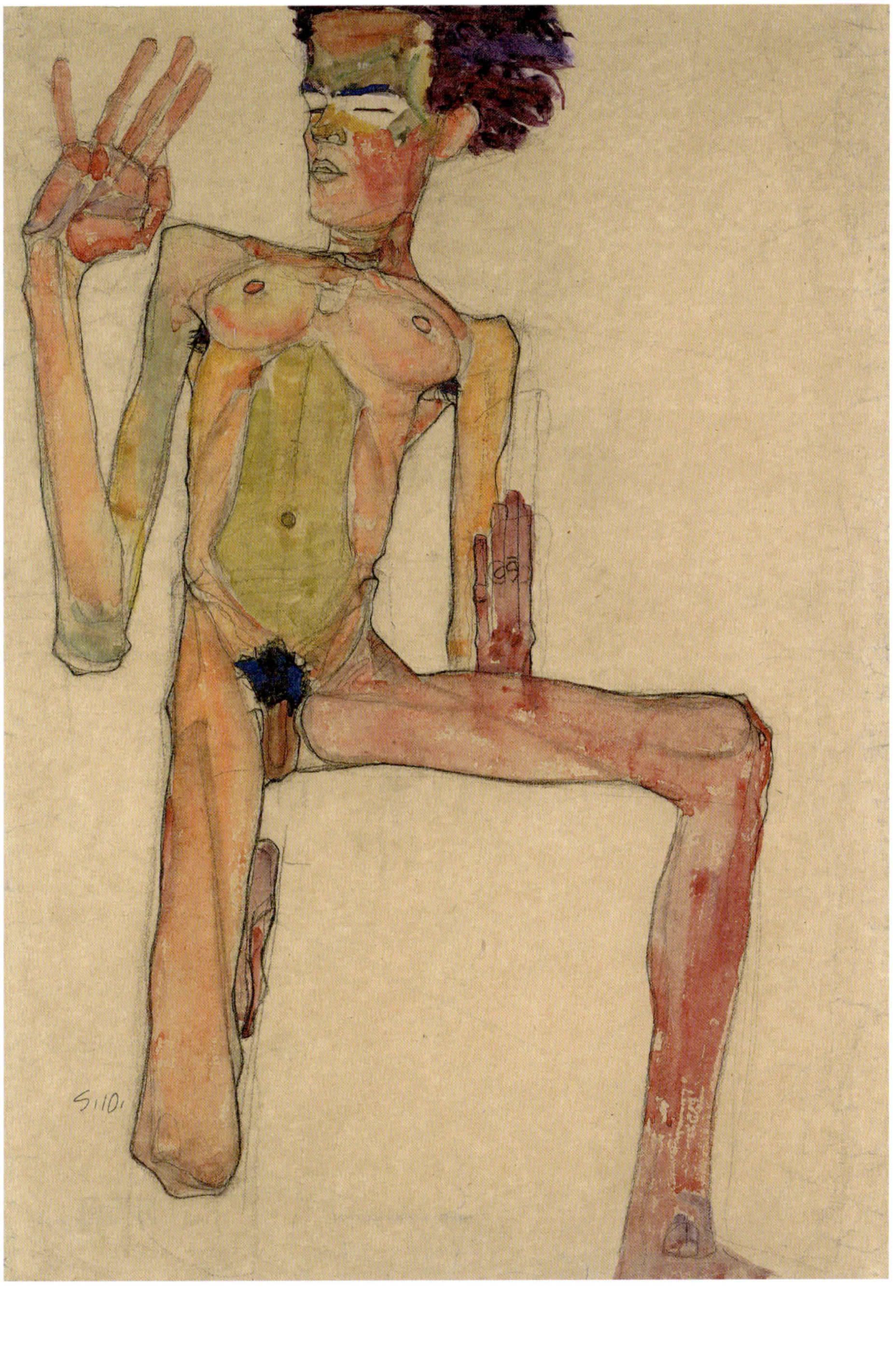

1910

COMPOSITION WITH THREE MALE NUDES

This sketch was undoubtedly created in connection to a large, seated male nude canvas painted by Schiele in the same year, which is also in the holdings of the Leopold Museum's collection (see p. 47). A remarkable aspect of this ink drawing is Schiele's technique of depicting the three figures as dark silhouettes. As a result, the gaze of the viewer is essentially focused on the contours of the bodies. Schiele additionally chose extreme postures and gestures, such as splayed and angled legs and unnaturally bent arms, as well as extremely slender waists. As a result, the very essence of the human figure transforms into a form that appears fragile and insect-like. In this grouping of three, the figures produce a somehow decorative tangle of contorted lines and planes. The formal allure of these silhouettes most likely sparked Rudolf Leopold's choice of the figure depicted on the right of the page to become the trademark for the museum he established. (FS)

Pencil, India ink on paper
19 × 20.7 cm
Leopold Museum, Vienna, Inv. 1459
K D.723

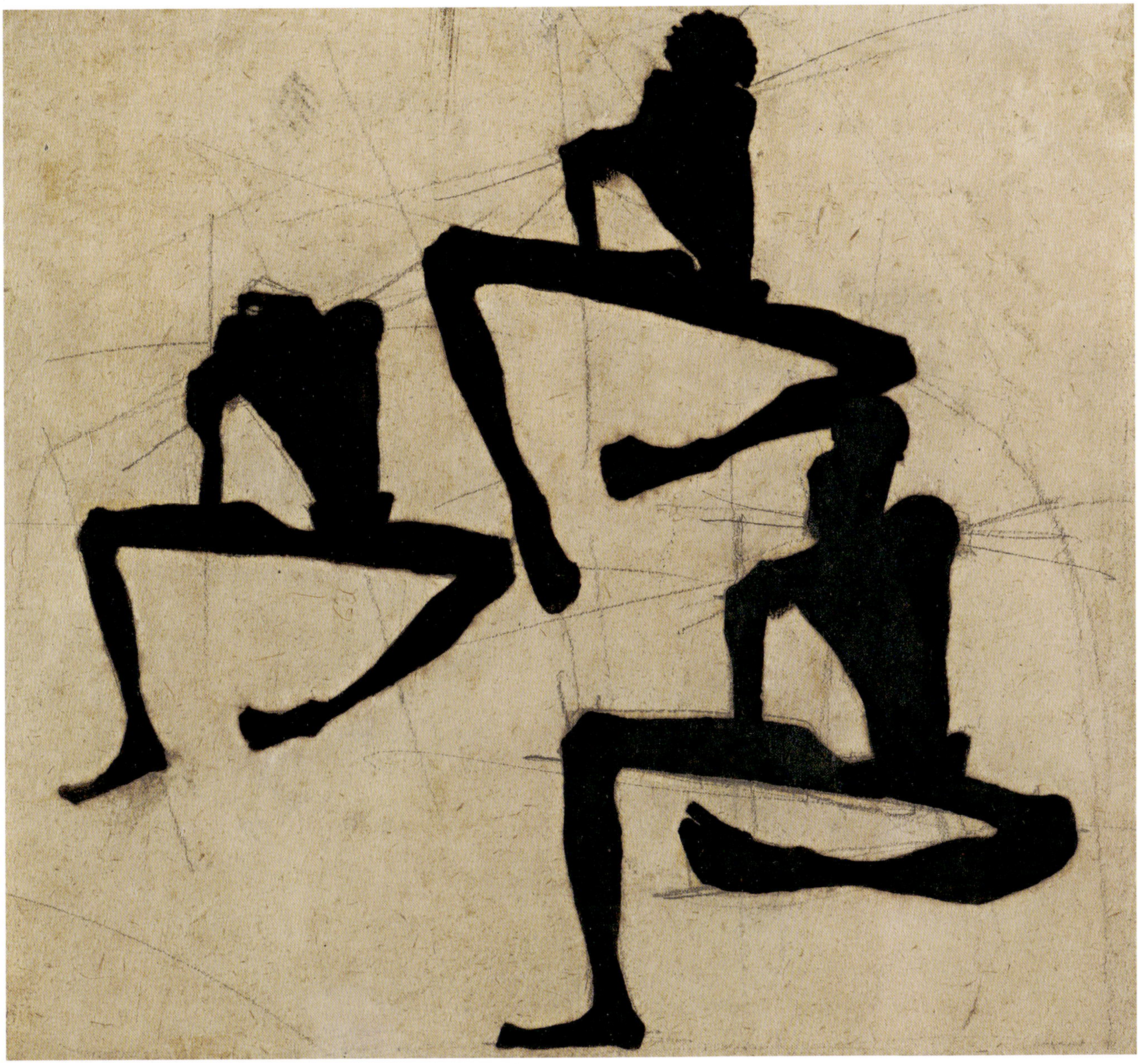

1910

SEATED MALE NUDE (SELF-PORTRAIT)

Of the four great 1910 nudes on canvas (L 140, 141, 144; K P.168, 196, 172) the seated one reproduced here and the standing male version, for which Schiele acted as his own model, were probably the last to be painted. Their angular, pointed outlines are still startling, but are clearly derived from a style he had developed in earlier works such as the *Autumn Tree with Fuchsias* (L 138; K P.158). The projections and hollows in the outline of the nude reproduced here seem to reflect the essential structure of the figure much more logically, creating striking breaks in the dynamic interplay of straight and curving lines. They are not merely ends in themselves, as they would come to be often enough in the years 1917 and 1918; rather, they are abstractions derived from the body's actual contours deliberately employed for their formal effect. The division of the body's surface into sharply defined areas in no way detracts from the overall structure. In many respects the figure has the quality of a woodcut.

The composition is exquisitely balanced. The splayed legs branch off from a columnar torso stretching up at an angle to the right. For balance, the head inclines in the opposite direction. To insure the integrity of the figure and guarantee its pictorial autonomy, its feet and any indication of the support on which it rests were simply omitted.

The flesh tones seem unnatural; they consist mainly of lighter and darker values of a greenish yellow set off by the orange of the rib cage and the reddish brown of the legs. These are in turn contrasted against the deep blue-black of the hair and various accents in red: the eye, the nipples, the navel, the genitals. The lighter yellowish tone of the trunk is bracketed by deeper shades above and below. The colors are all essentially sallow, and together with the angular projecting bone structure they suggest emaciation and weakness, but at the same time they reveal the essential structure of the figure. Here and there one becomes aware of a white aureole, but the lighter background as a whole is what gives the darker figure its vividness. Although Schiele frequently did not predetermine the sizes of the empty sections of his compositions, it is obvious in this case – as in the three other nudes on canvas and the portraits from this same year – that he placed the self-contained figure onto the white surface with great care. Its varying distances from the edges appear to have been calculated precisely.

Schiele never surpassed this figure in terms of composition and drama; all that he gained from here on was a richer sense of color. Form and expression have become as one. (RL)

Oil, opaque color on canvas
152.5 × 150 cm
Leopold Museum, Vienna, Inv. 465
L 145; K P.172

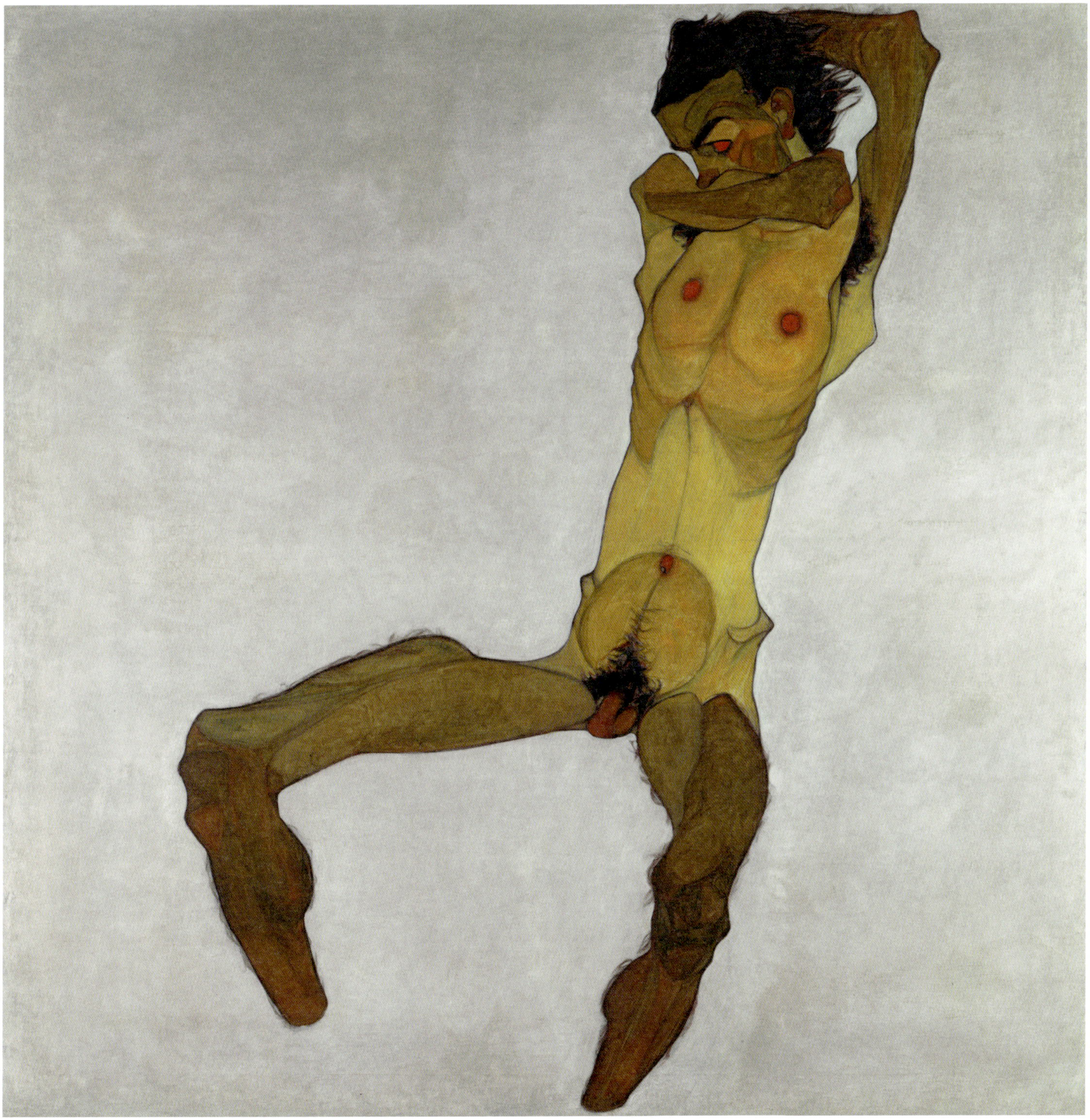

1910

THREE NUDE GIRLS

These three nudes were probably executed in the first half of 1910. The one in profile in the center, especially, is clearly indebted to the group *The Longing for Happiness* from Klimt's *Beethoven Frieze* (N 141). Despite numerous parallels, however, the differences are obvious. With his disciplined line, Klimt managed to give the outline of his emaciated nude the elegance of Jugendstil. Not so Schiele: the pose of his nudes is more nervous and hectic; his outline runs out to sharp points; the bodies' length is exaggerated.
It is also interesting to see how Schiele attempted to layer his figures in space, even though the overall concept is two-dimensional. To that end he placed one figure atop another and rendered them in progressively darker colors from left to right. The one on the right is also executed on a considerably smaller scale. (RL)

Black chalk, watercolor, opaque color on paper
44 × 30 cm
Leopold Museum, Vienna, Inv. 2316
K D.511

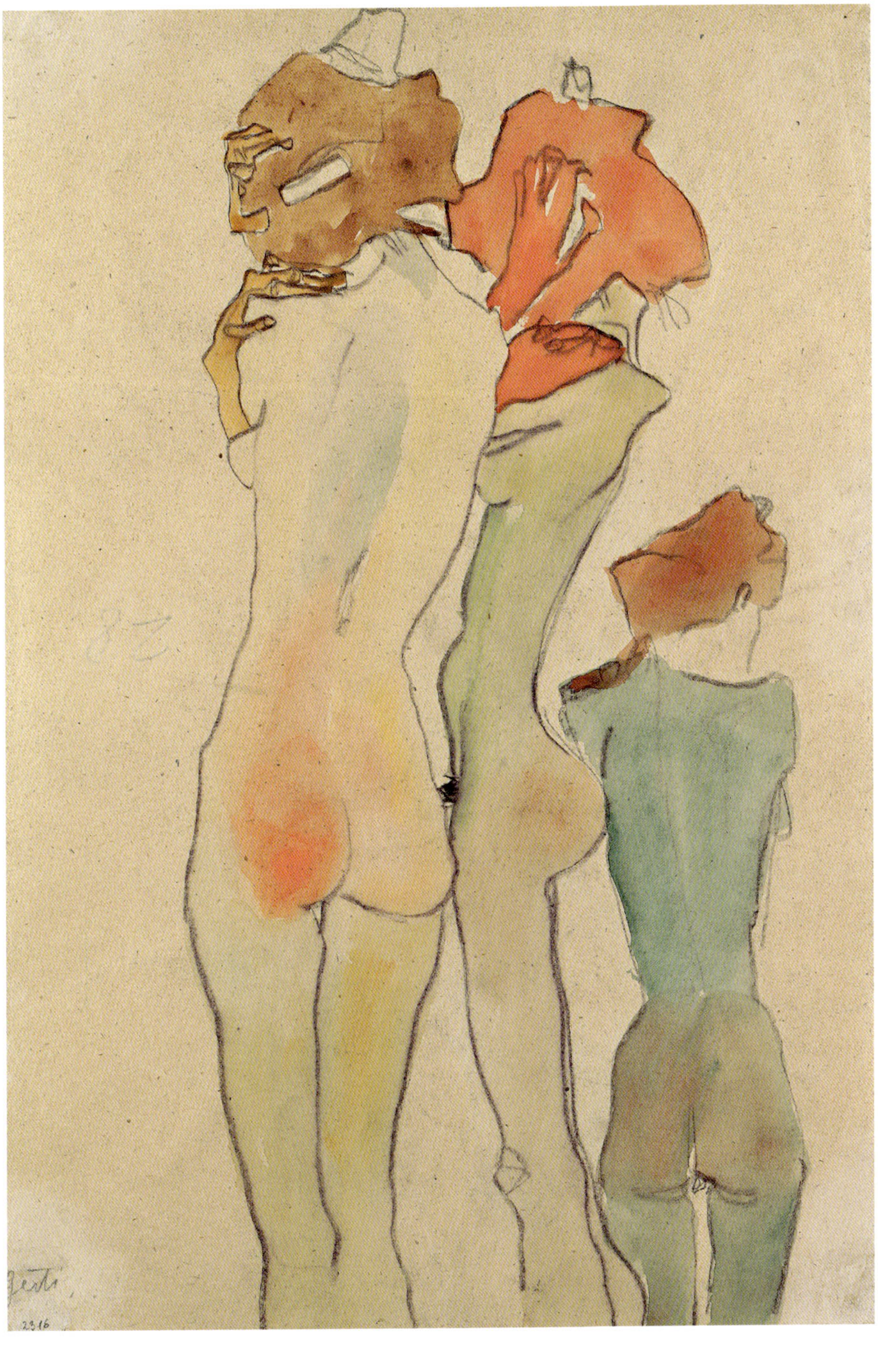

1910

FEMALE NUDE

This work depicts an overly slender, slightly protracted female body jotted down on the paper. This elongation is due especially to the position of the arms pressed tightly together and held up in front of the chest. The hands are unnaturally large and long, the fingers are balled together and the joints accentuated with dark colors. The arms provide a vertical axis to the curved body, while the beautiful face with closed eyes is turned to the right. This position of the head, along with the long, wavy hair, emphasizes the dreamy expression of abandon, which provides a peculiar contrast to the sitter's bony skinniness – one that is disconcerting and enchanting in equal measure.
The drawing and color of the hands, often splayed in a decorative manner and held next to or in front of the body, were of great importance to Schiele and were frequently used as a means of expression. The hands in the present rendering are perhaps "worker's hands" mentioned by Schiele in one of his poems of 1910 (ESAD, ID: 2): "The portrait of the silent pale girl. I loved everything. The girl came, – I found her face, Her unconscious, Her worker's hands, I loved everything about her." (EL)

Watercolor, black chalk on paper
44 × 30 cm
Leopold Museum, Vienna, Inv. 2316
K D.513

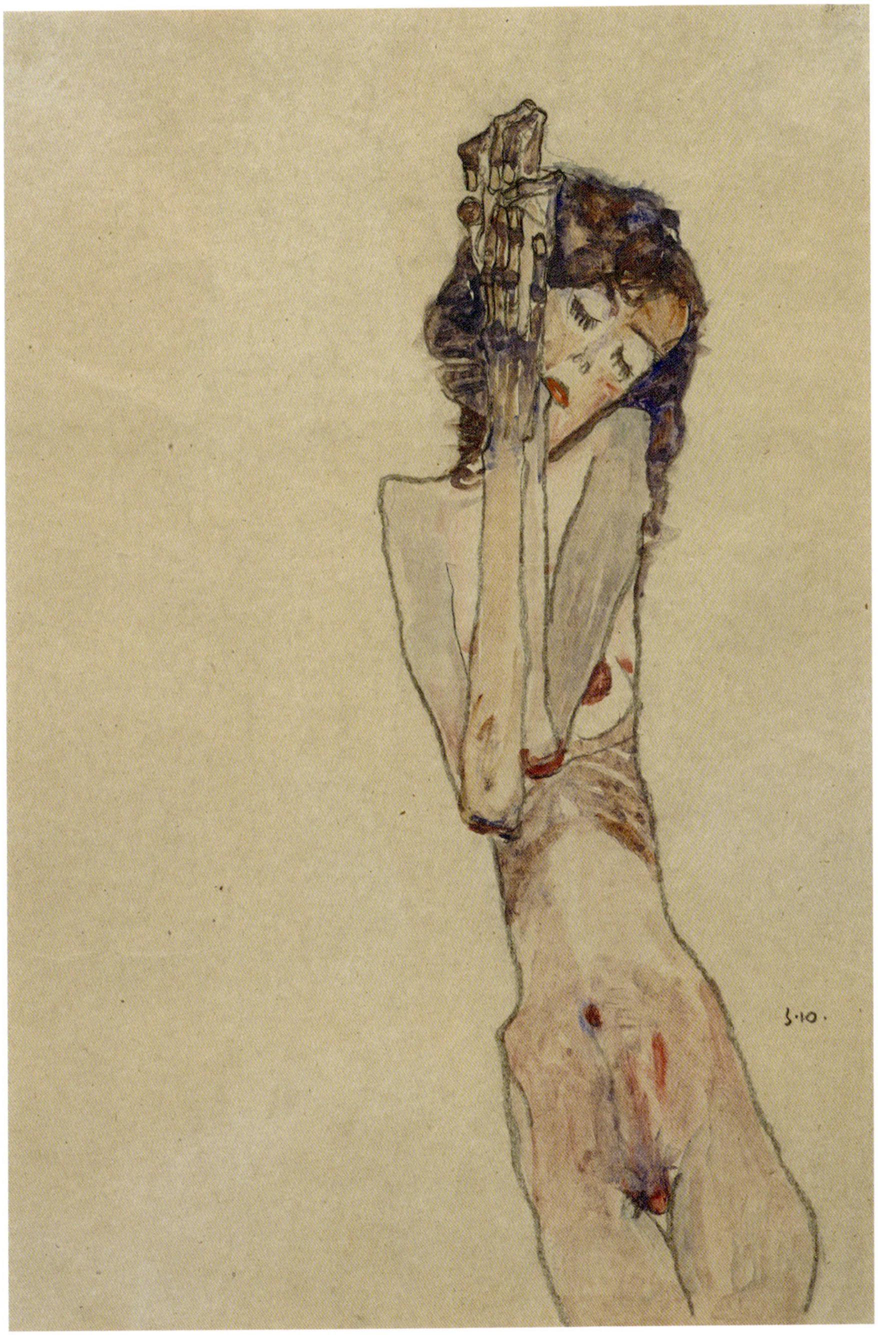
S.10.

1910

PREGNANT WOMAN, SITTING

Here Schiele painted the woman's belly a pale green, surrounding it with thighs, an arm, and an upper body in more realistic reddish brown tones. The face and hair are rendered in an even stronger reddish brown, heightened by the red of the lips and the swollen eyelids. In contrast to the *Nude Pregnant Woman, Reclining* (K D.528), the face is executed in detail, and the woman's gaze is altogether moving. (RL)

Black chalk, watercolor on paper
44.1 × 30.2 cm
Leopold Museum, Vienna, Inv. 2340
K D.540

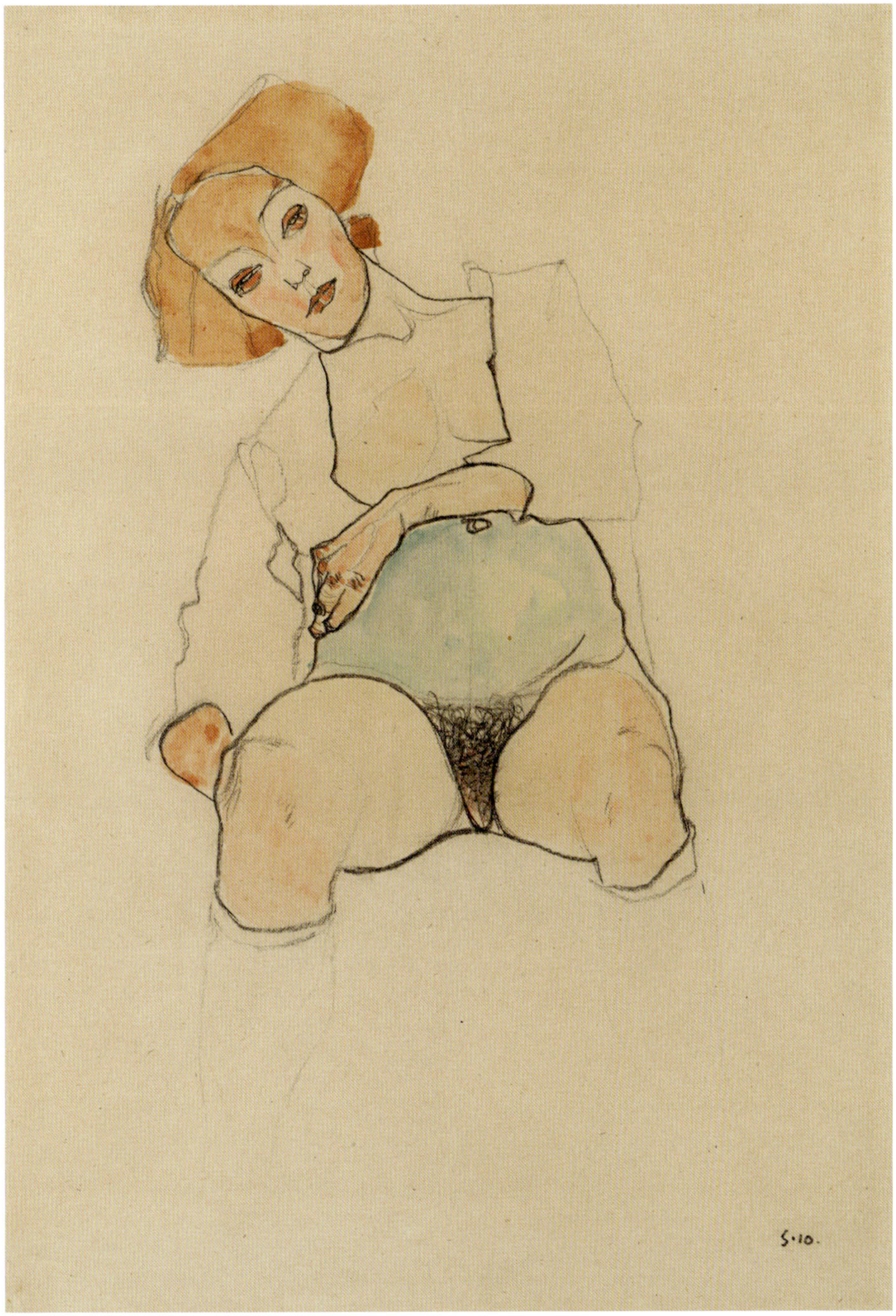

1910

NEWBORN WITH BENT KNEES

In the drawing and the colors of this work, Schiele masterfully captured the helplessness of a newborn infant. Although we see the face only in profile, we sense that the child is crying. Schiele exaggerated the reds and blues of the baby's skin, just as he exaggerated the deformation of its buttocks so soon after delivery. Needless to say, he was quick to utilize their flatness for its formal effect.

The placement of Schiele's monogram would suggest that the drawing was originally done in a vertical format, but that contradicts its character. He signed it in this way because the Vienna Secessionists favored either square or vertical formats. He too did most of his works in a vertical format, but up to the time of his death he habitually signed, retroactively, even his horizontal works as though they had been turned the other way. (RL)

Black chalk, gouache on paper
28.9 × 43.2 cm
Leopold Museum, Vienna, Inv. 1410
K D.387

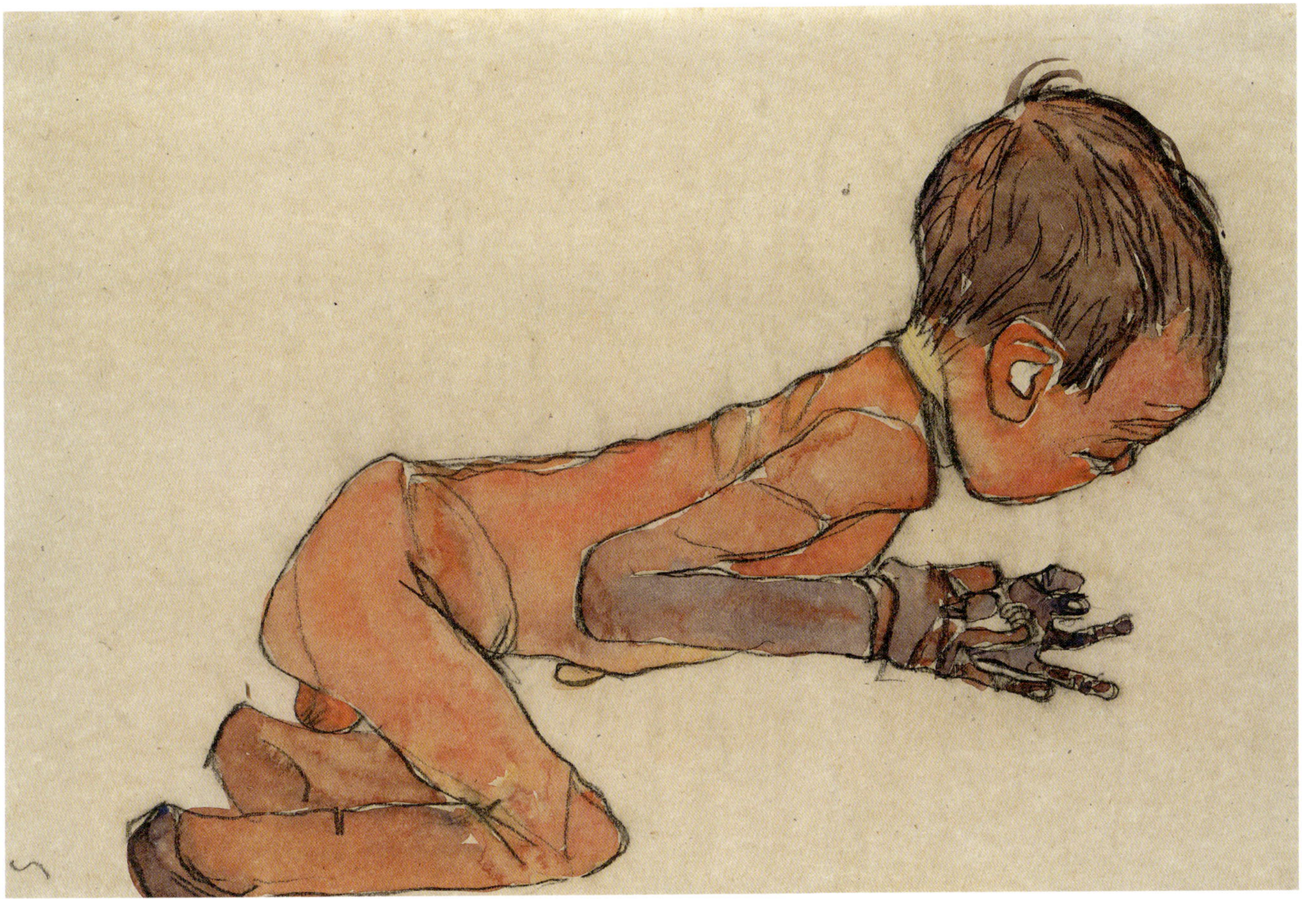

1910

MALE LOWER TORSO

This rather miserable figure has a deeply curved spine and pendulous buttocks. Schiele managed to heighten the sense of the grotesque with the fingers hanging down into the drawing from the top. The work has not been trimmed; this is the way Schiele meant it to be.

Every part of the figure corresponds to every other part. The buttocks, for example, relate to the pointed right knee, and that knee, in turn, is reflected in the angle of the heel below. The outline above the left kneecap has been scooped out to match the convex contour of the right calf. The resulting negative space is echoed by the one above the right knee. One is struck not only by the countless correspondences of line but also by the wealth of colors, each blending into the next and none confined to a specific area. A lilac-red passes through intermediary shades into the dark blue of the thigh, against which Schiele set off the genitals so that they virtually glow. Not only is this impressive in terms of painting; it also emphasizes – like the luxurious pubic hair – the sexual element.

With the blue of the right thigh, Schiele managed to separate the leg in space from both the genitals and the left thigh with color alone, a separation already suggested by the placement of the feet and the foreshortening of the right calf. Yet he made the right foot the same size as the left – perhaps even a little larger, owing to its central position and its importance in the overall composition – and in so doing caused the figure to seem somehow two-dimensional, with equally important elements more suggestive of a design. (RL)

Black chalk, gouache on paper
44.8 × 28.1 cm
Leopold Museum, Vienna, Inv. 1452
K D.675

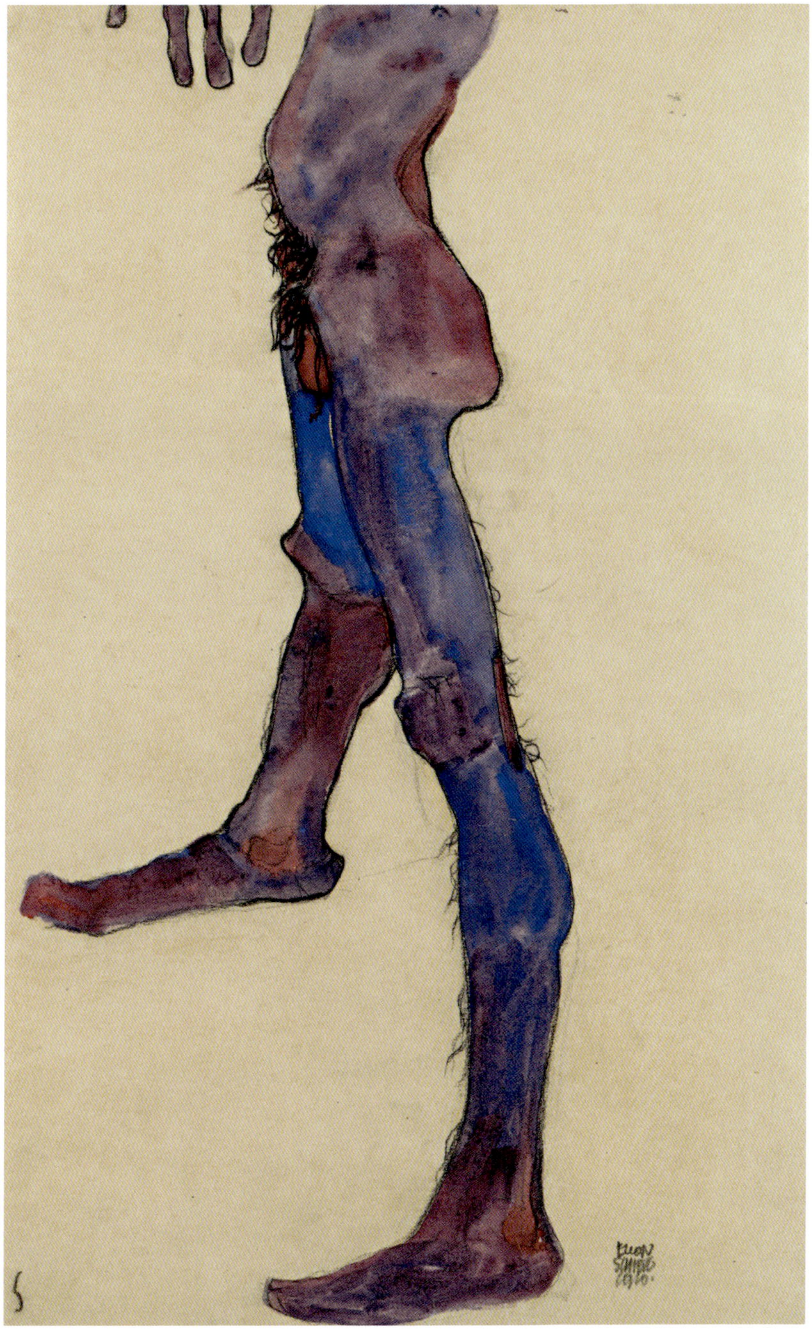

1910

THE GREEN HAND

In the soft lines of this drawing the influence of Gustav Klimt is still apparent to some extent. The young Schiele had been deeply impressed by the accentuated linearity and fragile corporeality of Klimt's draftsmanship. However, the idiosyncratic composition of Schiele's work and the curious fragmentation and autonomy of the woman's hand already clearly reveal the unexpected and disconcerting aspects of his expressiveness, which set in from 1910. That year Schiele first created drawings showing highly gestural and ecstatic figural compositions, which his contemporaries felt to possess a "Gothic" character due to their peculiar, angular contours and elongated proportions. An important means of heightening the discord in these renderings was the coloring, which Schiele usually only added after the drawing. The bilious green color of the hand in the present depiction serves to underscore the disconcerting isolation of this body part, which appears even more pronounced as the head of the model is not visible. This isolation and fragmentation of essential body parts would become a hallmark of Schiele's draftsmanship especially in his highly expressive phase. (FS)

Pencil, black chalk, gouache on paper
29.1 × 29.2 cm
Leopold Museum, Vienna, Inv. 2329

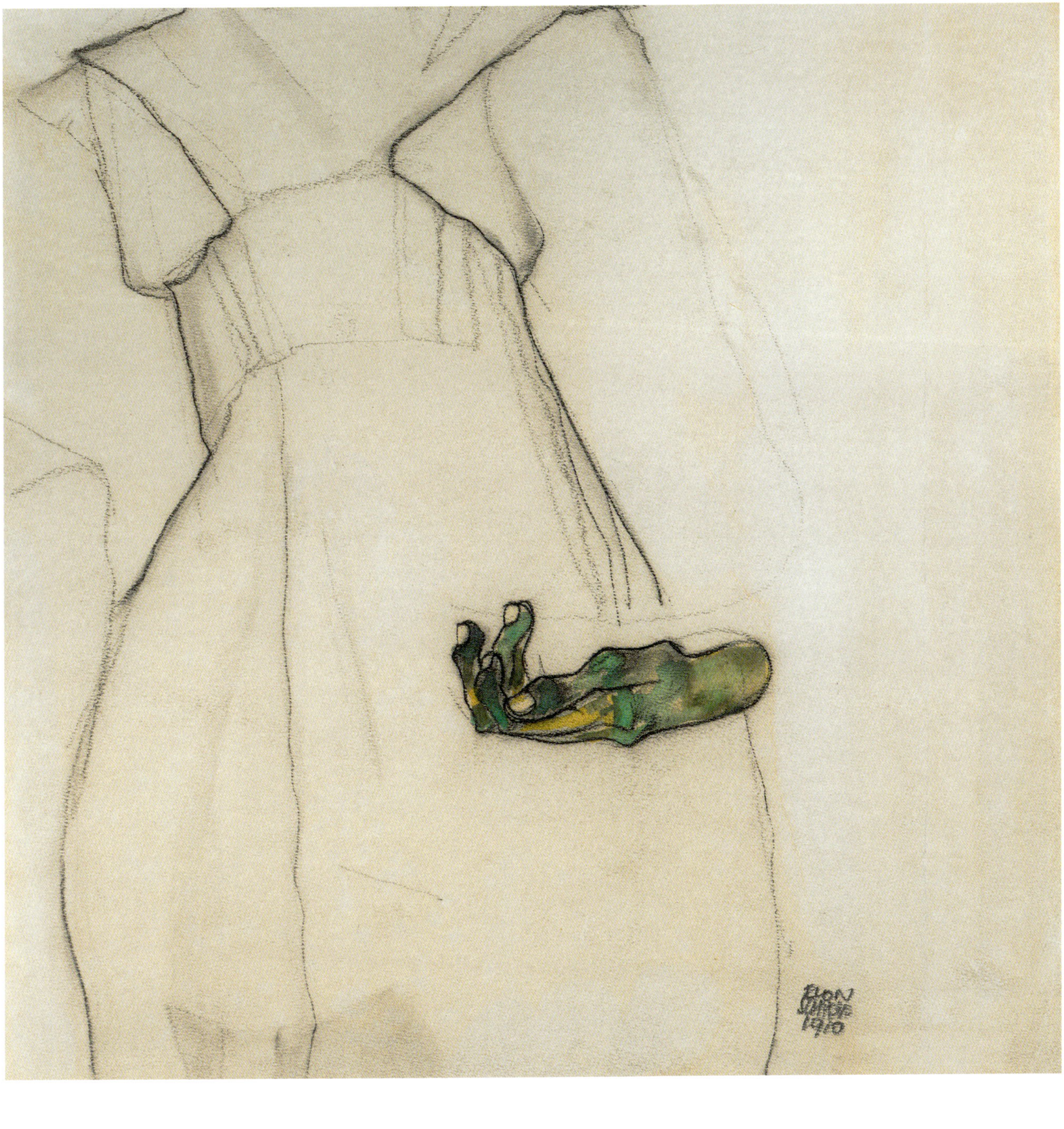

1910

MALE NUDE, PROPPING HIMSELF UP

The pictorial form is clearly defined. All of the elements are cross-referenced and reciprocally determinative. For this reason the right hand is simply omitted, for it would have created an accent Schiele did not want.
One is struck by the amount of color in the torso and especially the arms. For all their autonomy and exaggeration, these yellowish greens and oranges and even the red are juxtaposed with extraordinary success. The work calls to mind the Fauves in France, although Otto Benesch insists that Schiele had no knowledge of them at this time.
The colors may be improvised and the body unnaturally emaciated, even deformed; however, specific observations are perfectly believable – even the extremely hunched shoulder. This is precisely the way a skinny man's shoulder blade lifts when he leans on his elbow. (RL)

Pencil, black chalk, gouache on brown paper
45 × 30.7 cm
Leopold Museum, Vienna, Inv. 1451
K D.648

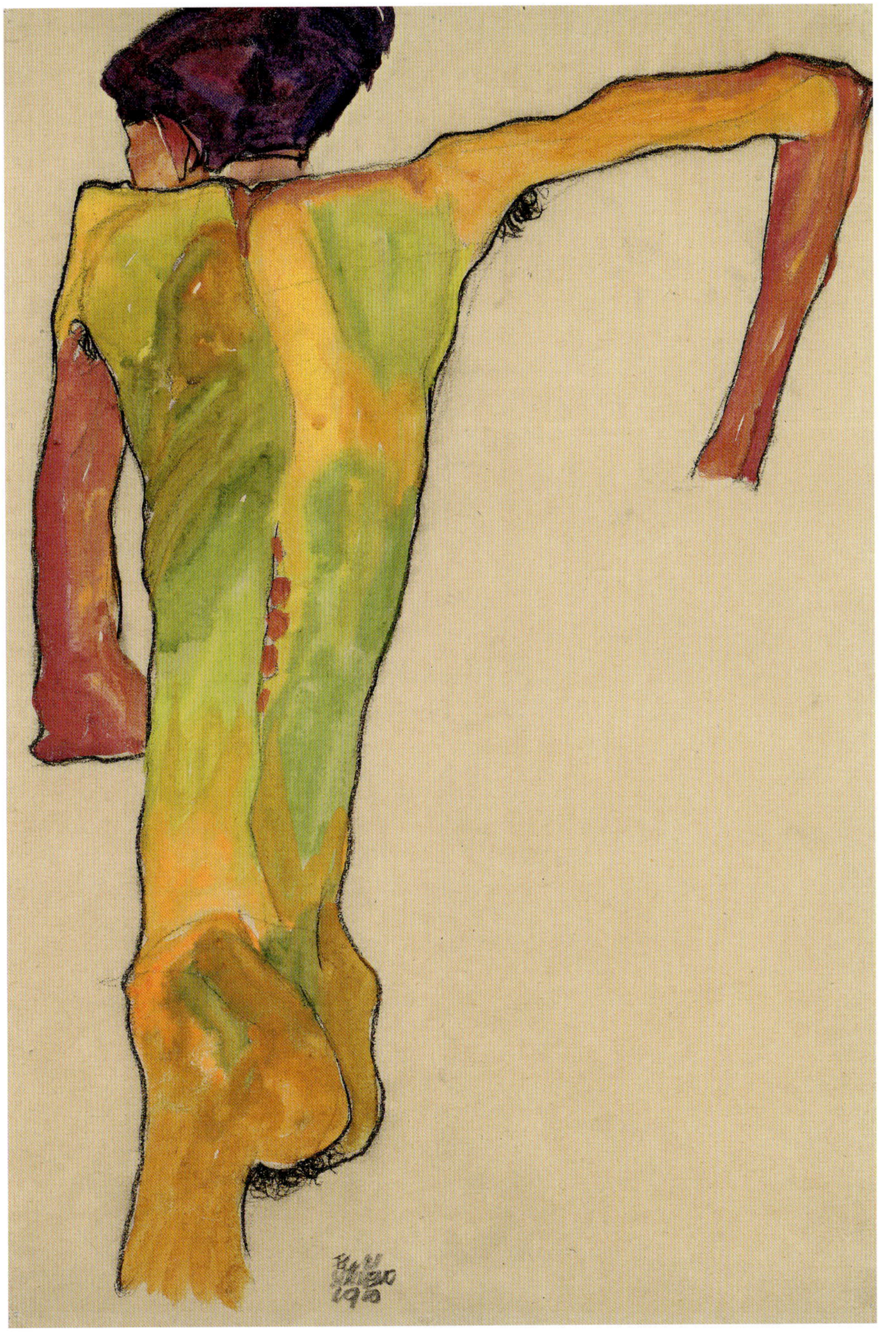

1910

KNEELING FEMALE IN ORANGE-RED DRESS

Schiele's younger sister Gertrude was the model for this drawing. The artist rendered her dress, stockings, and shoes in various shades of red, from orange to a bluish red – even adding a few touches of green. The folds of the sleeve are almost crystalline in structure. It is also important to notice the hand, which has been executed in an extremely painterly manner. A line leading from it to the hem of the girl's skirt traces Schiele's interest in the composition of the work.
Although the figure has been positioned on the surface with great care, one must not overlook its subtle three-dimensionality. This is no longer the sort of two-dimensional figure created by Jugendstil artists. (RL)

Black chalk, gouache on paper
44.6 × 31 cm
Leopold Museum, Vienna, Inv. 1453
K D.476

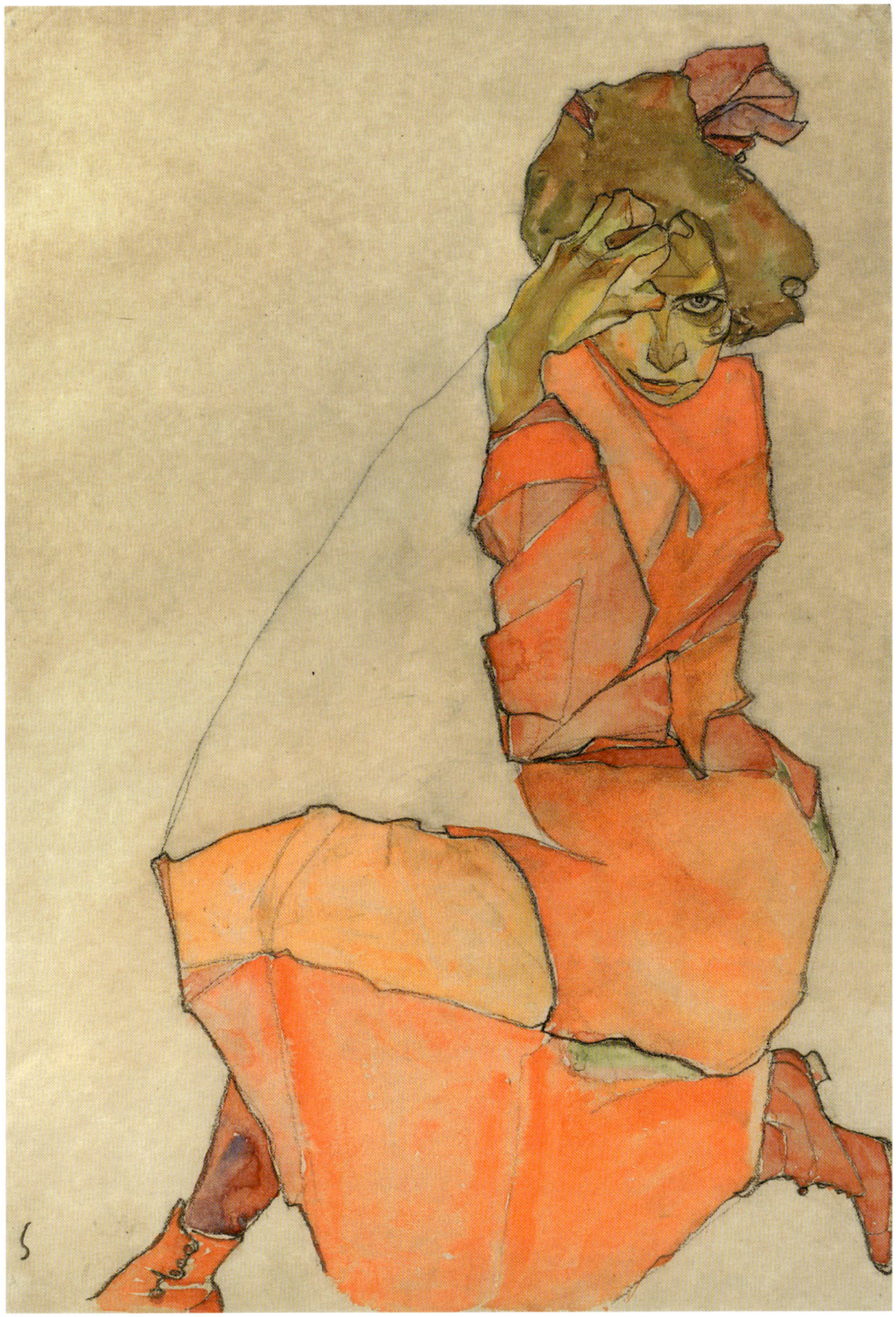

1910

ERWIN DOMINIK OSEN, NUDE WITH CROSSED ARMS

Schiele's painter friend Erwin Dominik Osen modeled for him on a number of occasions in 1910. This particular nude of him verges on the grotesque. The emaciated body is elongated, and the angular arms look like sections of some kind of pipe, as though Schiele were taking to the extreme the style of many works by the sculptor George Minne. The hands are abnormally large; the head appears to be separated from the torso. In terms of form, however, the line of the jaw where it touches the arm at an acute angle is carefully continued in the parallel upper outline of the left forearm and is precisely opposed by that of the right forearm. The tilt of the head is repeated in the angle of the right hand and especially the extremely long torso. These angles are balanced by the opposing movement of the relatively small buttocks.

Although the depiction is essentially scurrilous, in its formal construction nothing has been overlooked. Schiele's mastery of drawing is already evident in his wonderful outlines. (RL)

Black chalk, watercolor, gouache on paper
44.7 × 31.5 cm
Leopold Museum, Vienna, Inv. 2347
K D.598

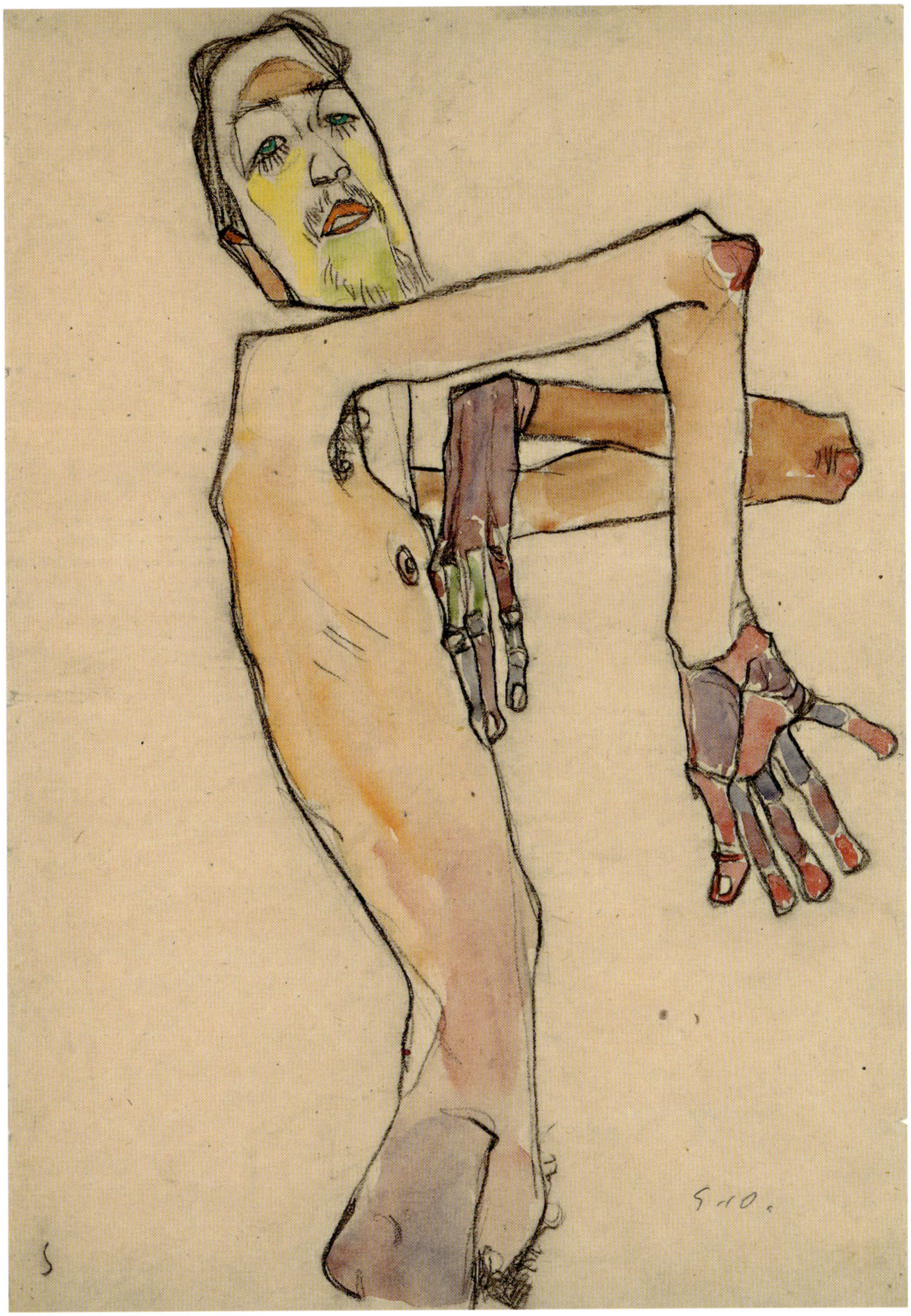

1910

ERWIN DOMINIK OSEN WITH FINGERTIPS TOUCHING ("MIME VAN OSEN")

This nude's columnar trunk, intersected by the hands forming a single horizontal line, seems to continue upward through the neck and head, the hair forming a sort of capital at the top. The tilted axis of the whole construction, relieved somewhat by the angled lines of the forearms, gives the composition a certain tension and restlessness. However, the almost level line of the hands holds it in check.

The detail in the drawing of the face and hands is impressive. They – and the navel – are the only areas to which Schiele added color, but this time in harmonious tones and not the exaggerated ones of the previous nude. (RL)

Black chalk, watercolor, gouache on paper
38.3 × 30.3 cm
Leopold Museum, Vienna, Inv. 2348
K D.600

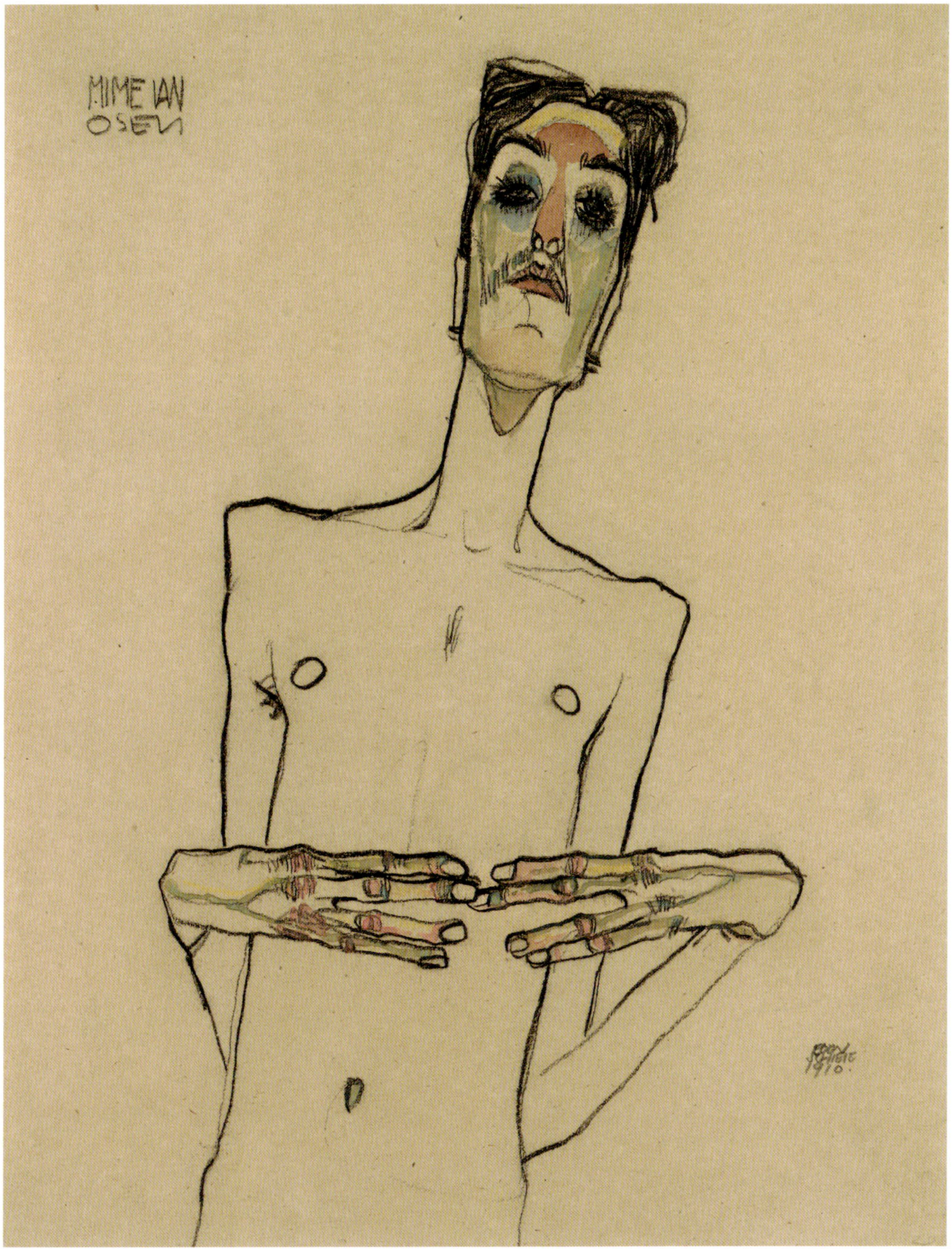
MIME VAN
OSEN
1910

1910

SQUATTING FEMALE NUDE

This impressive presentation of a nude is composed of opposing movements, and its internal structure, though minimal, is clearly executed. Crucial to its success is the decisive outline with the many small angles along its course. It is interesting how the lines of the face are taken up and continued by those of the neck.

Schiele succeeded perfectly with the obviously risky combination of colors in the head, the orange of the face interrupted by traces of green and contrasting with the lilac-red and blue of the hair. The body is mainly a yellow-ocher with occasional green and yellowish tones. Contrast is provided by the red of the nipples, the small spot of red in the navel, and the black crayon lines of the pubic hair. The surrounding white aura sets off the figure from the yellowish tone of the paper.

In 1910 Schiele's favorite paper for drawing was a light-colored brown paper, on which he generally drew with a black crayon. Depending on how it was stored, this sort of paper will appear more or less darkened today on account of its high lignin content. (RL)

Black chalk, gouache, opaque white on paper
44.7 × 31 cm
Leopold Museum, Vienna, Inv. 1456
K D.556

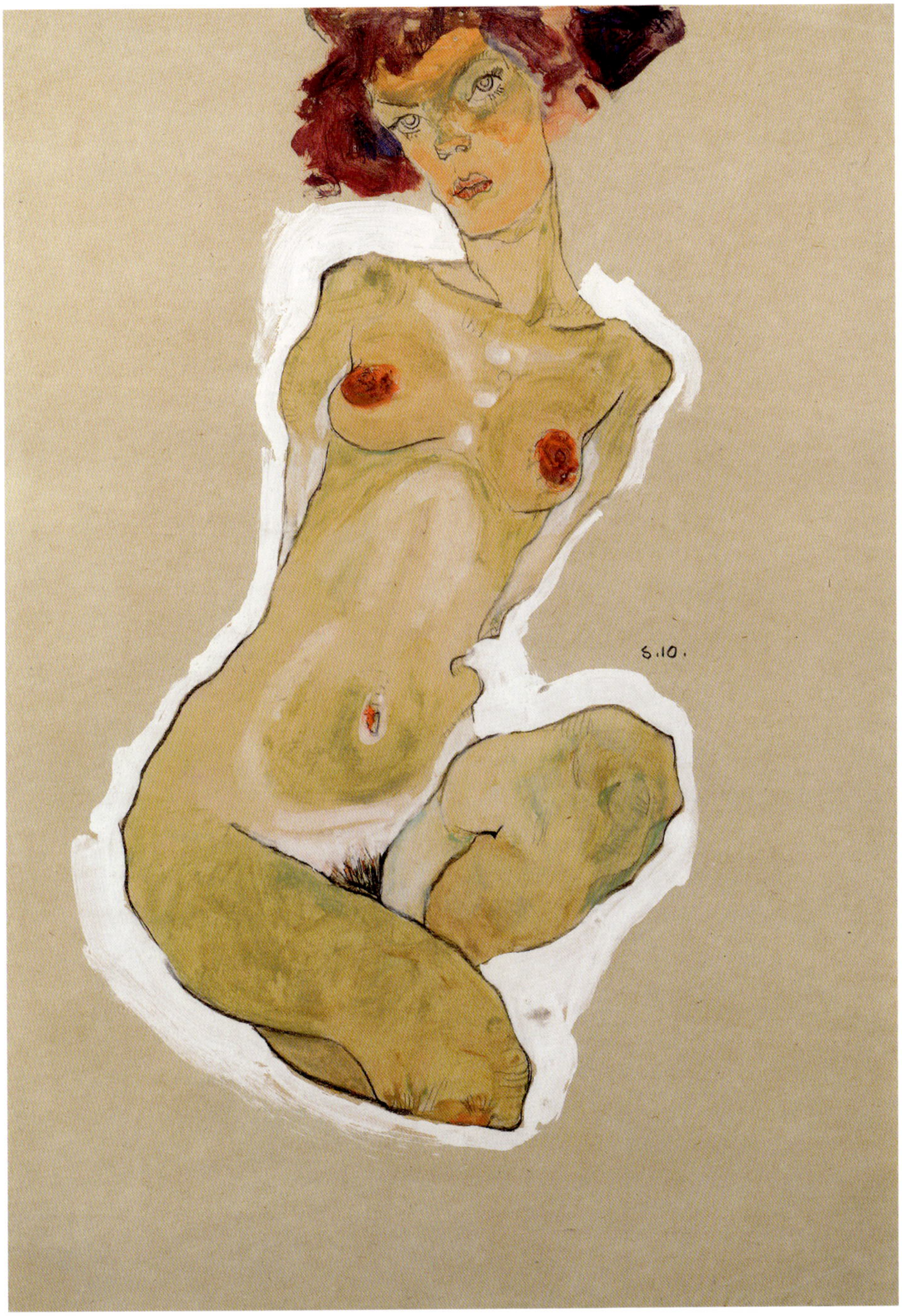
S.10.

1910

SELF-PORTRAIT WITH SHIRT

Only the figure is colored; the white shirt was simply left the color of the paper. The last joints of the fingers of the left hand are not shown, while the bent right hand is represented solely by the last two joints of the fingers and the fingernails. The lively outlines of these fingers are especially fascinating.
Here again all of the elements of the composition are interrelated; the hands refer to each other and together they anchor the whole. The hair looks like tongues of flame. This time Schiele gave the same light reddish brown to his eyes. (RL)

Black chalk, watercolor, opaque color on paper
45 × 31.6 cm
Leopold Museum, Vienna, Inv. 2317
K D.682

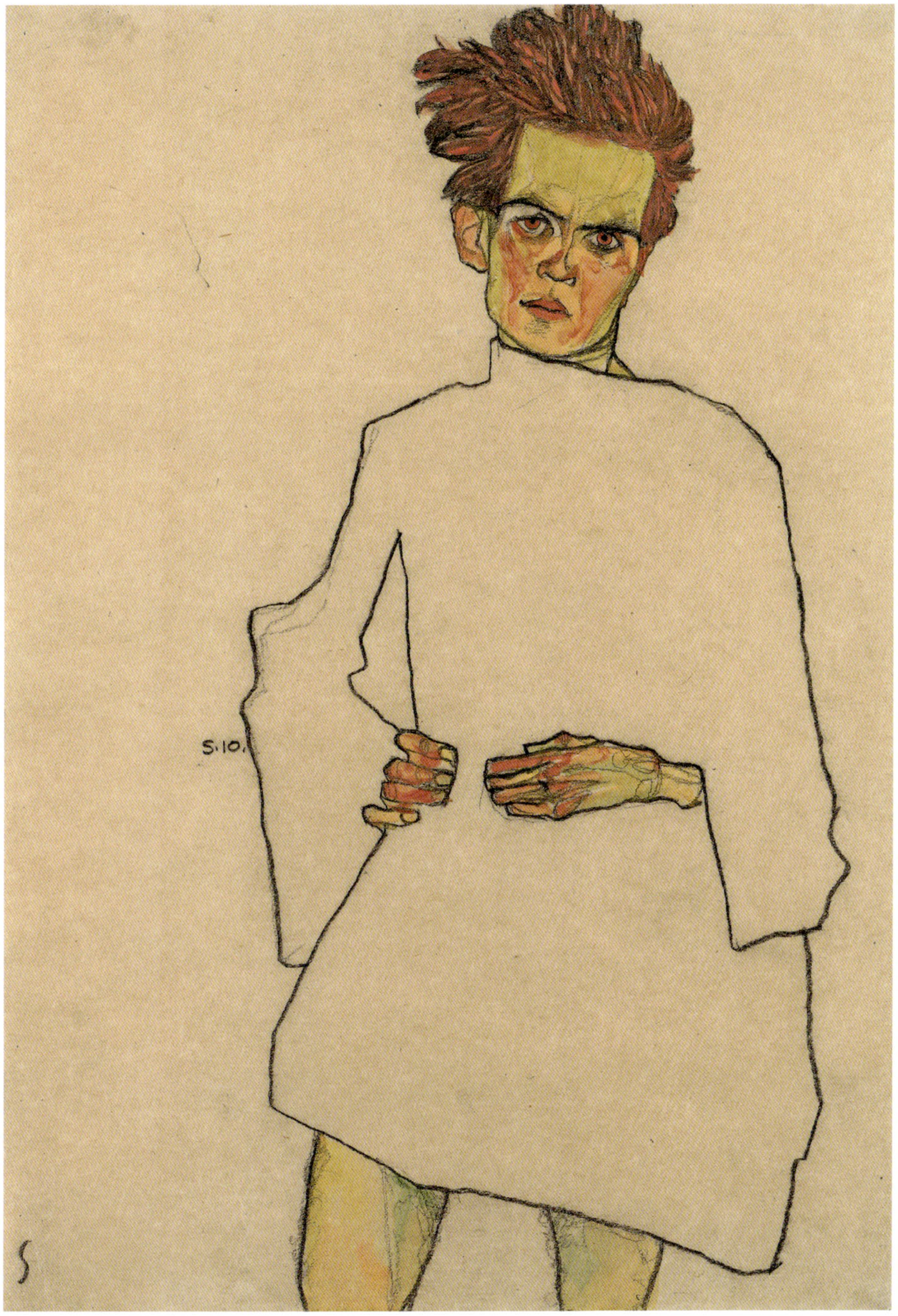
S.10.

1910

SELF-PORTRAIT WITH STRIPED SHIRT

This is perhaps Schiele's loveliest self-portrait in watercolor. A young man looks out at the world with large, questioning eyes. These eyes, the high forehead, and the full shock of hair are set apart from the lower part of the face also in terms of size in order to emphasize the predominance of the mind. The oversized head is carried by a delicate, still-adolescent body. The narrow-chested torso is only suggested, but the few lines are enough.

The sloping shoulders are barely indicated so that we are not distracted from the key elements in the composition. The large, colorful head is balanced by the equally colorful striped shirt-sleeve that has been deliberately separated from it by the uncolored body of the shirt. Of the right sleeve we see just a narrow triangle beyond the line of the chest.

One need only look at the impressive rendering of the hair or the modeling of the forehead and the temples to recognize that Schiele has by now become a masterful painter. The olive-gray of the forehead is set against the light red of the cheeks. Traces of blue help define the angle of the jaw. The bright red-orange ear stands out against the dark hair above it. These colors are unnatural, to be sure, but they have been applied in the proper relationships, so that the effect is altogether lifelike.

Even though the flesh tones are vivid, it is the eyes, with their dramatic contrast between light and dark that dominate the composition.

The work is a masterpiece in every respect, idiosyncratic and authoritative. Mature deliberation and intuition are evident in equal measure. (RL)

Black chalk, gouache on paper
44.3 × 30.5 cm
Leopold Museum, Vienna, Inv. 1458
K D.694

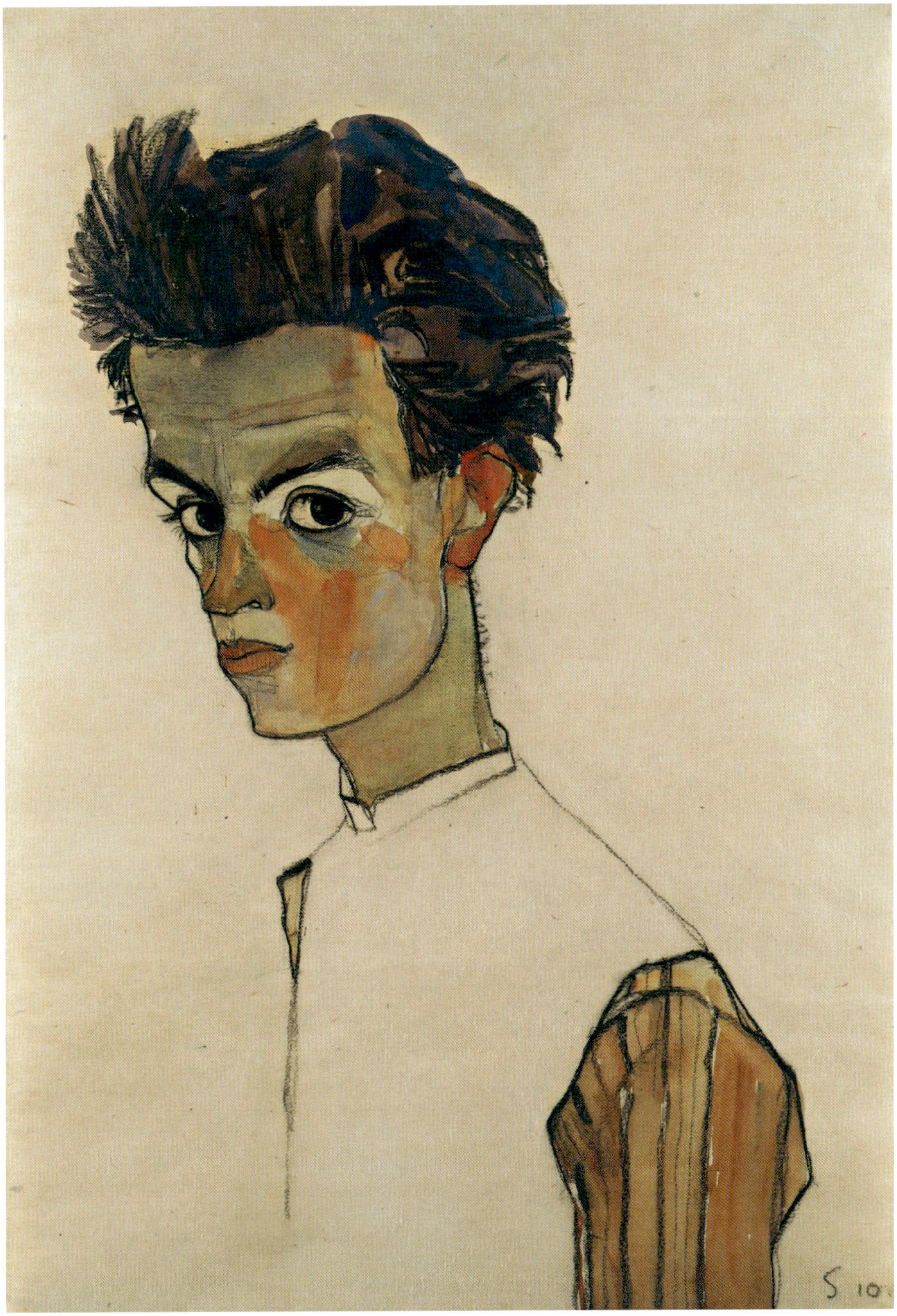
S 10

1910

NUDE SELF-PORTRAIT IN GRAY WITH OPEN MOUTH

One could hardly imagine a greater contrast between the quizzical face of the youth in the preceding self-portrait and this depiction. The naked man looks like he is being crucified and his face registers sheer horror. Everything is rendered in grim grays and black; only around the eyes is there a trace of yellow to heighten their expressiveness.

The arms are only suggested, so that the form remains self-contained. The composition is concentrated, the figure autonomous. (RL)

Black chalk, gouache on paper
44.8 × 32.1 cm
Leopold Museum, Vienna, Inv. 1460
K D.696

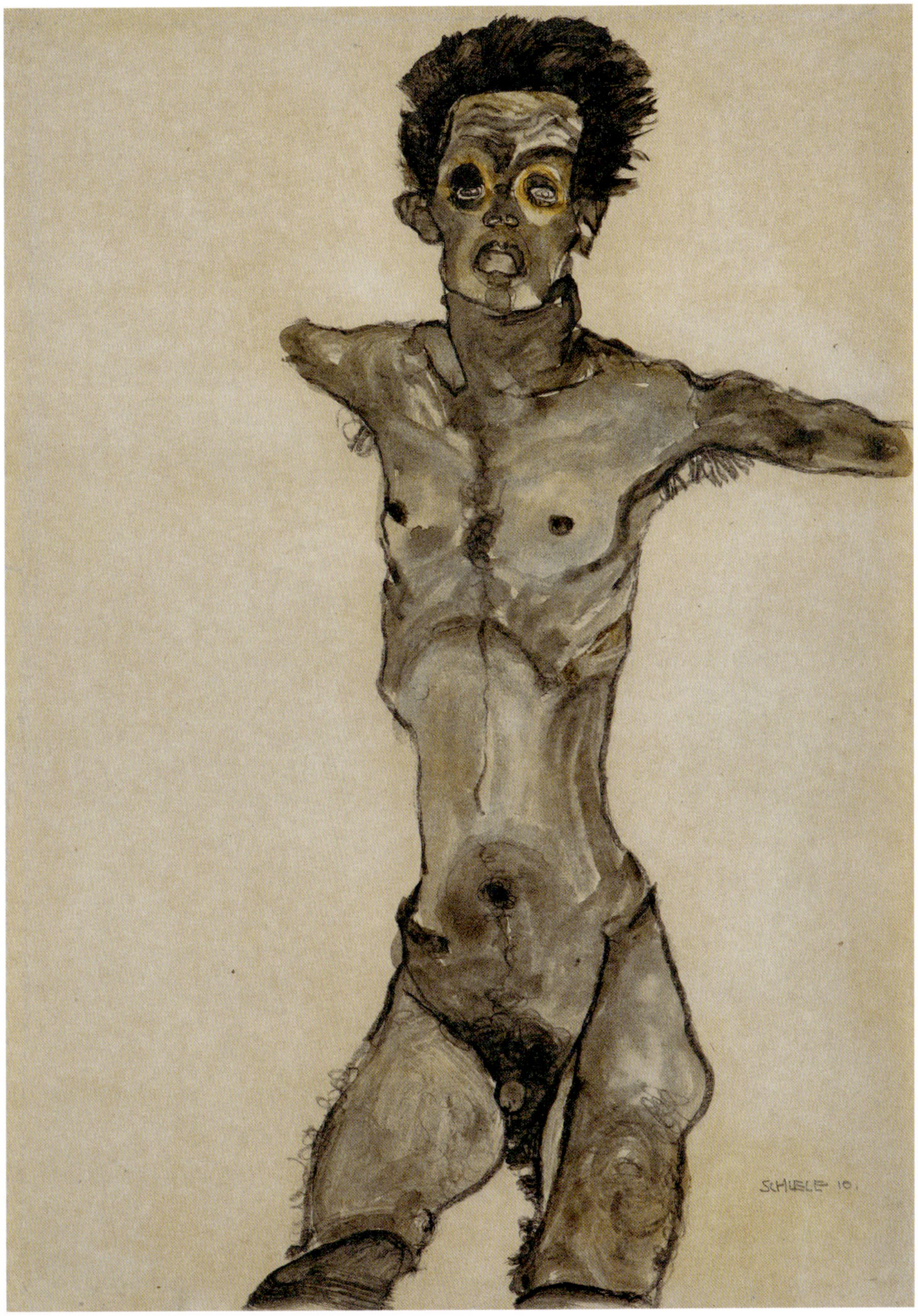
SCHIELE 10.

1910

GIRL IN BLACK DRESS WITH SPREAD LEGS

In a considerable portion of his work, Schiele shows himself to be obsessed with sex. This girl inspired him to make a number of erotic depictions, of which the one reproduced here is perhaps the most successful. Inside the dark hem of her skirt, virtually framed by it, the lighter area is as though set on a stage, the reddish, and therefore very noticeable, genitals surrounded by white and yellowish underwear.

Equally striking, however, is the degree of calculation evident in this composition and its considerable formal balance. The narrow wedge of the skirt stretched between the knees, with its strong, nearly straight lines anchors two triangles, one above and one below. The upper one consists of the sensitively painted gray-black blouse, the lower one of the angled legs. The feet provide a certain countermovement.

The colors in the work are especially delightful. Schiele juxtaposed the various shades from gray to black with those from orange to red – not to mention the touches of green in the skirt – and finally the white of the undergarments to the black and red. The face and hair appear precisely at the top of the figure's central axis, the exposed genitals at the bottom of it. In the one case the red is surrounded by a white aureole, in the other by the white of the underwear. The foreshortening of the face, although only lightly drawn, is masterful. (RL)

Pencil, gouache, opaque white on paper
43.9 × 30.4 cm
Leopold Museum, Vienna, Inv. 3664
K D.418

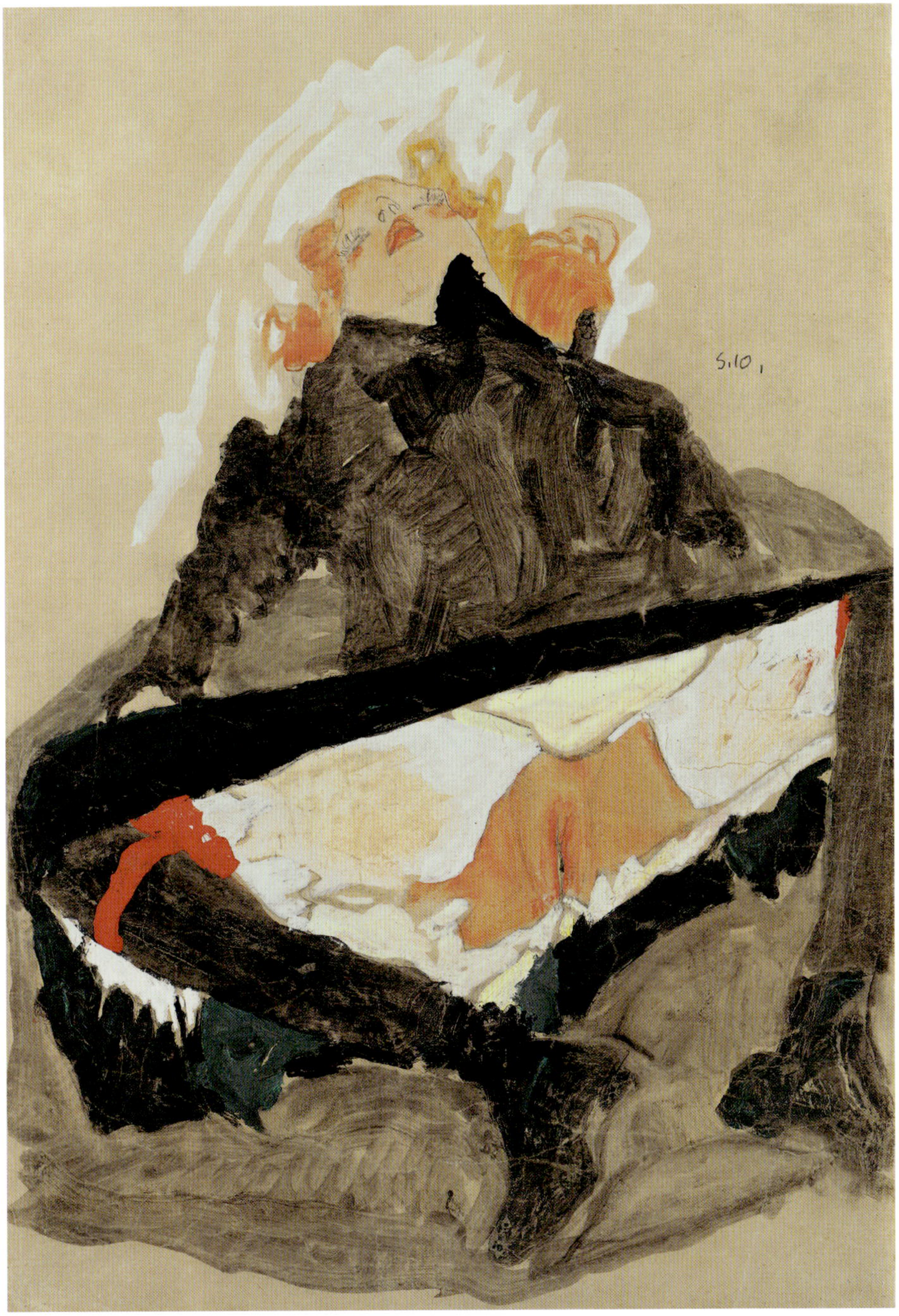
S.10.

1910

SELF-PORTRAIT IN BLACK GARMENT

A strange and mysterious man, wearing black, fixes the viewer with a glassy and melancholy gaze. Schiele has here drawn and painted himself very differently from the way he did only a short time before. He is no longer a boyish young man (see p. 73).

With the exception of the face, which has a pale yellow ground – part of the alienating effect of the portrait – the figure is painted in nothing but black and the many gradations of it made possible by diluting it with water. The right sleeve is solid black, the left one, by contrast, considerably lighter. The series of diagonal brushstrokes in a light gray next to it make it seem even less substantial. These brushstrokes serve to break the symmetry of the composition. At the same time, the nervous strokes – and the blottings surrounding the head – create a certain space for the figure. This is not a haphazard sketch; everything – even the retention of the dribble of black below the lapel – has been carefully attuned. The eye sockets have been left unpainted, as have the shirt collar and the hand. Here the light eye sockets, which in reality would have been darker of course, do not seem a mere artistic trick as they often did earlier (see, for example, the *Male Nude Kneeling, with Raised Hands (Self-Portrait),* L 140; K P.168), but rather accord with the spirit of the whole. The slight curve of the body and the predominantly gray tones with the brushstrokes still visible in the body of the coat give the figure a ghostly appearance.

The assured brushwork of this self-portrait represents one of Schiele's greatest achievements as a painter. (RL)

Pencil, gouache on paper
45.1 × 30.9 cm
Leopold Museum, Vienna, Inv. 1447
K D.699

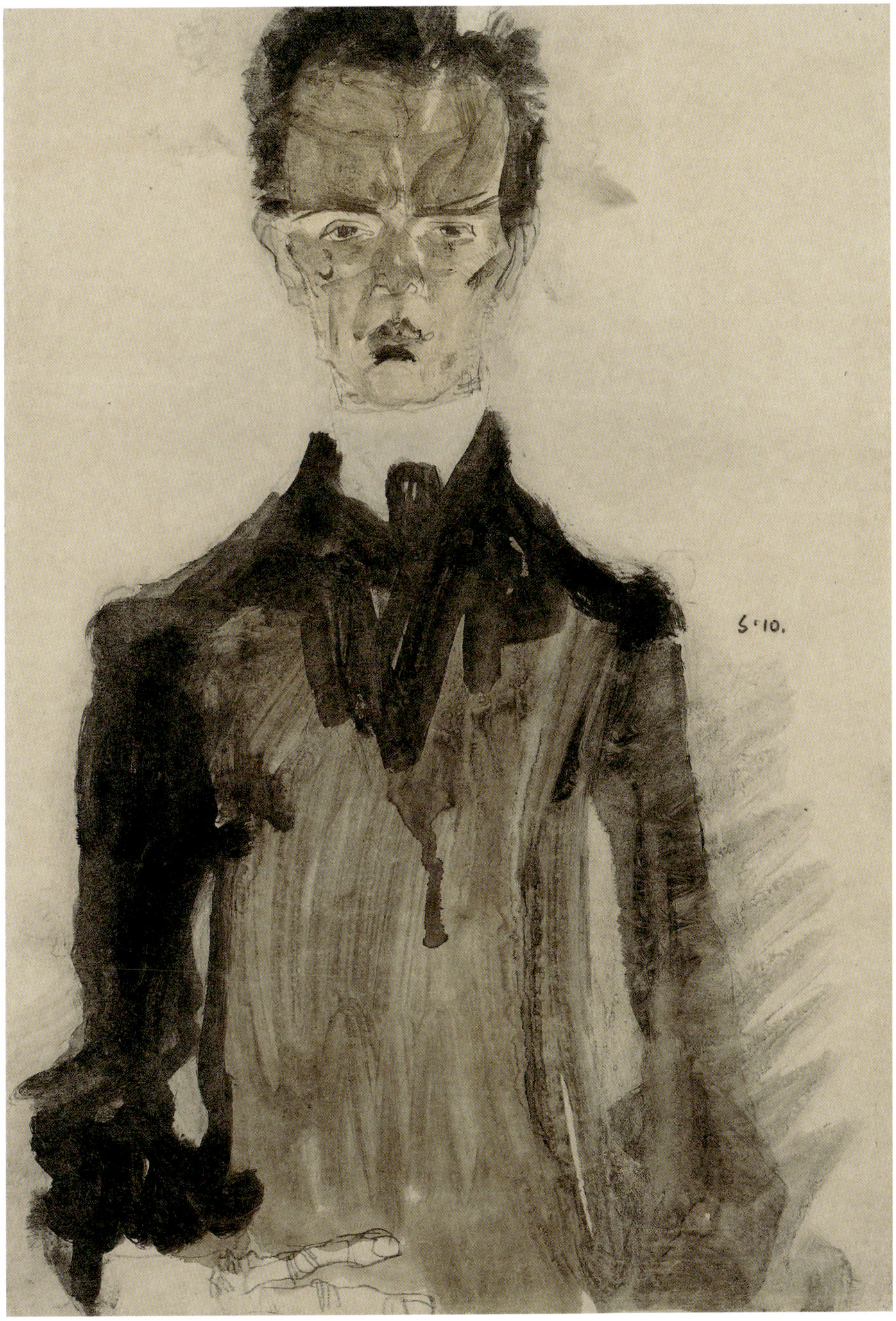
S'10.

1910

NUDE SELF-PORTRAIT

This sheet alone with works on both sides shows what amazing progress Schiele made in a single year. At the beginning of 1910 he was still a talented Jugendstil artist working in traditional styles; by the end he had broken through to a completely independent Expressionism. The self-portrait reproduced here also shows an advance compared to previous works of this year. He no longer paints the parts of the body in wholly different colors, as he did in the nude shown on p. 61; instead, he emphasizes the divisions important for the picture with almost graphic brushstrokes in a limited range of color.

Schiele's critics referred to works of his such as this as "rabbit pictures", as they found they resembled skinned rabbits in a butcher's display. When Schiele learned of this, he vowed to paint many more pictures of this kind. Today they could also serve as reminders of the concentration camps.

The anatomical exaggeration of this work is nevertheless balanced by the clear, calculated composition. It is fascinating how the formation of the torso, the rib cage with the arms – truncated so as not to distract from the form – relates to the pelvis, and how the column of the neck rises up out of the hollow behind the collarbones. The whole is crowned by a head painted in a chiaroscuro that is a masterful achievement.

The figure is set off from the buff tint of the brown paper by a white outline that registers its every contour. It too reflects the Expressionism toward which Schiele was heading. The resulting image is wholly his own, a moving, expressive cipher compounded of outline, color, and an exemplary composition. (RL)

Pencil, black chalk, gouache, opaque white on brown paper
44.9 × 31.1 cm
Leopold Museum, Vienna, Inv. 2320
K D.708

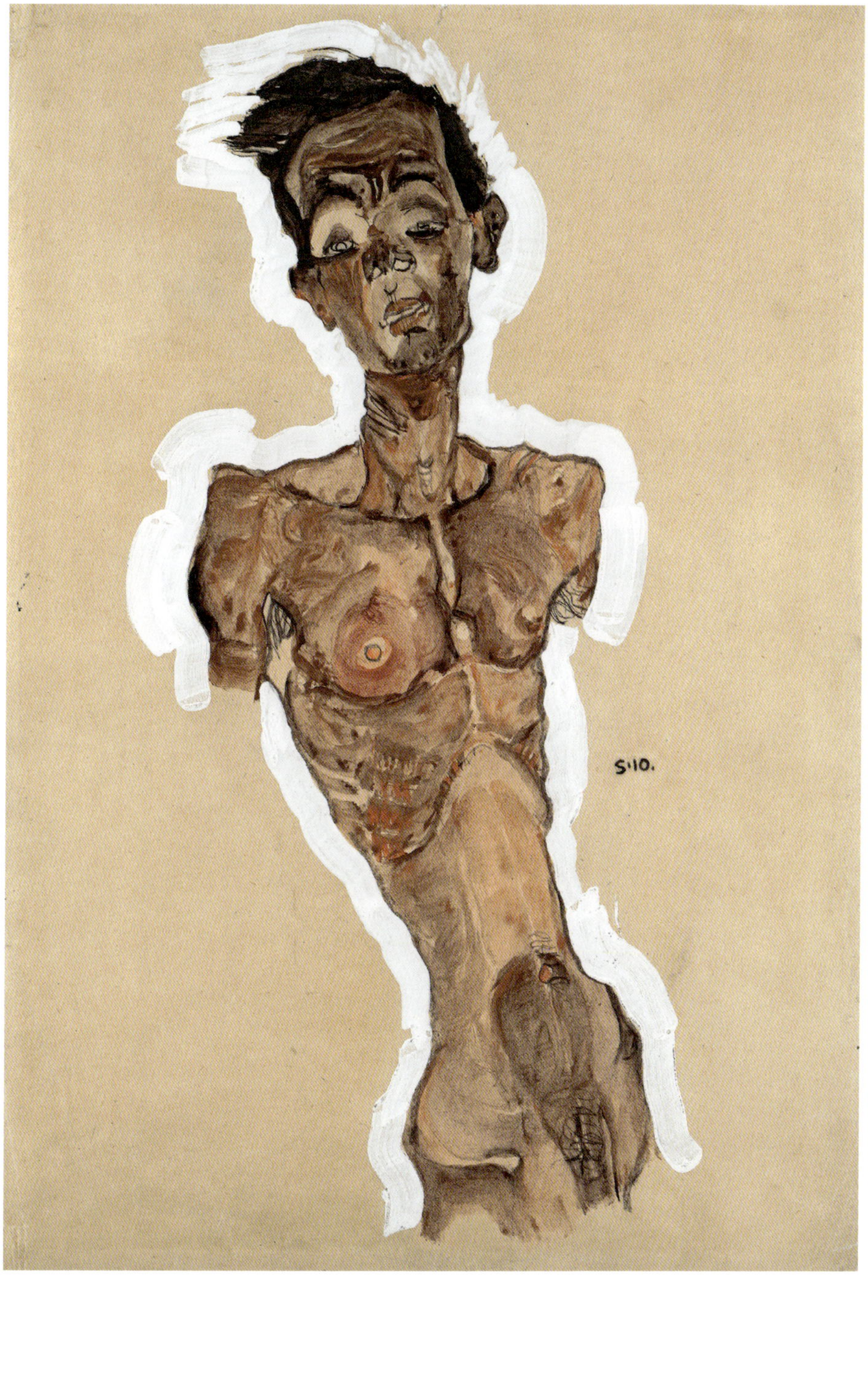
S.10.

1910

SELF-PORTRAIT, GRIMACING

Exaggeration is part of all of Schiele's self-portraits from 1910. Here the face is hideously contorted. Only the odd tooth is visible in the open mouth – although Schiele had perfectly fine teeth – the eyebrows are raised as high as possible, and the open shirt reveals his scrawny chest.
The deliberately unnatural coloring ranges from red to blue, and Schiele exploited that contrast in the jacket especially. There he also applied the color in a manner that clearly sets it apart from the flesh tones.
The apparent contrast between this unnatural coloring and the exaggerated drawing is reconciled by a strong sense of composition, and the result is definitely something new. (RL)

Black chalk, gouache on paper
45.3 × 30.7 cm
Leopold Museum, Vienna, Inv. 2312
K D.705

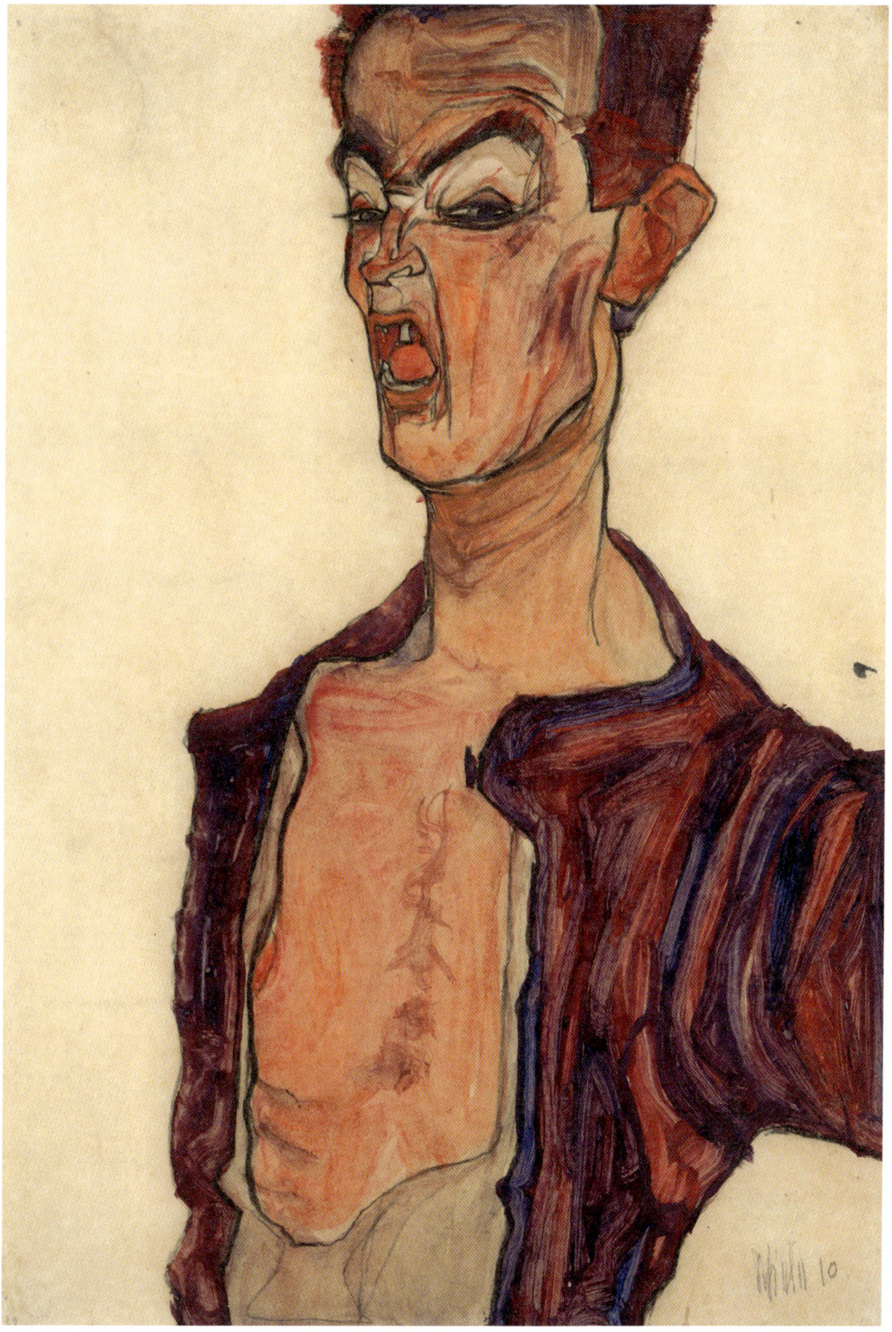

1910

GIRL WITH TILTED HEAD (GERTI SCHIELE)

It has not been noticed before, but Schiele used this drawing when painting the head of the *Dead Mother I* (see p. 87). Presumably his sister Gerti posed for the drawing, tilting her head to the side and slightly to the back. As a result – in contrast to the face in the painting – the face is slightly foreshortened, especially the nose. However, the line of the neck and the face, the angle of the cheekbone, the way the hair falls to the left and the shape of the lips are very like those of the mother in the work *Dead Mother I*. It is therefore highly likely that this pencil drawing was a study for the head in the painting.
Given Schiele's stylistic evolution, it is also clear that the drawing could only have been done in either November or December of 1910. (RL)

Pencil on paper
43.8 × 30.2 cm
Leopold Museum, Vienna, Inv. 1449
K D.586

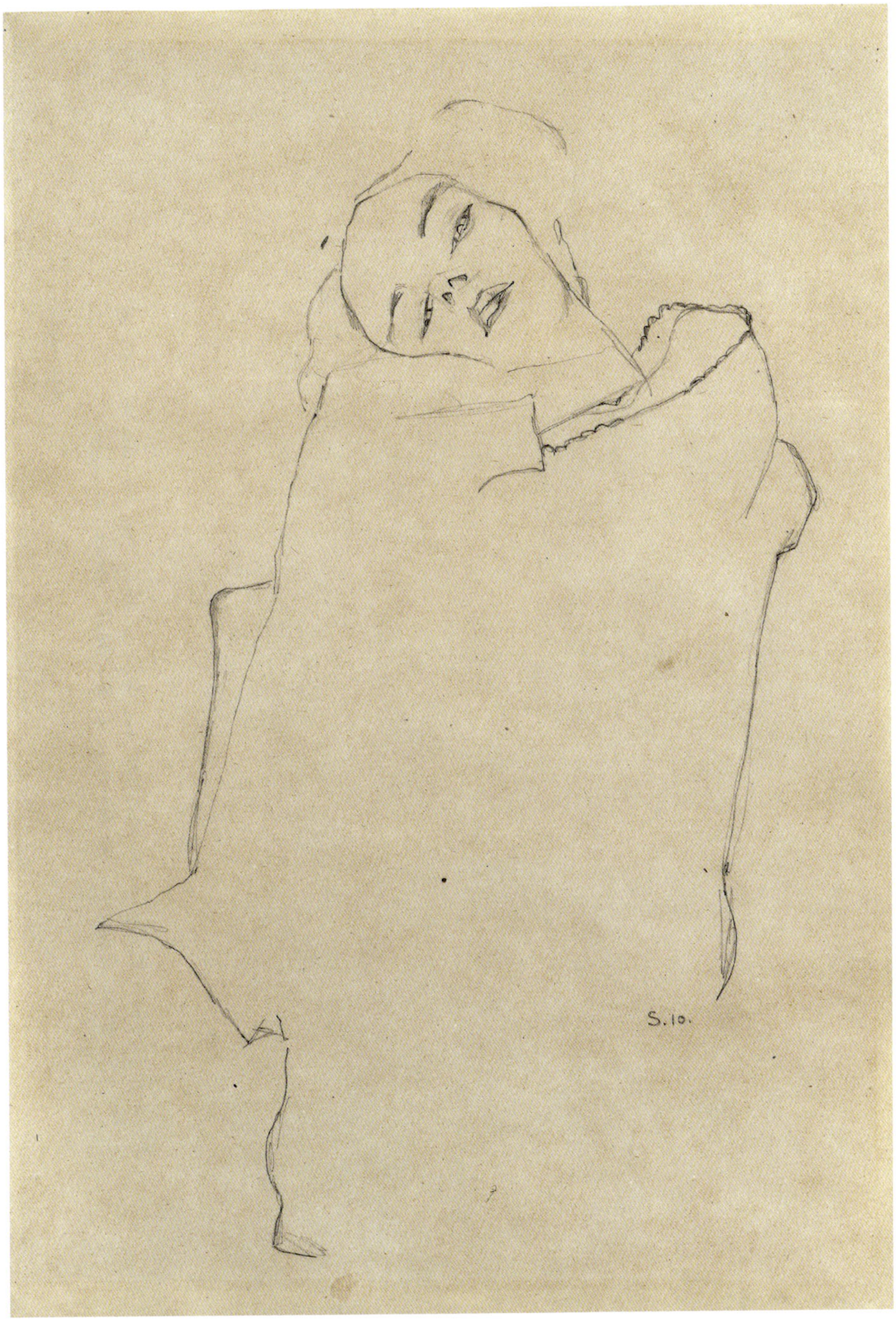
S.10.

1910

DEAD MOTHER I

Given its painterly style and the way color has been added as a means of heightening its graphic structure, this painting can only have been executed in either November or December of 1910. The fine pencil drawing visible in the hands is characteristic of this period. The three lighter and sharply defined areas – the mother's face and neck, her hand, and the child visible in her womb – are aligned along a slightly tilted axis rising upward from the lower left. The infant's head and hands essentially follow this axis, whereas the mother's face and hand lie perpendicular to it. This contrast and the tilted alignment of these most important elements of the composition create a sense of movement that is then held in check by the rest of the painting. The overall effect is accordingly one of self-contained harmony. The pale flesh tones of the mother's face and neck are abruptly cut off by the band of black beneath. Above it, however, between the face and the brownish and bluish black background, there is a somewhat lighter section comprising her hair and a thin, wedge-shaped portion of her dress. The painting thus alternates sharp contrasts with more subtle ones.

The mother's hair, which falls on the left, could have been derived from the *Pietà* that Kokoschka produced for the summer theater of the *Internationale Kunstschau* in Vienna in 1909 (see p. 9), but here its execution and the resulting effect are altogether different. Unlike Kokoschka, Schiele was concerned with subtler relationships, and he used this hair as a kind of crown for his composition.

Important inspiration for the tilted face cut off by a dark shape below came from Klimt's painting *Mother with Two Children (Family)* (N 188), which was exhibited in Venice in 1910. But if one compares this detail of the head in the two paintings and their overall concept, it becomes apparent that Klimt failed to adequately express the deeper meaning of this particular subject, especially in terms of color. The woman's vivid flesh color seems inconsistent with her deeply sorrowing pose. And the children, presumably helpless and threatened, look much too winsome.

Not so in Schiele's work. The inherent tragedy is communicated in every part of the composition. The child is truly helpless; the mother's features are visibly distorted by grief. Her eyes have glazed over. The skin colors, the washed-out face and hand of the mother and the orange and yellow-red of the infant, clearly contrast death and life. The latter colors virtually glow in contrast to the surrounding blackness.

The black strokes encircling the section containing the infant are not meant to suggest folds of the mother's clothing, but rather the impenetrable barrier that traps the helpless creature: the corpse of its mother, who even in death continues to press her hand to her body as though to protect her infant.

The tragedy is genuine, and it is deeply affecting. The artistic image is wholly expressive of the subject matter. This painting, executed in the final months of 1910, is one of Schiele's most riveting creations. (RL)

Oil, pencil on wood
32.1 × 25.7 cm
Leopold Museum, Vienna, Inv. 475
L 167; K P.177

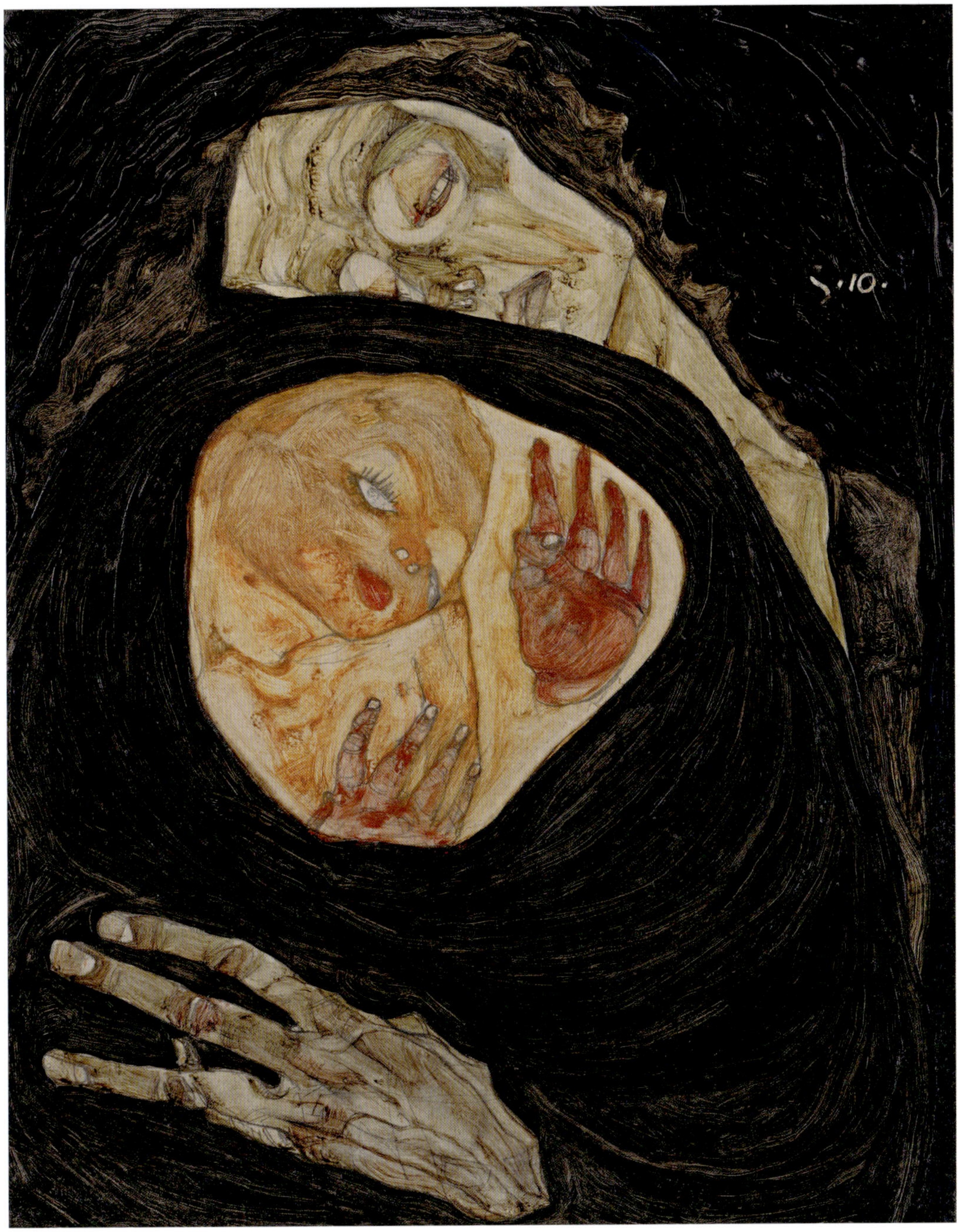
S.10.

1910

SITTING NUDE GIRL WITH STOCKINGS AND SHOES

The chair, the right arm, and the bottoms of the feet have been omitted for compositional reasons. We only realize that the girl is, in fact, sitting down from the notch in her right hip and thigh. Schiele achieved a degree of delicacy in this soft pencil drawing from late 1910 that he would never surpass.

The same girl, here posed innocently enough, also served as the model for some highly erotic images in late 1910 and early 1911. Some are simple drawings, others are colored with pigments that Schiele mixed, so as to produce more graphic structures, with Syndetikon, a common adhesive at the time made of carbohydrates and water glass. (RL)

Pencil on paper
55 × 35.7 cm
Leopold Museum, Vienna, Inv. 1390
K D.576

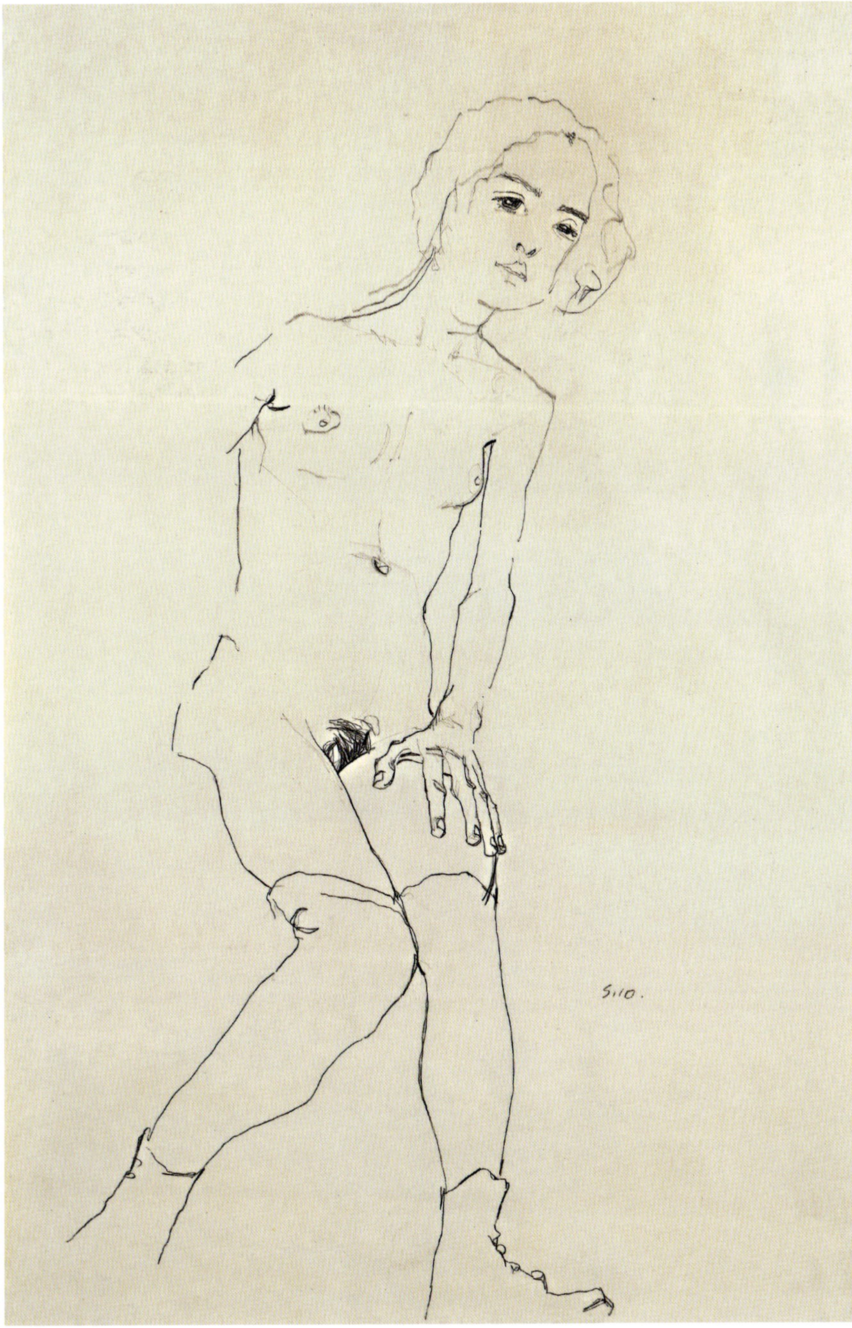

1910

SUN TREE

This is one of Schiele's most imaginative compositions in terms of color. Accordingly, he inscribed the work on the back with the title *Sun Tree*.

Compared with the drawings showing chrysanthemums (K. D.745–747) also created in 1910, this rendering shows the highest diversity of color. While the composition is held together by a graphic framework, this is eclipsed by the wealth of impulsively designed details and the exuberant vivacity of the colors. Despite the fact that numerous harsher tones dominate over muted green hues, Schiele managed to bring the coloring together to create a harmonious whole. The work was created in immediate proximity to the study for Schiele's *Thunderstorm Mountain (Chapel on Kreuzberg near Krumau)* (L 159; K. P.184, 185). This is illustrated not only by the identical application of the viscous opaque colors, a technique Schiele frequently employed to invest his brush strokes with a richer structure, but also by the occurrence of many very similar tones – for instance the same light blue-green used for accentuation.

Though Schiele let his imagination run wild in this rendering, the depicted flowers nevertheless appear very natural. (RL)

Black chalk, gouache on paper
39.5 × 31.5 cm
Leopold Museum, Vienna, Inv. 3663
K. D.748

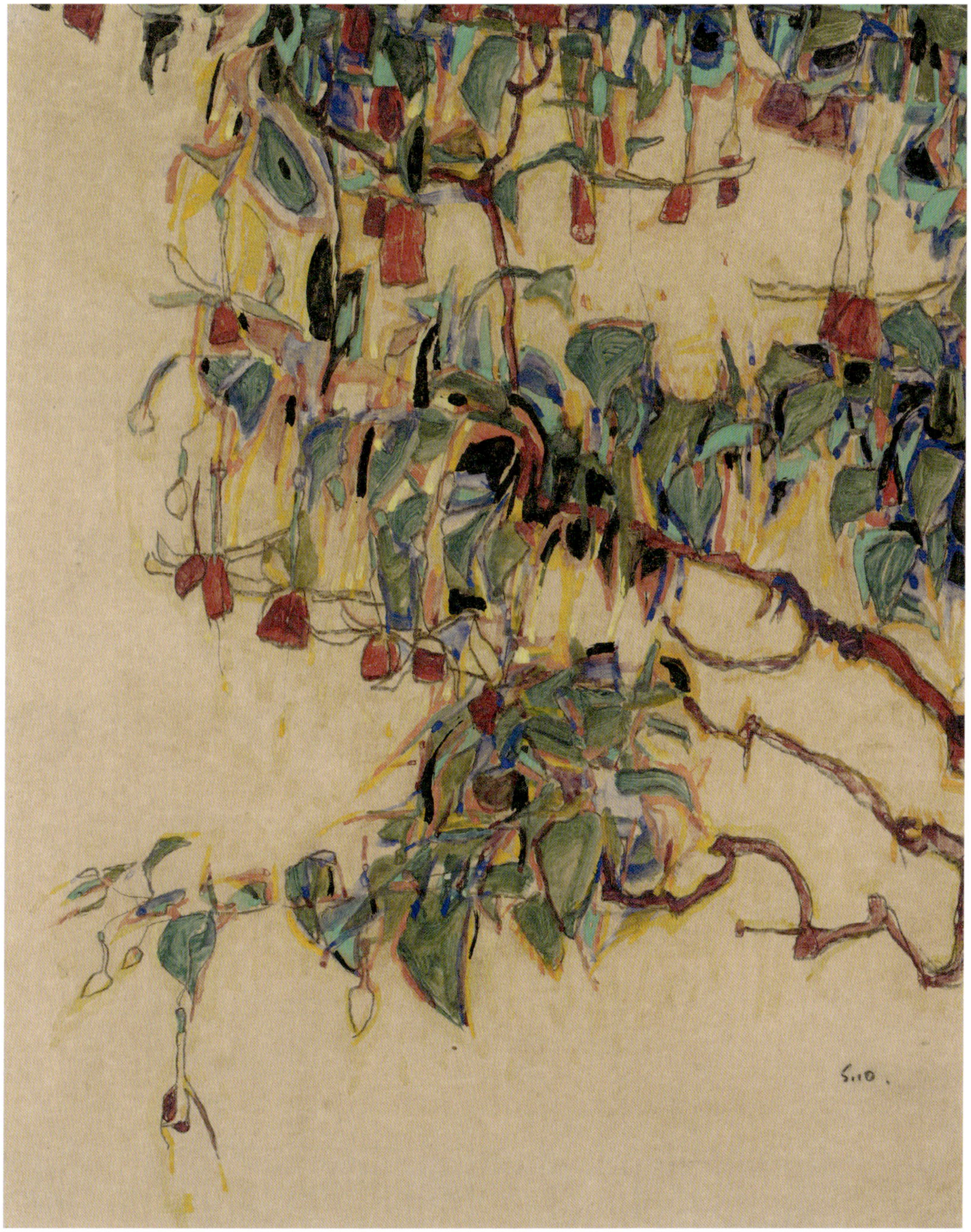

1911

THE LYRICIST

Schiele's *The Lyricist* – obviously given his own features – is not at home in the world and seems virtually crushed by its weight. He is a troubled, melancholy ecstatic. This is nevertheless communicated in an image of great formal discipline. Only Schiele would have been capable of combining the two. The first hint of such a composition is the ink and watercolor drawing of a *Girl Crouching in a Flower Meadow* (see p. 39) from roughly a year before, but here all traces of Jugendstil have been abandoned. The aureole that frequently surrounds the head in Klimt's portraits was included for purely decorative purposes. In Schiele's work, however, the aureole above the head is an element of the compositional structure.

The dark garment covers all but a narrow strip of the figure's left shoulder creating a shape that appears to be a long, thin neck (Schiele had already produced a similar effect in his portrait of the painter Karl Zakovsek, (L 148; K P.160)). The left hand appears unnaturally thin as well. Its lack of a thumb is a Schiele trademark; he frequently either omits the thumb altogether or draws it bent at a sharp angle or turned into the palm of the hand.

The line below the head and the neck serves as a kind of upper border for the composition, one that is supported by the right hand and the column of the nude torso. The displacement of this support to the side is balanced by the right thigh, the lower part of which was deliberately painted in vivid colors so that it forms a counterpart to the face.

The face was drawn with the brush, which again produced a wealth of formal correspondences in its details. If one compares this manner of drawing with the brush to that of van Gogh, one notes that in the latter the lines and dots inspired by Seurat are highly agitated, creating a swirl-like movement. Schiele, by contrast, produces a vivid yet carefully controlled complex of lines. It is ingenious how Schiele relates the slits of the eyes to the different curves of the eyebrows, extends these in turn into the lines of the nose, allows the upper lip to rise in two peaks toward the mismatched nostrils, has the rounded line of the lower lip mirror the upper line of the chin, and structures the latter as a triangle resting on the black garment.

Schiele's self-exposure, both psychological and physical, goes so far as to include the glans of his penis, which he exploits for its bright red color. That spot of red, another at the navel, and a third at the ear become focal points, growing lighter toward the top. Ultimately, the formal qualities of the drawing and the colors, for all their expressiveness, are of equal importance. The dramatic contrast of light and darkness that Schiele selected for his composition is enriched by a multitude of bright but harmonious colors placed with great bravura. (RL)

Oil on canvas
80.5 × 80 cm
Leopold Museum, Vienna, Inv. 450
L 172; K P.192

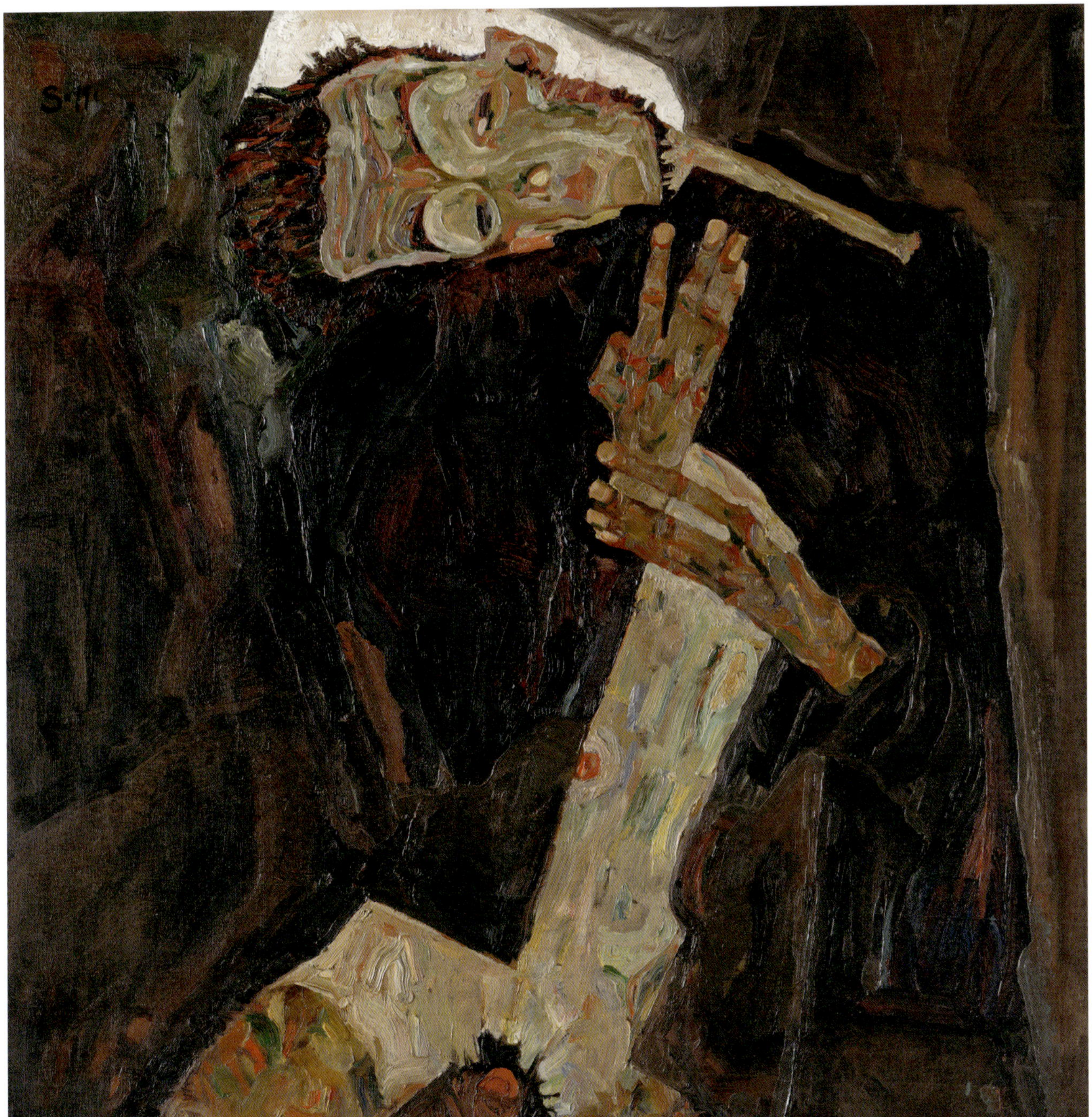

1911

SELF-SEER II (DEATH AND MAN)

Appropriately, Schiele also referred to this painting as *Death and Man*. The painter is sunk in meditation, his eyes closed. The red spots in the center of the lids suggest the intensity of his inward gaze. He sees himself and his approaching fate. His face appears a second time directly behind him, but this one is deathly pale, the mouth open, the cheeks sunken. It is the face of a corpse. The doppelgänger's bleached-out shroud billows up behind the figure and to his right. The agitated brushstrokes of the background and a mysterious eye-like object on the right heighten the sense of the uncanny.

Any number of artists have portrayed themselves in the presence of Death, the latter usually in the form of a skeleton – an image that the 20th century no longer finds frightening. Gustav Klimt even used the skeleton decoratively, arming it with a small red cudgel in *Death and Life* (N 193). Schiele was more up to date; even as early as 1911 the 21-year-old managed to depict Death in a way one might imagine it even today. That is why this painting is so disturbing.

Even with subject matter such as this Schiele maintained control, refusing to abandon his picture to formlessness and chaos. His composition is highly calculated, its forms clearly defined. It is particularly fascinating to see how he balances the strangely light area that backs his figure's right side with a few brushstrokes in a very similar tone roughly in the center of the opposite side.

The painting is dominated by shades of brown, which are everywhere enriched by traces of cinnabar-red, muted green, and black. In the drawing *Self-Portrait with Gown* (K D.942), which is related both to this painting and to the *The Lyricist* (p. 93), the arms also form a right angle. Here, however, the situation is somewhat puzzling: the section of the forearm below this intersection is the same color as the arm crossing it, a shade very similar to that of the figure of Death. Given the position of the left arm (imagine it somewhat elongated between the shoulder and elbow), it is possible that this is the arm of Death. Yet both the spread fingers of the other hand – the thumb, as so often, is bent sharply toward the palm – and their somewhat darker color make it clear that it belongs to the living man. In this period Schiele tended toward abstraction and frequently ignored anatomical accuracy for the sake of a more effective composition. (RL)

Oil on canvas
80.5 × 80 cm
Leopold Museum, Vienna, Inv. 451
L 173; K P.193

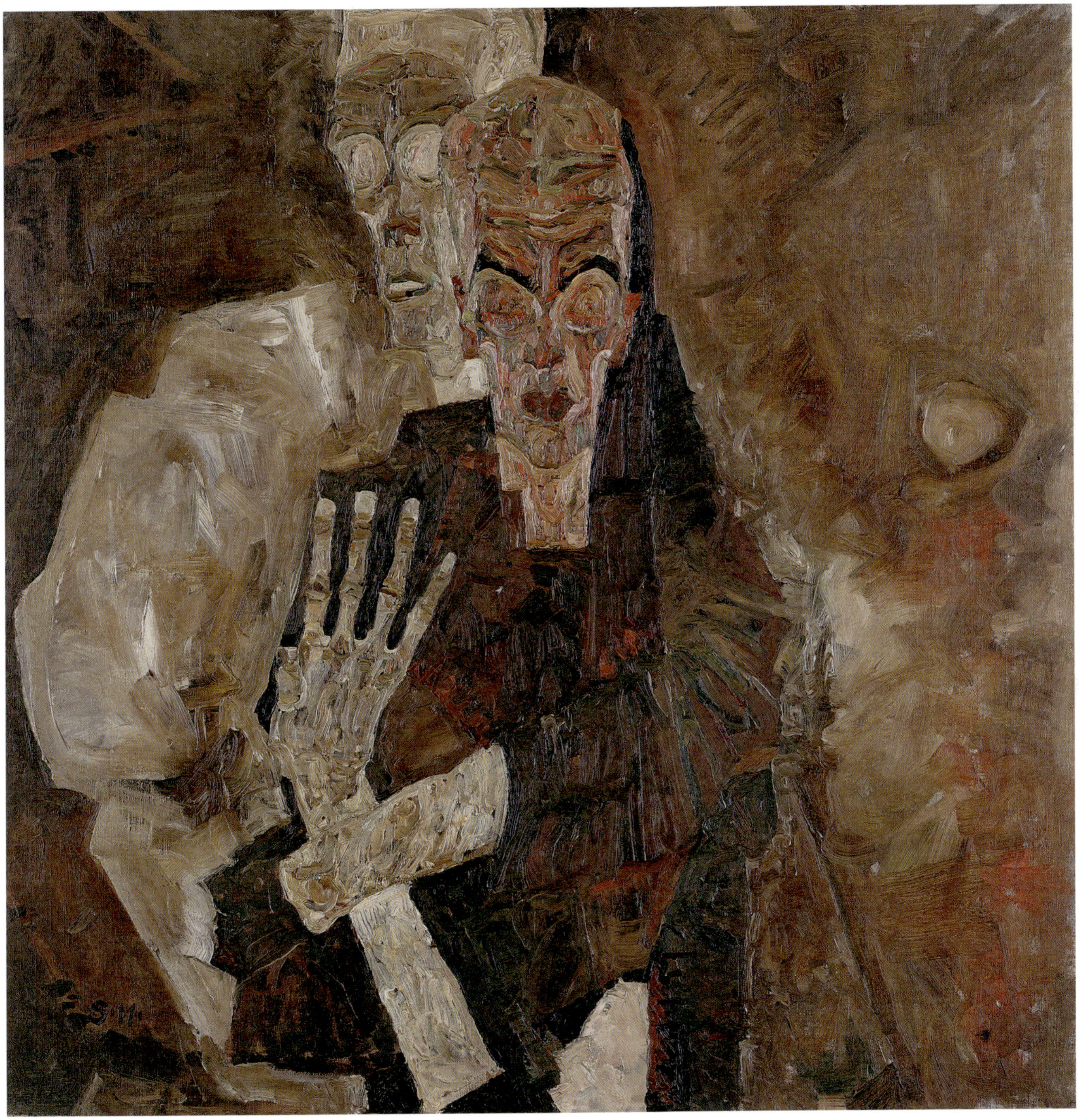

1911

GIRL WITH CROSSED LEGS

A woman with a catlike face – in underwear and skirt – sits with one leg resting on the other. We therefore see her lace bloomers and a bit of her pubic hair, which Schiele has rendered in a dark red. Emphasis on the genitals – whether out of lust or compulsion or both – is a constant in Schiele's work. The legs are so large because they are closer to the viewer and perspective demands that they be so; Schiele exploits the black of the stockings as a contrast to both the whiteness of the undergarments and the aureole surrounding the figure, important elements in his composition. The upper outline of the crossed leg forms a triangle with the hem of the skirt, one that is as though rotated to the left and backed by an irregular oval shape, possibly an armchair. In addition, the axis of the upper body and head slants slightly to the left. It is only the opposing direction of the left leg and the bend in the outline of the background oval next to it that solidifies the composition. The black of the stockings and the reddish brown and blue of the inside of the skirt stand out against the delicate gray of the oval background. The hair repeats these tones and is rendered with a similar fluid kind of painting. This is a very important feature, given Schiele's further development in 1911, whereas the sharper contrasts between the black, the red, and the white – the stockings and their garters, the undergarments, and the aureole surrounding the figure – are already familiar from works done in the last months of the preceding year. (RL)

Pencil, gouache on paper
53.5 × 36 cm
Leopold Museum, Vienna, Inv. 2342
K D.828

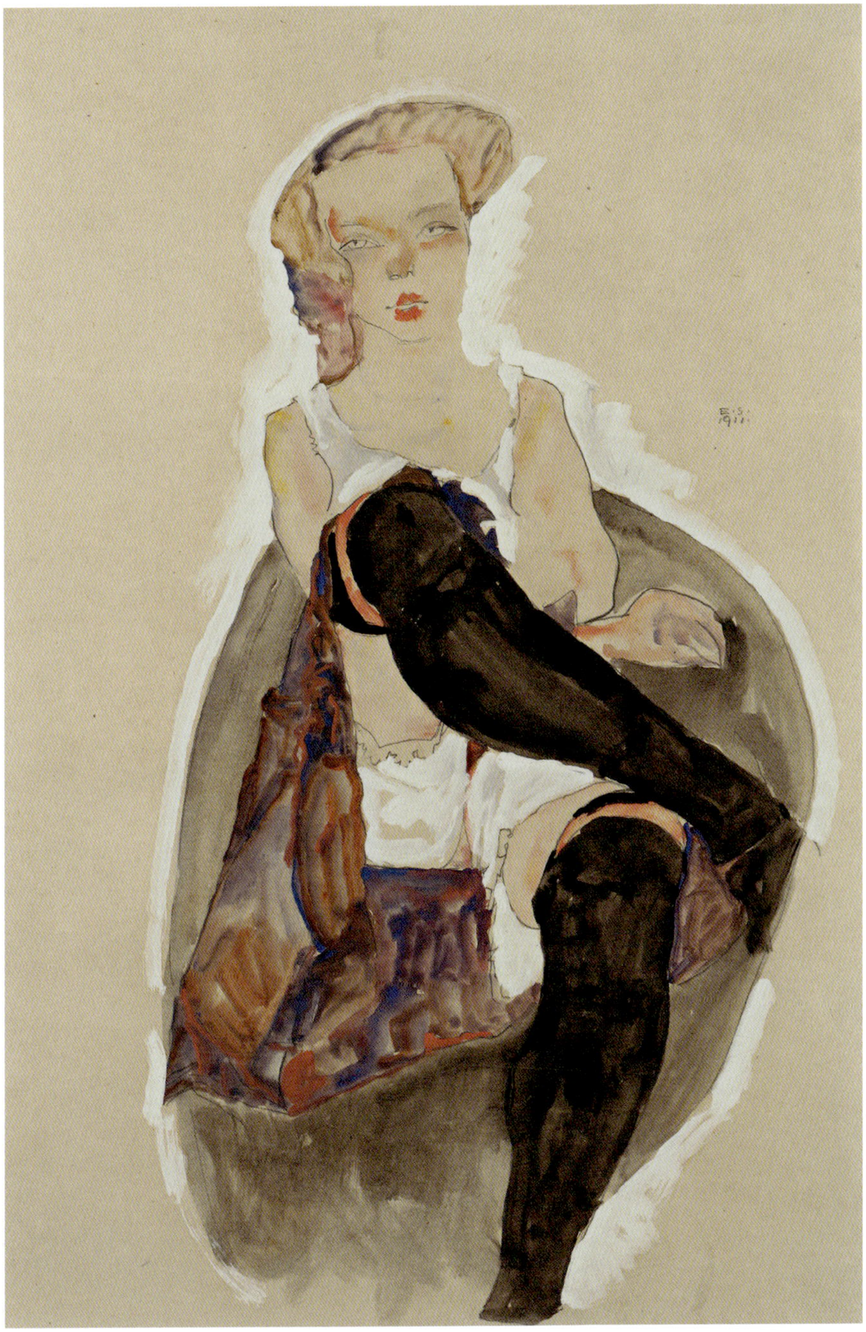

1911

SELF-PORTRAIT WITH SPLAYED FINGERS

This work is one of Schiele's most masterful self-portrayals in terms of color, form and liveliness of expression.
The delicate color nuancing is extraordinary. The way the colors run into each other is also typical of the year 1911, in which Schiele arrived at the pinnacle of painterly freedom. The unnatural lilac hues the artist often used to convey flesh tones in 1910 have disappeared. While the colors used to replace them at this stage of the artist's development by no means appear naturalistic either, the coloring of the depiction (especially as a whole) conveys quite a realistic impression.
The hair and face reveal the same gray-brown and bluish tones and have thus been subsumed into an entity. The trunk between the rib cage and iliac bone shows less coloring so as to separate and accentuate the more highly watercolored sections. Such concentrations of color can be found in the head, upper body, arms and hands, as well as the pelvis. As always, Schiele left the contour lines, which he often drew multiple times, visible, making the lines appear even more animated.
This vivacious immediacy is further expressed through the depicted's posture, which is that of someone halting in the middle of a movement as if taken by surprise. (RL)

Pencil, gouache, heightened with white, on paper
53 × 29.1 cm
Leopold Museum, Vienna, Inv. 1383
K D.952

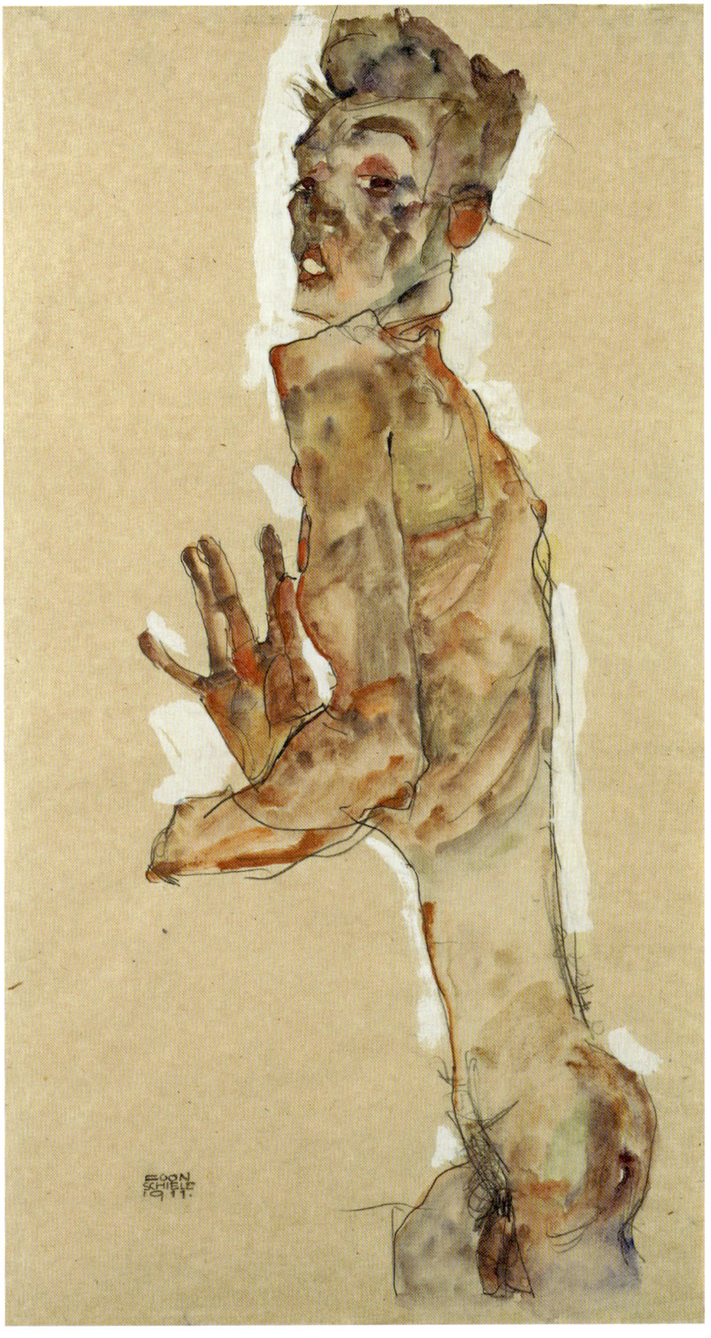
EGON
SCHIELE
1911.

1911

HOUSE AND WALL IN A HILLY LANDSCAPE

This picture was painted not long after the *Self-Seer II (Death and Man)* (see p. 95), as is clear not only from its style of painting, but also its colors. Here Schiele was even less concerned with reality, freely inventing whatever struck him as necessary. This wall and house with a small tower, and especially the bit of crenellation on the right, may have been seen in Krumau, but they have been placed in a wholly different setting, a hilly landscape with a fence extending toward the back. In addition, the right side of the tower surely did not slant inward this way in reality. Schiele chose to paint it like this for formal reasons, opposing the slant with diagonal lines, including those of the fence posts, running in the other direction. The composition seems to be much more abstract than that of the *Self-Seer II (Death and Man),* its painterly chiaroscuro more pronounced. Yet for all its abstraction, the somewhat mysterious scene makes a powerful impression. Schiele achieved much the same effect in a very different way in his *Autumn Tree in Stirred Air (Winter Tree)* (see p. 153). (RL)

Oil on canvas
52 × 43.7 cm
Leopold Museum, Vienna, Inv. 476
L 174; K P.208

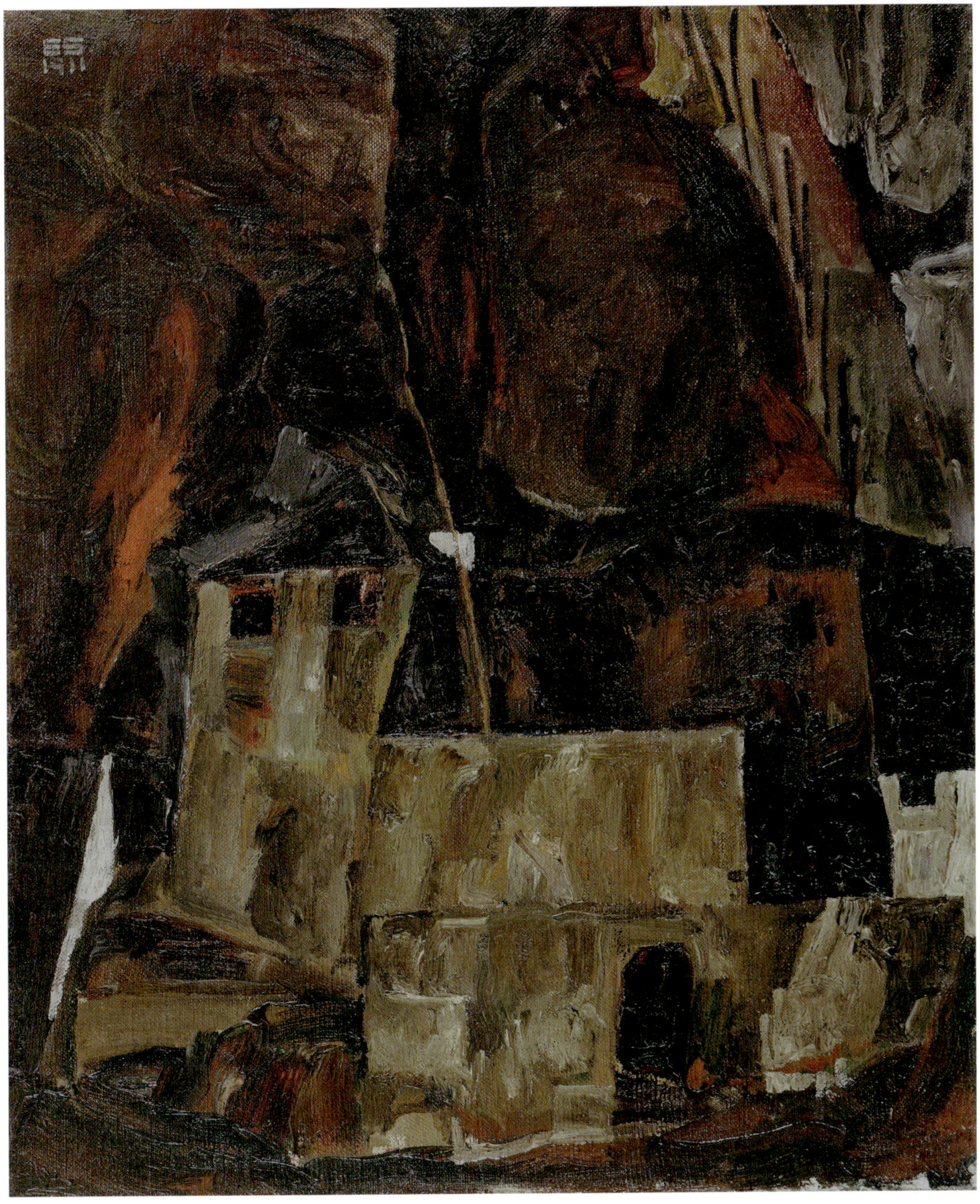

ES
1911

1911

BLACK-HAIRED GIRL WITH LIFTED SKIRT

The face with the dissolved blackish hair and the lower abdomen framed by the dark colors of the skirt (with the genitals surrounded by bright undergarments in the center) appear to be separated rather than connected by the neutral-colored upper body with its only minimal structure, and are thus juxtaposed.

Although certain details in this drawing are very similar to those on p. 97, the watercolors have been applied in a very different manner. Schiele's breakthrough into a more painterly style is especially apparent in his rendering of the hair, the face and the lifted skirt. The abundant hair is virtually monochrome, with only lighter and darker tones of a grayish brown-black, but painted with a remarkable degree of freedom that perfectly captures its texture. The pale face with delicately shaded red and gray around the eyes and on the cheeks and mouth forms a startling contrast. The dark skirt shimmers with color, even though its predominant tone is again a gray-black. The bottom edge of its larger section is tinted with a strong blue that recurs in a similar shade at the top of *Dead City III (City on the Blue River III)* (see p. 105), where it is also used to mark the boundary between light and dark.

In this drawing, Schiele transformed a girl's erotic fantasy into art, capturing it in a masterly display of painting. (RL)

Pencil, gouache on paper
55.8 × 37.9 cm
Leopold Museum, Vienna, Inv. 2307
K D.859

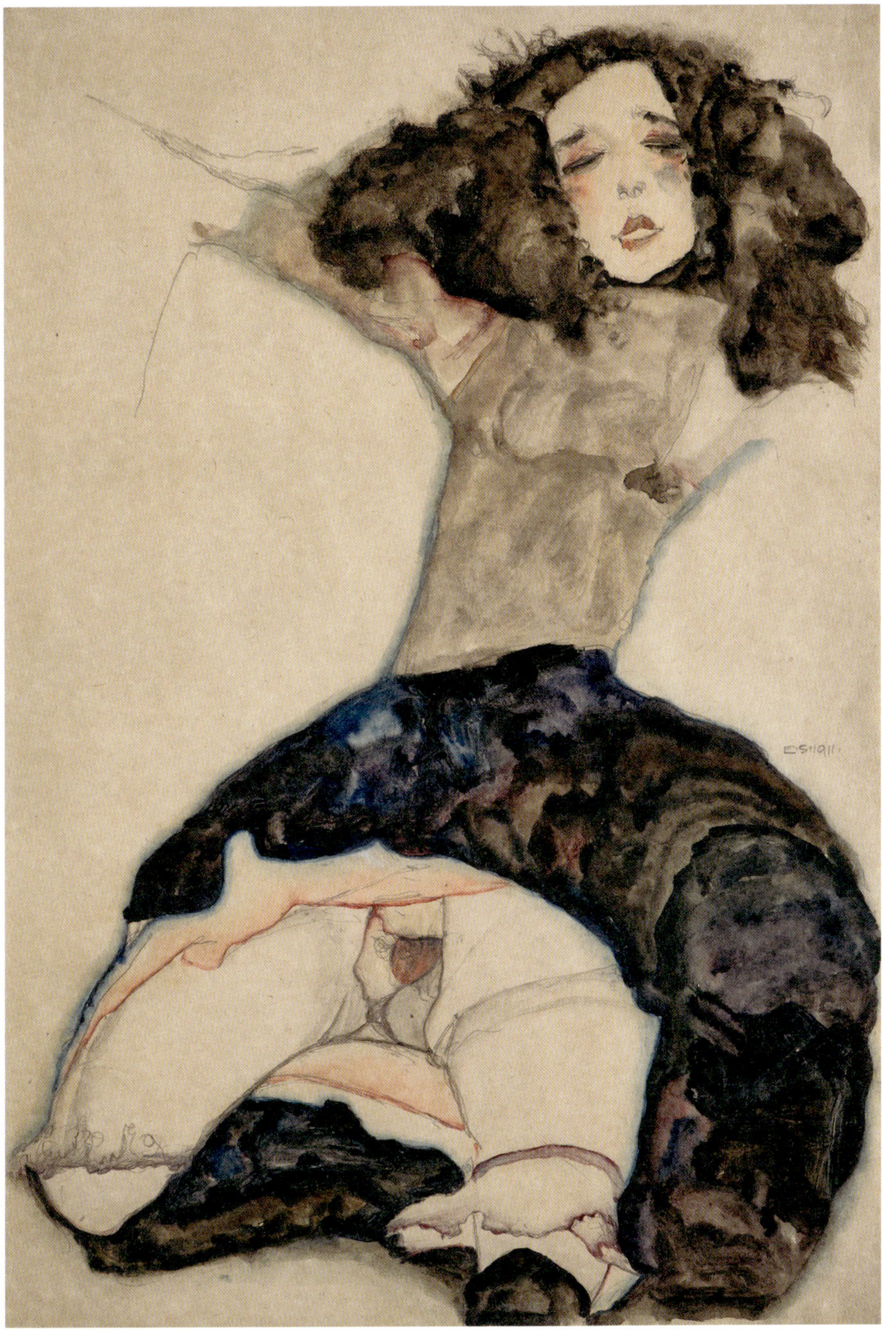

1911

DEAD CITY III (CITY ON THE BLUE RIVER III)

Schiele had already painted this group of houses in Krumau in the fall of 1910 (L 157; K P.183), and even then he had introduced changes into his motif. In 1911, as one of a series of small-format views of Krumau (L 177–180; L 183; K P.209–212, 214), he reworked the same subject on a small wood panel. It was probably this cityscape that Schiele referred to in a letter to Arthur Roessler dating from roughly the end of August 1911, saying that he had as yet held it back, and believed that it "is the most somber in color." (ESAD, ID: 371). In any case, the 21-year-old Schiele created with this painting a striking, fantastic vision.

Here the block of houses appears to have been pulled forward somewhat and isolated more completely than it was in the first version from 1910. The blue-black river still flows beside the houses to the left. The sides of the block form two lines that diverge slightly as they extend upward. The houses are here seen from a higher angle so that the roofs are elongated and the front-facing facades are foreshortened. (For compositional reasons, one wall, the narrow, windowless one at the top, has been lengthened.) This steeper vantage point and the change in the row of windows in the facade on the left from a horizontal to a slight diagonal heighten the three-dimensional effect, especially of the houses in front. This is apparent even in details, such as the shed that projects forward from the house in the center.

The striking arrangement of light and dark areas in this painting of 1911 results in a more self-contained composition. The colors, mainly dark, sonorous tonalities enlivened in places with more intense shades, produce a rich pictorial uniformity. Note the greenish blue that edges the light narrow wall at the top and the touch of carmine pink to the right of it, next to which is a somewhat wider patch of grayish blue. Light reflections shimmer from the roofs; some of them almost appear to be in motion. (RL)

Oil, opaque color on wood
37.3 × 29.8 cm
Leopold Museum, Vienna, Inv. 460
L 182; K P.213

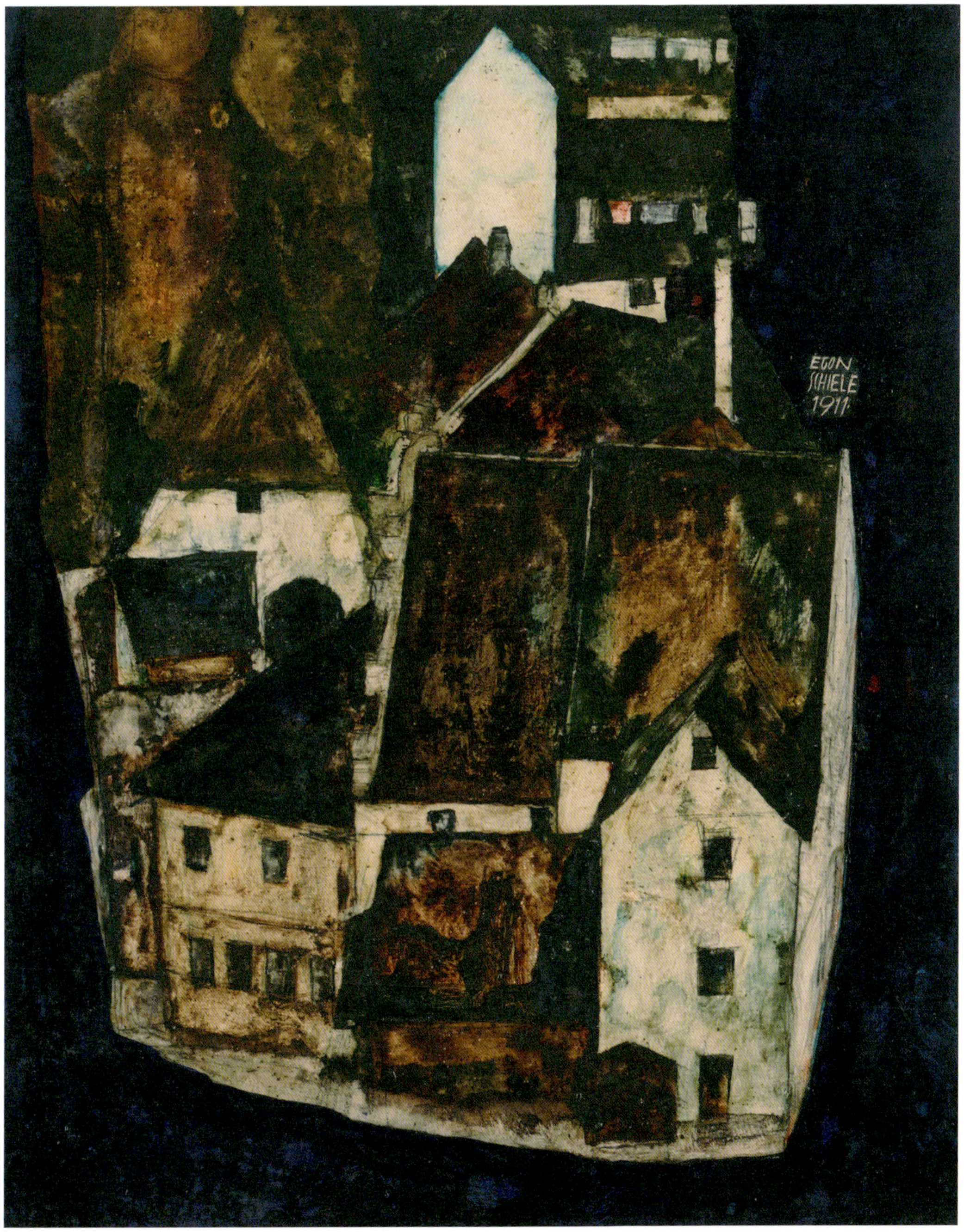
EGON
SCHIELE
1911

1911

REVELATION

Against a dark background rises a pyramid-shaped, steep structure, in which the following can be discerned – two faces, the naked back of a boy, a foot as well as four splayed fingers. The male and female figure as well as the boy are woven together through seemingly almost abstract sections of drapery reminiscent of medieval stained-glass windows, while something hitherto concealed appears at this moment to be revealed to the boy.

This mysterious character of the depiction is further emphasized by the diverse nuancing of the colors and the different treatment of the painterly material. Brightly luminous colors applied like a glaze are contrasted with densely painted sections as well as areas in which Schiele scratched or wiped off the paint. This surface enrichment is visible particularly in the sleeve of the male figure as well as in the two faces. In the faces, Schiele at times reversed areas of light and shade: while the eye sockets are lit up, the lids and noses appear dark. "The image must emanate light, the bodies possess their own light, which they consume in life", Egon Schiele wrote about his painting in a letter to the dentist Dr. Hermann Engel, the first owner of the work (ESAD, ID: 141). (RL)

Oil on canvas
90 × 84.5 cm
Leopold Museum, Vienna, Inv. 477
L 195; K P.203

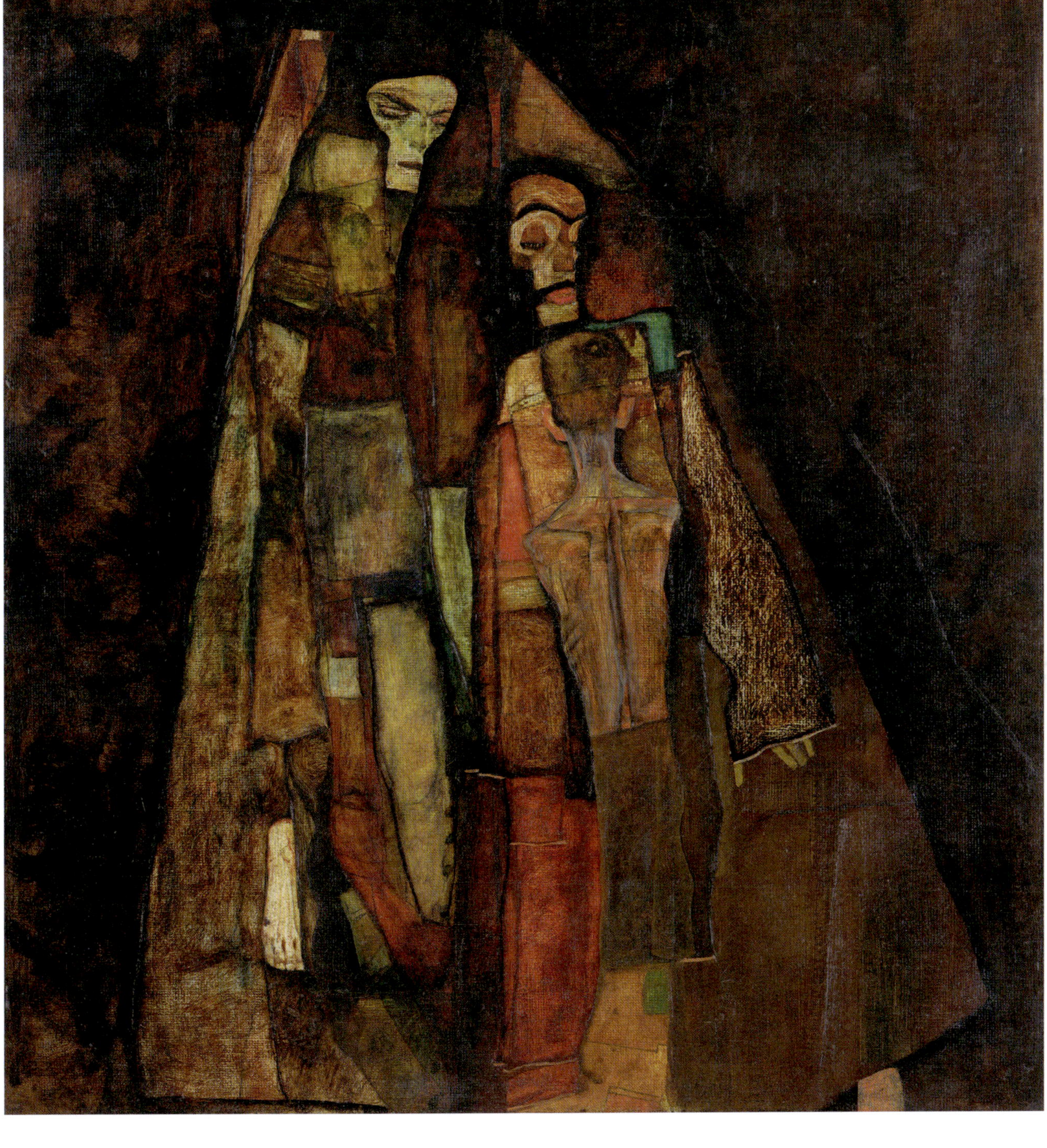

1911

"ANTON PESCHKA!"

In this painting the more intense blue, red-violet and violet tones are achieved with thicker pigments. Schiele used them to create more graphic structures in those areas, contrasting them against the lighter shirt painted in watery colors with a tendency to run. The head, torso and arms of this very painterly portrait are still quite recognizable as reflections of the reality before him, but in the areas rendered in black – the trousers – and violet and various shades of blue, Schiele invented more freely. These colors are contrasted with the browns, ochers, and oranges of the hair and flesh tones.

The painting seems somehow restless owing to the great variety of colors and the different ways in which they have been applied, yet the face of his model, comfortably seated with his eyes closed, has an expression of inner calm and manly earnestness. (RL)

Pencil, gouache on paper
44.5 × 30.4 cm
Leopold Museum, Vienna, Inv. 1381
K D.934

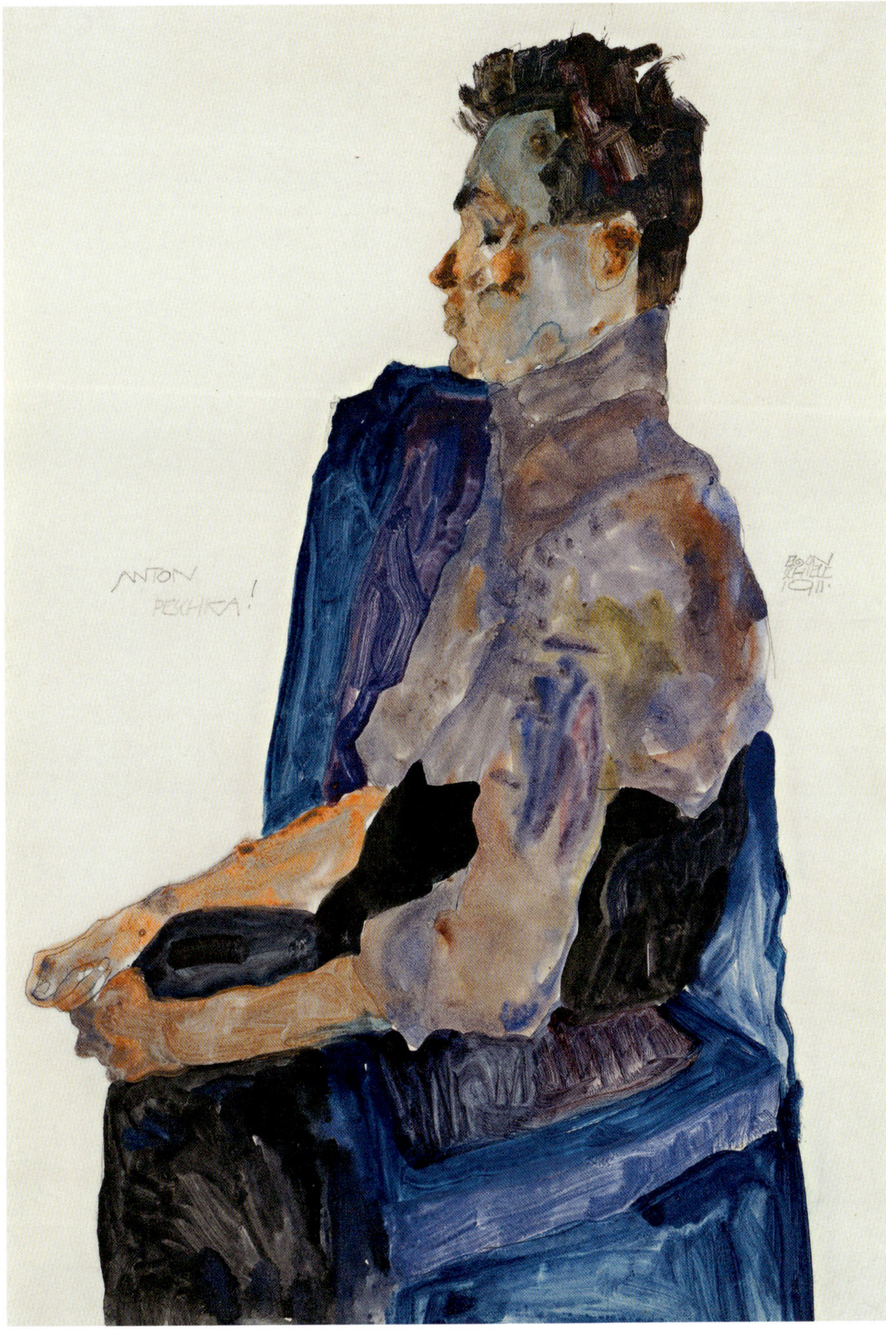
ANTON
PESCHKA!
1911

1911

"MOA"

This rendering of a dancer swathed in bright fabrics is noteworthy in that it demonstrates how far Schiele distanced himself from his early indebtedness to Klimt. Because this type of draped figure was a virtual trademark of the older painter, it is readily apparent how very differently Schiele has approached it. In Klimt's paintings, the areas of decorative fabric become stiff and architectural; Schiele treats them not as ends in themselves, pictures-within-pictures, as it were, but as flowing elements integrated into the diagonal pose. Their surfaces and bands of color seem to be in motion and therefore evoke a dancer's movements.

Just as Klimt frequently topped his ornamental drapery structures with a highly realistic face, Schiele has also rendered the face and hands in a more literal way, using a different style of drawing and painting from that employed for the drapery. The face is left almost entirely free of color and, because of the contrast with the black hair that frames it, seems even lighter than it is. The eyes are deep black and highly expressive. The lower lip and the nostrils are exaggerated so as to balance them.

The similarity to Klimt in this deliberate contrast between a realistic face and abstract, decorative drapery is only superficial. Schiele was by this time more concerned with the expressive potential of his art and had long since rejected the lovely illusions of his mentor. (RL)

Pencil, watercolor, opaque color on paper
47.8 × 31.5 cm
Leopold Museum, Vienna, Inv. 2310
K D.906

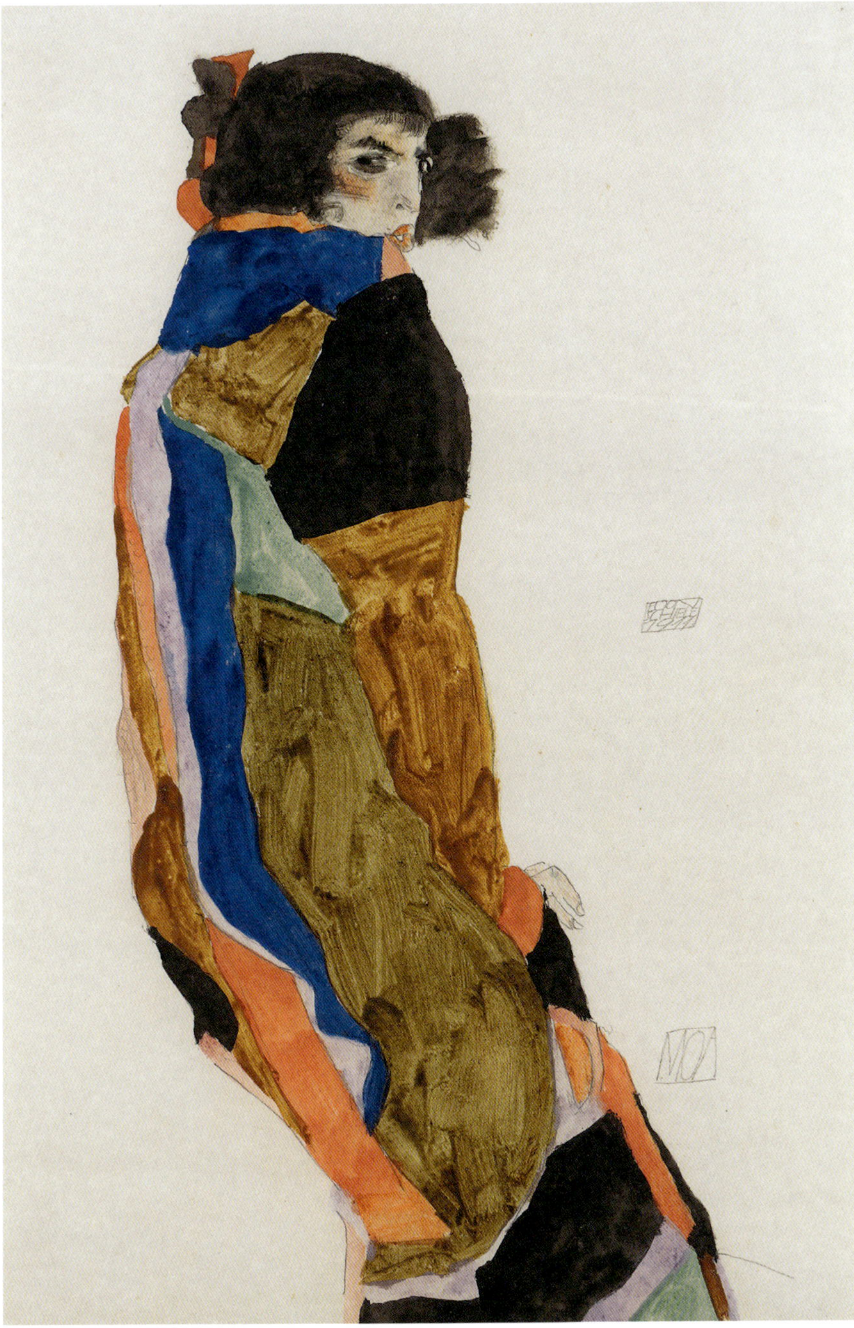

1911

LANDSCAPE WITH RAVENS

In this piece of landscape surrounded by a fence, the fence is black, the landscape dark and autumnal. The sky, by contrast, is extremely light and in places, where the paint is thinly applied, the black underpainting shows through, toned down by a wash of white. The underpainting is entirely visible in a black strip running down the right edge from the top to roughly the center. This strip is an important part of the composition; it serves as a wall and becomes a kind of foil, causing the fence to appear much smaller by contrast and therefore farther back.

This strip also has another function in that it counters the overriding symmetry of the arrangement. Other elements counteracting this symmetry are the unequal distances of the two sections of fence on the left and right, the corner in the fence, shifted slightly to the left, and the hill in the middle distance, which appears to be steeper on the left side. These are balanced by the opposing angle of the light reddish brown area, which has already been mentioned, and the more substantive fence on the left side. The interplay of these various elements adds a certain dynamism to an otherwise potentially static arrangement.

In this fall landscape in warm colors, the small tree has been stripped of most of its leaves and all but a single fruit. On the hill stands a windblown shack, with an even more rickety arbor structure in front of it. A black fence marks the boundaries; above it is a cold sky with crows. One can almost hear their cawing. In such a context the clothesline poles suggest the crosses in a cemetery.

The sense of looking down on the scene from high above is heightened by the way the land beyond the hill lifts upward, coming to a point at the corner of the fence: a landscape seen as a cathedral.

This high vantage point, from which all of the elements of the landscape have equal value, also occasions something fundamentally new. The old landscape conventions of foreground, middle distance and background are no longer valid. With this picture Schiele also created a psychological statement: autumn's decay has become symbolic of life's impermanence. (RL)

Oil on canvas
95.8 × 89 cm
Leopold Museum, Vienna, Inv. 527
L 191; K P.216

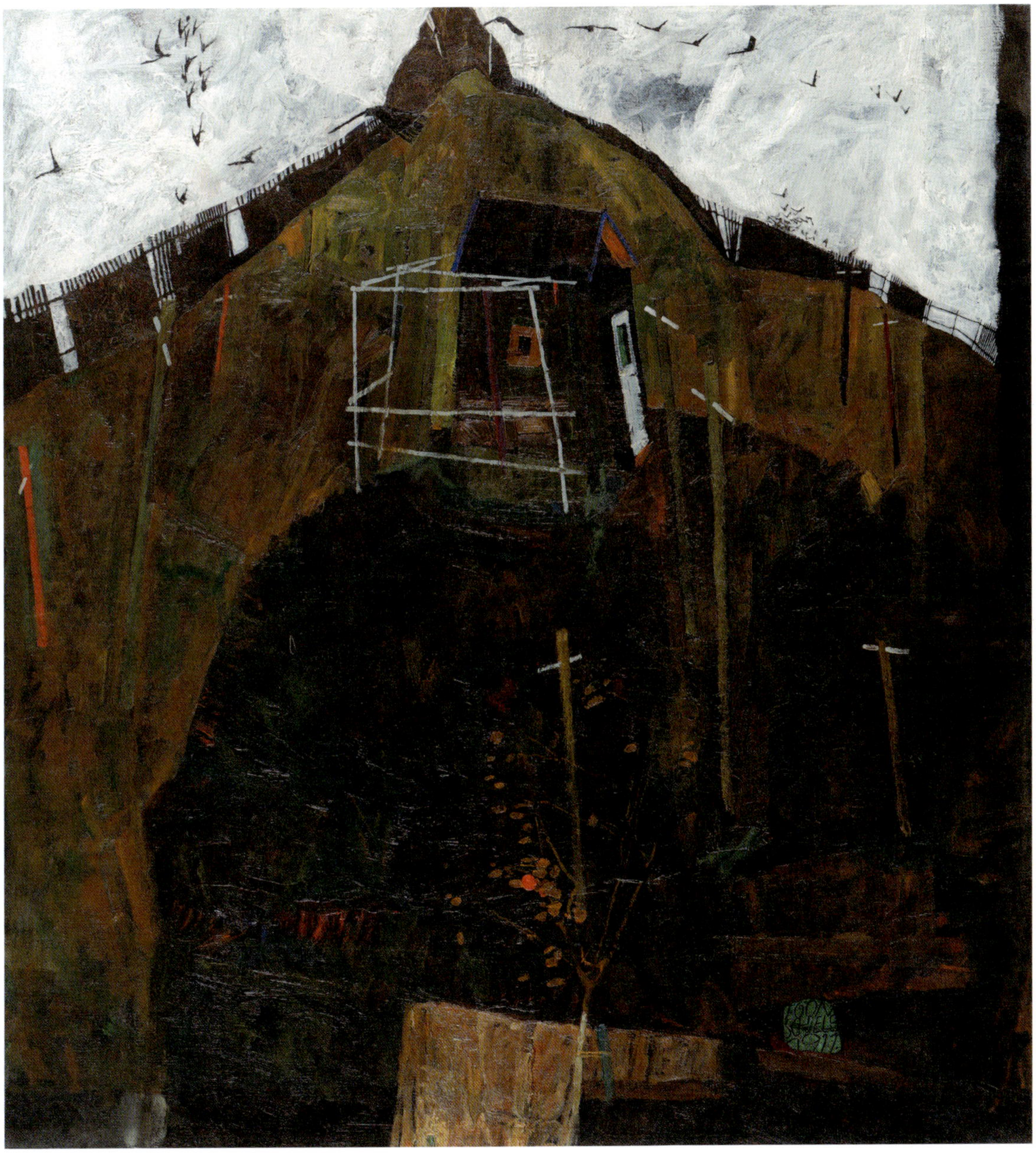

1911

SEMI-NUDE (SELF-PORTRAIT)

Schiele here presents himself as either despairing or dying. The agitated contour lines – both those drawn with a pencil and the ones painted with a brush in black – are similar to those of the painting *Pregnant Woman and Death (Mother and Death)* (L 198; K P.202), but this composition, filled with tension, appears to have been executed in a single sitting. The detail of the wavy furrows across the forehead – some traced with pencil, some with a brush – shows the great similarity in style between the two works.

Schiele painted the face in the same shades as those used for the exposed portion of the body. Oddly, he even used the same colors for the cloth wrapped around the body from the waist down. The color alone ensures the continuity of this tilted figure from top to bottom. (RL)

Pencil, gouache on paper
44.7 × 31.4 cm
Leopold Museum, Vienna, Inv. 1445
K D.950

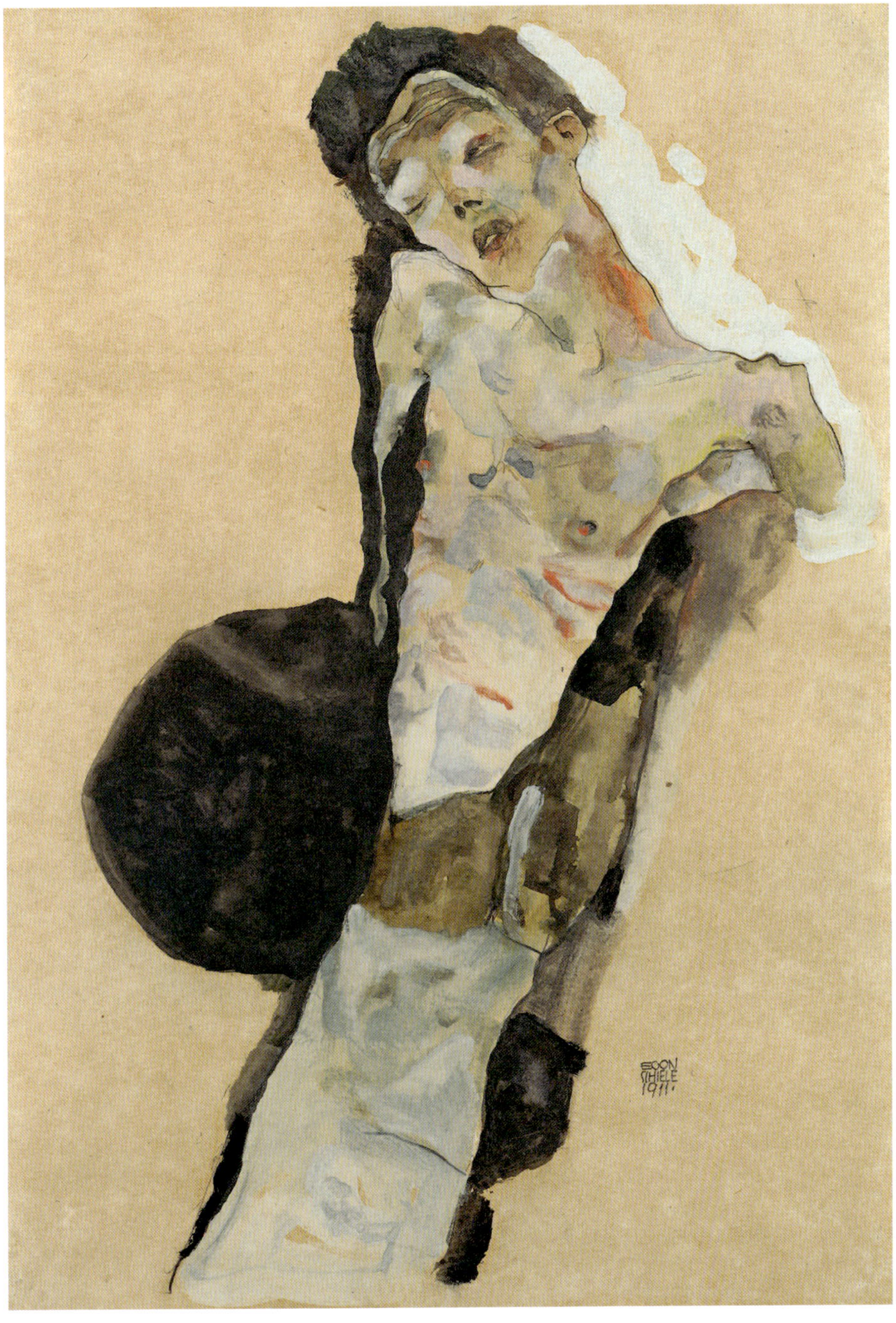
EGON
SCHIELE
1911.

1911

STANDING FEMALE NUDE WITH ARMS CROSSED ON HER CHEST (MOA)

This is a nude drawing of Moa (see p. 111). Here Schiele elongated still further her already very slender body. It narrows to an extremely small waist, then widens again in the pelvis so that the two sections are vividly contrasted. The graphic focal point in the bottom half of the picture is the pubic hair, in the top half the shading above the eye – not, as in most other drawings, the eyes themselves.

The lines, as is typical of Schiele's drawings in this period, are almost like music: note how the single line traces the body's contour down from the left shoulder at a diagonal, changes direction at the waist, follows around the hips and buttocks, and finally resumes its original direction.

The contours, with their pleasing succession of larger and smaller waves, seem to obey abstract pictorial laws, yet they leave no doubt about the shapes of the various parts of the body. A number of formal parallels are visible between these lines and the major divisions of the body. Note, for example, the similar angles describing the two elbows, also the way the indentation at the waist on her left side is repeated on the right elbow. It was precisely for the sake of this parallel that the right arm was drawn so very long. The resulting difference in height of the two elbows also enhances the illusion that we are seeing the figure from below and gives it a distinct three-dimensionality. The lower body, seen from above, projects the same sense of three dimensions, in no small part because of the perspective rendering of the pubic hair. An imaginary diagonal joins the right and left elbow, an opposing diagonal the right hip and the curve of the left buttock; together they suggest the twist of the figure in space.

What makes the figure resemble a piece of sculpture, finally, is the great sensitivity of Schiele's line, even though it is only an outline drawn on a two-dimensional surface. (RL)

Pencil on paper
47.8 × 32 cm
Leopold Museum, Vienna, Inv. 1446
K D.909

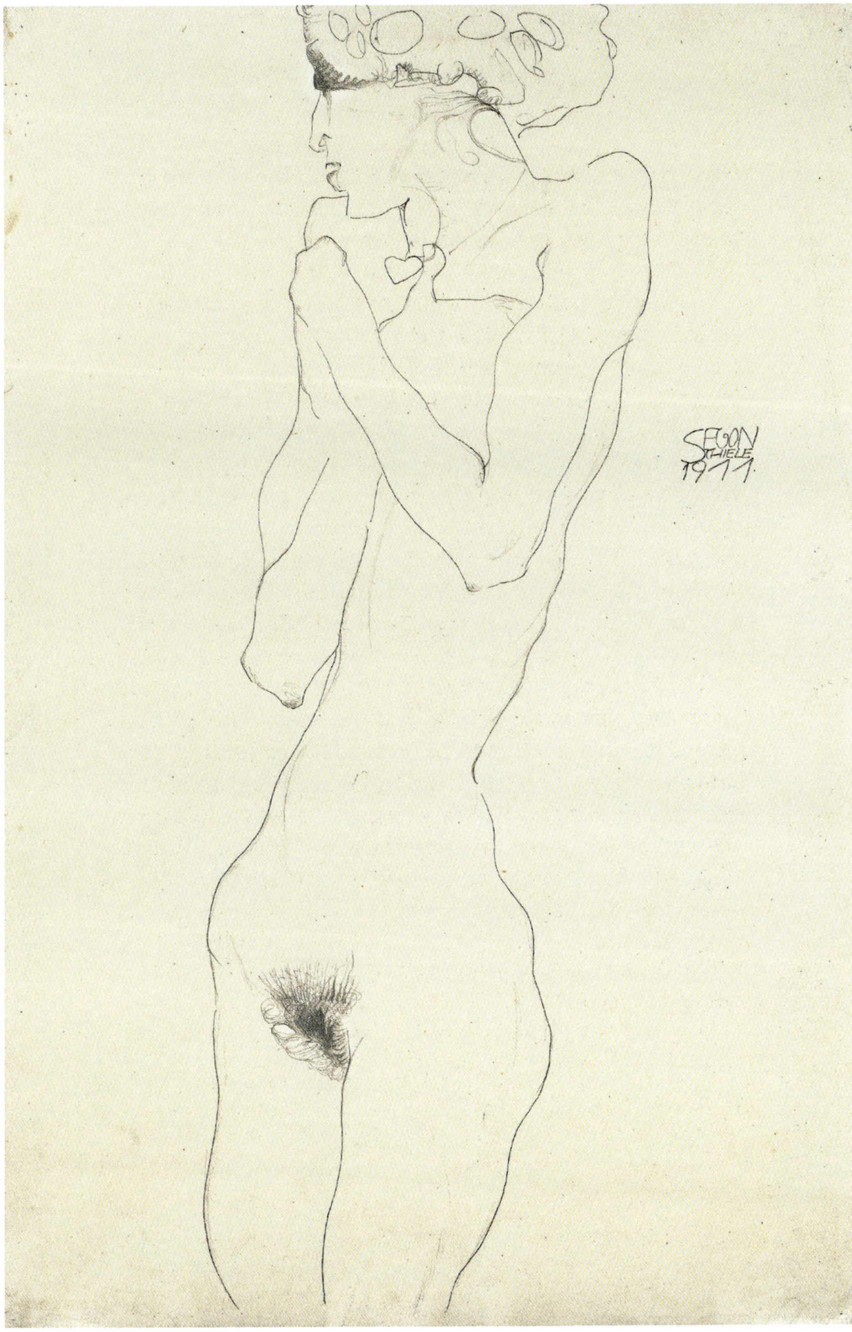
EGON
SCHIELE
1911.

1911

SMALL TREE IN LATE AUTUMN

The consistent curve of the hill mirrors the shape of the crowning branches of the tree, which are painted in similar tones. At the same time, nothing could be a greater contrast to the imperturbable solidity of the hilltop than the tree's frail, windblown silhouette.

Because the lower part of its trunk has been limed, the top of the tree and the center section with its bluish trunk and one large limb cantilevered out to the right seem cut off from the ground and are therefore juxtaposed to it. In terms of color, the olive and reddish brown of the dead grass contrasts with the blue tones of the center section of the tree. A bright, pearl-gray sky serves as the backdrop for the hopeless struggle of this defenseless tree. It is being whipped by the wind, as one can see from the moving clouds. The trunk of the tree is hideously twisted, its natural growth having already been checked in two places. In the upper one the trunk has thickened, forming something like a head from which the thin branches reach upward like wildly gesticulating arms. The branch that extends out to the right below this can be seen as a leg, the limed trunk the other leg.

The tree has become a symbol of man's fate; there is virtually nothing comparable with its anthropomorphism in the Expressionism of the time. It almost seems that the poor tree is dancing. Essentially, however, the image is a dramatic symbol of man's isolation and vulnerability in the face of hostile forces; the dance is a dance of death. (RL)

Oil on wood
42 × 33.5 cm
Leopold Museum, Vienna, Inv. 459
L 199; K P.222

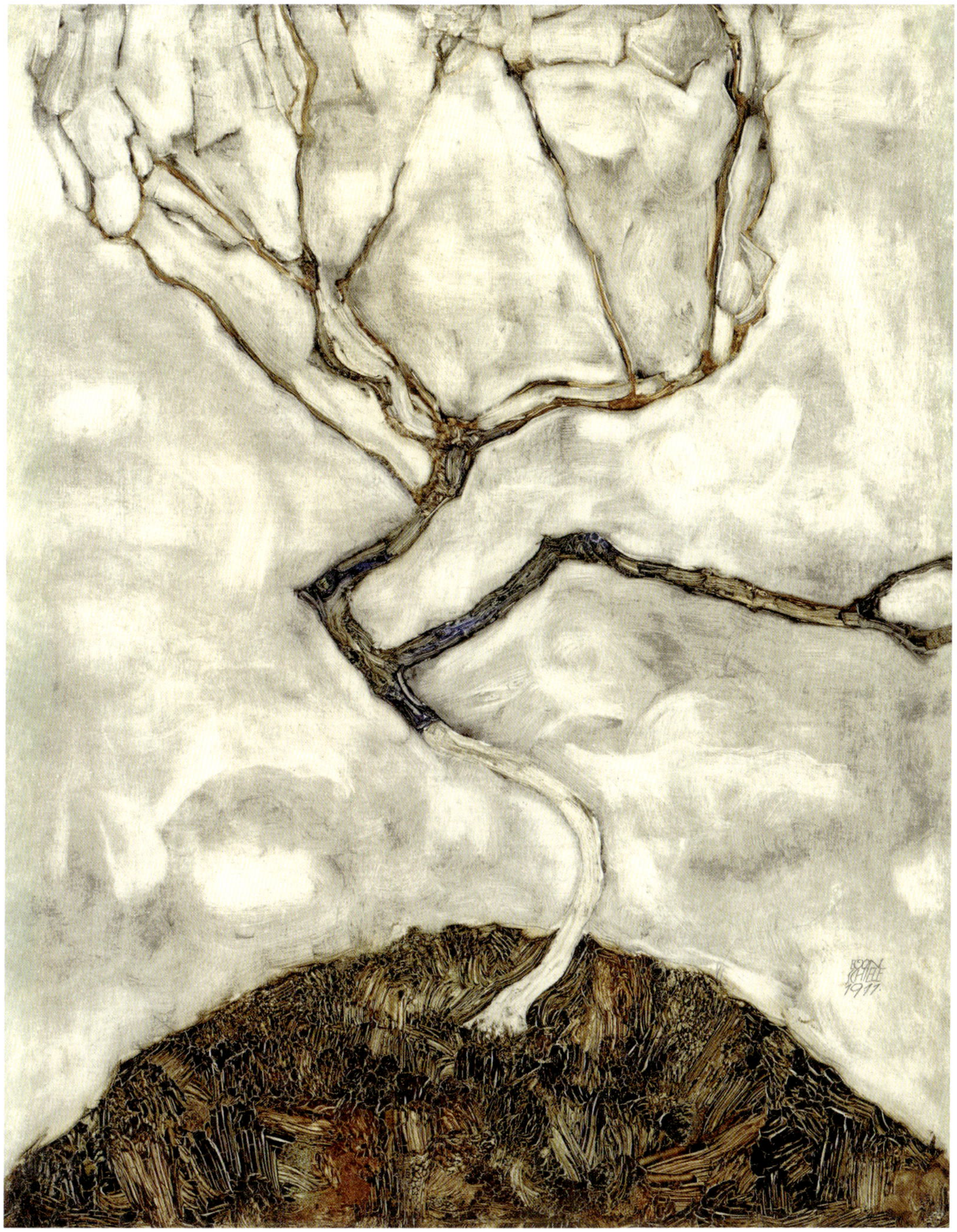

1912

NUDE SELF-PORTRAIT.
STUDY FOR THE *SEMA PORTFOLIO*

This is one of the artist's studies for the lithographed self-portrait he contributed to the *Sema Portfolio*, which was published in Munich by Delphin Verlag in April 1912. A letter dated January 23, 1912, suggests that he had already finished these studies. The presence of the moustache also helps to date the work to the first weeks of 1912.
Schiele first drew this figure in black ink, and then added washes to it with great verve, in places adding still more drawing in the wet ink with the tip of the brush handle. (RL)

India ink, brush on paper
46 × 29.1 cm
Leopold Museum, Vienna, Inv. 1440
K D.1160

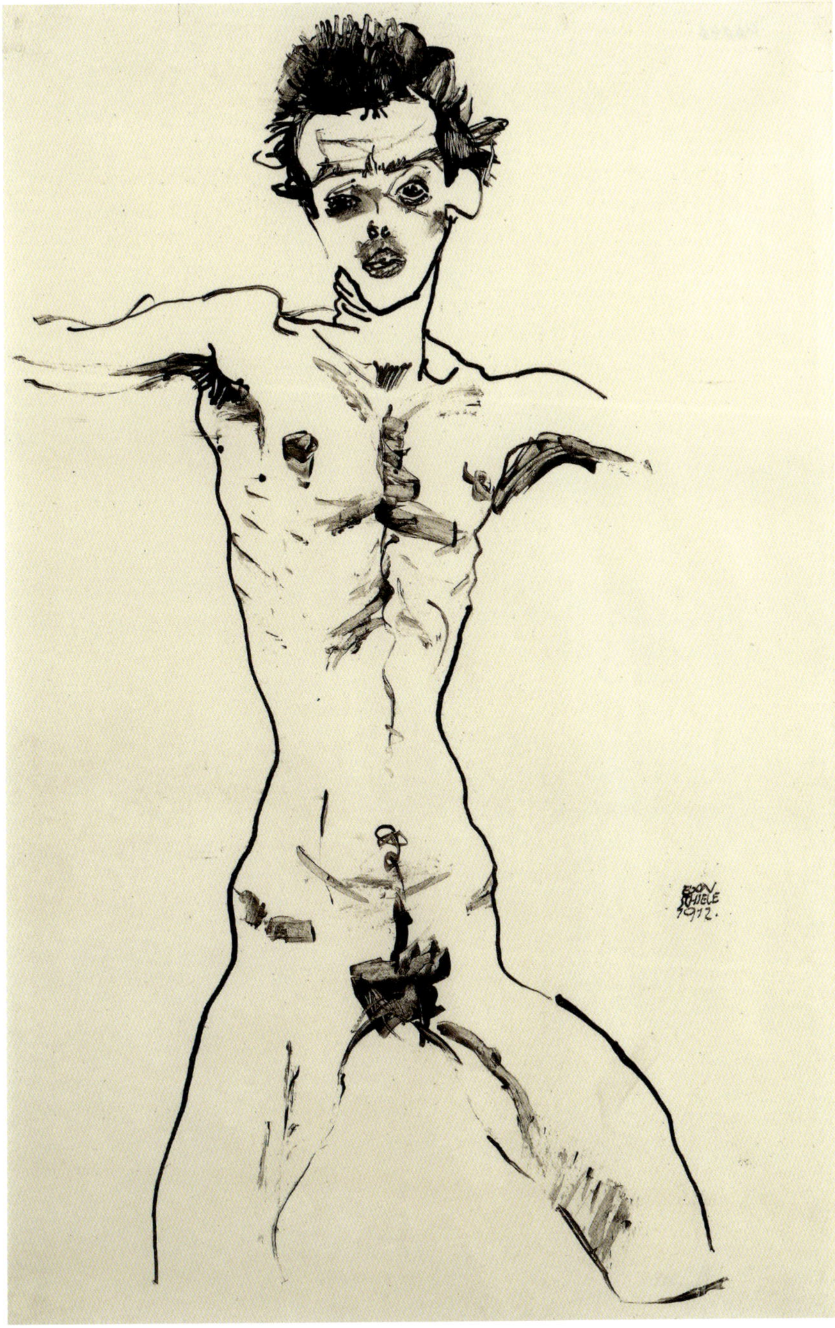
EGON
SCHIELE
1912.

1912

SELF-PORTRAIT WITH LOWERED HEAD

This man seems grotesque, mysterious and miserable all at the same time. The head bends forward, the eyes gazing up through his eyebrows. The whites of the eyes are therefore like crescent moons, glowing brightly against the dark skin tone of his face. The skull is powerful, but the cheeks are sunken. A neat moustache is perched above the blue-red lips. It would appear that Schiele painted himself with the light behind him. In any case what interested him was the contrast between the dark forms of the face, the bare chest, and the hand, and the white of the background and the only slightly shaded drape. The sharp angle between the head and the right shoulder mirrors the one formed by the spread fingers – only one of many formal parallels in this highly impressive composition. Schiele's painterly sensitivity is just as apparent in his signature application of pigment as it is in his juxtaposition of the various tonal values.

The self-portrait study *Self-Portrait in White Monk's Habit* (K D.1171) for the double figure of *The Hermits* (see p. 125) was done a short time after this painting. Schiele had a moustache only from the late fall of 1911 to the first weeks of 1912, and he conscientiously recorded it in his depictions of himself. He used this same pose in the later study and in the larger composition of *The Hermits,* where the hand with spread fingers is placed on his right hip. (RL)

Oil on wood
42.2 × 33.7 cm
Leopold Museum, Vienna, Inv. 462
L 202; K P.228

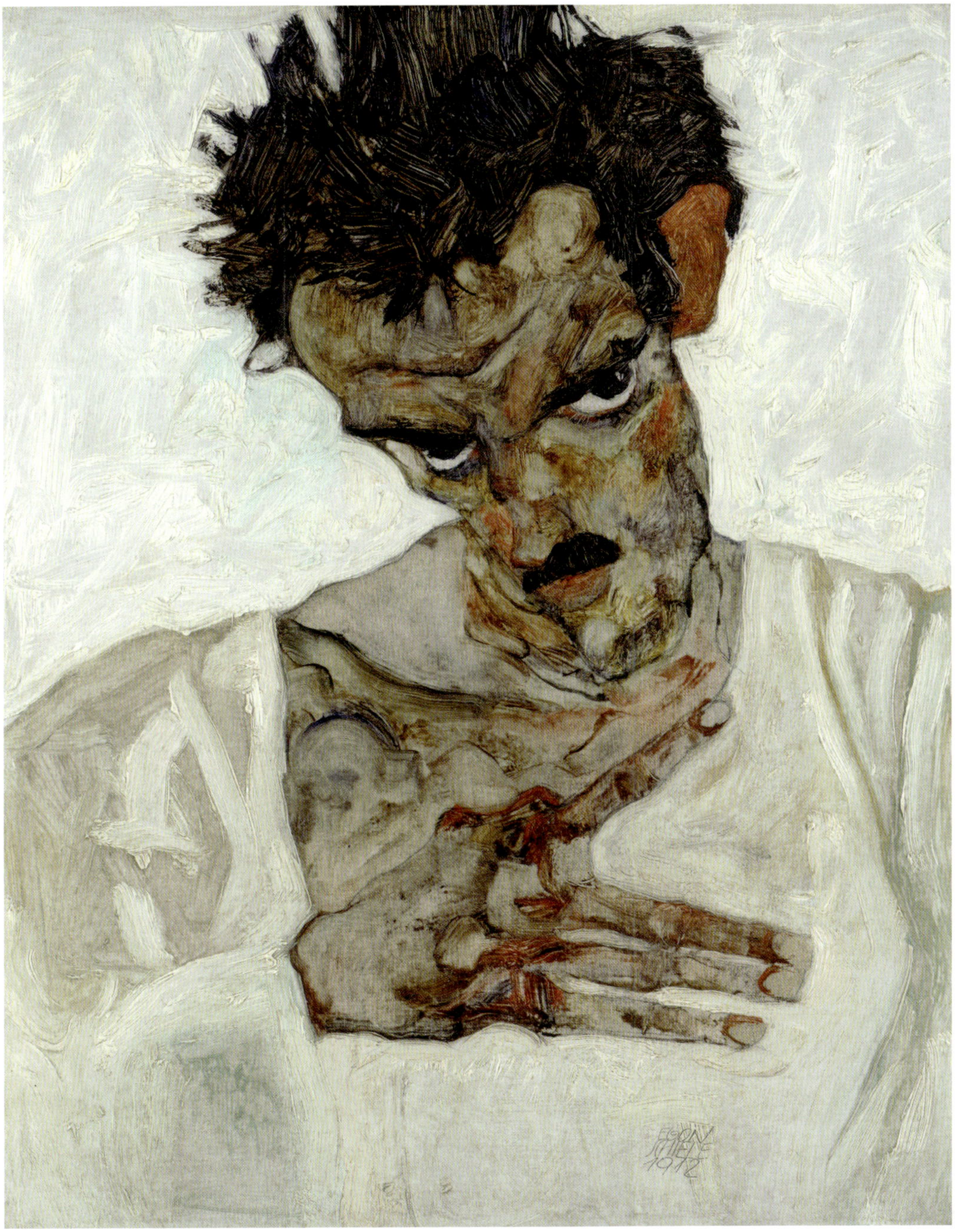

1912

THE HERMITS

In this painting Schiele merged two lifesize figures into a double image. The faces are clearly those of Schiele and Klimt, but these citations are not intended to be taken literally. In a long letter he wrote about the painting to Carl Reininghaus, Schiele makes no mention of the fact that in it he had portrayed himself and Klimt (ESAD, ID: 45): "I admit that you are right for once: in the large painting one cannot properly see exactly how the two are standing [...] the indistinctness of the figures, which are perceived as folded together [...] the bodies of world weary men, suicides, but bodies of men of feeling. I see the two figures as resembling a cloud of dust, like the earth, which rises of itself, only to collapse in exhaustion. In a picture that is not intended to have this meaning, one would see the poses of the figures emphasized, but that was not the intention here."
Schiele's attempt to defend his picture to one of his collectors was unsuccessful; he never managed to sell the work. The grandeur of his creation, its unique combination of monumental, almost abstract forms and highly dramatic expressiveness, was not appreciated.
Essential to the composition is the diagonal center axis of the large, dark, almost abstract robed figure rising up from right to left. The two heads incline even further in the same direction. This movement is opposed by the hill in the background, the white line that rises up from the flower, and the foot, which is obviously juxtaposed to Schiele's face. The wonderful contours of the "cloak" were not easily achieved – Schiele changed and reworked them in various ways – but they appear to be so natural that one accepts them as the product of a single inspiration. The hands of the younger "hermit", exquisite in their drawing and coloring, stand out against the blackness of the cloak.
The left hand clutches a portfolio that is scarcely visible against the dark cloak. With it Schiele wished to suggest only that he was carrying with him a collection of his drawings. This time Klimt, the other "hermit", has his eyes closed. Is he asleep or dreaming? He wears a wreath of autumn fruit around his brow, as though he had already enjoyed the harvest. The sensual, full lips in Schiele's face are in marked contrast to the sunken cheeks, the furrowed, angular brow, the crown of withered thistles, and the painfully wide-open eyes. A single rose bush pushes up from the ground to the left of the double figure, its blooms fading, its stems wilted.
These living figures have been infected with a "sickness unto death". Every element of the painting is calculated to express a wholly tragic world view. Both the idea and its execution are filled with passion. Schiele was by no means exaggerating when, in that same letter to Reininghaus, he wrote that the painting "was created from nothing but the most heartfelt emotion." (RL)

Oil on canvas
203.8 × 189.7 cm
Leopold Museum, Vienna, Inv. 466
L 203; K P.229

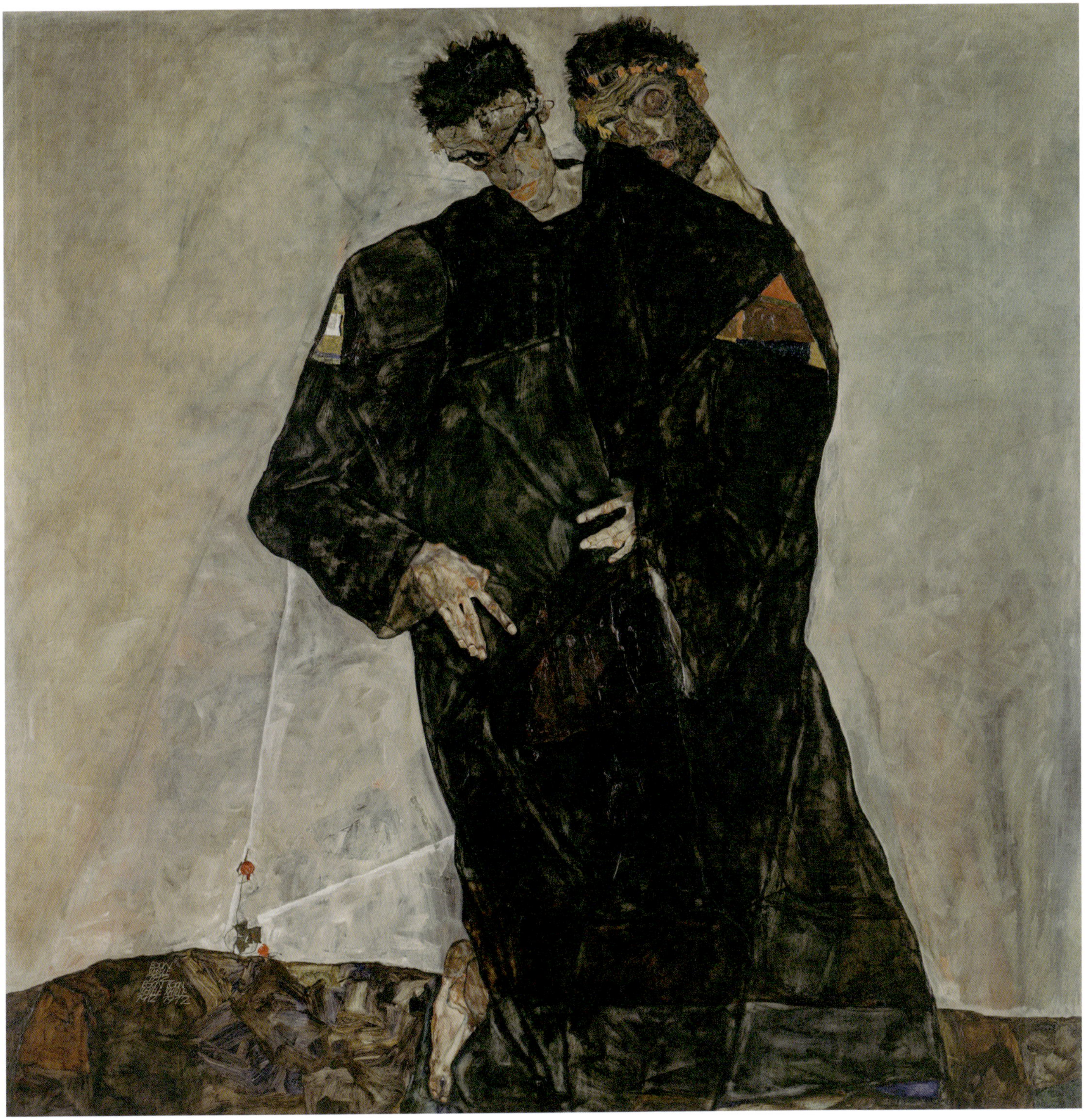

1912

MOURNING WOMAN

This woman's face is the picture of sadness. Her cheeks are sunken (an impression reinforced by the black scarf partly covering the right cheek) her nose is extremely narrow, her skin pale, her eyes large and dark, welling with tears. The sallowness of the face seems even more extreme in contrast to the red of the mouth and the black of the eyes, clothing, hair and kerchief. The upper edge of this head covering is asymmetrical, oddly flattened on the left. Behind it we see part of a man's face. That face and a thin triangle of reddish ocher behind it complete the curve begun by the kerchief and hair on the right. Schiele is suggesting that the woman has this man – himself, in fact, an artist touched by madness – on her mind. It is he who is the cause of her sorrow. There is no longer anything beautiful in the world, not even the red rose, which has wilted, in front of a cold patch of chrome-yellow. The effect of the striped ribbon to the right of the head is very different; its colors glow mysteriously.

The model for this woman's head was Schiele's companion, Wally Neuzil. Although Wally was blonde with blue eyes, she was unquestionably the model here. When the colors of a given composition or subject matter required it, as here, Schiele simply gave her dark hair and eyes (see, for example, K D.1196). Schiele doubtless based the man's head on himself. It is interesting to note his awareness that his companion mourned him, the brilliant but disturbed artist.

This small painting is one of Schiele's most expressive works and is virtually without parallel in his oeuvre.

Careful stylistic analysis unquestionably reveals that the *Mourning Woman* was executed before the so-called idyllic portraits and also before *Cardinal and Nun (Caress)* (see p. 141). Most important, Schiele painted all of these pictures *before* he was sent to prison. Accordingly, neither the *Mourning Woman* nor *Cardinal and Nun (Caress)* can be thought of as a reaction to that event.

Study of the Schiele letters indicates that for months after his imprisonment, Schiele painted no pictures at all, both for psychological and financial reasons. He managed to begin painting again only in December 1912, and the first works from that time were by no means the *Mourning Woman* and *Cardinal and Nun (Caress),* but rather a pair of paintings based on motifs from Krumau like *The Small Town III* (see p. 155). (RL)

Oil on wood
42.5 × 34 cm
Leopold Museum, Vienna, Inv. 461
L 201; K P.224

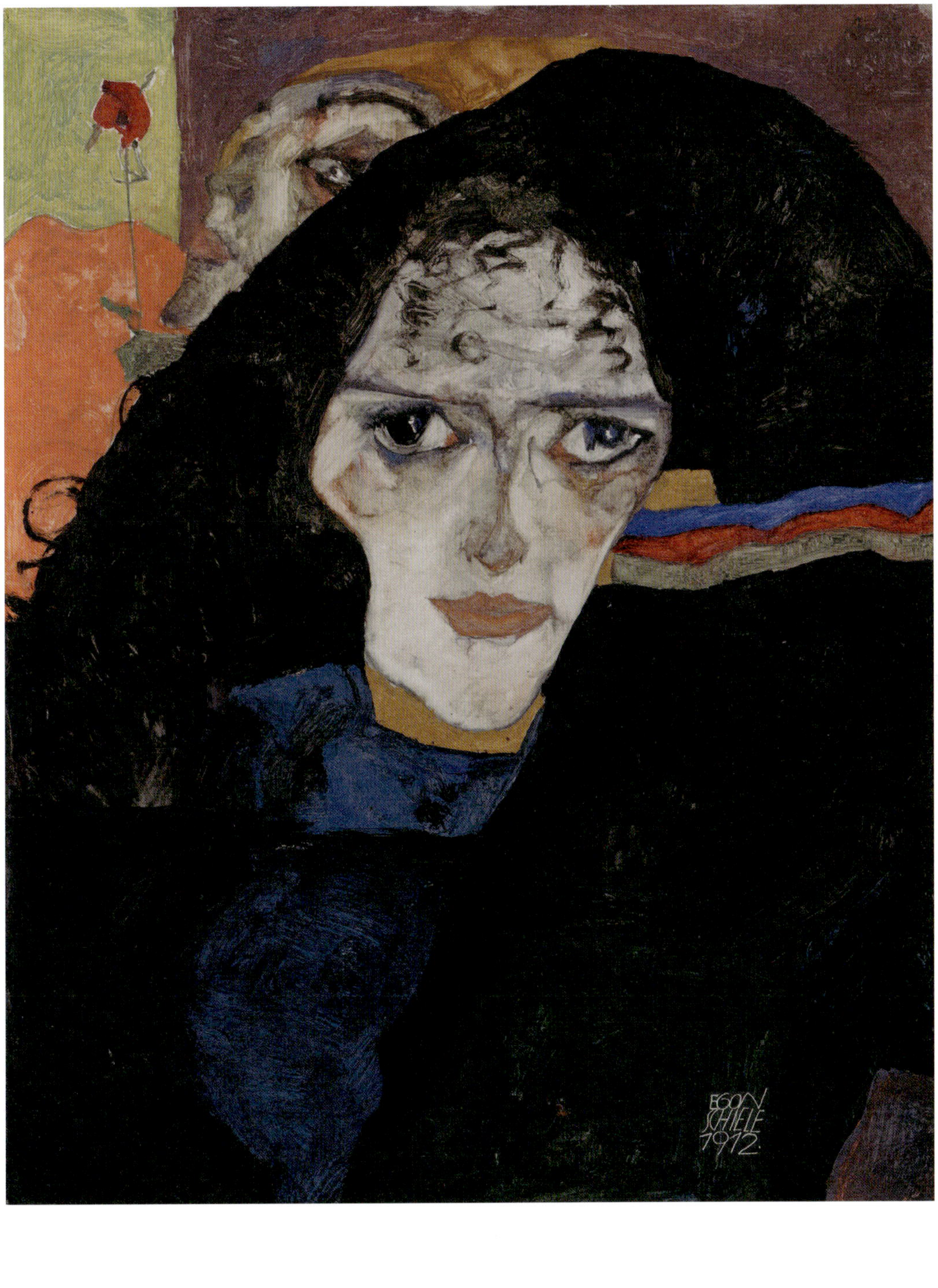
EGON
SCHIELE
1912.

1912

EMBRACE

Schiele gave these two intertwined figures a common outline, simply ending the woman's thigh with a curving line and leaving the man's leg undefined.
Within this overall form the man's body is darker, the woman's lighter – the only aspect of the drawing that has anything to do with convention. But the man's skin is painted in vivid colors, ranging from bright blue to brick red. Inside the preestablished contours of the limbs, the painting is quite free. The merging colors and wavy outlines link this work from the beginning of 1912 to typical pictures from 1911.
The man's dark hair forms the center of this dynamic composition. Otto Benesch relates that his father, who owned this drawing, told him that Schiele here showed himself with one of his models. (RL)

Pencil, watercolor, gouache on paper
31.9 × 46.8 cm
Leopold Museum, Vienna, Inv. 2376
K D.1147

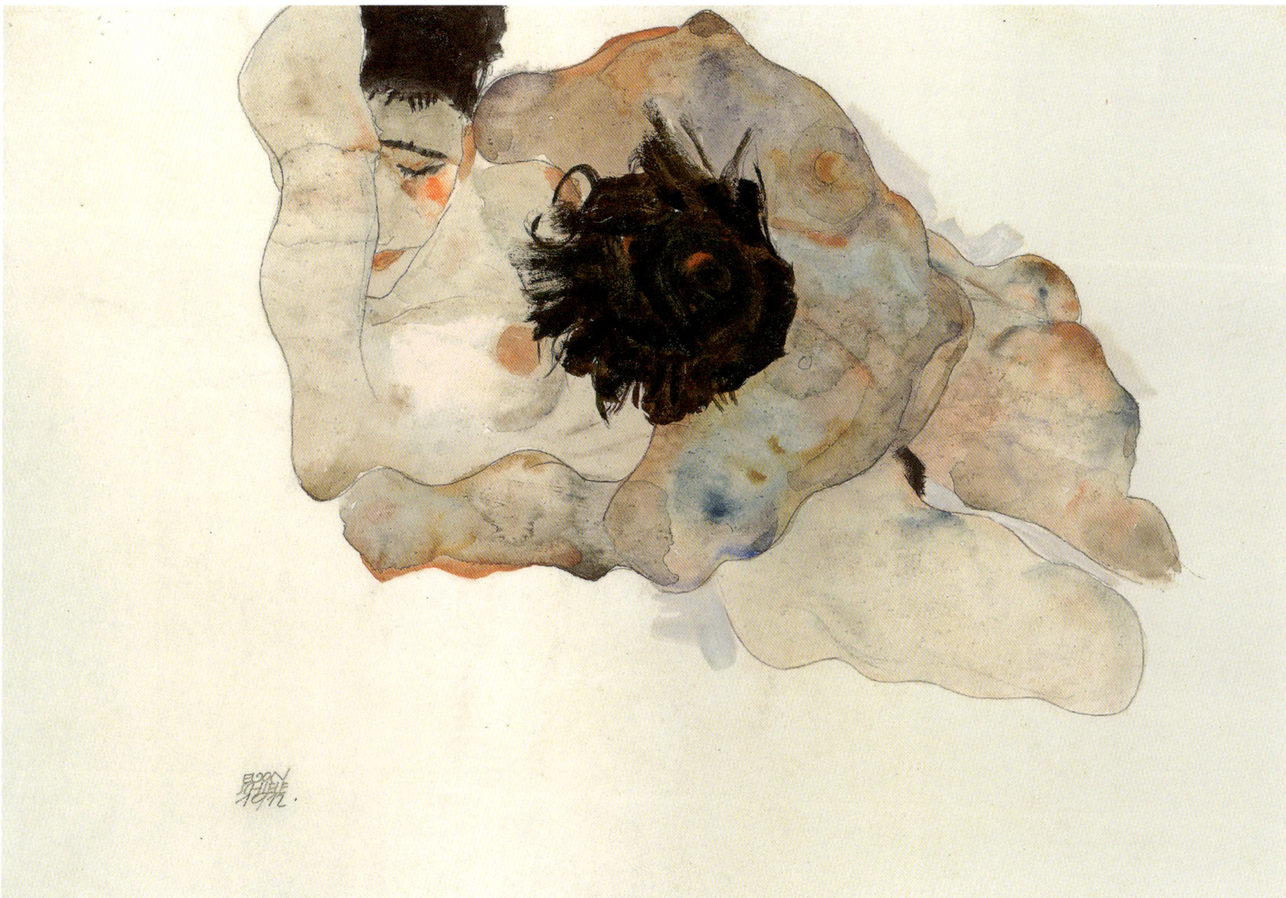

1912

MOTHER AND CHILD

The composition of this painting resembles that of an icon, but here there is none of the hieratic solemnity of such works. Two faces and two hands stand out against a dark, highly agitated background. The child seems to be staring out with horror at a hostile world, one to which the mother has resigned herself. Her eyes and mouth are closed, her cheeks sunken. The two heads are pressed against each other and connected by a common white collar. Their bodies are as though hidden in shadow, the child's only suggested by the way the mother's hand has been placed protectively around its right shoulder.

The vivid colors of the faces and hands resemble those of the watercolor on p. 129, but are much more expressive. In some areas Schiele clearly painted with his fingers, leaving prints in the wet pigment. The mother's head is surrounded by a deep, glowing blue. (RL)

Oil on wood
36.5 × 29.2 cm
Leopold Museum, Vienna, Inv. 652
L 205; K P.225

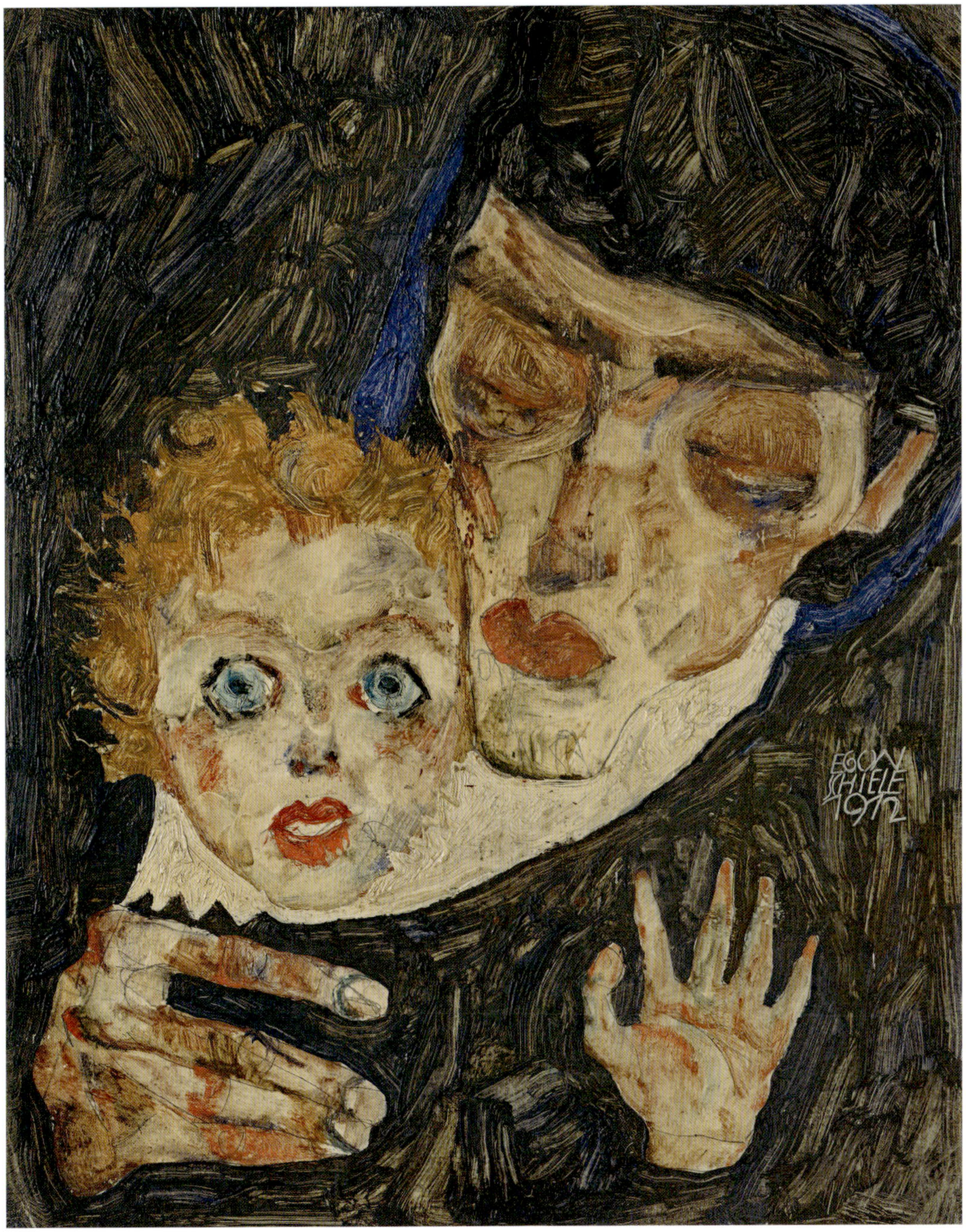
EGON
SCHIELE
1912

1912

SELF-PORTRAIT WITH RAISED BARE SHOULDER

The face is filled with horror: the mouth hangs half open, the eyes are wide. Panic has been channeled into painting, the agitation evident even in the way the pigments were applied. In some areas Schiele used a brush, in others his fingertips. With the tip of the brush handle he scratched the "scar" on his forehead.

The skin color – ocher, red-brown, and red – resembles a person who has been badly burned. The line of the jaw is traced with a suggestion of blue – a delightful contrast. The almost white background and the only slightly darker drape set off the silhouette of the head, neck, and right shoulder. The left shoulder is covered, so as not to detract from the diagonal sweep of the opposite shoulder and head, the major elements.

The bare shoulder is turned directly toward the viewer. It appears as though it has been thrust up from the bottom edge of the painting. By contrast, the head and hair are cut off by the top and right edges. The sense of being pressed into a corner – a universal human feeling, in this case autobiographical – is thus literally reflected even in the arrangement of the composition. (RL)

Oil on wood
42.2 × 33.9 cm
Leopold Museum, Vienna, Inv. 653
L 209; K P.227

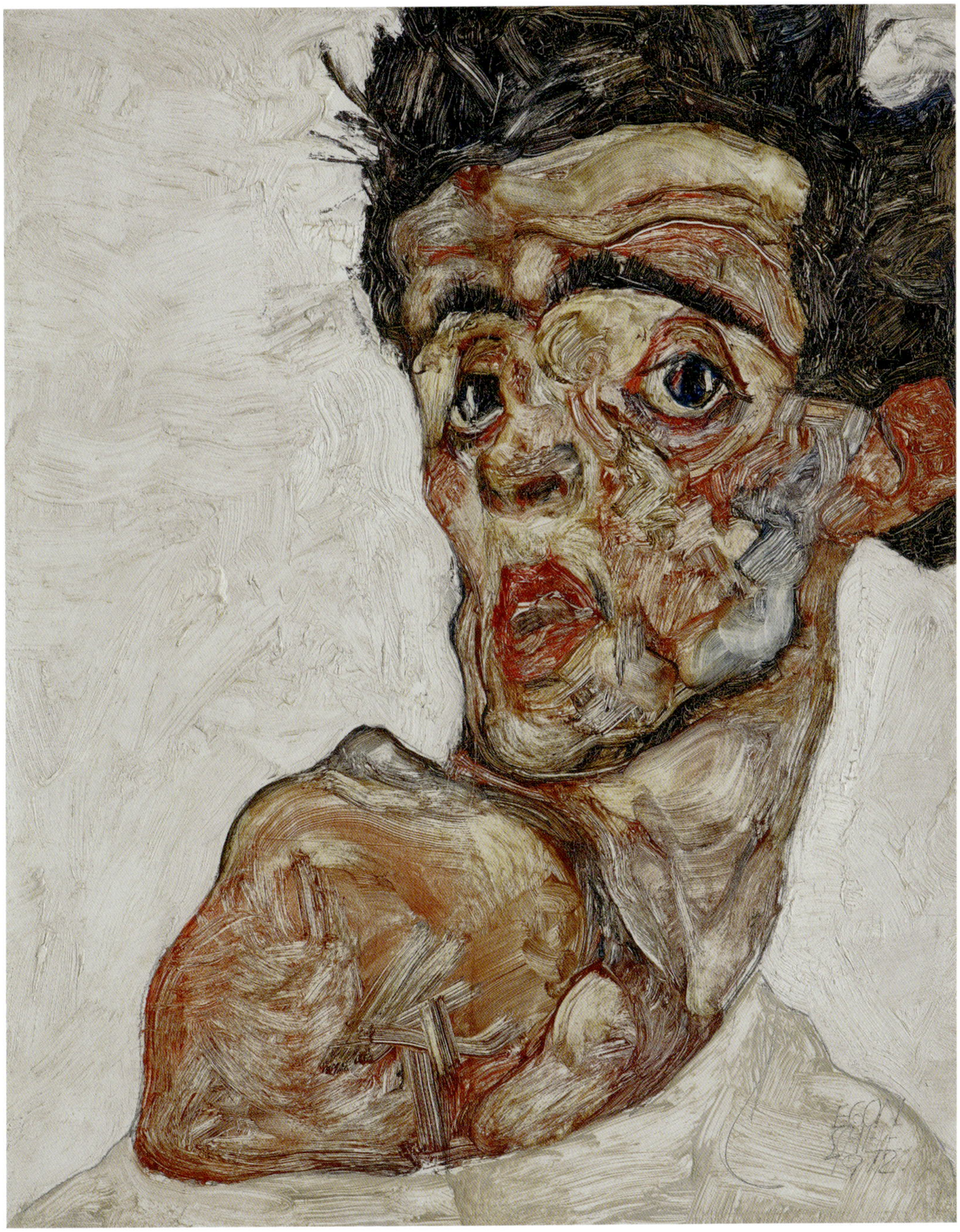

1912

NUDE SELF-PORTRAIT, CROUCHING

The artist here drew himself crouched in a highly contorted pose. His upper body, head and left arm twist in one direction, his buttocks and legs in the other.
The lowered head with its expressive face is rendered in greater detail. The furrowed brow, the few curly lines that describe the hair, and even the waviness of the body contours in some areas are reminiscent of drawings Schiele had done the previous year. Most of the undulations in the outlines have been suppressed, to be sure; all in all his drawing has become more realistic. The contours are drawn with verve. Schiele's mastery is amply demonstrated in the bravura rendering of the foreshortened right foot. (RL)

Pencil on paper
47.8 × 30.3 cm
Leopold Museum, Vienna, Inv. 1444
K D.1165

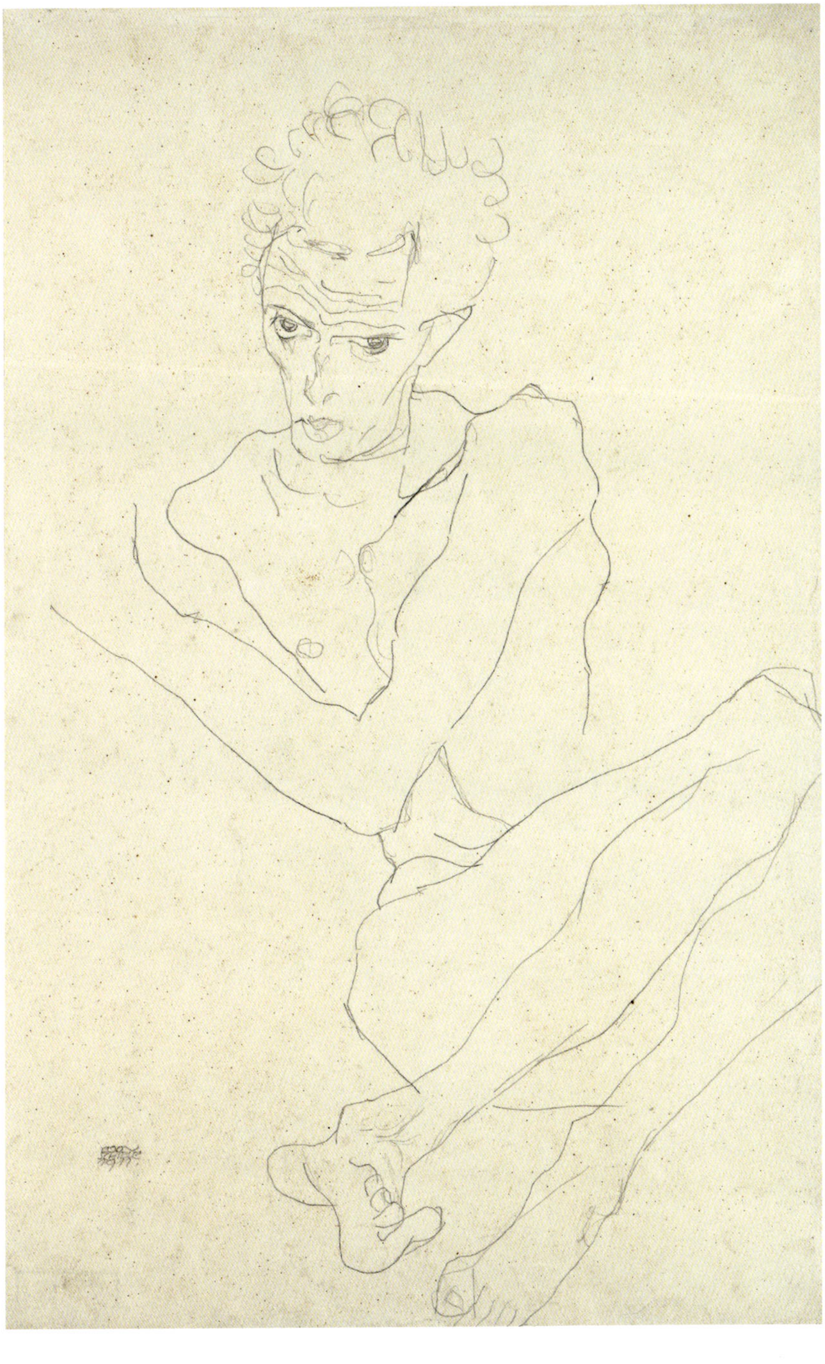

1912

KNEELING WOMAN WITH A GRAY CAPE (WALLY NEUZIL)

In this lively watercolor study of Schiele's favorite model in this period, Wally Neuzil, he juxtaposed the reddish flesh tone to the gray-black of her dress. The folds of the fabric are wonderfully rendered, so that it appears that light is falling on them from above.

It seems odd, but this study of a female model clearly served Schiele as a pattern for the figure of the cardinal in his painting *Cardinal and Nun (Caress)* (see p. 141), even though the head is here turned and resting on the right shoulder. This head was also used for the painting *Portrait of Wally Neuzil* (see p. 147). Perhaps even more remarkable is the fact that the face of the nun bears an astonishing similarity to the one in the *Self-Portrait with Raised Bare Shoulder* (see p. 133). The position of the dark eyes is the same, as are the wavy form of the bridge of the nose and the placement of the nostrils. Unlike some painters of the second half of the 19th century – Michael von Munkácsy, for example – who frequently searched among hundreds of subjects for a suitable type for a painting, Schiele utilized whatever was at hand, even regardless of gender, reworking whatever he borrowed from his studies in such a way as to make it altogether convincing. (RL)

Black chalk, watercolor, gouache on paper
46 × 31.2 cm
Leopold Museum, Vienna, Inv. 2350
K D.1125

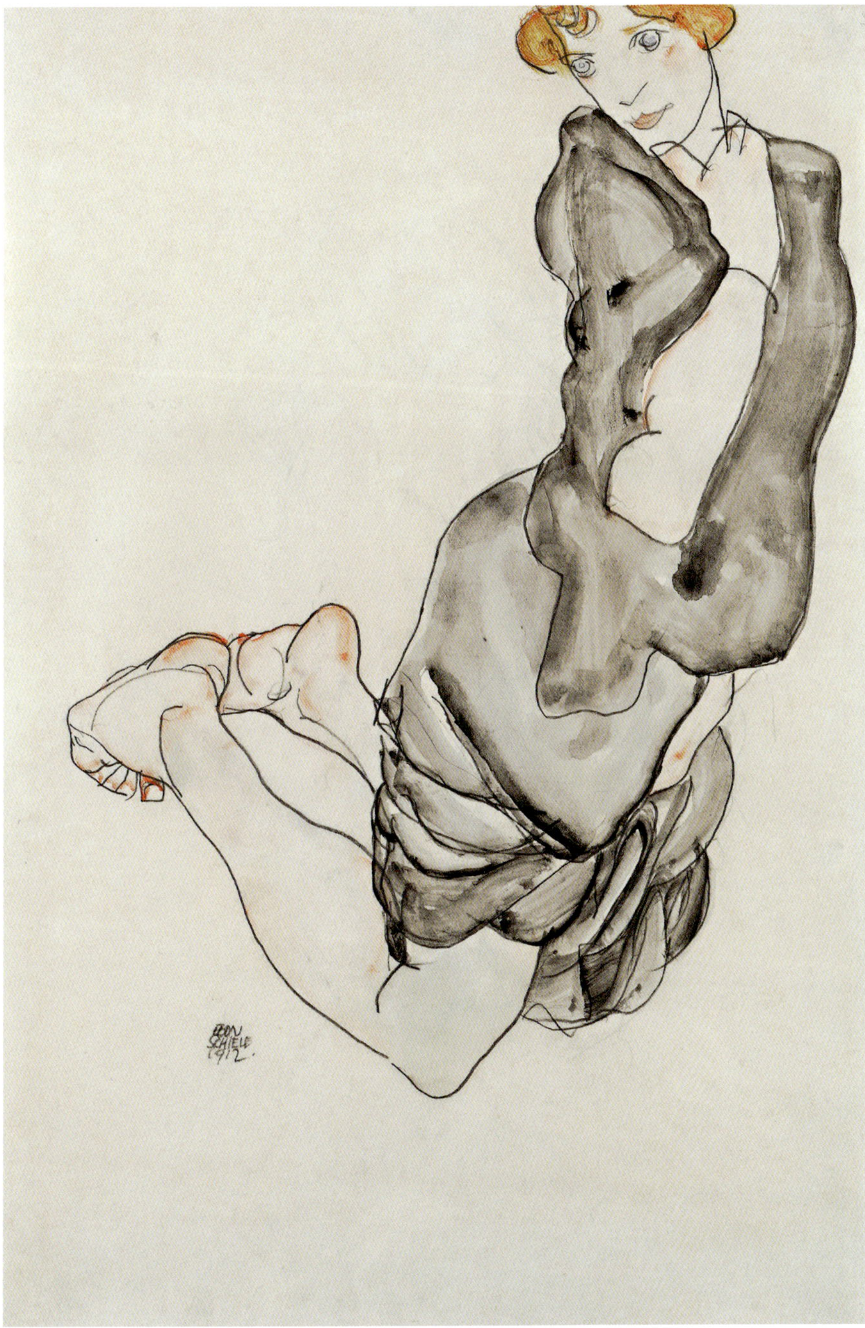

1912

NUDE OLD WOMAN, STANDING

The depiction shows an old, naked woman, her consumed, tired body with limp breasts and a wrinkly stomach – she is by no means beautiful. However, the figure is drawn with sensitive, thin lines, her head is slightly inclined, one hand on her face implying that she is lost. Schiele's mastery is revealed in the surface painting, the heightened parts, and the way the buttocks and joints, her face and hairstyle have been emphasized by means of gray, cloud-like brushstrokes. Nothing was euphemized here, but everything was rendered with harmonious naturalness.

The work is reminiscent of the old woman in the painting *The Three Ages of Woman* (N 168) by Gustav Klimt. In this work, Klimt presented the witheredness of old age in an almost dramatic contrast to the bloom of youth. However, owing to his genius hand and his natural rendering, Schiele's work is not off-putting but rather depicts a spiritual farewell to youth and beauty. (EL)

Pencil, gouache on paper
44.4 × 30.8 cm
Leopold Museum, Vienna, Inv. 2352
K D.1109a

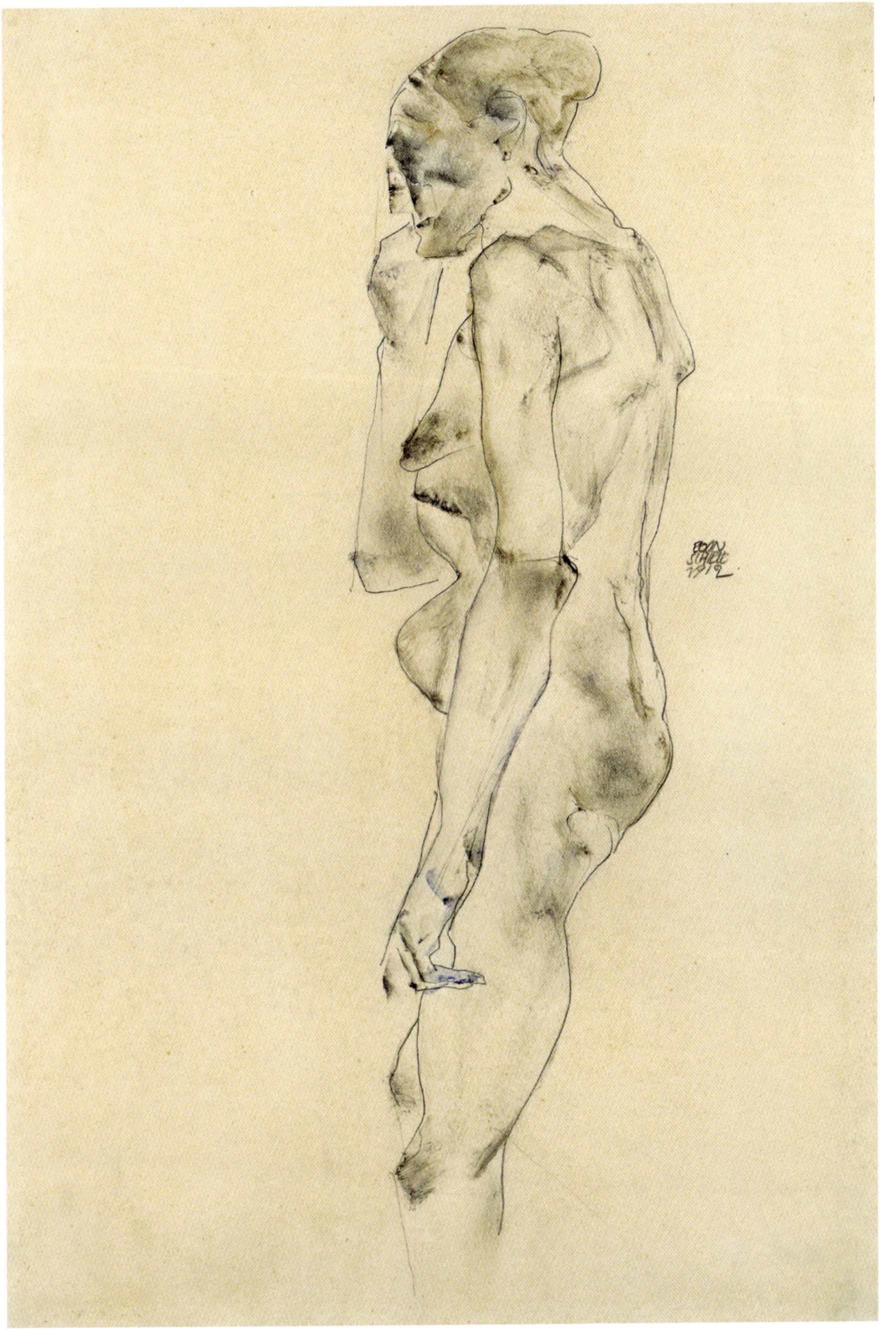

1912

CARDINAL AND NUN (CARESS)

The shocking subject matter is fixed within a strict formal arrangement, and the expressiveness of the work is inseparable from its magnificent structure. The dominating triangle shape, with its base at the bottom edge of the painting, incorporates three smaller triangles.

Red, black, and the contrasting light flesh tones of the two bodies predominate. The red shows the richest variety of shading. In those areas where it achieves a bright cinnabar, it takes on an uncommonly exciting radiance. Perhaps the only other painter in the 20th century to paint a red as expressive as this was Chaim Soutine. Unlike him, however, and without sacrificing any of its intensity, Schiele presents the color in shapes that are highly controlled.

Another triumph is the rendering of the cardinal's feet. They were drawn with great precision, yet they are incredibly expressive.

Particular importance was given to the poses of the two hands; both are captured in the gesture of prayer, a reflection of the pair's vocation. His palm is reverently placed against her body, hers against his. Schiele referred to this picture – not without sarcasm – as *Caress*. The nakedness and coarseness of the two pairs of legs are deliberately set off against the nun's habit and the cardinal's robe, as though Schiele wished to suggest that carnal desire cannot be suppressed, but rather breaks through all of our denials and prohibitions. The nun, her eyes wide, looks terrified. The cardinal's expression is more ambiguous. With his face, his red cap, and his strangely curved neck, it is very likely that Schiele meant to suggest the male organ. One is justified in this assumption by the fact that Gustav Klimt explained to his friends – Schiele being one of them – that in the neck of the man in his painting *The Kiss* (N 179), he had meant to evoke not only the potency of the figure but also the back of the penis.

Unquestionably, Schiele's *Cardinal and Nun (Caress)* is a paraphrase of Klimt's *The Kiss*, but it was only the subject matter of the latter that inspired Schiele's response. He completely reworked the motif, *both* in terms of content and form. The idea in Klimt's painting that a girl who gives in to a kiss is already at the edge of the abyss, is no longer especially apparent in Schiele's picture. In his work the abyss yawns for both figures. The nun, to be sure, is in greater danger than the cardinal owing to her position, but her legs are firmly braced. Schiele transformed Klimt's flower-filled meadow into bare earth interrupted only by strips of grass that are fixed elements in the pictorial structure, the man's static calm and the woman's nestling against him into an exciting forward thrust and counterthrust. A paradisiacal idyll, with tender submission on the part of the female, has become a picture of terrifying compulsion: Jugendstil has been transformed into Expressionism. (RL)

Oil on canvas
70 × 80.5 cm
Leopold Museum, Vienna, Inv. 455
L 210; K P.232

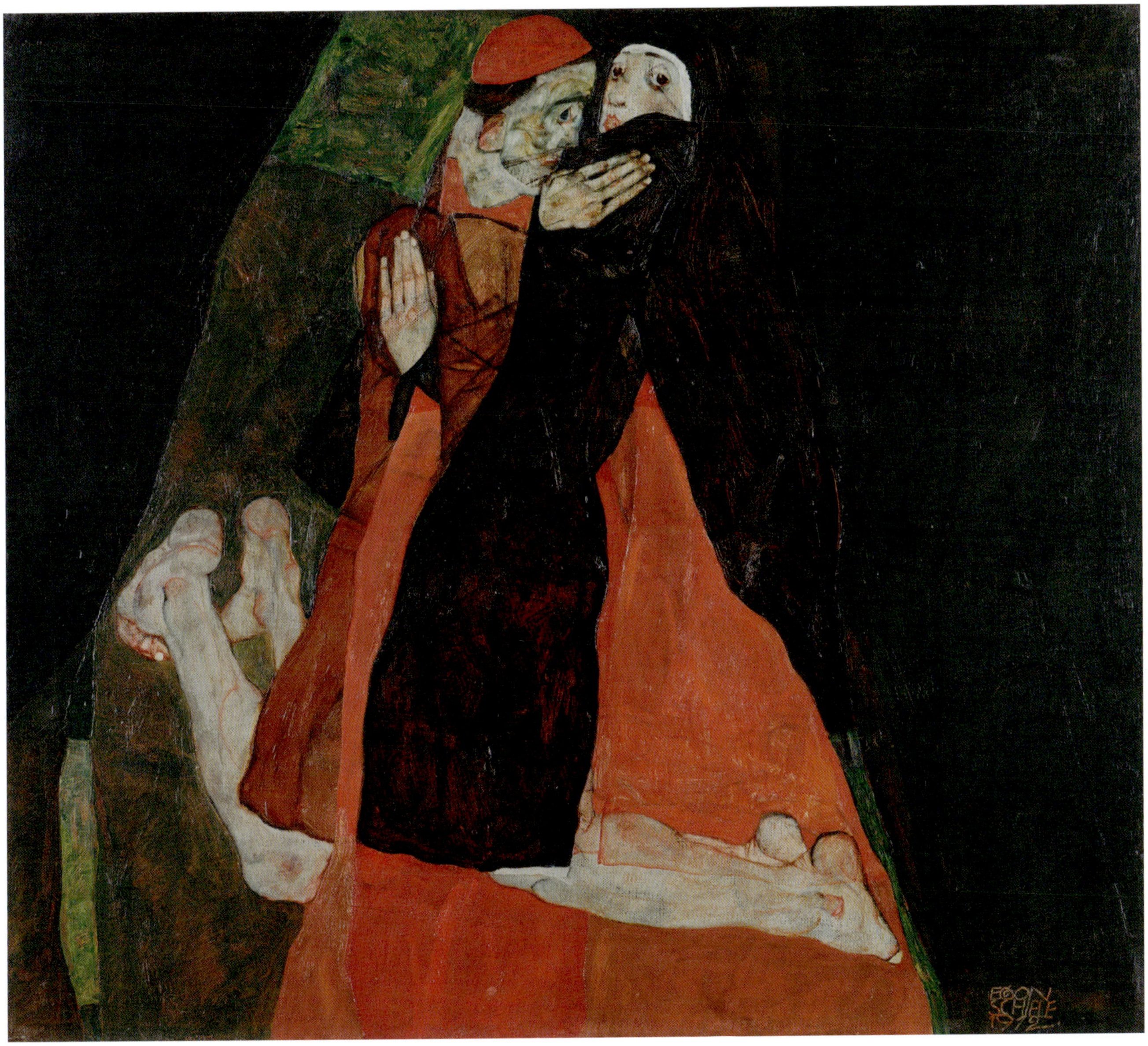

1912

NUDE WITH BLUE STOCKINGS, BENDING FORWARD

Schiele brilliantly met the challenge of this picture, the foreshortening of a nude figure seen at an angle from above. The woman's body is described with sensitive contours and at the same time the picture is given a clear structure. The curving line of the spine is all-important in the composition.

The touches of color along the outlines, the shading lines next to them in some areas, and the delicate painting within the figure give it a distinct three-dimensionality.

The overall coloring is as vivid as that of the oil paintings created at this time, for example, *Calvary* (see p. 149), or *Portrait of Wally Neuzil* (see p. 147). (RL)

Pencil, gouache on paper
37.5 × 28.9 cm
Leopold Museum, Vienna, Inv. 1441
K D.1088

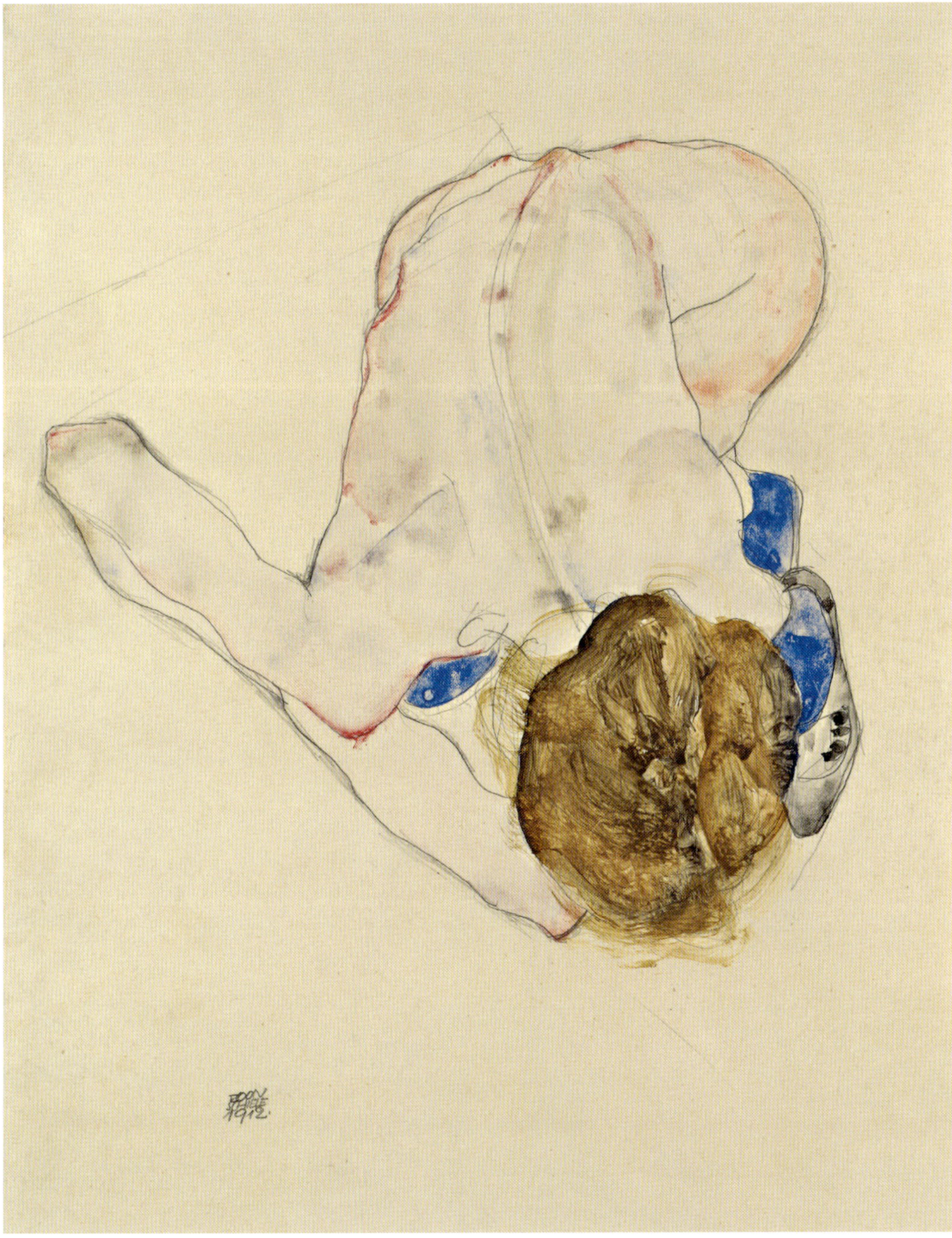

1912

SELF-PORTRAIT WITH CHINESE LANTERN PLANT

This is one of Schiele's most popular self-portraits. The complex interrelationships between the pictorial elements – one shoulder dropped, the other hunched, the head inclined to the side, the Chinese lanterns and their curving stems and dried leaves – are magnificently controlled. The hair and the torso are deliberately cut off by the edges of the painting and are thus juxtaposed.

The head is supported by a slender, slightly curved neck. The fragility this suggests is continued in the way the head turns in one direction, the eyes gaze in another, and in the expression of pain on the face. Note the odd, wine-red pupils and the moss-green of the irises. All of this is totally convincing.

Schiele's sensitive drawing is apparent in numerous details. For example, the line of the left shoulder is continued by that of the right side of the jaw, which, after it angles upward, parallels the outline of the neck. His painting is equally deft; the placement of the colors in the face and neck is masterful – another reason why this self-portrait is so appealing.

Schiele here portrayed himself exactly as he was: a hypersensitive man and artist. (RL)

Oil, opaque color on wood
32.2 × 39.8 cm
Leopold Museum, Vienna, Inv. 454
L 211; K P.233

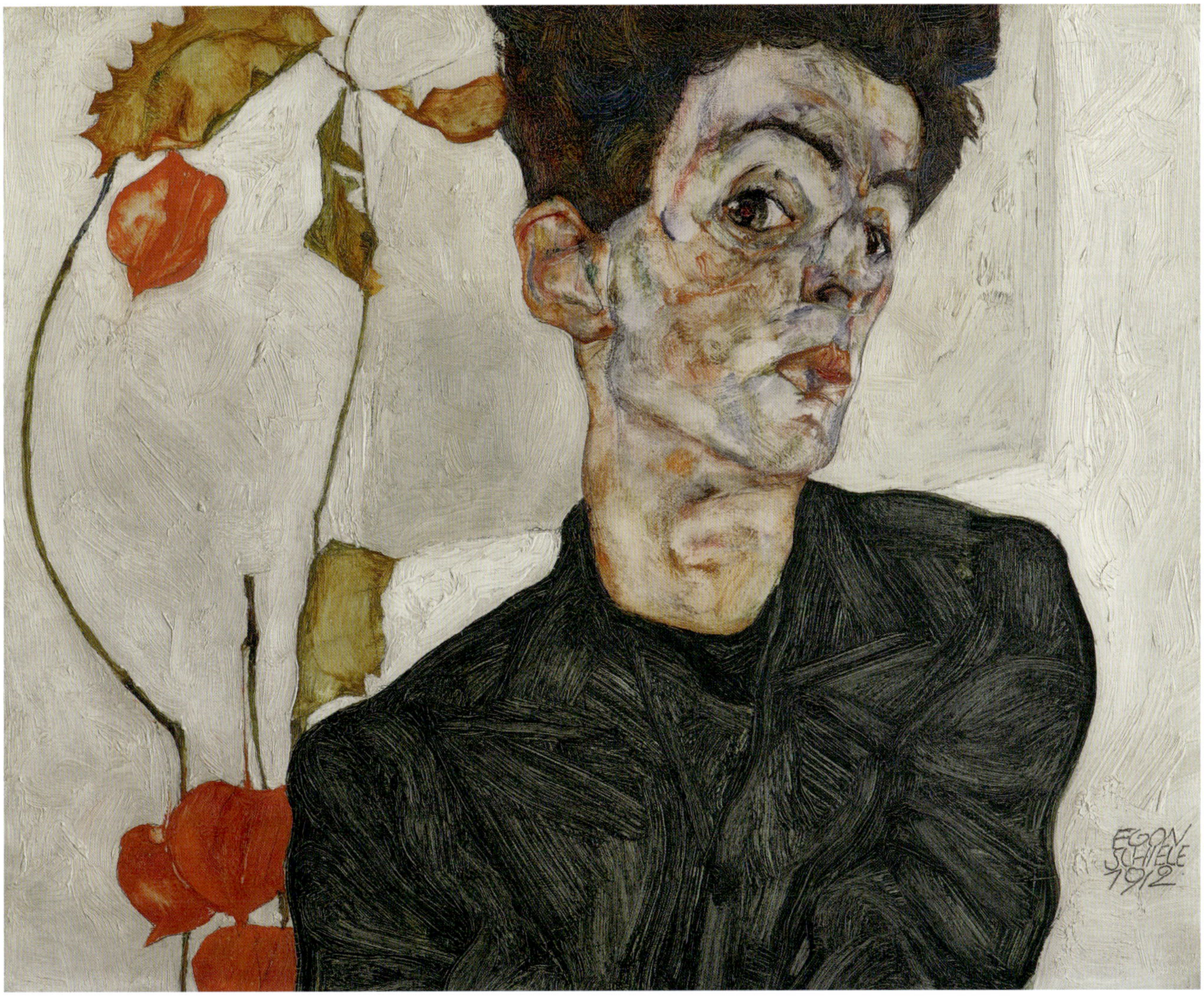
EGON
SCHIELE
1912

1912

PORTRAIT OF WALLY NEUZIL

Schiele painted this portrait of his companion as a counterpart to his *Self-Portrait with Chinese Lantern Plant* (see p. 145).
The arms rest next to the slender body.[3] The head is tilted forward, the eyes overlarge. Yet the radiant gaze has something melancholic about it. Again Schiele used physical details to express meaning, depicting psychic need convincingly.
The strictly balanced composition utilizes in part geometric shapes: the right cheek virtually forms the base of a half-circle that begins with the chin, extends around the left cheek, and is then only suggested as it passes through the hair. An echo of this is the slightly curved stem of the plant, the upper part of which corresponds to the outline of the hair just across from it. Similarly, but more markedly than in the self-portrait, behind the head a light gray shape is set off from the otherwise white background, its outline carefully attuned with the composition as a whole.
The color harmony is extraordinary: orange, ocher, and blue; white, light gray, and black; and red and green produce an impressive consonance. (RL)

3 | Schiele adopted the contours of the shoulders and arms and the lace collar from a colored drawing of Wally (K D.1118) – reworking them, of course – but not the face. The face is based on the one in *Kneeling Woman with a Gray Cape (Wally Neuzil)* (see p. 137). In this work it is quite sketchy, but in all of the essential elements the two are very similar. The face in the drawing from which Schiele borrowed the arms and the lace collar is the one that he transformed into the *Mourning Woman* (see p. 127).

Oil on wood
32 × 39.8 cm
Leopold Museum, Vienna, Inv. 453
L 212; K P.234

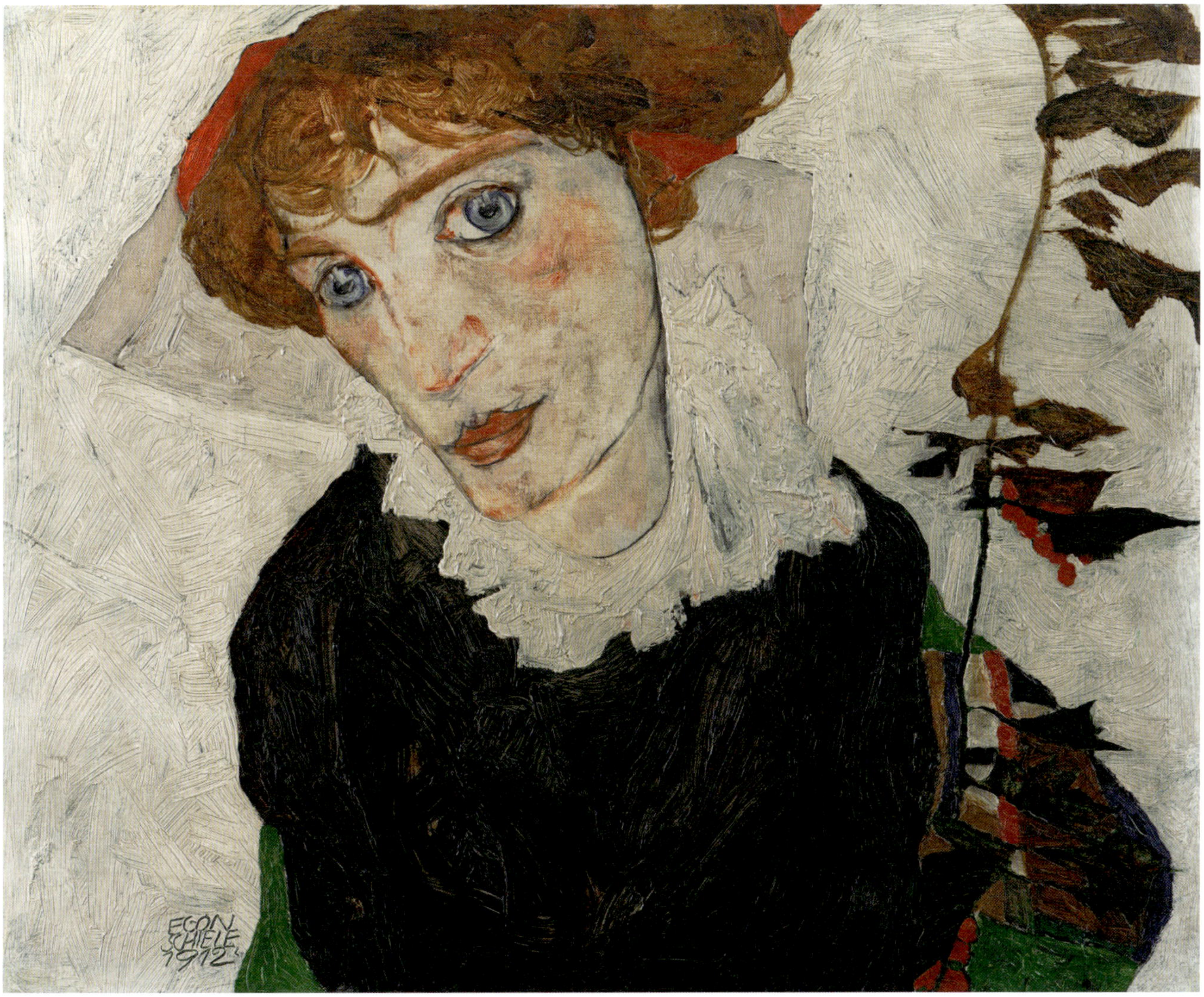
EGON
SCHIELE
1912

1912

CALVARY

There are only two renderings by Schiele which depict a rising sun: the work *Autumn Sun I (Sunrise)* (L 220; K P.236), which the artist also called "Sunrise", among other titles, and the painting *River Landscape with Two Trees* (L 231; K P.264), the atmosphere of which clearly evokes a rising sun, though we do not know what Schiele himself called the work. Otherwise, this artist, who was decidedly more interested in depicting decline, be it evening or late autumn, much more often captured a *setting* sun or the atmosphere *after* sunset.

This is also the case with the present rendering. The meadows appear to be hit by the fading light, which the artist expressed using predominantly warm colors blurring into one another. These hues include only a little blue as a complementary shade. A similar blue, with the addition of a cool red hue, was used especially for the depiction of the two lower bands of clouds. Thus, the warm-colored foreground is contrasted with the sky rendered in cool shades. Separating the two sections is an area of almost dazzling white, against which stand out colorful tree props with little leafless trees, a small station of the cross and, most importantly, three crosses. These crosses with their nailed-on bodies are placed before a hill, presumably meant to represent Golgotha, and are so askew that one feels that no one cares for these old Calvary symbols anymore or pays them any attention. The tree closest to them seems to be about to fall over. These many small trees with their supports, which appear more and more skewed to the left and finally "disappear" behind a hill, generally contribute greatly to the atmosphere of decline.

It was only in the depictions of this time that Schiele rendered the ground especially in a completely unnaturalistic manner, much like he did in *Trees in Winter* (L 216; K P.241), *Bare Trees* (L 217; K P.242) and in *Autumn Sun I (Sunrise)*.

The avid Schiele collector Heinrich Benesch repeatedly visited the artist's studio and – according to his son, the later Director of the Albertina – chose this very rendering of a *Calvary* among the aforementioned, stylistically related works. Even by an objective observer it can be deemed the most eminent among them. For aside from the "painterly painting", as it were, the work also boasts the most successful compositional structure. (RL)

Oil, gouache, pencil on canvas
81.7 × 80 cm
Leopold Museum, Vienna, Inv. 480
L 215; K P.240

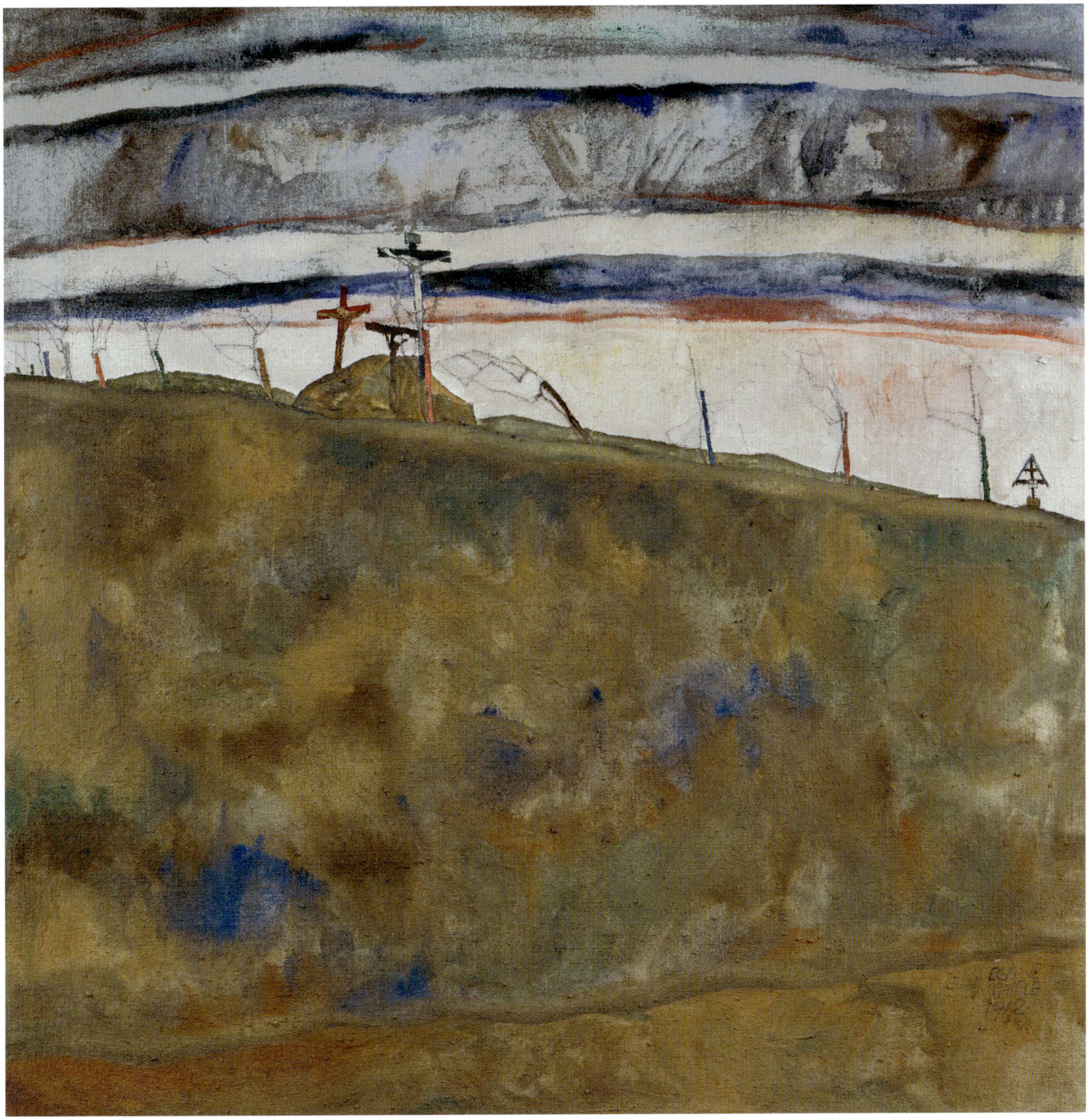

1912

DEURING CASTLE

This small castle stands above the city of Bregenz. Schiele painted it in August 1912, from the square in front of the parish church of St. Gallus. The tower on the left, with an octagonal top story, was added onto the essentially medieval complex in the second half of the 17th century.
Schiele contrasted the castle's ocher walls and reddish roofs with basically cooler colors dominated by a light blue-green and an ultramarine. He applied these vivid colors describing the dense foliage that surrounds the castle almost in the manner of an Action painter. (RL)

Pencil, gouache on paper
31.5 × 48 cm
Leopold Museum, Vienna, Inv. 2373
K D.1216

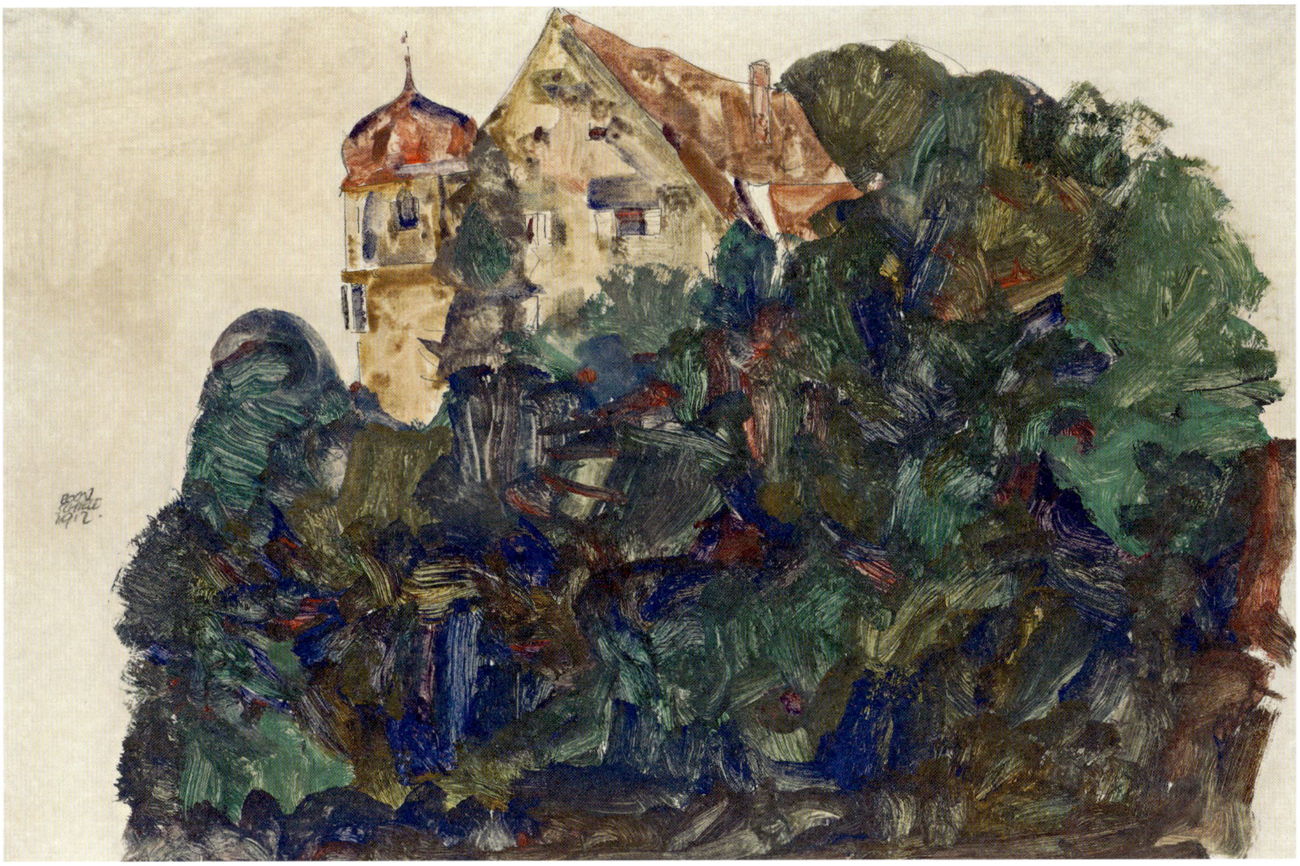

1912

AUTUMN TREE IN STIRRED AIR (WINTER TREE)

At first glance, many people see this painting as an abstraction. This is because the background clouds and the connection between the tree's branches and the ground are not immediately perceived. Schiele deliberately left the limed trunk a lighter color so as to isolate the branches from the strip of ground at the bottom and the distant range of hills for the sake of contrast between light and dark and the play of colors. The separation is even more complete than that in the painting on p. 119. In their isolation, the forms of the branches are also dramatically juxtaposed to those of the earth below.
The longer one studies this painting, the more realistic it seems. The different shapes of the branches reflect different responses to life. The wind bends the topmost ones like whips and causes the thinner ones that branch off from the one rising nearly straight up in the upper left to flutter like flags. Others have become crippled in their tedious struggle, and those in the lower right have apparently given up, as they hang down exhausted.
The bluish black of the chain of hills above the light reddish ocher field sets it off and relegates it to the far distance.
Never before – or after – did Schiele paint a sky with such sensitivity, such a nuanced array of tonalities. The lightest areas are like halos surrounding the tree's last leaves. Areas like these frequently appear in stormy skies in early winter, and country people call them "snow lights," recognizing that they signal the approach of a blizzard. Yet they, too, like so much else in the picture, are not rendered realistically. In this landscape Schiele managed to capture altogether convincingly the raw energy of a storm in late autumn. With this tree, totally exposed and threatened, he also created a symbol of human existence. (RL)

Oil, pencil on canvas
80 × 80.5 cm
Leopold Museum, Vienna, Inv. 449
L 221; K P.239

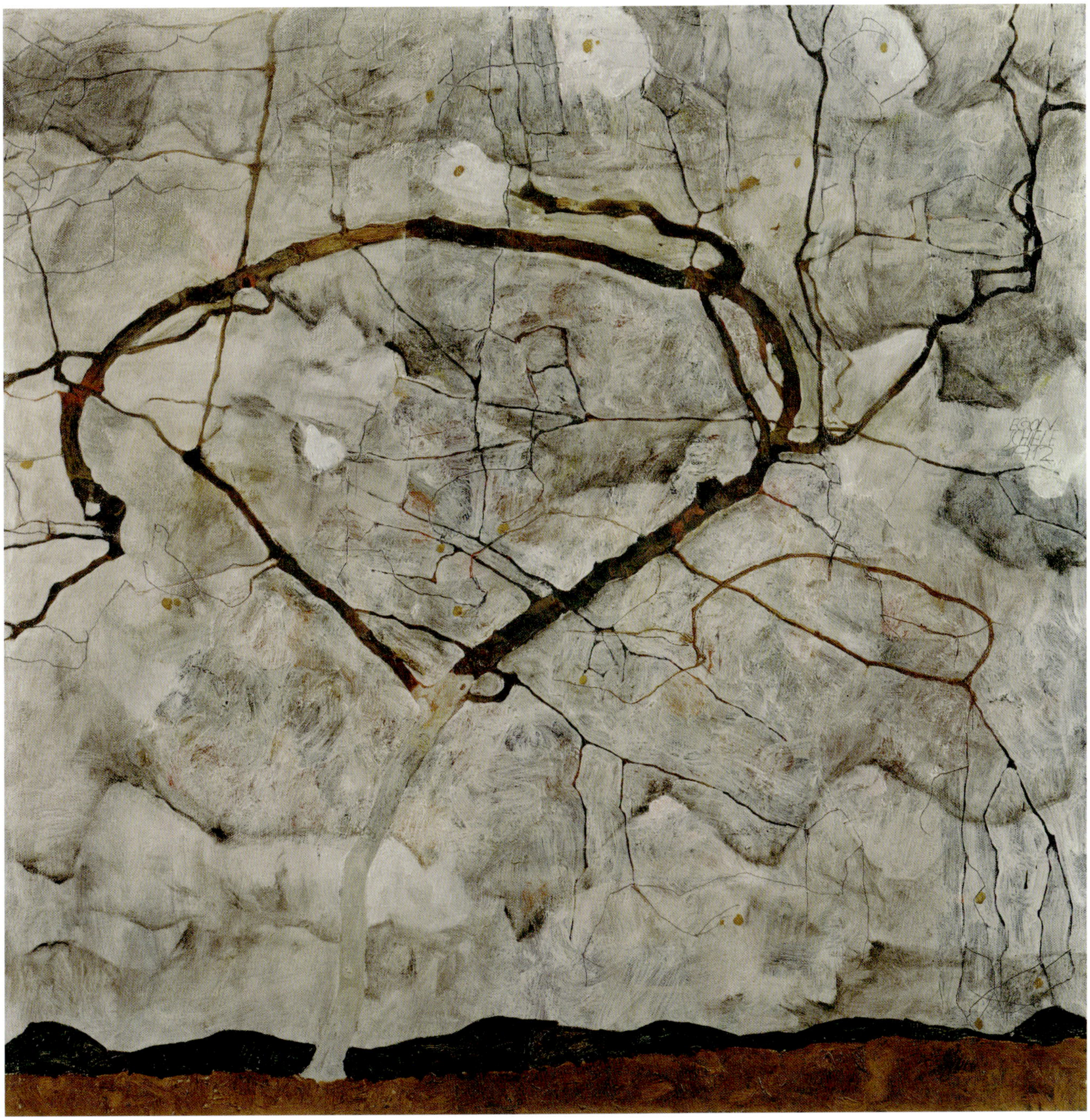
EGON
SCHIELE
1912

1913

THE SMALL TOWN III

After his time in prison it took Schiele a long time before he was able to begin painting again. Not only was he shaken by the experience, but he also lacked a proper studio and probably the money with which to secure the necessary materials. For the first two paintings he undertook, he had to use canvas that had been stitched together from two smaller scraps. On November 16 he wrote to Arthur Roessler that "with the most primitive of materials" he had "almost finished a few paintings." (ESAD, ID: 530).

It is a sign of Schiele's mental state at this time that neither this painting nor the *City in the Twilight (The Small Town II)* (L 226; K P.260) was inspired by fresh impressions. Unlike any of his other cityscapes from these years, they were pieced together from sketches of Krumau motifs and from invented structures. There is no single location in Krumau from which even those buildings that can be identified appear as they do here. The one that is most recognizable is St. Jodocus Church, upstream with its wall facing the Vltava and its adjacent structures in the center at the top. But even here Schiele has changed the facade's color to red and the facades of the houses to the left of it have been twisted so that they continue upward at an angle rather than facing the same way. The buildings to the right of the church, and especially the crenellated wall beyond them, have been changed considerably. For all of these changes, whether in color, shape, or orientation, the church and the structures on either side of it are the only part of the city that Schiele left in something like its actual configuration. The large building just to the right of the center, with two tall white chimneys, is clearly the Jesuit seminary, even though it too has been reworked. The crenellated wall below it and to the left may recall the facade of Krumau's City Hall. In use since roughly 1650, it is made up of four Gothic houses, but in Schiele's painting there appear to be only three. And, in fact, the City Hall building faces in a different direction in relation to the Bader Bridge, visible in the upper left, which connects the old town with the new.

The roofs are gray-black, the facades more colorful. A black river winds between them. At the top of the picture the stream is narrower, at the bottom it has widened and shows shifting reflections. The roofs of the many buildings are tall and steep, almost like hats, and many of the windows below them look like eyes. It is as though we were looking at as many faces.

The lovely colors of the facades of the houses and the blackness of the river – both freely invented by Schiele – complement each other. The result is a harmonious whole. (RL)

Oil, soft pencil on canvas
89.9 × 90 cm
Leopold Museum, Vienna, Inv. 482
L 227; K P.261

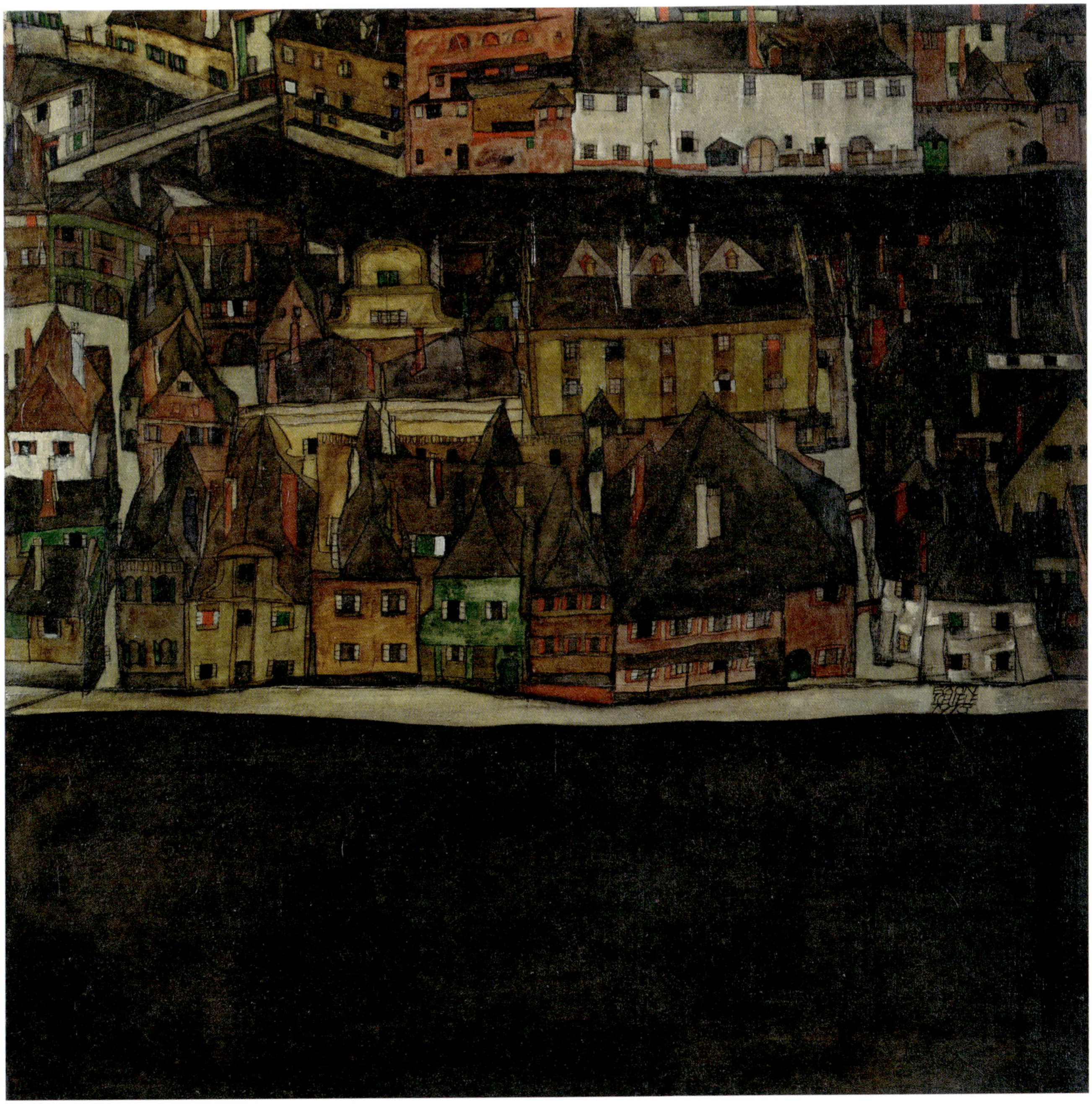

1913

RECLINING BOY (ERICH LEDERER)

The boy is lying in an upholstered chair, his head resting against the back. One is struck by the drastic turning of his head, which, seen from above, looks extremely odd against the flat yellow behind it.

To judge from Schiele's stylistic evolution, this drawing, with its highly charged but sensitive lines, must date from the beginning of 1913. The subject matter confirms such an assumption.

The rigid lines of the drawing and the application of painting to only a part of it reveal a definite step in the direction of abstraction. Schiele painted only the back of the yellow chair, and as a result one does not at first recognize it for what it is. Its right arm would also be puzzling – unlike the left one, which is clearly connected to the back – if the lines describing it, angled up from the body, were not traced in the same telltale yellow-ocher.

The light-colored face stands out in three dimensions against the deliberate flatness of the chair. The strongly contrasting dark hair and eyes, and even more the softly painted shadows, are also typical of Schiele's work from early 1913. (RL)

Pencil, gouache on paper
31.8 × 48.1 cm
Leopold Museum, Vienna, Inv. 1408
K D.1224

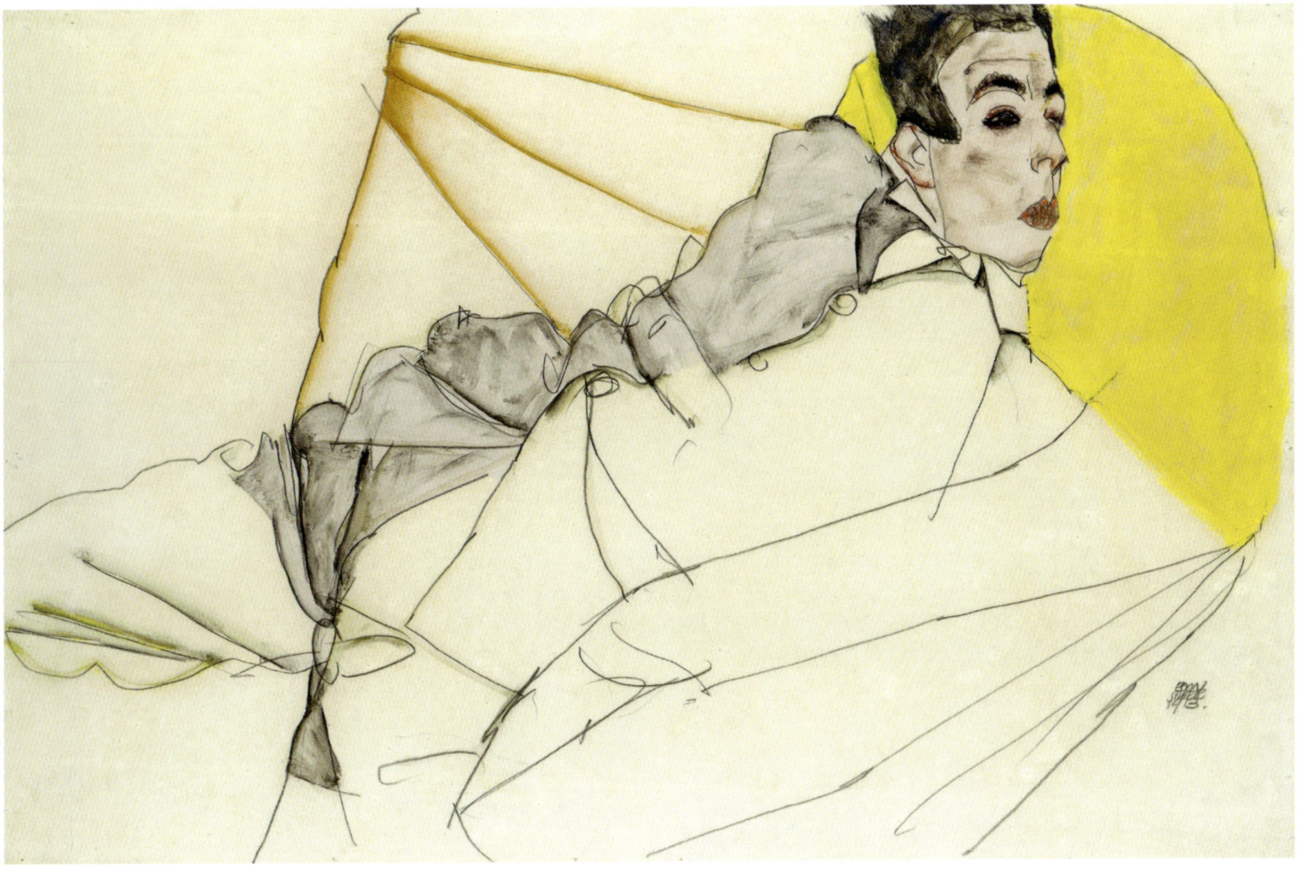

1913

SETTING SUN

In Schiele's early years, the season depicted in his landscapes always conformed with their actual period of execution. In the case of his mature paintings, this connection no longer held. This is true of the present landscape, *Setting Sun*. Based on Schiele's letters, it is safe to assume that this so profoundly autumnal depiction of 1913 was not done until April or early May of the following year – when spring was in the air. The motif that inspired Schiele to this painting was the coastline near Trieste and two outlying islands. Two small trees project above the hilly area in the foreground, their crowns intersecting sea, islands and sky. Otherwise the painting is composed largely in terms of horizontal strata and lines. This lends it a sense of calm, but also of melancholy, to which the strange colors contribute.

Many artists before and after Schiele have depicted sunsets. Almost all have rendered the play of colors in warm gradations dominated by orange. Not so Schiele. Light carmine red and a compartively dark steel blue dominate the upper area of the composition, in an interplay that has a simultaneously cool and exciting effect.

Although by the laws of optics the isolated mountains would stand in shadow when the sun is in this position and be visible only as a black mass, Schiele has rendered them as if they were translucent, lending them a crystalline character. They are subsumed with sky and sea into a colored unity. This was done not only for aesthetic reasons but perhaps even more to find a compelling visual solution to the task Schiele apparently set himself. The overall brightness of the upper area, broken only by thin branches and foliage, is contrasted to the pervading darkness of the lower section. This is dominated by grayish purple and dark green, only the small yellow flowers, rendered as circular ornaments in one last recollection of the Vienna Secessionist style, providing lighter accents. Otherwise everything is plunged in gloom and, one senses, it has grown cold – the leaves seem to have stiffened with cold and the nearly bare tree, as if with a shudder, has drawn its frail branches together into a narrow crown.

Differently than in 1911 and 1912 but with no less power of expression, in his new style Schiele managed to create an emblem of the transitory nature of all things.

Everything seems to lie under a cloak of hopelessness and melancholy. Even the magic of the sky and the rocky islands is doomed to pass. Bluish veils have descended over the sun, whose light shines through only in two narrow bands. The question arises whether the light and warmth-giving sun might not sink into the sea never to rise again? This borderline situation is convincingly evoked here. (RL)

Oil on canvas
90 × 90.5 cm
Leopold Museum, Vienna, Inv. 625
L 235; K P.265

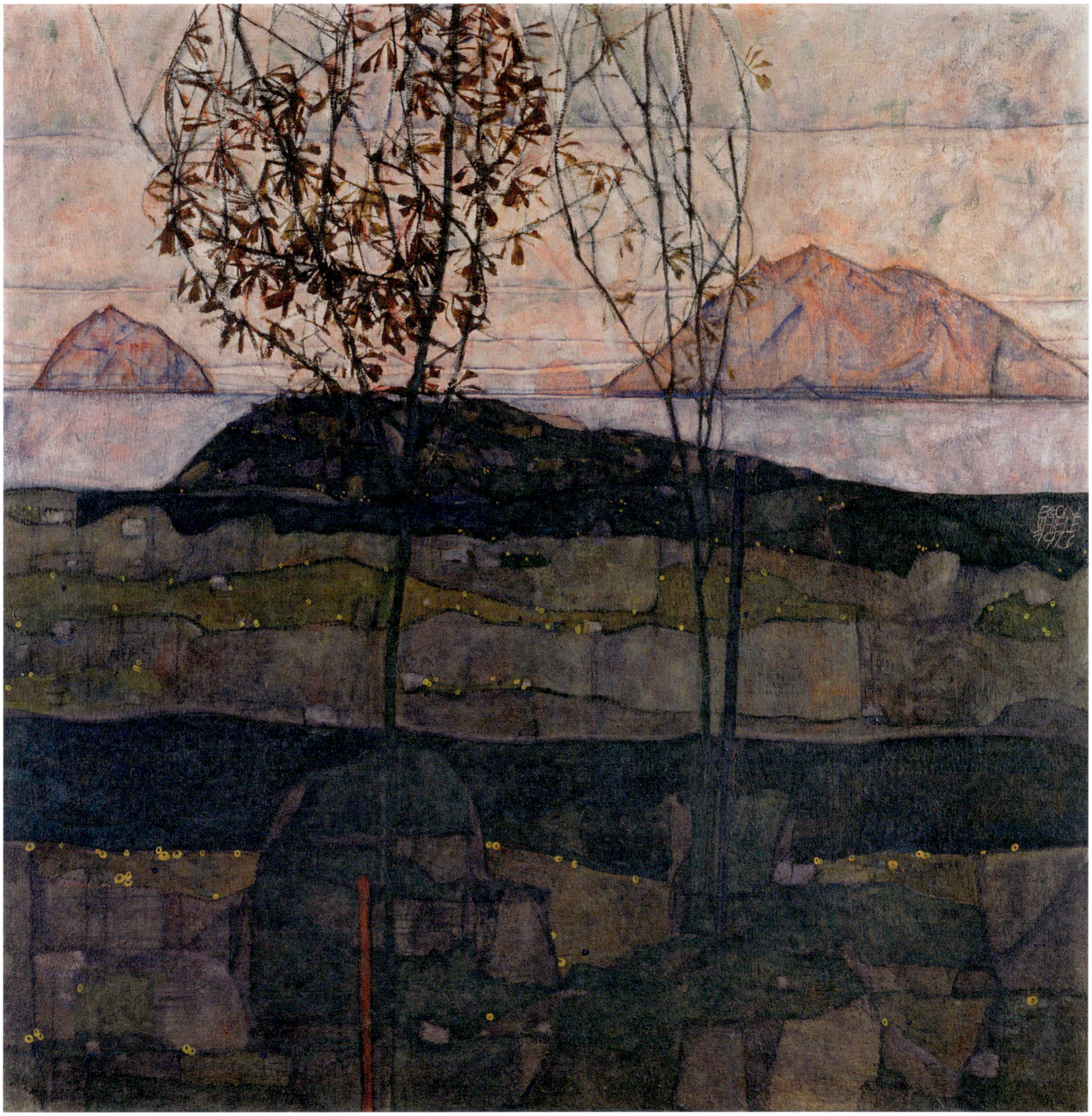

1913

REAR VIEW OF A FEMALE HALF-NUDE WITH CLOTH (FRAGMENT)

In 1913 Schiele was working on the painting *Conversion* (L XLIX; K P.XLIII), measuring approximately 200 × 300 cm. It appears that the painting was never completed and was eventually cut up. Only a few fragments have survived, including the female nude from behind with drapery. In his essay entitled "Remembering works by Egon Schiele which no longer exist"[4], Otto Benesch related: "It was the most enormous canvas he ever held in his hands. It depicted a group of about twelve, almost lifesize figures, viewed from above, standing or striding on the ground and loosely filling the pictorial space. While the figures were fictitious, they were inspired by real people. Friends and people close to Schiele could be discerned, including Klimt, my father, and, in the traits of a boy, I recognized myself. They were all clad in long habits like ones worn by monks. Female nudes, viewed from the back, also appeared".

In several letters to the collector Carl Reininghaus, Schiele discussed the "painting with the striding figures and prophets", mentioning a figure assuming "the gesture of a clairvoyant witnessing a religious sensation" as well as "a praying, divine man in the middle of the painting" who appears to depict Schiele himself (ESAD, ID: 61, 64). Many preparatory drawings, especially of the "striding figures" created using pencil and gouache have survived. They all show decisively drawn out contours and distinctive outlines of the naked body parts. This allowed Schiele to not only define spatiality but to also convey the impression of striding. (RL)

4 | Otto Benesch: "Erinnerungen an Bilder von Egon Schiele, die nicht mehr existieren", in: Otto Kallir (ed.): *Egon Schiele. Œuvre-Katalog der Gemälde*, Vienna 1966, pp. 37–38.

Oil on canvas
192 × 52.5 cm
Leopold Museum, Vienna, Inv. 654
L 237; K P.254

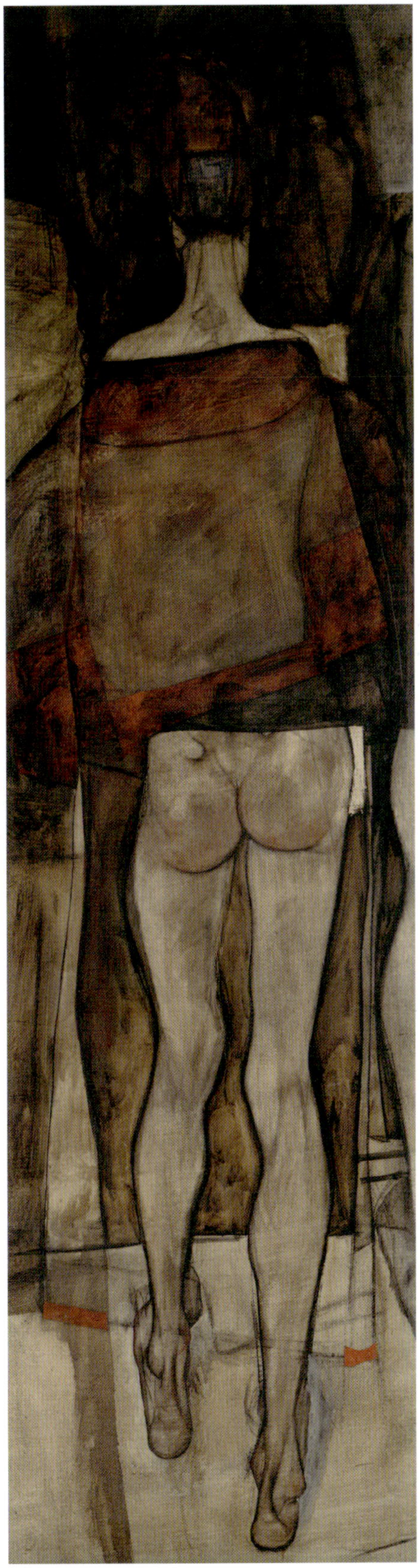

1913

STEIN ON THE DANUBE II

Of the two works by Schiele depicting the town of Stein as seen from the Kreuzberg, with the Danube and the far shore, only the smaller version (L 233; K P.267) reflects the actual situation to any extent. As in the other small version showing Stein from the opposite bank of the Danube, Schiele has depicted the parish church only rudimentarily and with a schematically simplifed roof, perhaps with an eye to emphasizing the tower of Frauenberg Church opposite as the dominating element.

The large version, executed months later – as the present author already pointed out in a publication of spring 1959 – is built up of several components. Visible in the foreground is the building complex of the Minorite Monastery and Church, and to the left, Frauenberg Church – which is in fact taller and, above all, lies approximately 250 meters farther west.

The three-aisle pilaster basilica of the former Minorite Church has round clerestory windows, depicted here as horizontal ovals, and is abutted by the choir on the east. Schiele has foreshortened both and depicted the roof of the choir a great deal higher than it actually is. Visible at the southwest corner of the choir, as in reality, is a church tower with a Baroque onion dome. Yet as we can see from certain details, this is not the dome of the parish church, as we would expect on the basis of the actual topography, but that of the Minorite Church. The main reason why Schiele chose to locate not the parish church but the Minorite Church to the right of Frauenberg Church, was recognized by my wife, Dr. Elisabeth Leopold. In order to emphasize the soaring tower of Frauenberg Church, which seems to extend over the entire width of the Danube, it was "necessary" to set a small church beside it – the Minorite Church, which appears to crouch behind the exaggeratedly high roof of the choir. Located adjacent to it on the west are two smaller buildings (the two "Salzstadel" built in 1598). Schiele has depicted only one of them, which rounds off the composition on the right. In reality, however, this building, too, does not stand west of Frauenberg Church but far to its east.

Schiele succeeded in blending these diverse separate motifs into a unity so convincing that viewing the picture, we feel that the local scene must have looked just like this and no different. (RL)

Oil on canvas
91.5 × 91.5 cm
Leopold Museum, Vienna, Inv. 479
L 240; K P.269

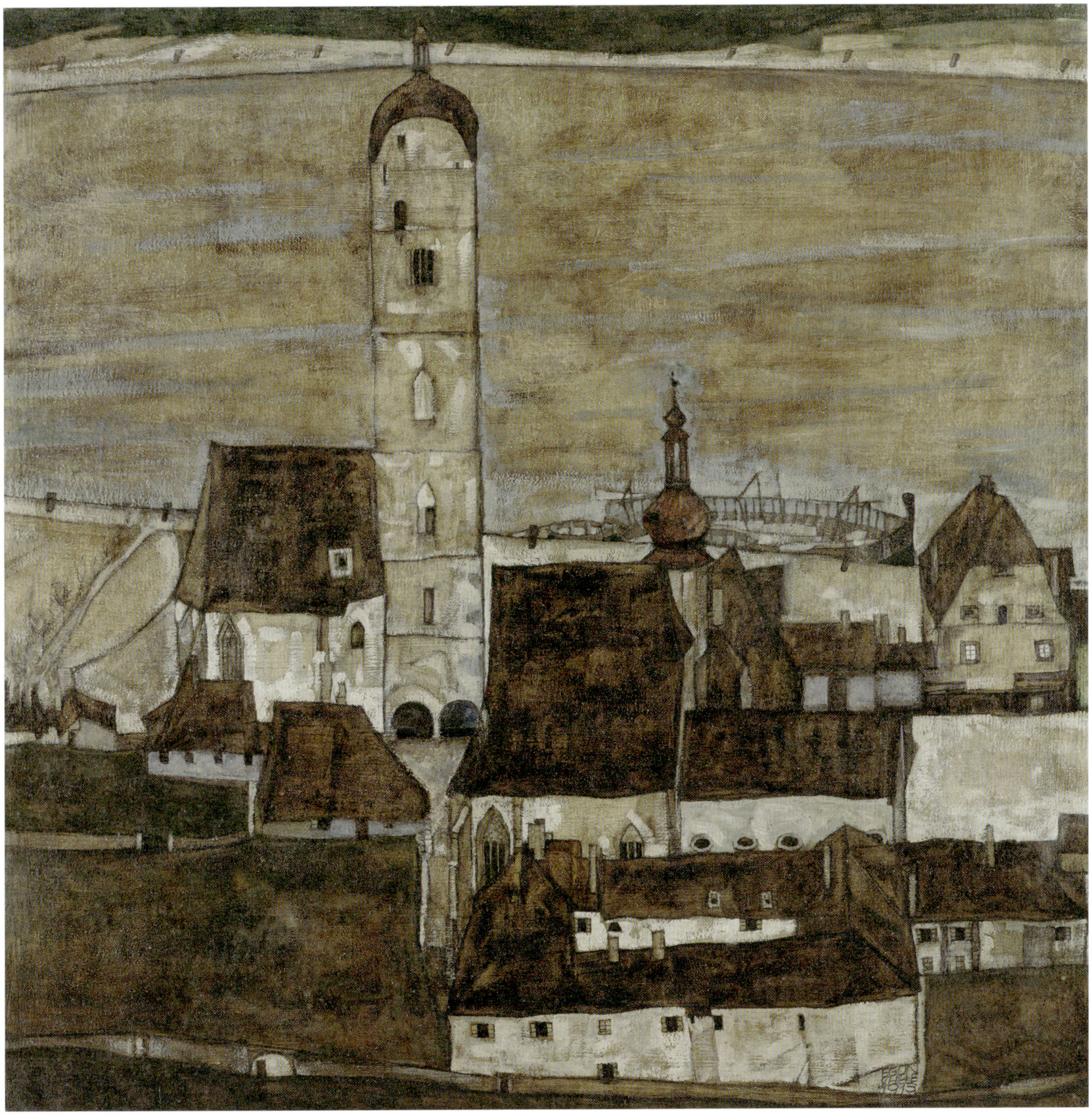

1913

MOTHER AND DAUGHTER

This is a tense but extraordinarily self-contained composition. The dominant diagonal axis of the elongated girl's body is balanced by the vertical braid and the roughly opposite diagonal described by the mother's forearm and the upper part of the girl's right arm. The tilt of the mother's face, the girl's face, and the outside contour of the left hip and thigh also help to stabilize the composition.

The drawing of the girl's body, with its shoulder sloping to the right and the braid hanging down her back, is particularly impressive.

Her skin color, enlivened by delicate tones of red and gray, is set off against the scarlet-red of the mother's dress. The hair of both women is an identical blonde. (RL)

Pencil, gouache on paper
47.9 × 31.1 cm
Leopold Museum, Vienna, Inv. 1436
K D.1298

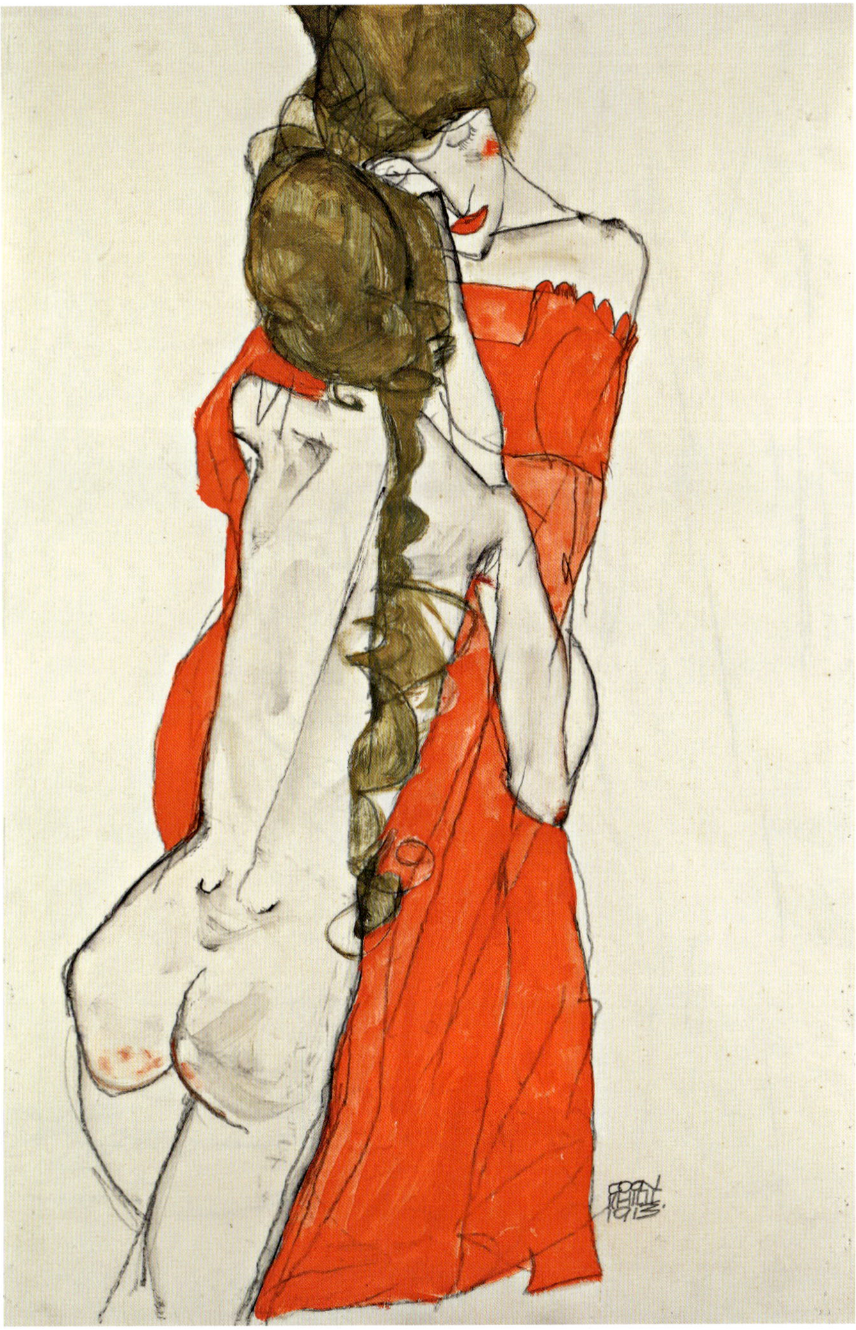
EGON
SCHIELE
1913.

1913

KNEELING GIRL ON RED PILLOW

This kneeling girl appears to have been caught in motion. Her expression and the extreme tilt of her head – cut off as it is by the top edge – give the impression that she is afraid of bumping against something above her. One can see from the outline of the mattress on which the girl is kneeling how carefully it was incorporated into the composition. Props such as this are rare in Schiele's work. His figures are usually shown standing, sitting, lying, or kneeling without the slightest indication of their surroundings. Here he provided a base for this fragile, angular figure so as to underscore the sense of dynamic movement. The pillow between her legs, painted bright red, helps to explain the position of the right calf and foot extended away from us.

Especially notable are the short, fanned lines suggestive of ribs. Although anatomically incorrect, they are justified in the context of the composition and are thus perfectly acceptable.

All of the elements in the arrangement are cross-referenced, but in an inconspicuous way, so that one's first impression is that of a living, moving figure. (RL)

Pencil, gouache on paper
47.4 × 32 cm
Leopold Museum, Vienna, Inv. 1438
K D.1285

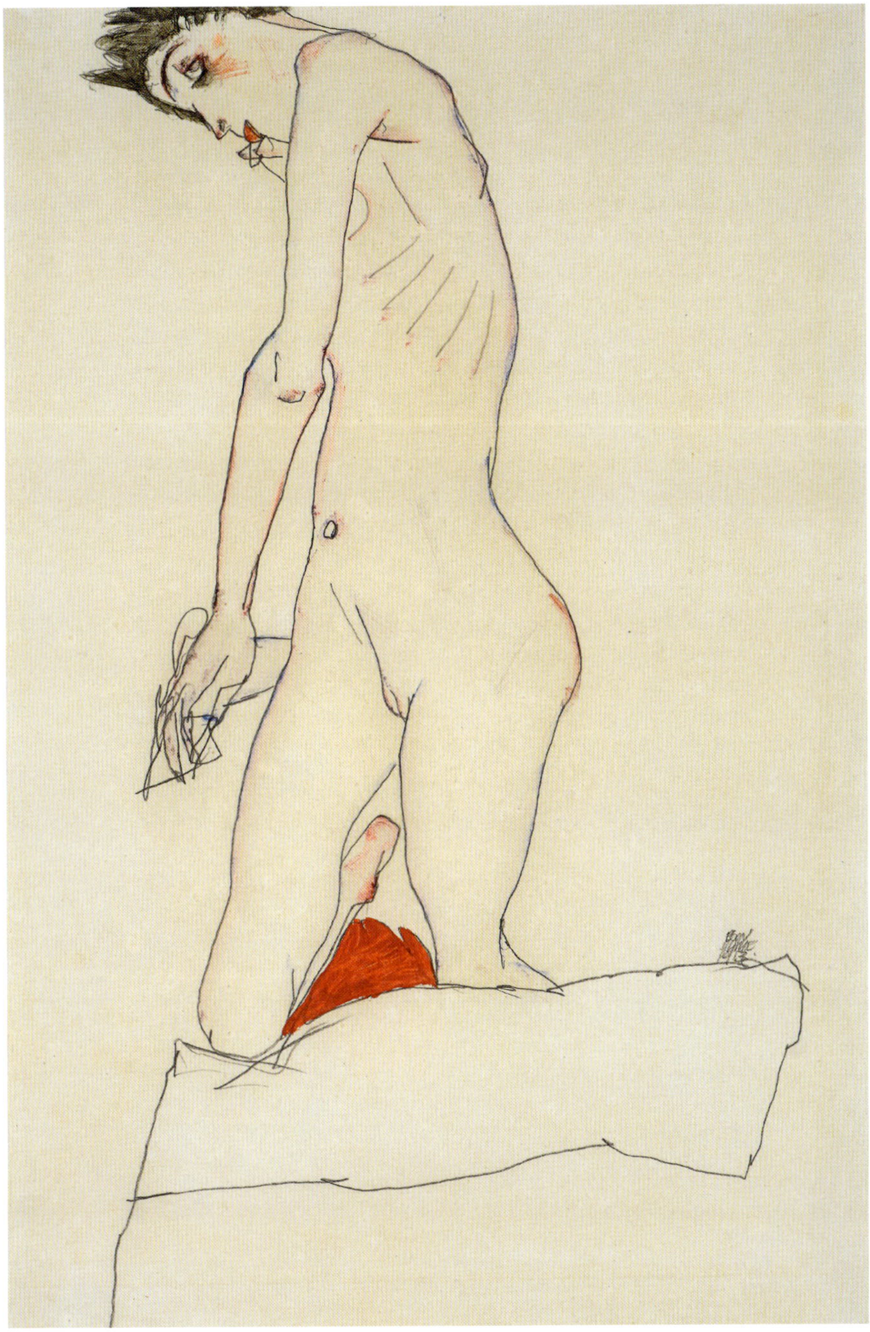

1913

RED BLOUSE

In this work Schiele produced an exciting contrast between the flat, brilliant scarlet of the blouse and the fully three-dimensional body. He depicts only a torso, but formally it strikes one as "complete," a self-contained composition.
The open blouse serves to frame the naked body. Shading here and there along the outlines of the legs and arms lifts them off the paper and places them in space.
Just as the shoulder and head are cut off at the top, the left foot is cut off at the bottom. Thanks to this formal juxtaposition, one does not perceive their absence as a deficiency. Nor does one register the highly casual rendering of the hands, for they serve as key elements in the composition. The right hand appears at the apex of a roughly triangular shape only interrupted by the naked body, its curved base formed by the left arm and sleeve. The spread legs form another triangle, the point of which is represented by the pubes, which are executed in three dimensions in contrast to the flat surface of the blouse. It was not only for formal reasons that Schiele made this part of the body the center of his composition. (RL)

Pencil, gouache on paper
48 × 31.2 cm
Leopold Museum, Vienna, Inv. 1433
K D.1394

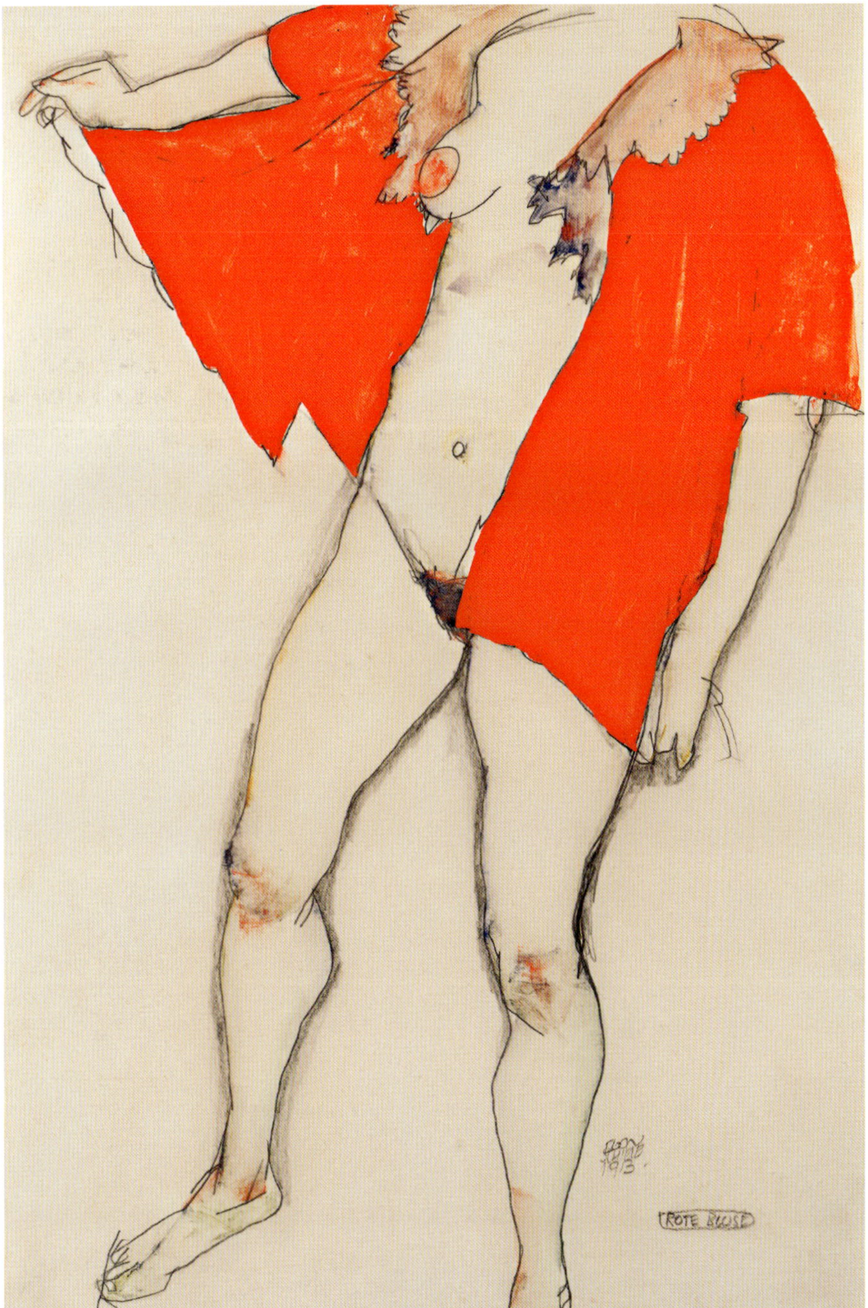
1913
ROTE BLUSE

1913

OLD GABLE

Schiele first explored this old structure with its crumbling masonry and derelict roof in an earlier pencil drawing from 1913 (K D.1474), made during his summer vacation in Carinthia. In that work he included its ground floor as well. In this version it was omitted; a carefully executed painting of this subject only suggests the ground floor with narrow strips of olive and orange across the bottom.

The warm-colored masonry is surrounded by blackish tones, here and there mixed with blue. At the bottom of its opening there are touches of brick-red so intense that one might almost take them to be the flames of an open fire. The soaring roof makes one think of a chapel.

Schiele produced a number of studies of buildings in pencil and gouache on paper, but this is surely the most impressive of them. Otto Benesch reproduced it in color in his 1950 Schiele portfolio. It even surpasses the very beautiful study *Old Houses in Krumau* (K D.1691). Both works once belonged to Otto Benesch. (RL)

Pencil, gouache on paper
32 × 48.6 cm
Leopold Museum, Vienna, Inv. 1413
K D.1473

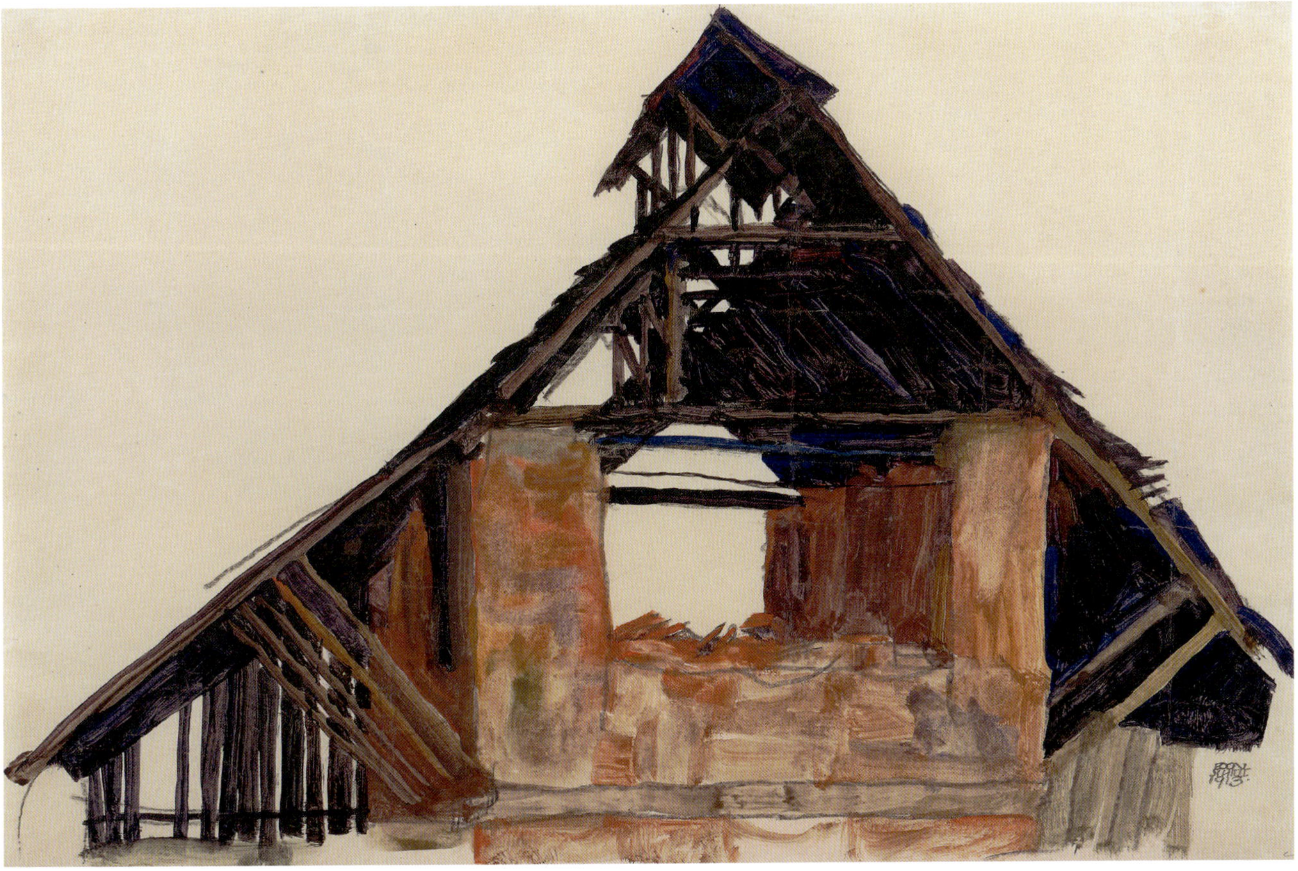

GIRL (FEMALE NUDE WITH YELLOW CLOTH)

The basic symmetry created by the upper body and the legs extending out from it at roughly right angles is enlivened by the tilt of the head to the side and especially by the differently proportioned thighs, which form a common axis sloping down toward the right. The sharp downward movement of the left leg below the knee also introduces a certain imbalance. Since the outline of the left thigh as it was first drawn from life failed to provide the important axis just mentioned, Schiele altered it. He also changed the position of the head, but – as in all such cases of which I am aware – made no attempt to erase the original lines.

The angle of the right knee does not correspond to that of the left one, which has been deformed into a point, as it serves as a counterbalance to the straight outside line of the left calf. The projecting angles become important elements in the two-dimensional design, but at the same time they reflect the figure's extension in space. This drawing is an early and very typical example of how Schiele chose to restructure the body so as to produce geometric forms, much as the French Cubists were doing, though in a very different manner. Unlike them, he preserved its natural appearance.

The skin tone is essentially that of the paper itself, to which hints of brick-red and gray-black have been added. Despite these delicate touches of painting, it is the graphic element that dominates the work. The more heavily painted areas of the cloth and hair are firmly anchored in the overall structure. (RL)

Pencil, gouache on paper
31.2 × 47.8 cm
Leopold Museum, Vienna, Inv. 2381
K D.1278

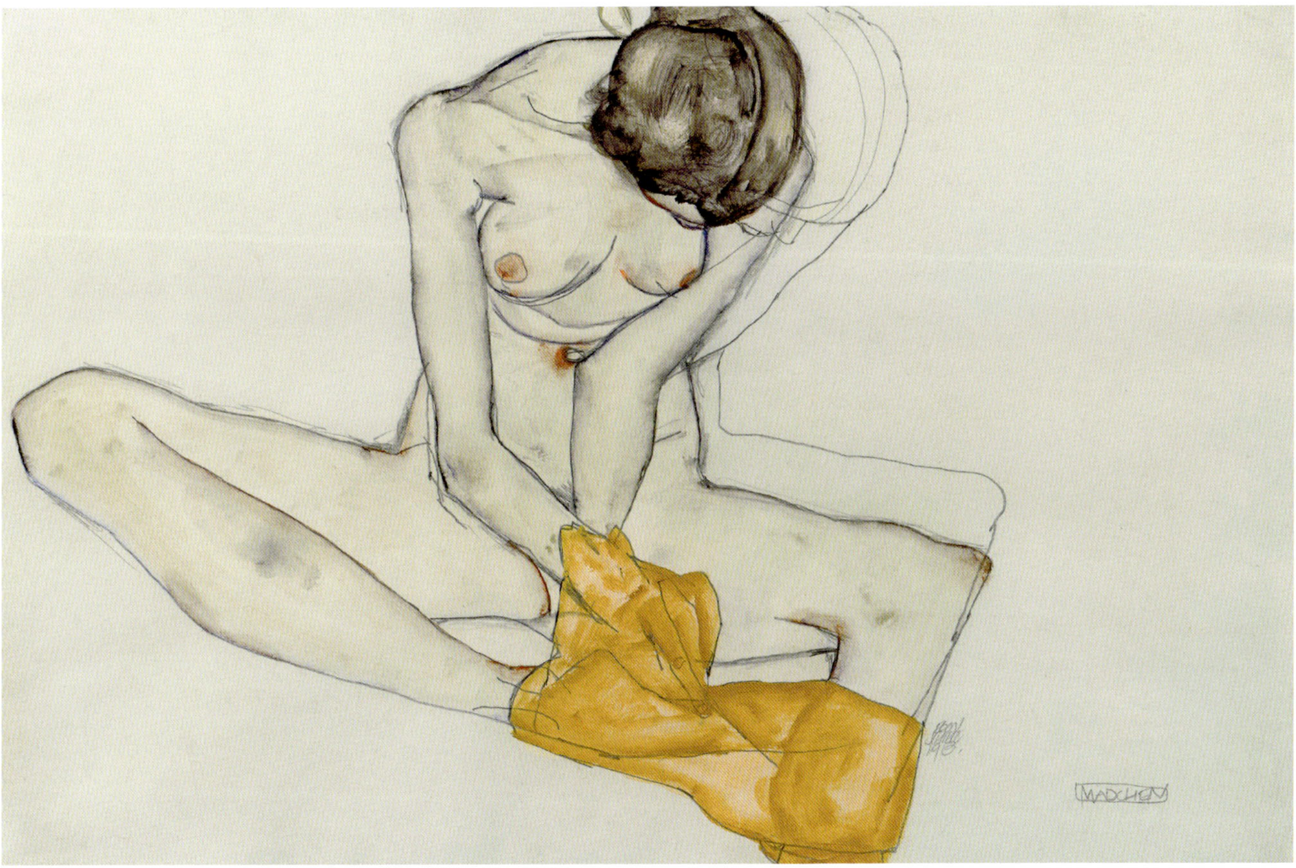
MADCHEN

1913

BEFORE THE MIRROR

Schiele rarely painted such a luminous green as the one used for this woman's shirt. It contrasts sharply with the body, with its accents of intense color, and serves to accentuate its nakedness. The ugliness of the woman's face, her sex, and her deformed thigh and knee are balanced by the beautiful colors and expressive lines of the highly satisfying composition. This is a fine example of Schiele's habit of depicting the ugliness of a body unflinchingly, even exaggerating it.
The tilt to the right of the upper body, the head and the hands introduces a distinct imbalance to the arrangement, but it is just checked by the opposing tilt of the pelvis. This "just" was Schiele's intent, and it is what makes the work so lively and impressive. (RL)

Pencil, gouache on paper
48.3 × 31.1 cm
Leopold Museum, Vienna, Inv. 1435
K D.1362

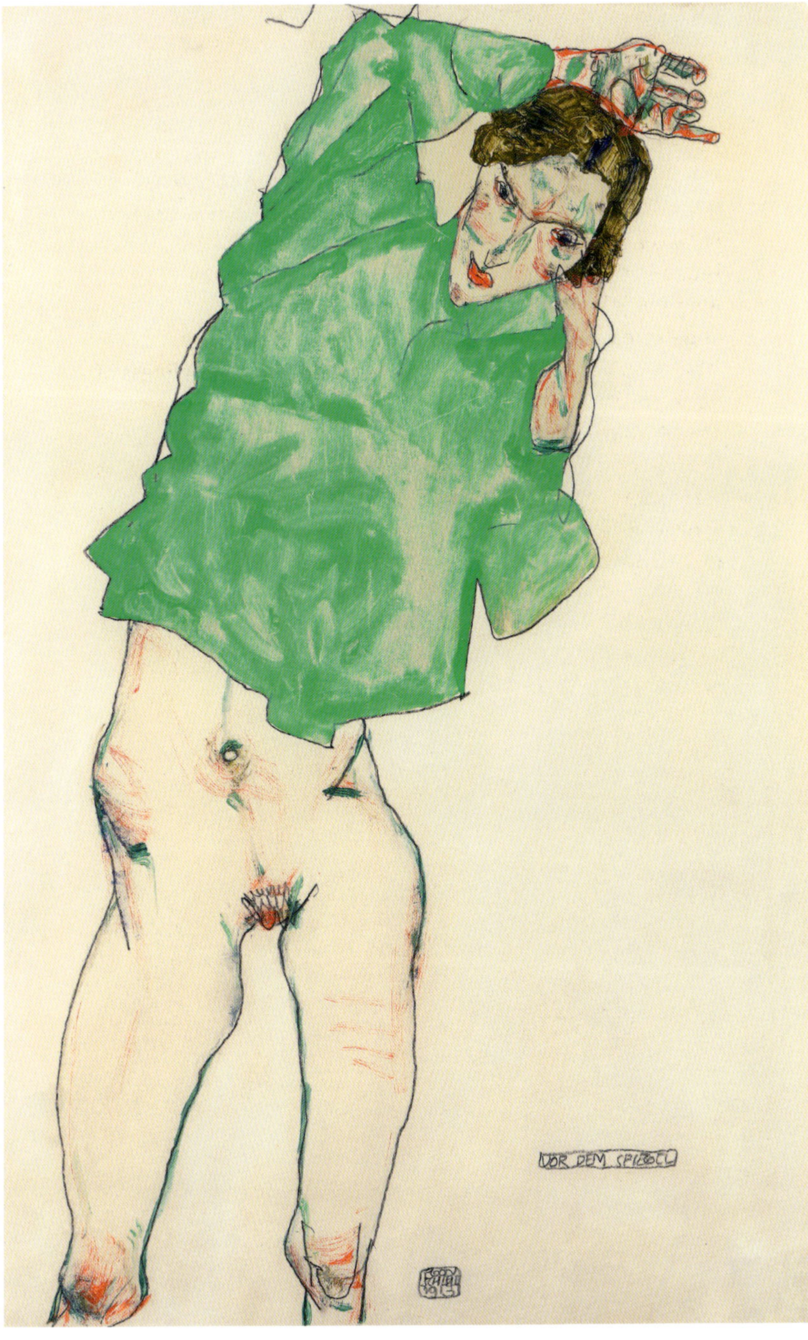
VOR DEM SPIEGEL

1913

THE DANCER

The arms of this strange, dancing figure are caught in hectic, angular, rhythmic movement. The rest of the composition underscores his complete abandon. The firm pencil lines appear to have been laid down in a trance, sharp contours alternating with descriptive scribbling. There are many zigzags and lines crossing each other. The painting is equally expressive: even less concerned with reality, it reflects both the dancer's excitement and that of the painter. Most of the work is done in bright colors. Here there are only touches of the piercing blue-green that is so prominent in most drawings from this period. Red, ocher, blue, and brown predominate, applied in either simple dots or drawn-out strokes of the brush. The leftward extension of the right forearm and that of the head behind the hunched left shoulder do not completely counter the essential instability of the tilted figure. This is, of course, deliberate, and it helps to express the excitement of this man utterly absorbed in his dancing. (RL)

Pencil, gouache on paper
48 × 32.2 cm
Leopold Museum, Vienna, Inv. 1434
K D.1414

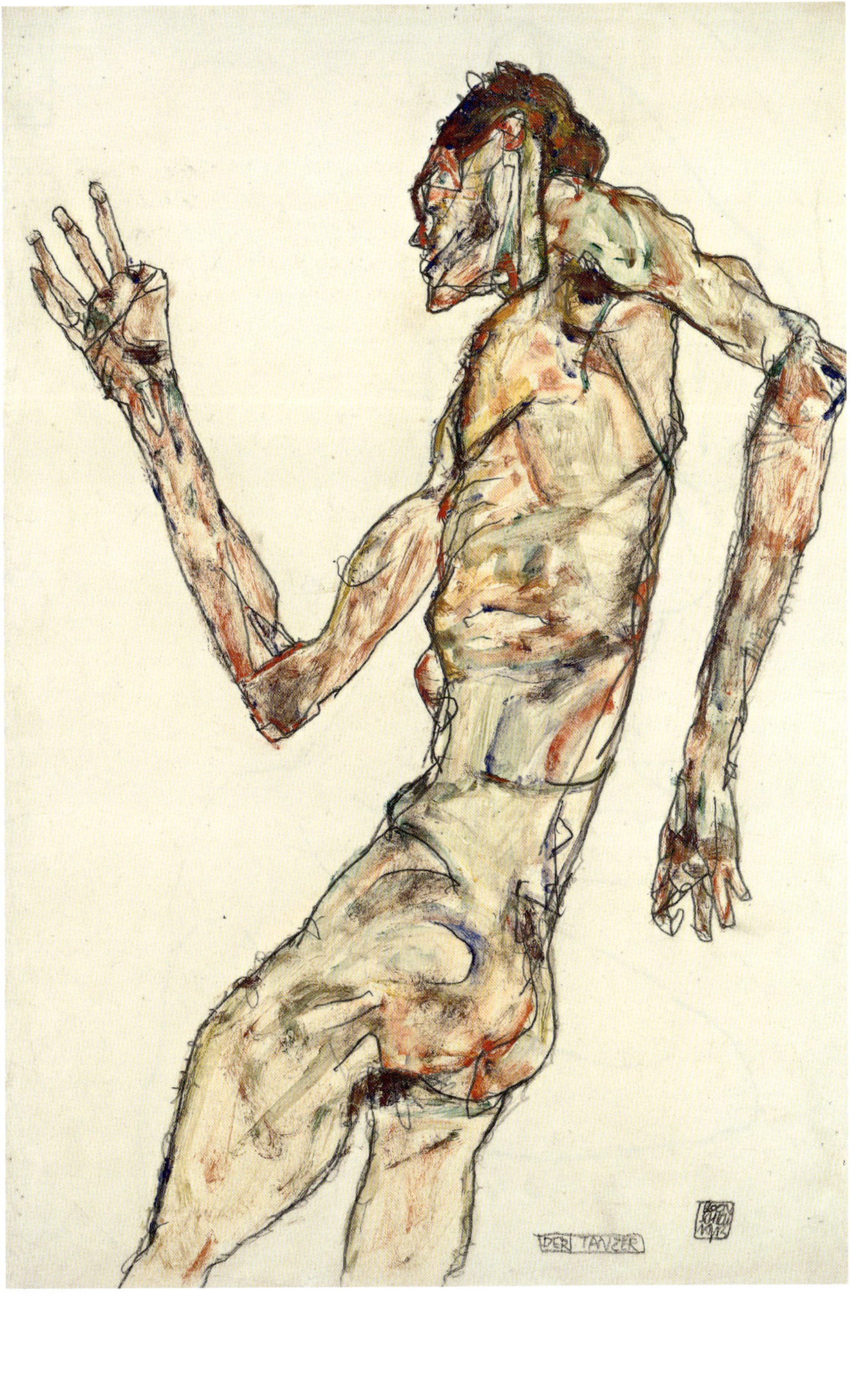
DER TANZER

1913

DEVOTION

This rendering depicts two striding figures wearing shirts that look like short, habit-like cloaks. The fingers peering out from underneath the left sleeves of both figures appear helpless, the one raised, overly slim arm with the tensed up fingers seems to hold no strength. Equally emaciated are the faces and the collarbone region of the right figure which looks as if there was no flesh but only bone underneath the skin. (Formally, this area is juxtaposed with that of the chin.) These individual traits match the instability conveyed by the inclined posture and the even more slanted thighs offering no real support to the depicted. While this precariousness is thus made formally visible, it is at the same time rendered more stable by the strict togetherness of the two protagonists. Their outlines approach each other most closely slightly underneath the center. While they diverge towards the top and the bottom, their heads are once again inclined towards one another. The parts that have been left blank between the figures provide interesting negative forms related to the silhouettes of the figures. A comparison of this rendering with the *Double Portrait of Heinrich and Otto Benesch* (L 234; K P.250) reveals intriguing similarities and differences between the two works. Such a comparison also clearly illustrates how much progress Schiele had made in his new style throughout the year 1913; how much stronger the creative logic behind the equally stringent composition of the work *Devotion* had become. The compositional complexity of this work applies to the whole as much as it does to individual details – the right figure, which can be likened to a tensed bow, precisely mirrors the figure to the left with its head, the long outline of the shirt and the thighs. The bent hand of the figure on the left corresponds equally precisely to the omitted part of the clothing, while also relating to the chin in its upper outline. Distinctly though all the individual parts were composed in relation to one another, the composition on the whole appears informal and natural, with the inspired coloring further contributing to the vivacity of the overall structure. The painterly animation of the hands and the vehement application of color on the naked skin correspond to the lines drawn in an agitated manner. (RL)

Pencil, gouache on paper
48.3 × 32 cm
Leopold Museum, Vienna, Inv. 2311
K D.1418

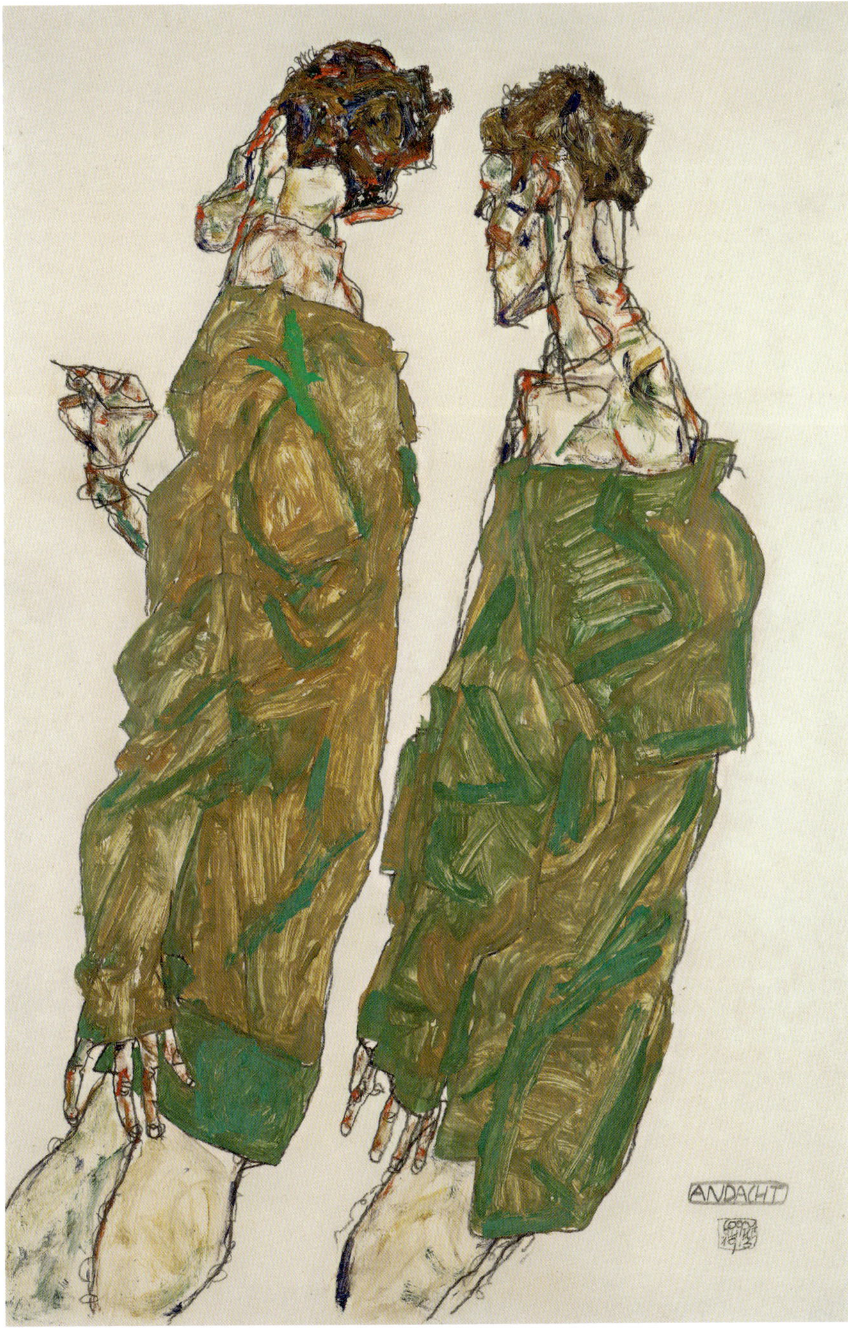
ANDACHT

1913

PREACHER (NUDE SELF-PORTRAIT WITH BLUE-GREEN SHIRT)

Schiele's presentation of himself in this drawing is rather strange, even scurrilous. His head bends forward from the body at nearly a right angle parallel to the extended right forearm. (For the sake of the formal relationships in the composition, the forearm was deliberately drawn much lower than anatomical reality would allow.) He gazes downward fixedly, apparently at his genitals, which are emphasized by a touch of red. Do the gaze and the extended hand have something to do with the word "preacher", which was subsequently inscribed on the drawing? Erich Lederer recalls that Schiele generally gave very little thought to the inscriptions that commonly appear on his drawings from 1913, inventing them only after the works had been completed. Some of them are perfectly appropriate, but others seem somewhat arbitrary.

The excessive weight of the head and arm stretching toward the left is partially balanced by the forward angle of the right thigh, the similar angle of the left forearm, and the billowing of the shirt to the back. To relate the extended head and arm to each other, Schiele bent the right hand upward slightly so that its axis converges with that of the head. This also serves to close off the composition to the left. The light skin color with accents in red is contrasted to the darker blue-green of the shirt.

The distinctly geometric tendency of the drawing is apparent in the many lines that appear to be arcs of circles in the body and the neck as well as in the contours and details of the face, especially the odd pair of angles on the cheek – the one on the left intersected by a vertical line – and the interesting rendering of the eye area. (RL)

Pencil, gouache on paper
47.1 × 31.3 cm
Leopold Museum, Vienna, Inv. 2365
K D.1441

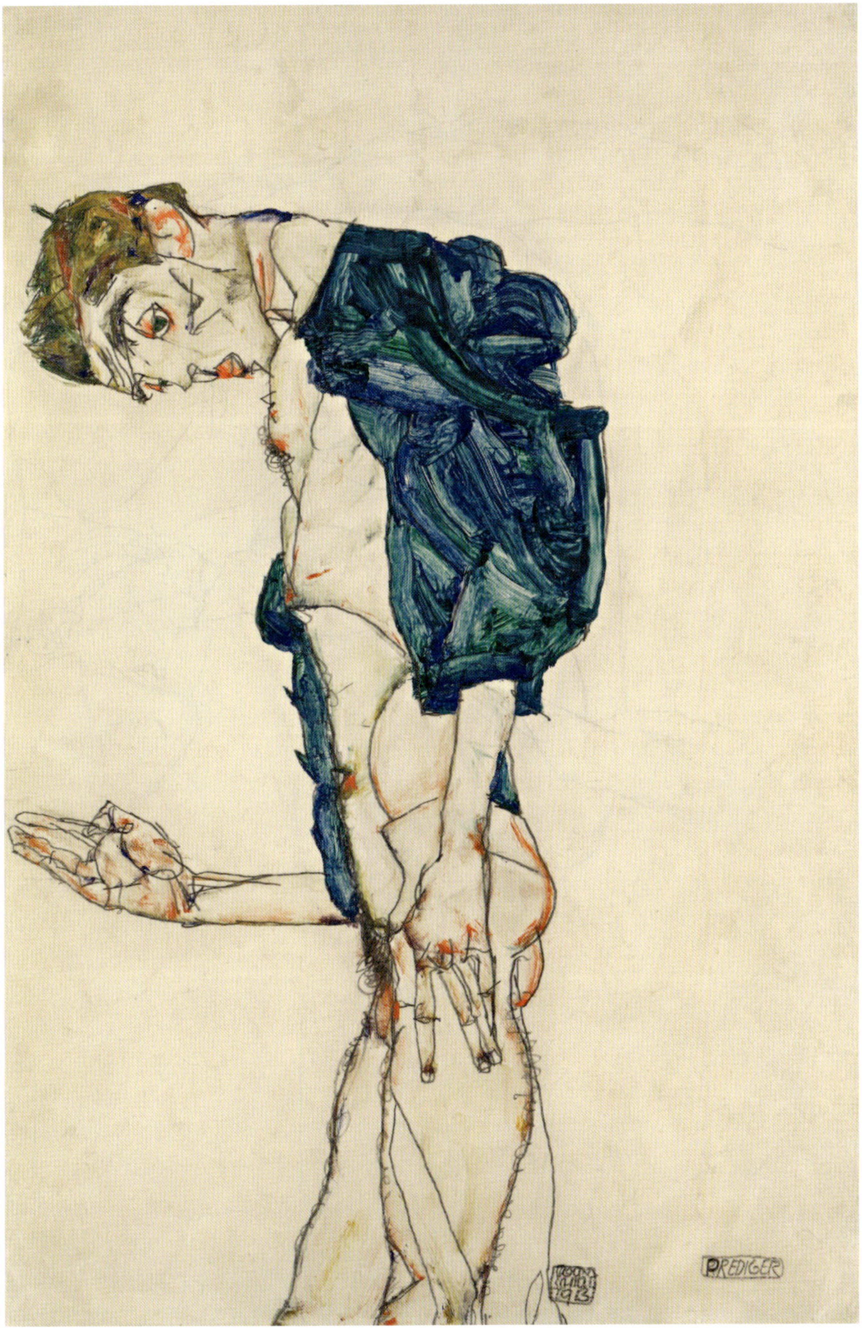
PREDIGER

1914

KRUMAU ON THE VLTAVA (THE SMALL TOWN IV)

When Schiele sketched these Krumau houses extending from the Vltava to the City Hall square, he was looking down on them from the top of a tower. He then distributed their roofs and facades, separated by narrow alleyways, across the surface of his painting. Although the composition of the work reflects a great concern for two-dimensional design, the houses retain their spatial integrity. The picture is therefore a very typical and pleasing example of the new manner of composition apparent in Schiele's work beginning in 1913.

The facades of the row of houses in the foreground are actually perfectly aligned, but Schiele has set each one slightly behind the next until they reach the street. The building on the right is pulled forward and painted a yellowish tone to match the color of the one on the far left. The essential boundaries of the composition are set by these two houses and the back wall of the City Hall facade at the top, which is painted a similar yellowish color. These three buildings mark the angles of an isosceles triangle. Across the very top, to close off the composition, Schiele added a strip of green that has nothing to do with the actual scene. At the bottom there are broader stripes extending across the whole canvas. The deep black one along the bottom edge represents the Vltava. Above this solid base of buildings, the houses with their white, orange, violet, gray, and red facades below dark roofs take on a life of their own. Two narrow alleys slice through them. The facades of the smaller cluster on the right side of the street are highly varied and presented with extreme foreshortening. These structures are more brightly colored; with the exception of the one at the top end, even their roofs are lighter in tone. By contrast, the quarter bounded by the two vertical streets, with its dark roofs and highly varied facades, seems more block-like and solid.

Many of the facades have only two windows that look like eyes. The ones in the horizontal violet strip of wall appear to be leering at us from under the large hat of the roof. Just above that roof is the back wall of the City Hall building. Schiele structured its varied gables with great sensitivity. The high walls and warped roofs, the small windows, and the lively, freely invented colors convey the image of a sleepy town forgotten by history. This painting is perhaps the only cityscape by Schiele in which there is no trace of pessimism or sense of the tragedy of old age. All we sense is a gentle melancholy. (RL)

Oil, black chalk on canvas
99.5 × 120.5 cm
Leopold Museum, Vienna, Inv. 655
L 244; K P.278

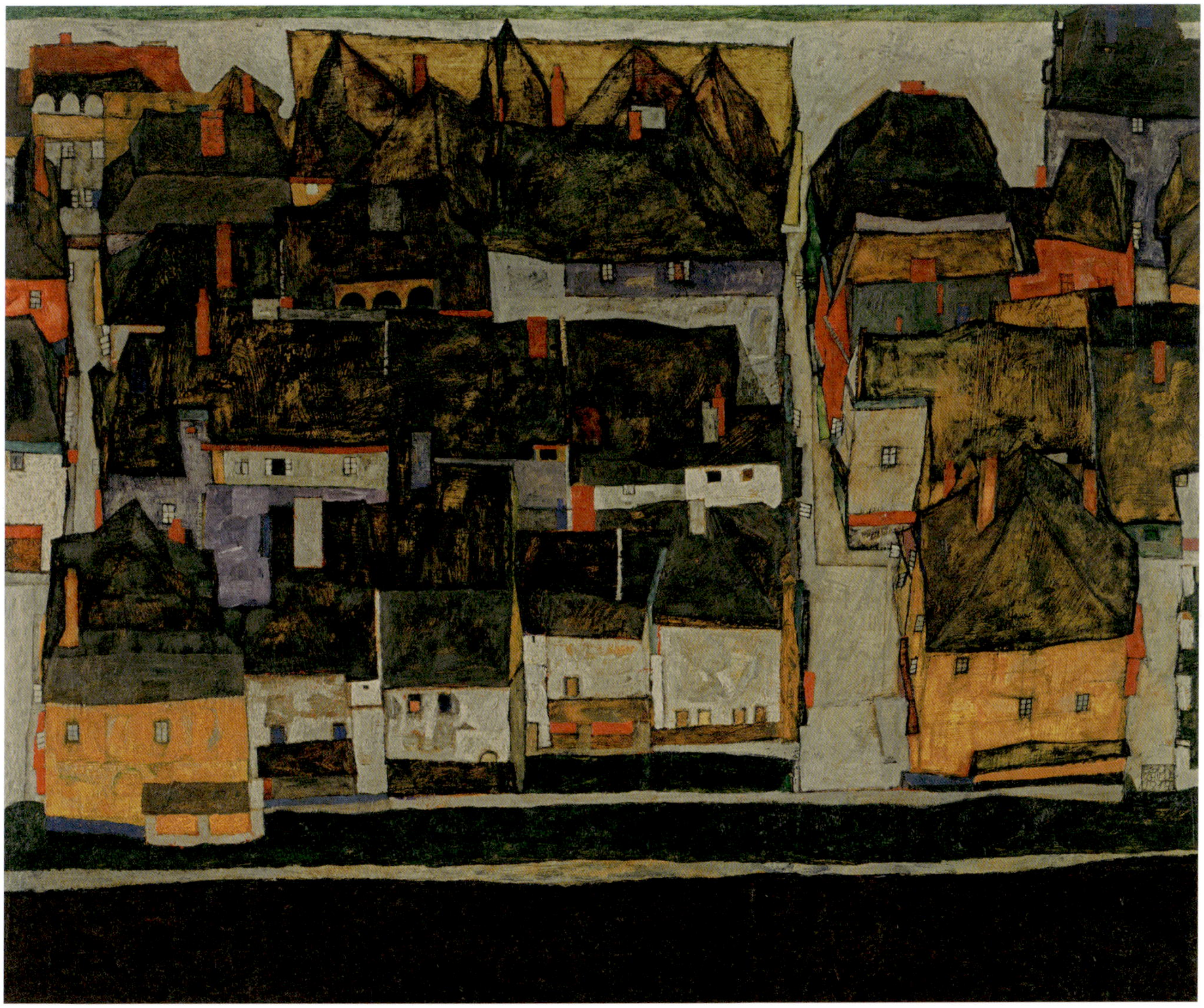

1914

HOUSES BY THE SEA (ROW OF HOUSES)

Schiele gave this painting three different titles: "The Houses by the Sea", "Houses by the Sea" and "Row of Houses". The painting boasts an only seemingly simple composition made up of several horizontal zones, the most important one formally and in terms of content crossing fairly precisely through the center of the depiction. The group of houses appears to be standing on an elongated strip which delimits it sideward in a block-like manner. This area stands out from the others particularly on account of its brightness but also because of its stronger spatial effect. This effect is achieved in two ways: firstly by means of an irregular, alienating perspective – several roofs and gables are viewed from a much steeper angle than the house walls turned towards the beholder – and secondly with the help of the dark strip of terrain behind it which appears to be pushing the block of houses forwards, as it were.

Despite the planar composition, distance and proximity are conveyed without the aid of foreshortening, initially through the varying density of the strips of terrain in front of and behind the houses. The impression of far distance, meanwhile, is achieved through the shading of the horizon line and the darker sky above it. The merging of sea and island by means of a single strong line was done not merely for formal reasons. In conjunction with the rather uniform treatment, this area is stripped of its actual reference, creating a sense of anxious uncertainty. The sea and islands have become a wall, while the line has become a border. Behind it appears to be the end of the world, or, worse still, nothingness.

The row of houses, which has been removed from its different surroundings and thus rendered significant, has been placed into the same borderline situation. It represents a last bastion of human population in a desolate terrain. Only the foreground is relieved by small poles in a subdued red as well as by patches in a harsher red hue. The five houses are a vivid metaphor for the exposedness of human existence. In order to express this portentous threat Schiele anthropomorphized the house walls, investing each with physiognomic details: hatches are turned into eyes, rows of windows become mouths. The sense of tranquility conveyed by the overall composition made up of horizontal zones is thus interrupted by five menacing and at the same time threatened "faces".

These ensouled forms are supported by similarly soulful colors and painting. The uniformity of the drawing of the background depicting sea and air is underscored by the color – an only slightly varying bluish gray. The predominantly dark coloring of the terrain, by contrast, is made up of different green tones and particularly of a garish red, which contributes to the nervous atmosphere, with the ghostly pale house walls flaring up against this somber backdrop. Sensitive dents and scratches on the facades increase the sense of restlessness conveyed by these "faces". Different shades of reddish brown, orange-ocher and an odd yellow further contribute to the unreality of this setting. (RL)

Oil on canvas
99.5 × 119.7 cm
Leopold Museum, Vienna, Inv. 452
L 248; K P.281

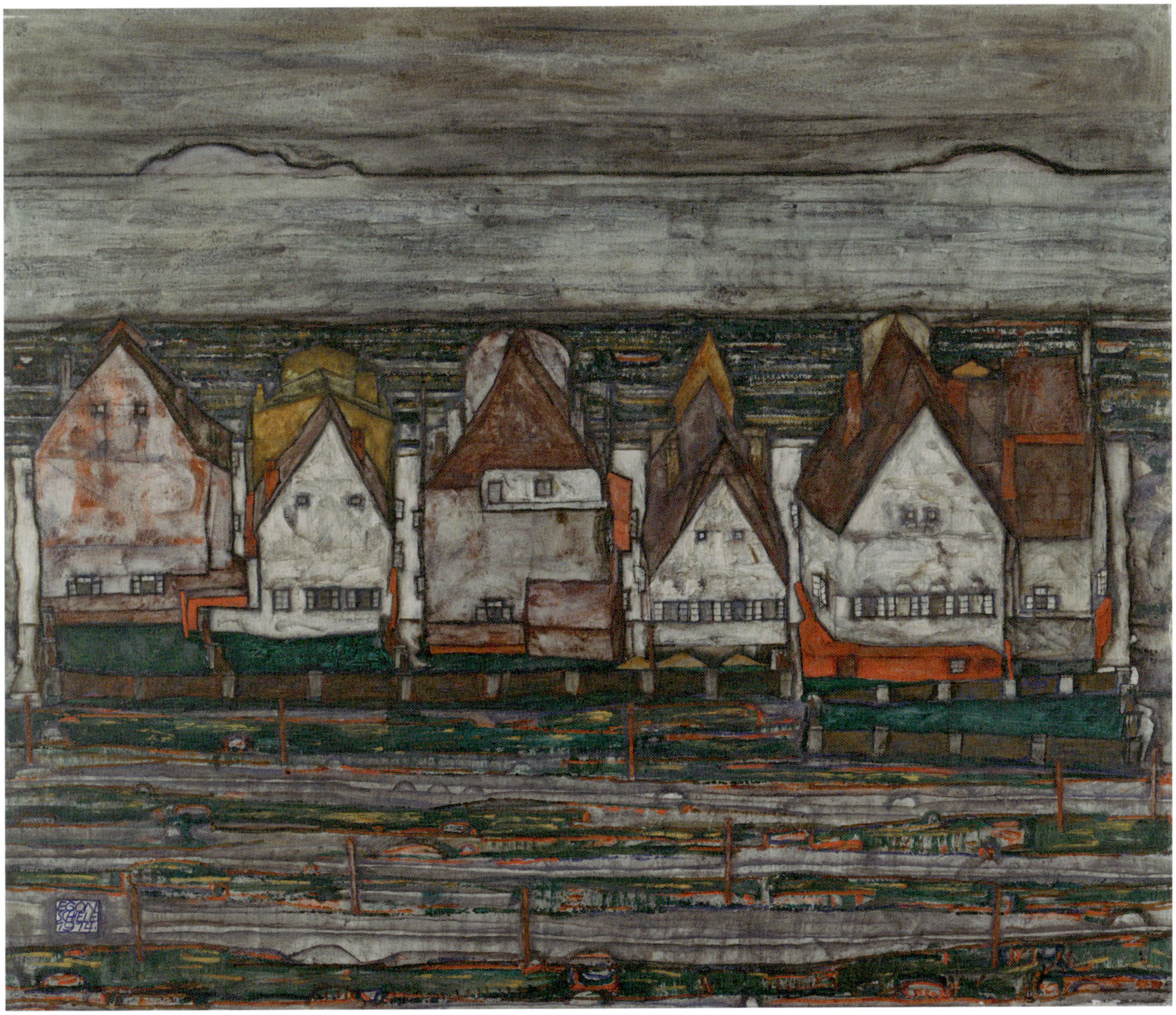
EGON
SCHIELE
1914

1914

STILL LIFE WITH BOOKS (SCHIELE'S DESK)

This work depicts Schiele's desk in his studio on Hietzinger Hauptstraße from a steep aerial view. This way, the objects on the desk, which Schiele transformed into a towering structure, appear as if they had been fanned out. The depiction is dominated by the vertical. The curtain, the books, notebooks and sheets of paper, the candle holder and the rocker blotter all follow a longitudinal axis that deviates only marginally from the perpendicular. They appear more strongly inclined towards the horizontal line, including the uppermost rustic miniature wooden horse, which has been placed slightly sideways. This results in a marked pull towards the right, compensated on the one hand by the writing utensils and on the other by numerous stripes of curtain initially running from the bottom towards the top left. The red equestrian figurine and the folder at the lower end of the canvas related to it in terms of color also have a counterbalancing effect. At the same time, the positioning of these two red highlights serves to make the notebooks and books in the depiction appear more cohesive.

Schiele once again proved his mastery not only in the overall composition but also in the finer details: how voluminous does the curtain appear, for instance, especially as Schiele deliberately refrained from any kind of shading and achieved the spatial effect only through the brilliant drawing of the stripes. The three-dimensional effect of the individual objects on the desk was further elicited by the fact that Schiele applied layers of varying density of a gypsum and chalk mixture onto the painting surface in their places, thus pre-shaping the sheets of paper, folders and rustic toys. That way, he created areas of relief which alternate in a lively manner with the objects painted onto a flat surface. Schiele availed himself of this technique also for other works created around that time.

Fine though the choice of predominantly subdued colors may be, it is doubtlessly the chiaroscuro that is responsible for the exciting overall composition of this painting. Creating this effect, Schiele not only used simple black and white shades. Rather, the dark colors range from jet black to dark gray (enriched by different shades of green and reddish brown), while the light spectrum covers shades of white, yellow, light gray, olive and brown.

The notebooks and folders, the candle holder, the writing paper, the big old book and the faded small volume at the very top – they are all invested with a sense of melancholy which seems to be linked to a formally stringent composition. This combination is a characteristic of Schiele's oeuvre. (RL)

Oil on canvas
117.5 × 78 cm
Leopold Museum, Vienna, Inv. 458
L 253; K P.297

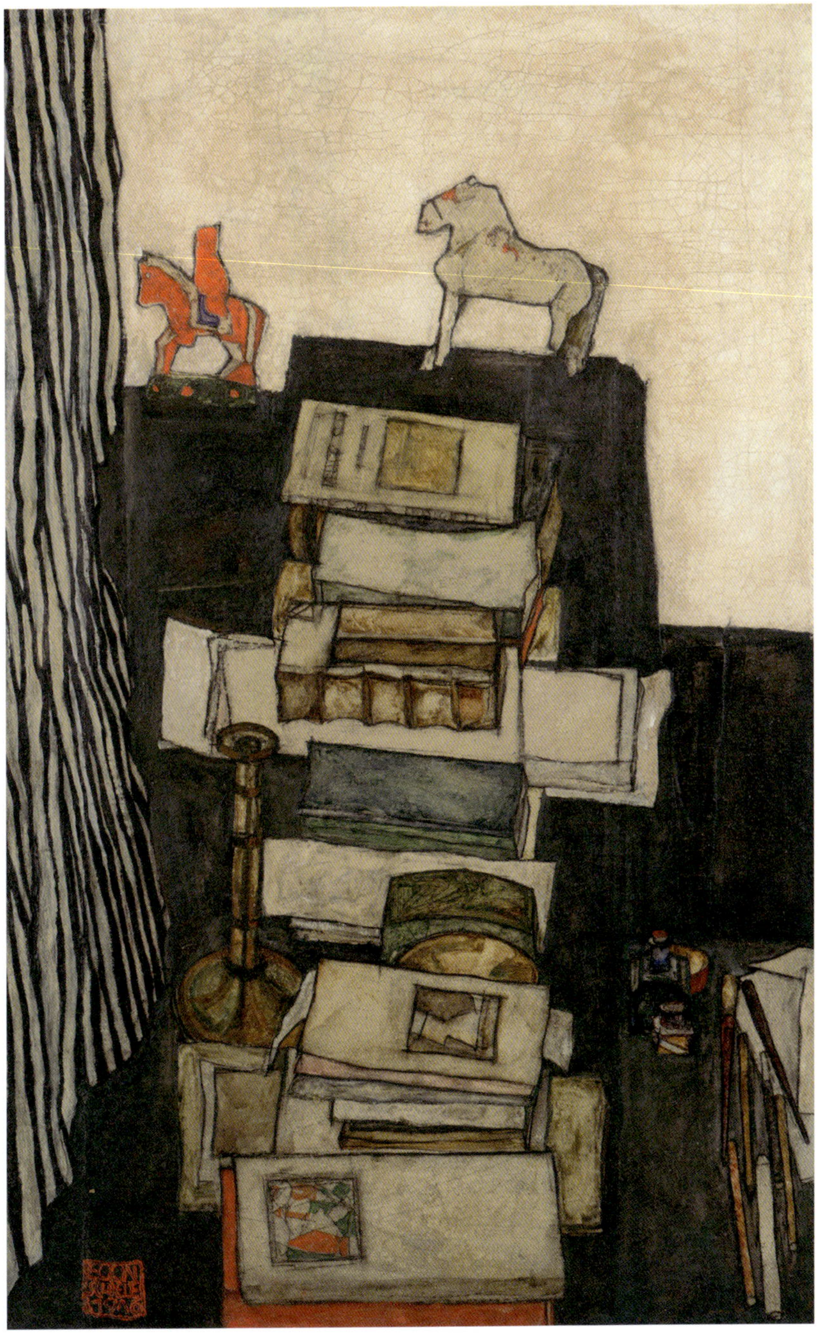

1914

EMBRACING COUPLE

These two figures, pressed together, appear to be dancing. The woman, seen from the back and wearing a hat, stands in front, while the man behind her faces forward. His brow is captured with one continuous line. His jaw, chin, and lips are also perfectly rendered in shorthand by a single line that twice changes direction but is never interrupted. The nose is also only a simple acute angle. These and other details are typical examples of Schiele's concentration in his drawing on the graphic essentials.

Much more important for this drawing is the arrangement of the two figures, its unusually dynamic conctruction. The woman's back and right leg form the main axis, while her neck, head, and left leg bend in the opposite direction. Her body dominates the compostion. The man's figure is only secondary, his limbs serving as harmonious variations on hers. The contour of his left side and thigh provides a fascinating counterpoint to the line of her body just to the left of it. The round outline of his wrist echoes the sharp curve of her raised left shoulder. Incisive lines – like some of the ones here – are occasionally found in Schiele's drawing beginning in the second half of 1912. (RL)

Pencil on paper
45.6 × 28.1 cm
Leopold Museum, Vienna, Inv. 2364
K D.1670

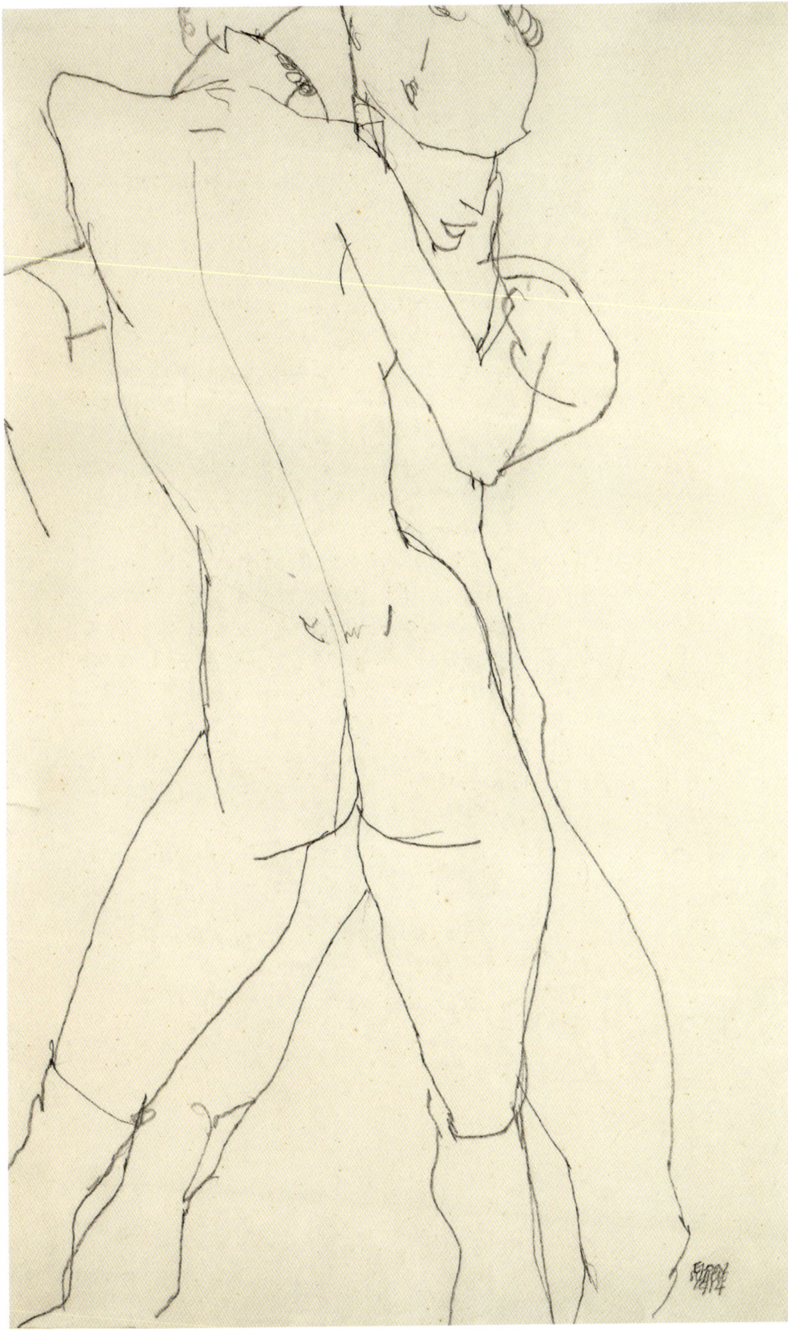

1914

CROUCHING WOMAN WITH GREEN HEADSCARF

Schiele used this same model a number of times in the first half of 1914. Here her upper body, right shoulder, and head are bent forward. Her nakedness is set off and emphasized by the stockinged calves and the lighter and darker fabrics. Her spread legs and the curving cloth over her head call to mind a yawning bivalve exposing its light-colored insides. Her nipples, painted like the navel in a bright orange, protrude between her arms. There is something animal-like in her gaze. A bit of pubic hair is visible at the point where her right arm crosses her left thigh. Schiele masterfully exploited the overlapping and perspective foreshortening that resulted from his looking down at the figure from above. His fondness for geometric shapes is particularly apparent in the distinctly triangular face and in the many lines that could be parts of circles or ellipses. The curly lines accompanying many of the contours help to define the position in space of the various parts of the body. The kerchief, painted in contrast to the face and hair as an essentially flat form, has a similar function. (RL)

Pencil, gouache on paper
47 × 31 cm
Leopold Museum, Vienna, Inv. 1431
K D.1500

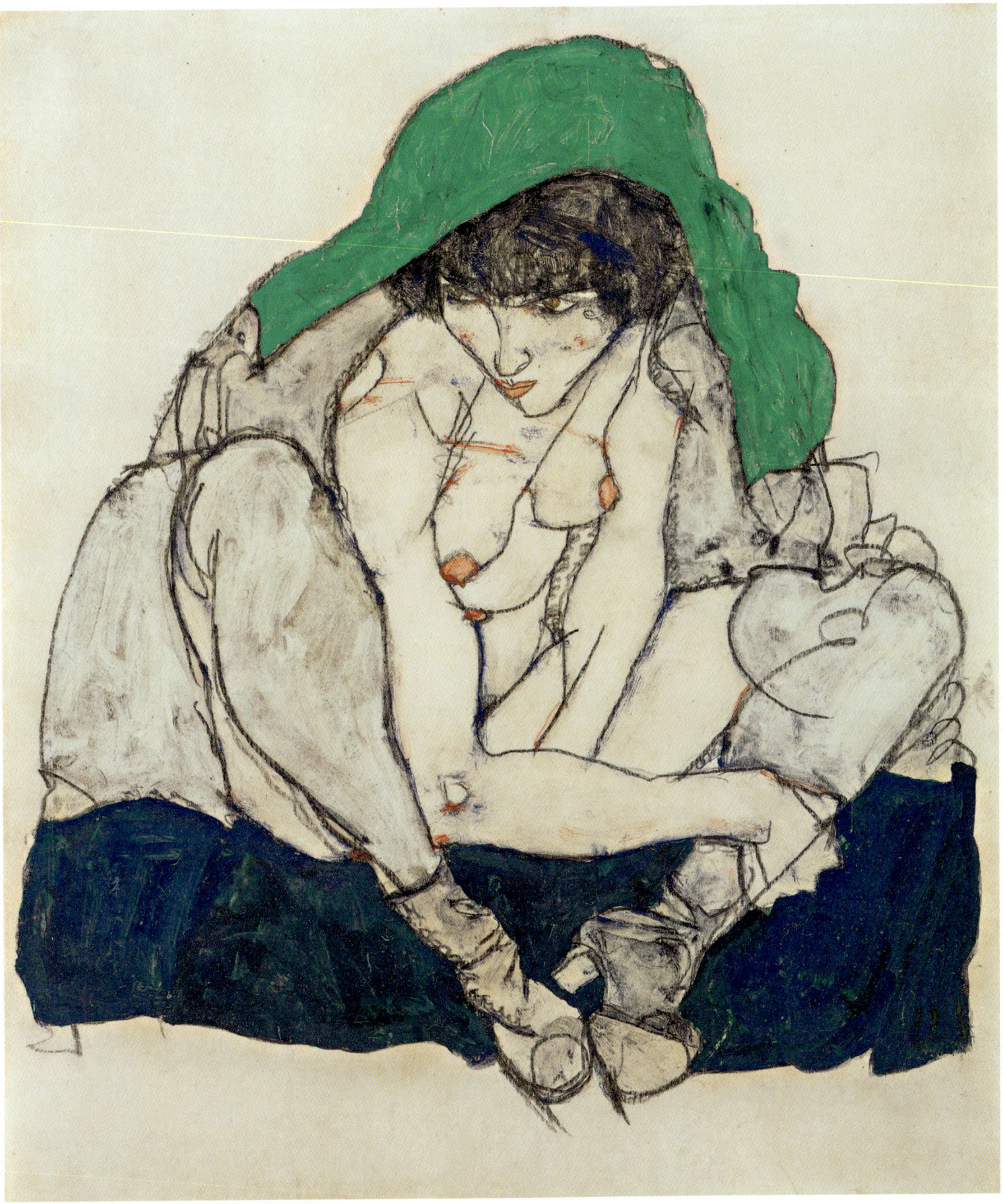

1914

STANDING NUDE GIRL WITH ORANGE STOCKINGS

The wiry hardness of these lines is made even more pronounced by the coloring. The drawing reveals a definite similarity in style to that of the *Blind Mother* (see p. 197). Note, for example, how the neck area is rendered as a triangle.

The same interest in geometric forms is also apparent in the construction of the body. It is seen essentially from the front, the legs far apart. Its symmetry is slightly relieved by the twist of the head to the side and a slight turning of the upper body in the opposite direction. To accentuate this change of direction, Schiele emphasized the collarbones, which are clearly visible beneath the skin, with added color. Imaginary lines drawn through the hands and the breasts would roughly parallel their slight deviation from the horizontal. The breasts have been treated as a major element in the composition. The nipples, lips, and stockings are painted in the same bright orange, which adds stability to the whole. The painting of the rest of the skin, by contrast, is extremely delicate. (RL)

Black chalk, gouache on paper
48.5 × 32.1 cm
Leopold Museum, Vienna, Inv. 1429
K D.1488

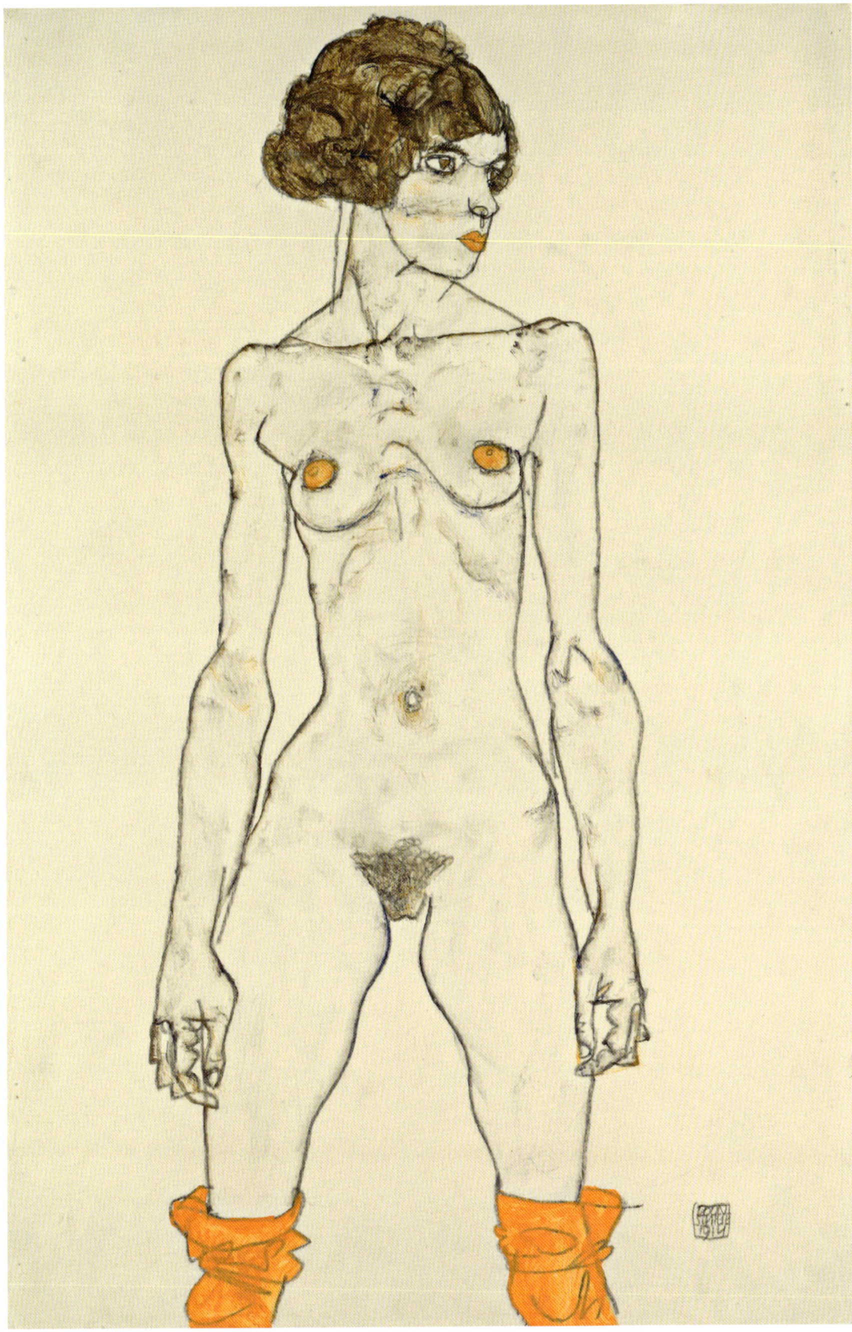

1914

SQUATTING WOMAN. STUDY FOR *BLIND MOTHER*

This interesting drawing is related both to the *Blind Mother* (see p. 197) and to the engraving *Squatting Female (Troubles)* (K G.7b), produced some months later. Schiele was inspired in this motif by Auguste Rodin's bronze *Femme accroupie*, which depicts a woman crouched in an almost identical pose with her right hand resting on her left ankle.

With the outlines of the body, arms, and legs, Schiele recorded the essentials of the pose and the formal correspondences between the various parts of the figure. The only areas worked out more fully are the feet and the head, both of which are rendered in a highly geometric manner. The basic shape of the face is a triangle, with a semicircle above it for the skull. The lines of the eyes, the nose, and the right cheek appear to be sections of ellipses. Hatching and spiral lines, some tighter, some more open, describe the hair. The toes and the spaces between them are also represented by tiny geometric shapes, while the kneecap is indicated by a larger semicircle.

Small rows of lines like the ones perpendicular to some of the longer lines in the feet and either abutting or intersecting them are found in many drawings executed after this time (see especially p. 207). Schiele relied on them to indicate spatial values. (RL)

Pencil on paper
46.2 × 28.5 cm
Leopold Museum, Vienna, Inv. 1432
K D.1511

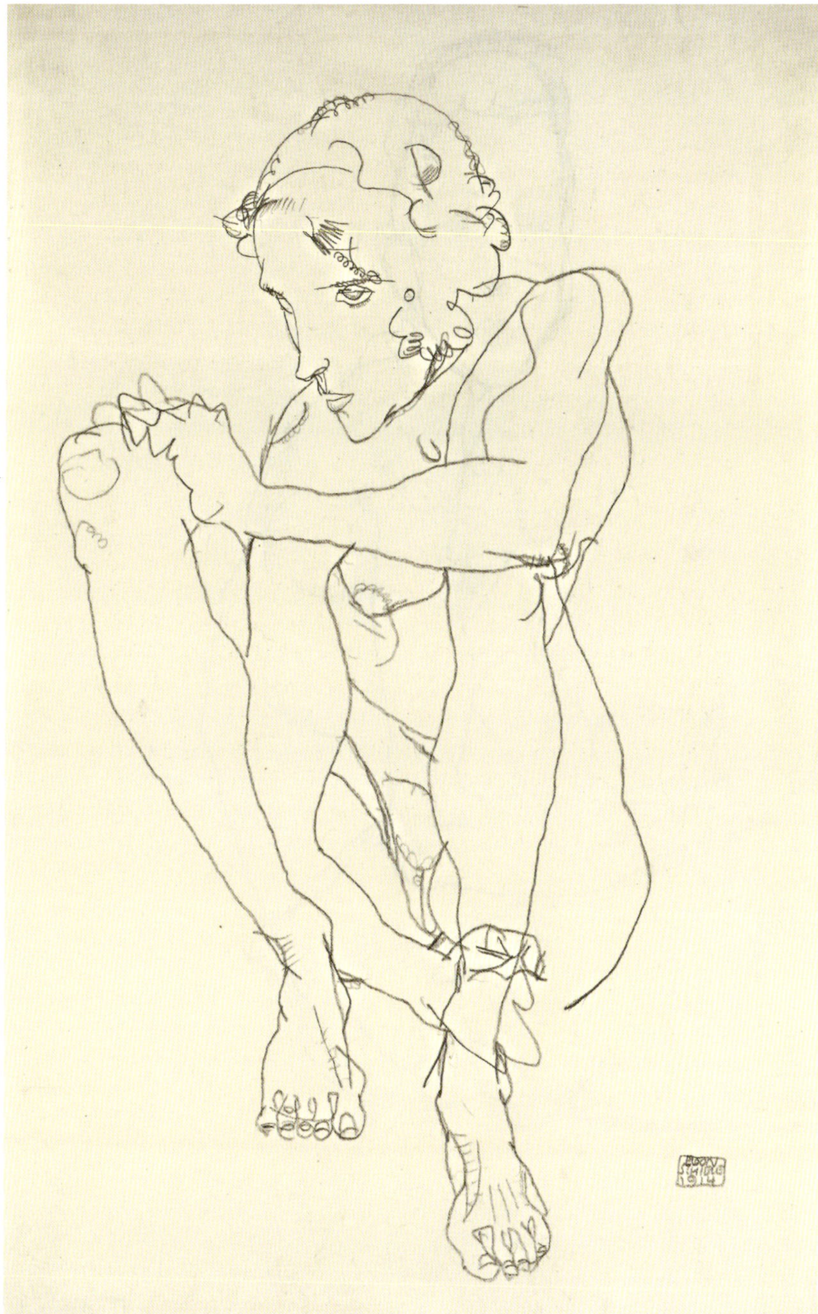

1914

BLIND MOTHER

A woman is nursing two infants, crouched in what appears to be an extremely uncomfortable position, her upper body bent sharply to the right between her widely spread legs. It would be difficult to assume such a pose, and one would think it hardly an ideal one in which to cradle and nurse two babies. Yet the complex, highly angular figure in the center of this composition is an uncommonly compelling, self-contained image, a powerful commentary on the hopeless situation of a mother who is blind. Her pose and the lifeless emptiness of her eyes are altogether pitiful. The figure – most notably the raised left shoulder – was inspired by Auguste Rodin's bronze *Femme accroupie*. Schiele has the shoulder loom up from between the legs like a mountain peak, becoming the highest lighter area in the whole composition. To emphasize this, he deliberately toned down the crown of the woman's head, which is nearly bald, like the heads of the infants; its form is related to those of the bent knees. For compositional reasons, the rendering of this body is very taut. Everything that is soft and feminine in Rodin's nude, such as the delightful swelling at the nape of the neck, has disappeared. Despite the considerable importance of geometry, there is still no sense of excessive formalism, for both the composition as a whole and all of its details are filled with dramatic intensity.

In addition to a slightly brighter green, the red accents in this strip of cloth are the only strong colors in the painting. Everywhere else the dominant tones are more muted, though they produce a definite chiaroscuro. Some of these tones are cooler, some warmer. The mysterious background and the equally warm shades of the cradle, with darker shading applied to a yellowish ground – these surfaces have the reassuring texture of old parchment – contrast dramatically with the ice-cold skin tone of the mother and the heads of the infants. This, too, serves to demonstrate her tragedy. Light and dark areas overlap, as do cold and warm ones, and all are skillfully intermeshed. All of the elements in the picture are clearly identified with regard to both texture and volume, so that the structure of the whole seems more logical and believable than that of any of Schiele's other paintings, whether earlier or later. (RL)

Oil on canvas
99 × 120 cm
Leopold Museum, Vienna, Inv. 483
L 247; K P.272

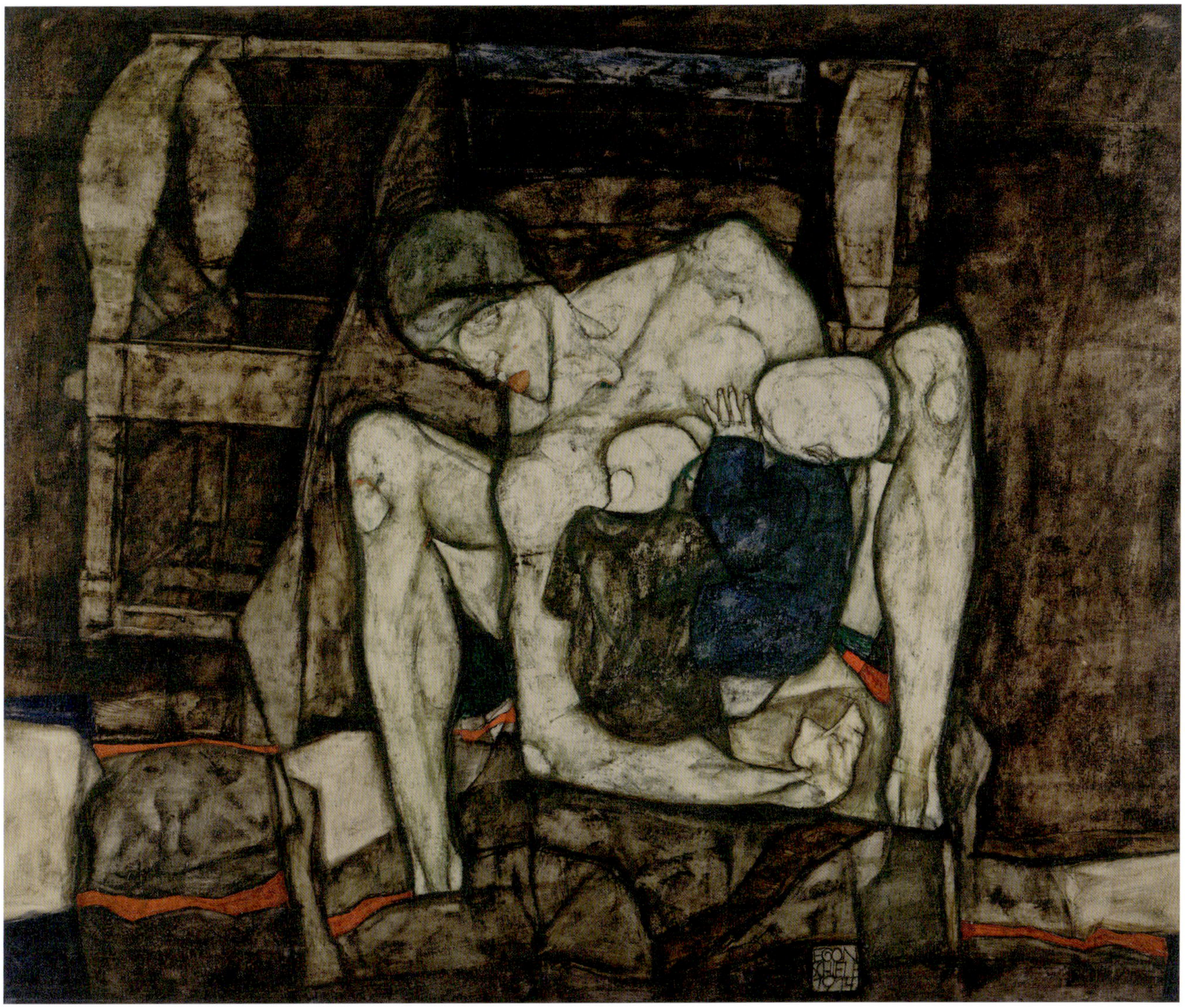

1914

CROUCHING NUDE GIRL

This woman has bent her upper body down between her spread knees, locking her arms over her legs and placing the soles of her feet together. The artist has exploited her pose – the way the body, arms, and legs seem interwoven – to produce an unusually self-contained, three-dimensional figure. One hardly notices various deviations from anatomical accuracy, as they are perfectly justified within the composition. The left arm, for example, is unnaturally elongated and the elbow extends beyond the foot's silhouette, forming a counterpart to the right knee peeking up behind the head. This in itself is invented, for it could scarcely have been seen in a pose such as this. That knee is crucial to the composition, for it continues the contours of the right arm and the left thigh.

The figure's contours are emphasized by the coloring. While they serve to define the thigh, they also roughly divide the shape formed by the thigh and trunk in half. Thus the curve of the lower back echoes the lower line of the thigh. That line, in turn, mirrors the outline of the adjacent calf. The long curve of the back is also juxtaposed to the left elbow, which is farther away. One could compile a whole catalogue of such correspondences. The consistent coloring – unnatural though it is – contributes considerably to the integrity of this figure. (RL)

Black chalk, gouache on paper
31.3 × 48.2 cm
Leopold Museum, Vienna, Inv. 1398
K D.1608

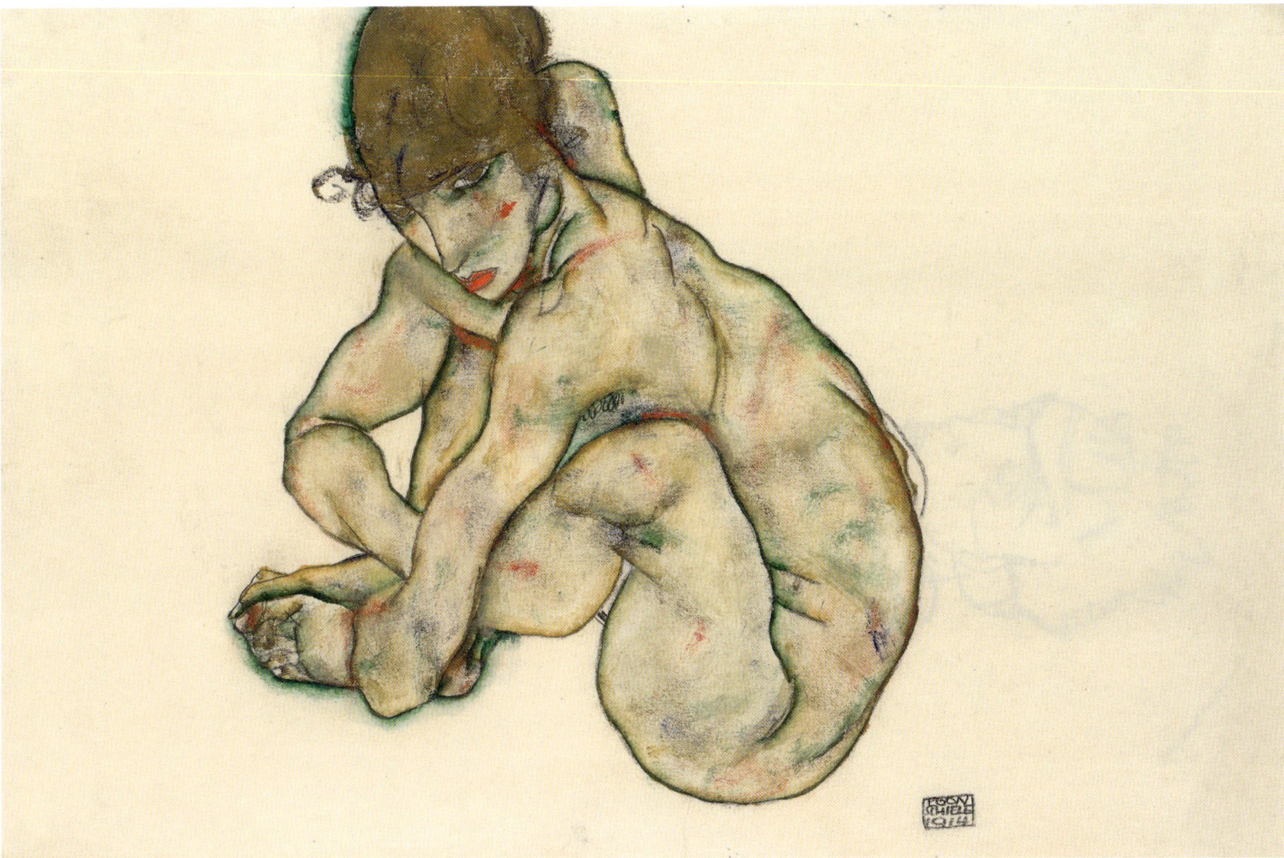
EGON
SCHIELE
1914

1914

TWO PEOPLE LEANING TOWARDS THE RIGHT

Between 1914 and 1915 Schiele created three large-scale paintings: *Mother with Two Children II* (see p. 235), *Death and the Maiden* (L 266; K P.289) and *Levitation (The Blind II)* (see p. 241). The two latter depictions especially feature the so-called "Schiele face", which also appears in the drawing *Two People Leaning Towards the Right*. Schiele, who often used himself as a model, tried out several compositions with different postures for his large-scale paintings. Thus, this drawing could have served as a preliminary study for a canvas. It depicts what appears to be his last embrace of Wally, his faithful partner of many years – Schiele's arm clasps her face, the inclination towards the right likely indicating a departure.

The drawing is perfectly beautiful, Schiele signed it in the right place for the composition and thus left it as a completed work. For his paintings *Death and the Maiden* and *Levitation (The Blind II)* he sought and found another posture for the figures, yet the "Schiele face" in the drawing and the face of the lower figure in *Levitation (The Blind II)* resemble each other very closely. In the painting, the eyes of the lower figure are wide in terror, but they also reflect curiosity about where man goes after death. (EL)

Pencil on paper
31.8 × 47.3 cm
Leopold Museum, Vienna, Inv. 5267
K D.1657a

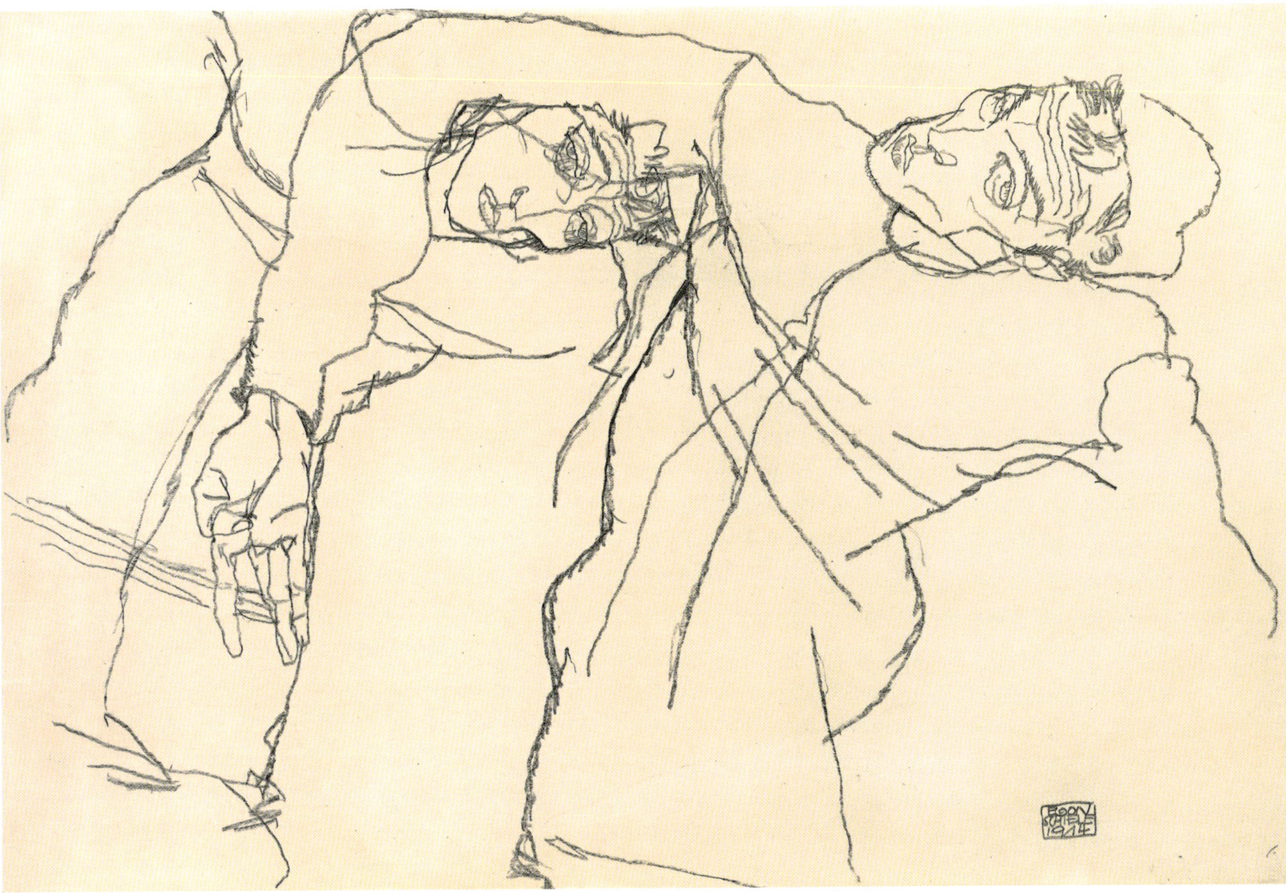
EGON
SCHIELE
1914

1914

RECLINING WOMAN WITH RAISED RIGHT LEG

The model has here assumed a pose she could not have sustained for long. Accordingly, Schiele worked more swiftly than usual, as is perfectly obvious from countless details in this powerful drawing.

In addition to producing a highly successful composition, the artist may have wished to tell us something more. By placing the model's hand on her genitals and having her gaze in that direction, he suggests that she is masturbating. Even in this rapid and highly spirited drawing, the use of geometric shapes, such as the triangle for the woman's face, is unmistakable. (RL)

Pencil on paper
31.6 × 48 cm
Leopold Museum, Vienna, Inv. 1395
K D.1579

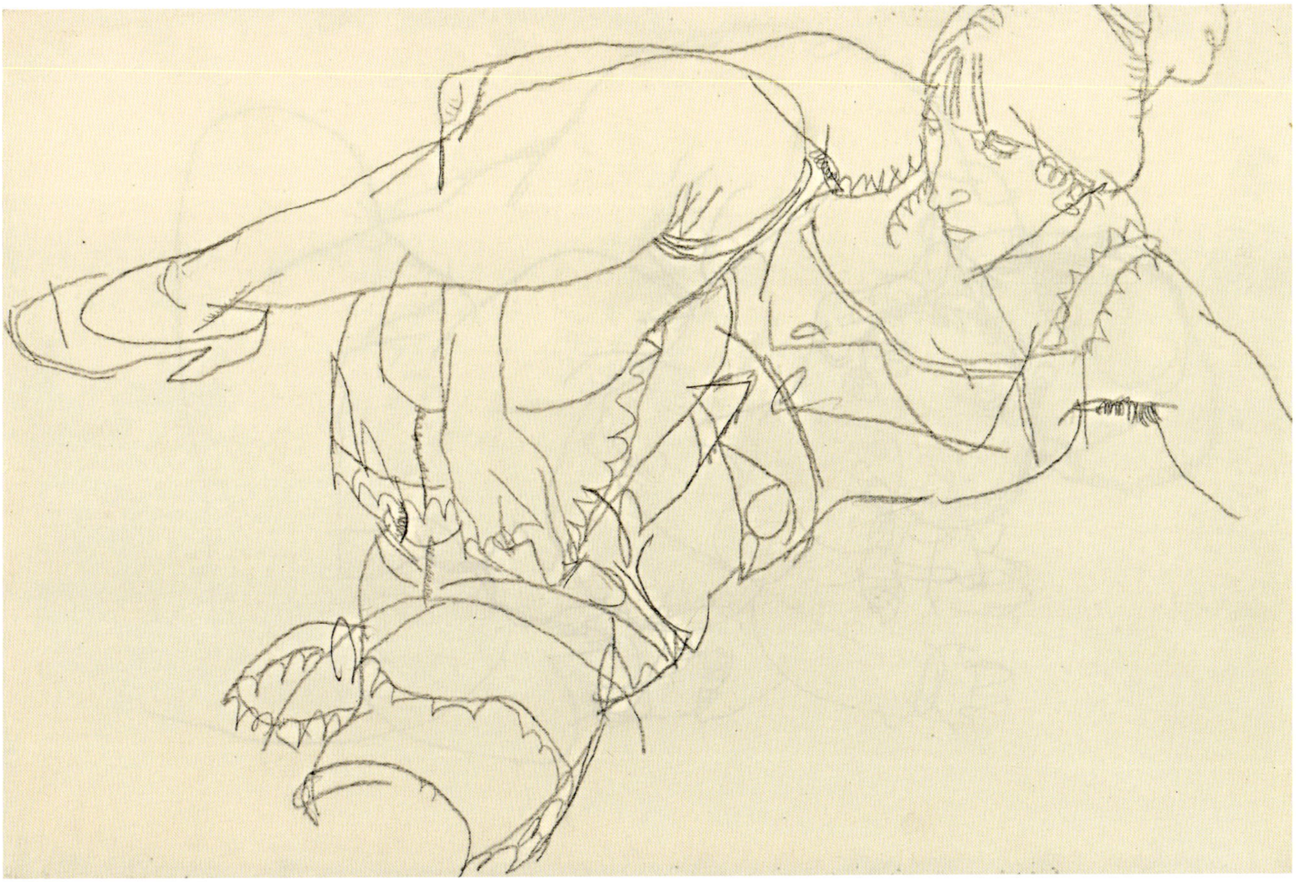

1914

NAKED GIRLS EMBRACING

These two nude girls have their arms around each other. Although Schiele had one of them place her left thigh between the other one's legs, where a bit of pubic hair is visible, and although the "clothes" around the legs at the bottom suggest that the last veils have fallen, there may be no particular subtext to any of this. If there is any message, it is that even when constructing such a purely formal composition Schiele could not refrain from including a suggestion of sexuality.

The faceless figures placed next to each other in a purely ornamental manner make it obvious that they were of no particular interest to the artist. The heads are almost brutally cut off by the edge of the sheet, just like the fabric at the bottom. These two more intensely colored areas serve to close off the composition above and below. What is essential is what falls between them: the almost identical bodies and their intertwined limbs. By this time in Schiele's work the outlines were no longer required to describe the complex structure of a figure by themselves. Internal drawing and painting have become more important. Schiele chose to suggest the flesh tones with an unnatural dark brown, in some places shading it with a bit of black. This helps to unify the composition. To describe the internal structures, he applied the same color with a dry brush. Color contrast is provided by occasional smudges of blue-green and completely unnatural accents in red and blue. All of these serve to draw attention to the structural arrangement of this brilliant composition. (RL)

Pencil, gouache on paper
48.4 × 32.4 cm
Leopold Museum, Vienna, Inv. 1426
K D.1606

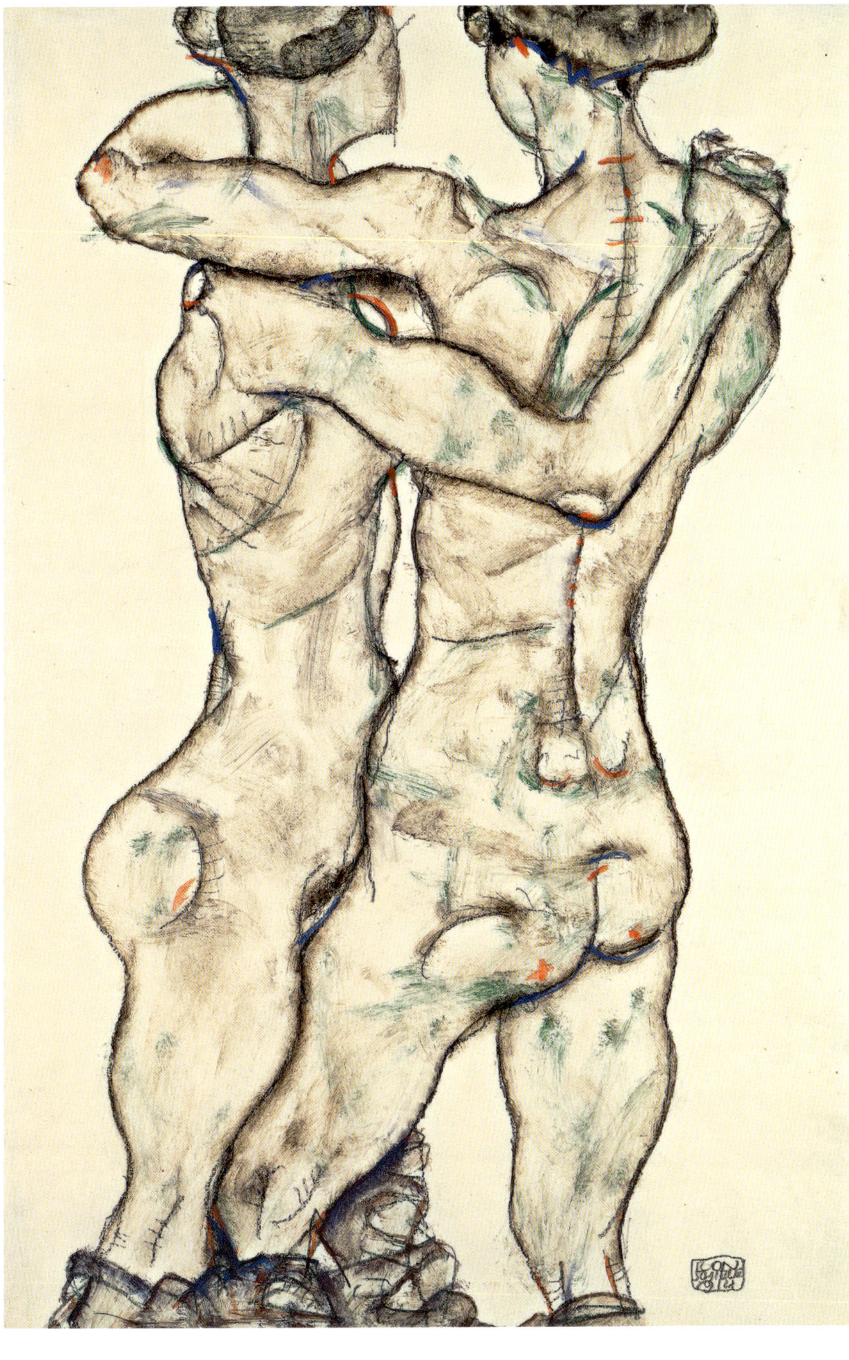

1914

RECLINING WOMAN WITH RAISED SHIRT

This nude is lying down, but the signature was placed in such a way as to suggest that the drawing was done in vertical format (see p. 55). Many of the lines of the drawing are bordered or intersected by rows of perpendicular hatching, which had begun to appear already in the second half of 1913. Here, in one of the loveliest examples of this technique, they are especially numerous. Much like the smudges and short strokes of color in Schiele's watercolors of the same period, these pencil shadings lend volume to the various forms and serve to fix them in space. That function is especially apparent along the center line of the torso and in the folds of the fabric.

The head and face have been greatly simplified to reflect geometric shapes: they are described with only a simple oval outline, a few curving lines for the hair, two semicircles tracing the lines of the brows and the sides of the nose, and finally a short angled line for the tip of the nose. The eyes are missing altogether, but the other lines in the face are so accurate that their absence is not disturbing in the least. The artist's fondness for geometry is even apparent in the *mons veneris*, where short curving lines alternate with tiny rows of spirals. These bring into focus the graphic area on the left side of the composition, both as subject and form. Its counterpart on the right side is the chemise, with its brilliantly executed, highly three-dimensional folds. (RL)

Pencil on paper
32.2 × 48.2 cm
Leopold Museum, Vienna, Inv. 1409
K D.1550

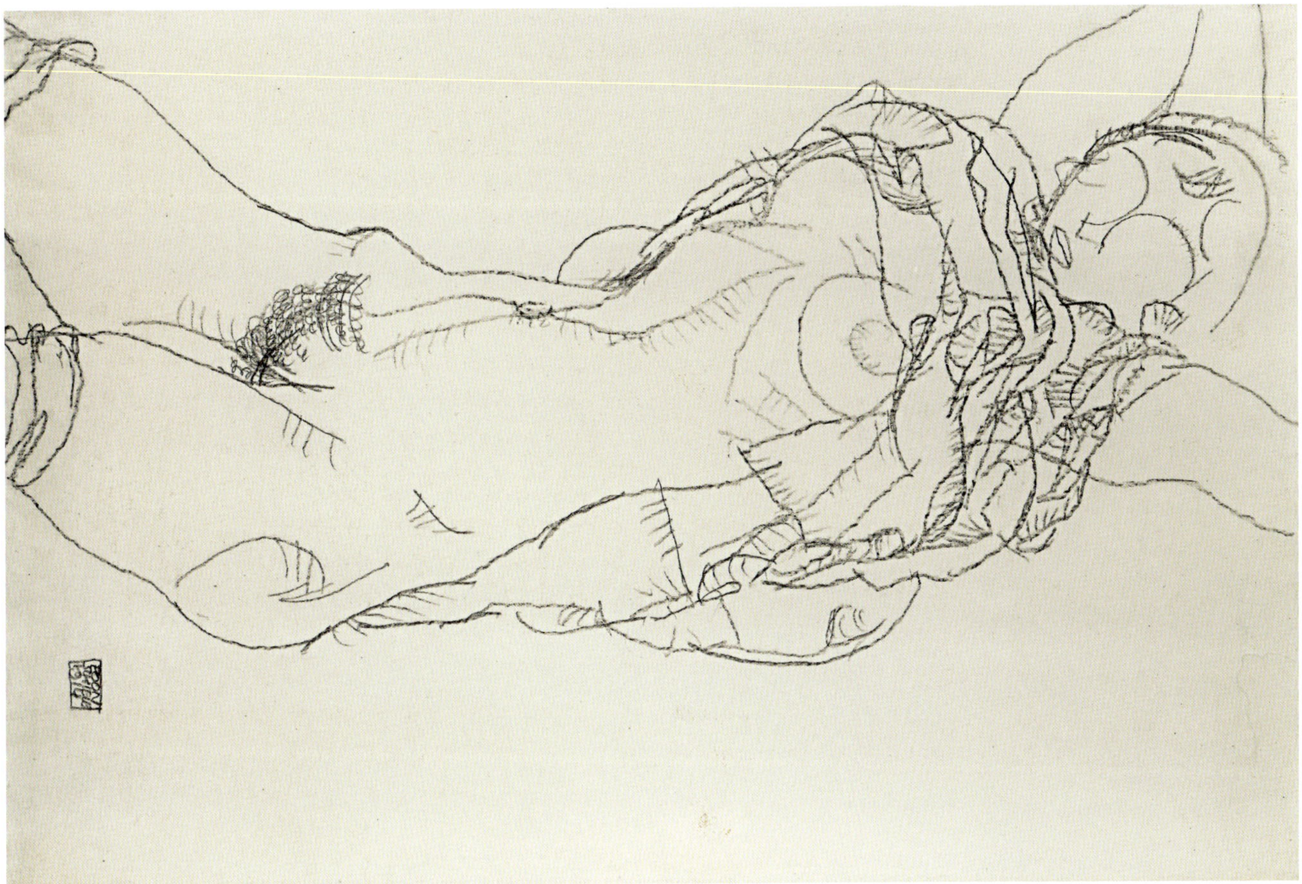

1914

SITTING SEMI-NUDE WITH BLUE HAIRBAND

This is an outstanding example of Schiele's ability to combine precise drawing with equally explicit coloring. His geometric bent is clearly apparent in many of the details, both in the outlines as well as in the internal structures. In the jacket, especially, these forms are emphasized by the coloring, which is most intense next to the lines. The combination of cool blue-green and blue also underscores the constructive quality of the drawing. Schiele allows this combination of tones to dominate over the browns and scattered reddish tones of the flesh, the ashen brown of the hair, and the brick-red mouth. (RL)

Pencil, gouache on paper
47.4 × 31.3 cm
Leopold Museum, Vienna, Inv. 1425
K D.1594

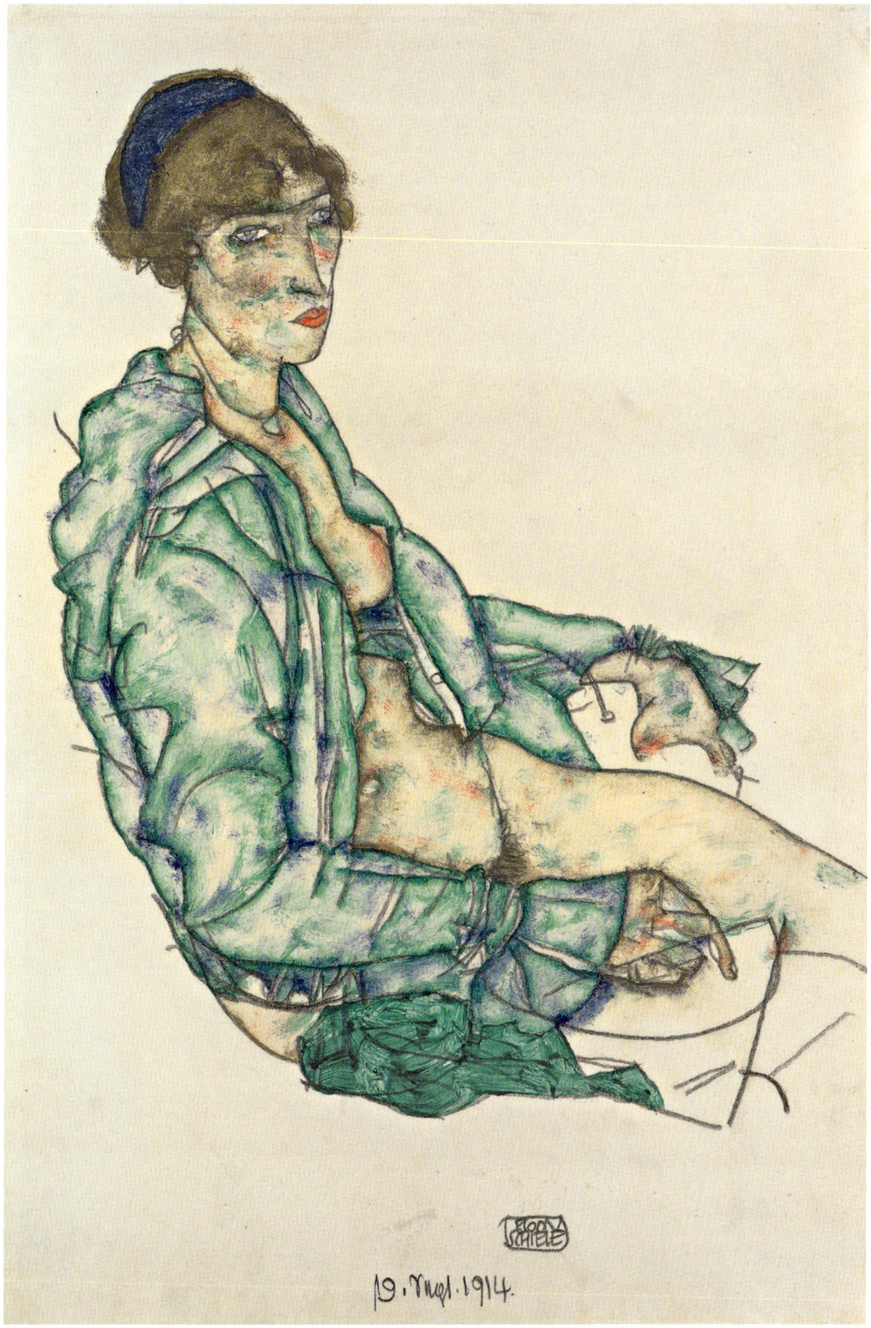

1914

SITTING FEMALE NUDE WITH RED GARTER, SEEN FROM THE BACK

The flesh of this seated figure is rendered with various shades of brown and touches of blue-green and brick-red. With these Schiele not only captured the tone of her skin but identified the volumes and functions of the various parts of her body with great success. It is this free and loose way of painting that makes the drawing so fascinating. By minimizing her sexuality in this back view, Schiele was able to concentrate on the rhythmic sequence set up by her knees, her shoulders and her head. (RL)

Pencil, gouache on paper
44.2 × 30.1 cm
Leopold Museum, Vienna, Inv. 2338
K D.1614

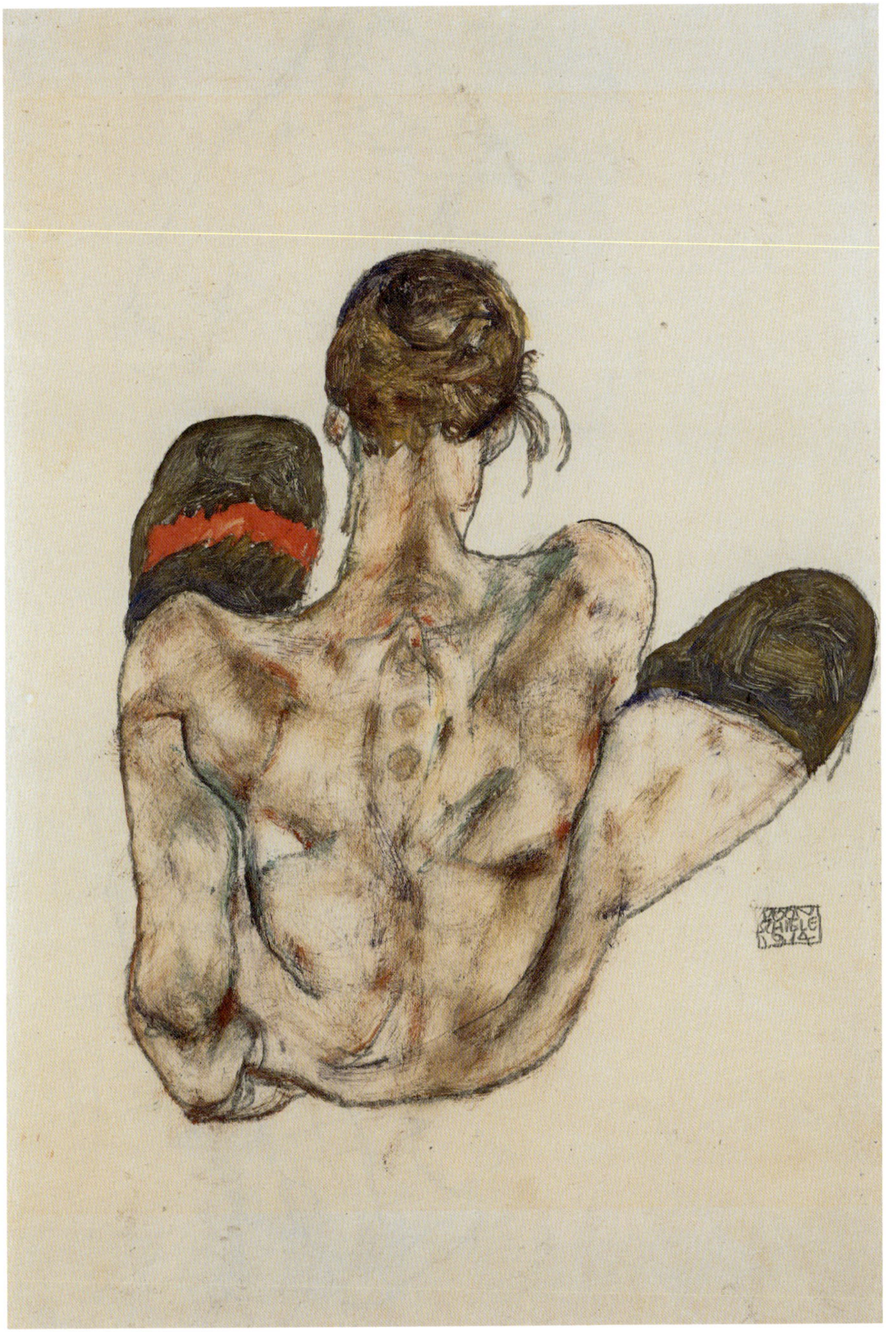

1914

MOTHER AND CHILD

One of the special features of this work is the way the figures are enveloped by the painting as if by shading. Much like the accompanying fine strokes alongside the outlines, which appear especially frequently in works on paper created in 1913, this makes the group of figures stand out from the background in a three-dimensional manner.

The bodies of the mother and the child were composed in opposite directions, while Schiele gave the child's body clad in an orange-colored dress an interesting spindle shape. The execution of the details reveals a strong tendency towards geometrization, which can be observed in the naked arms, in the mother's thighs visible beneath her dress and especially in the drawing of the two faces and their outlines.

All formal aspects – however impressively executed – are eclipsed by the work's expressive content. The mother and child appear to be burdened by a sad fate: the mother's head is bowed in deep resignation, her eyes cast down, while the child's head is held high, its eyes wide open. Schiele captured a mother and child in a similar depiction in 1912 (see p. 131) – the face of the mother especially reveals almost the same state of mind. However, the look in the child's eyes in the 1912 depiction expresses sheer horror, while it appears sadder and somehow hollower in this work.

The different mental states of the mother and the child are expressed by the diverging posture of the heads and the closed versus the wide open eyes and are further reflected in the varying colors of their hair and dress. And yet, a certain similarity in these colors highlights the bond between mother and child. The warmer ocher color of the child's curls is reflected in the mother's paler ashen hair. The lively orange hue of the child's clothes has faded in the mother's dress almost completely, which is dominated by muted tones.

The work's allegorical character is evident. In it, Schiele illustrated the tragic nature of human existence in two different stages of life. (RL)

Pencil, gouache on paper
48.2 × 31.9 cm
Leopold Museum, Vienna, Inv. 2313
K D.1673

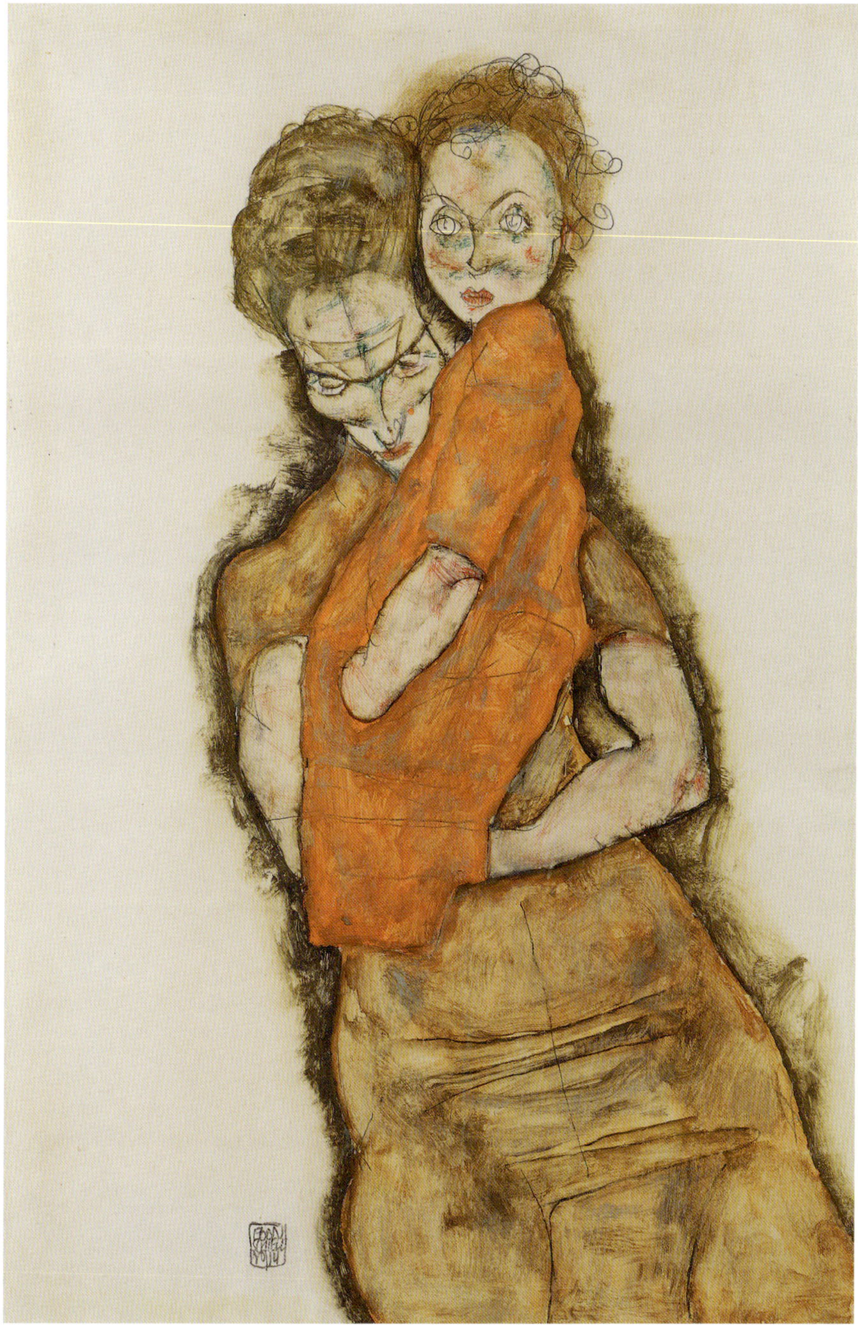

1914

CRESCENT OF HOUSES IN KRUMAU. STUDY WITH COLOR SPECIFICATIONS FOR *CRESCENT OF HOUSES II (ISLAND TOWN)*

It is easy to pick out this complex of Krumau houses, built on a curve, from the many others one looks down upon from the Schlossberg. To emphasize the curve, Schiele left out a number of other structures or only included suggestions of them. These fragmentary suggestions, such as the roof outlines and one façade in extreme foreshortening in the foreground, have an importan function. They effectively enhance the sense of looking down from a height and give some indication of how far away the main cluster of houses actually is.

The sweeping line of houses flows upward and back into the depth of the picture's space. With its many angled lines facing the river, the formal emphasis turns toward the left, which Schiele corrected by placing the bridge and houses on the other side. In addition, the line formed by the structures and turning to the right from the tall double house helps to anchor the thrust of the curve to the left.

The lines describing these roofs and walls appear to be quite straight-forward, but they are, in fact, drawn with great sensitivity, varied not only in their shapes but also in their intensity. This alone adequately captures the three-dimensional forms of the structures, even though Schiele's masterful manipulation of perspective also comes into play. The sense of space would have compromised the wonderful effect of pure line. The few patches of shading he did use serve merely as accents in this superb drawing.

The letters visible here and there on the walls of the houses are color notes for the large paintings of such a curving row of houses that Schiele was planning. The first two of these (see p. 233; L 258; K P.291) were executed in 1915, the third and last (L 284; K P.331) in early 1918. (RL)

Pencil on paper
43.7 × 31.9 cm
Leopold Museum, Vienna, Inv. 2308
K D.1696

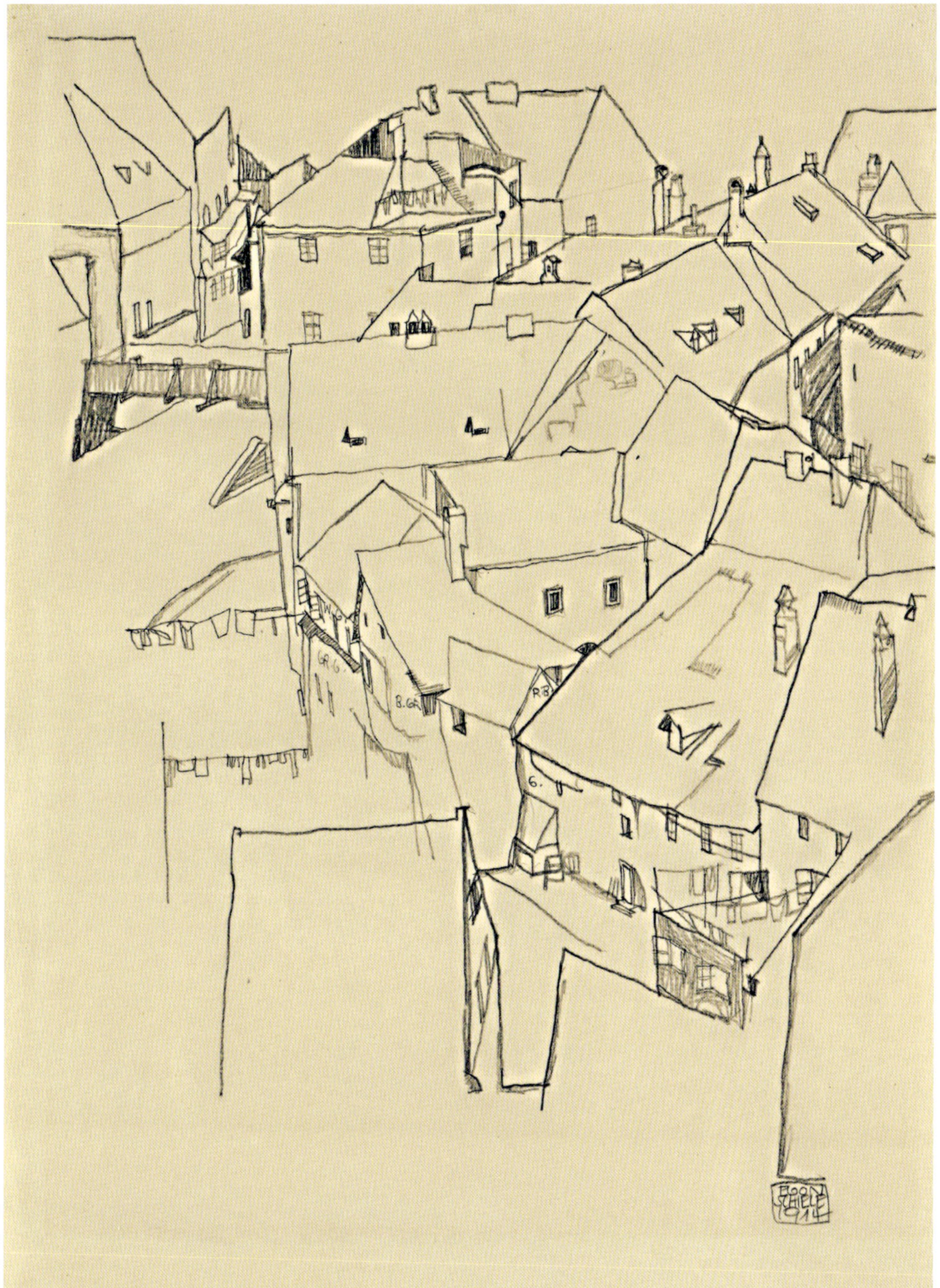
EGON SCHIELE 1914

1914

HOUSE WITH SHINGLE ROOF. STUDY FOR *HOUSE WITH SHINGLE ROOF (OLD HOUSE II)*

Schiele's motif in this drawing was a house that one can still see in Krumau. It is squeezed in between other structures, as both a preliminary sketch for the painting (Sketchbook 1914) and this detailed drawing clearly indicate. In the painting, Schiele omitted the structures beside and behind the house and placed it in an imaginary landscape.

Schiele enriched his drawing by applying different degrees of pressure to his pencil and by providing it with an off-center focal point in the one window he completely blackened. The delicate short lines beneath the curve of the bridge directly below that window reappear in a very similar context in the drawing of the model Poldi reproduced on p. 219. (RL)

Pencil on paper
43.3 × 31.8 cm
Leopold Museum, Vienna, Inv. 1428
K D.1694

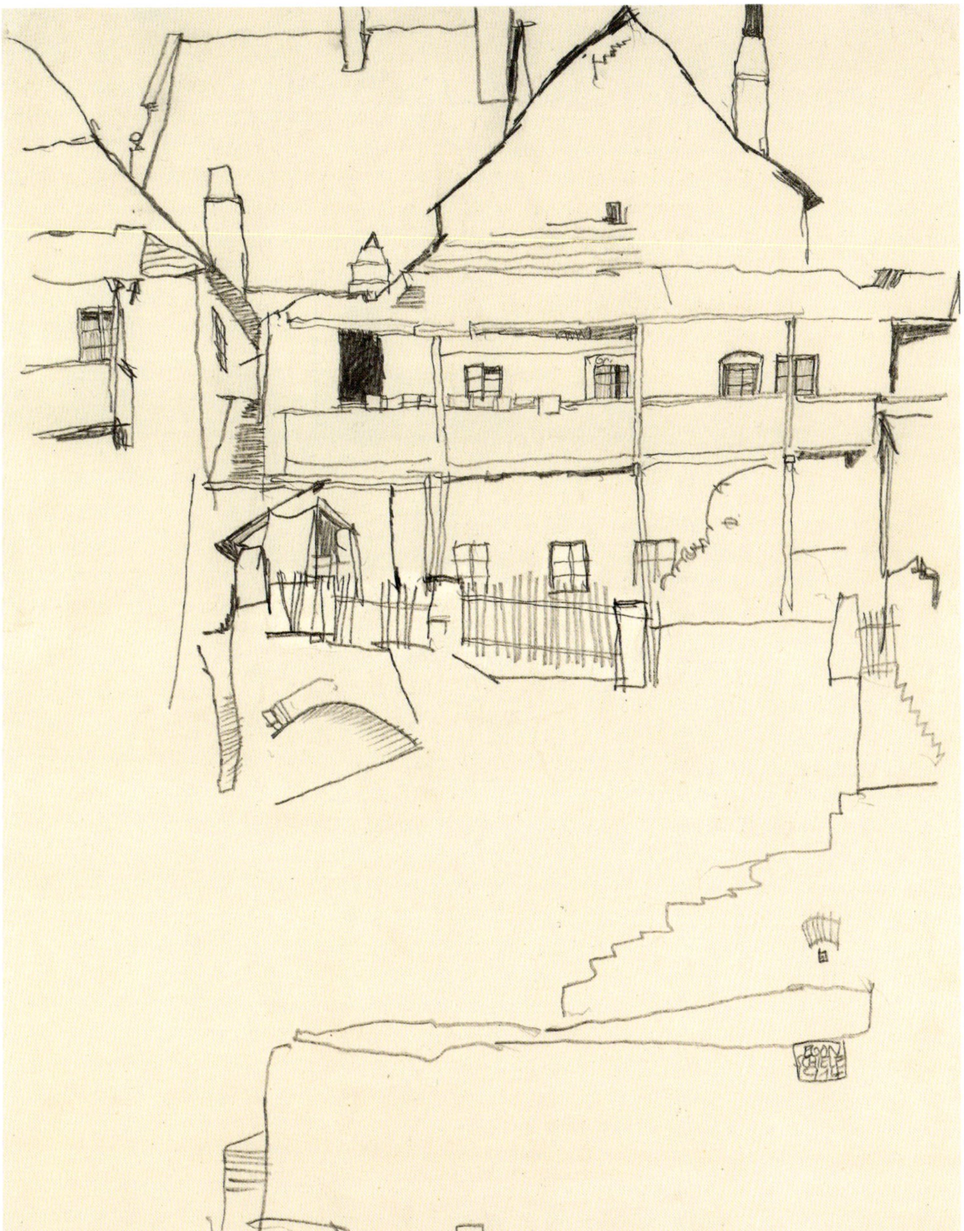

1914

"POLDI"

There are a number of known drawings of this model named Poldi. The depiction of her face here is one of the most brilliant examples of Schiele's masterful draftsmanship. The clarity and sensitivity of these lines are unsurpassed. In addition, Schiele superbly captured her expression; one sees in it the strain of having to maintain a specific pose for a long time. Poldi doubtless bent her left thumb in such an artificial way at Schiele's request.

Everything has been omitted that might have detracted from the ornamental outline of this seated figure. Some of the folds of the blouse she has shrugged off are rendered with double lines. Roughly parallel lines such as these are common in the drawings Schiele executed between 1914 and 1916, and occasionally appear in his paintings as well. They are generally found in the description of fabrics, but are also sometimes used to mark contours important to a composition. Again, the rows of short or longer strokes placed close together next to important contours can be seen in architectural studies from this period. (RL)

Pencil on paper
47.5 × 31 cm
Leopold Museum, Vienna, Inv. 1427
K D.1519

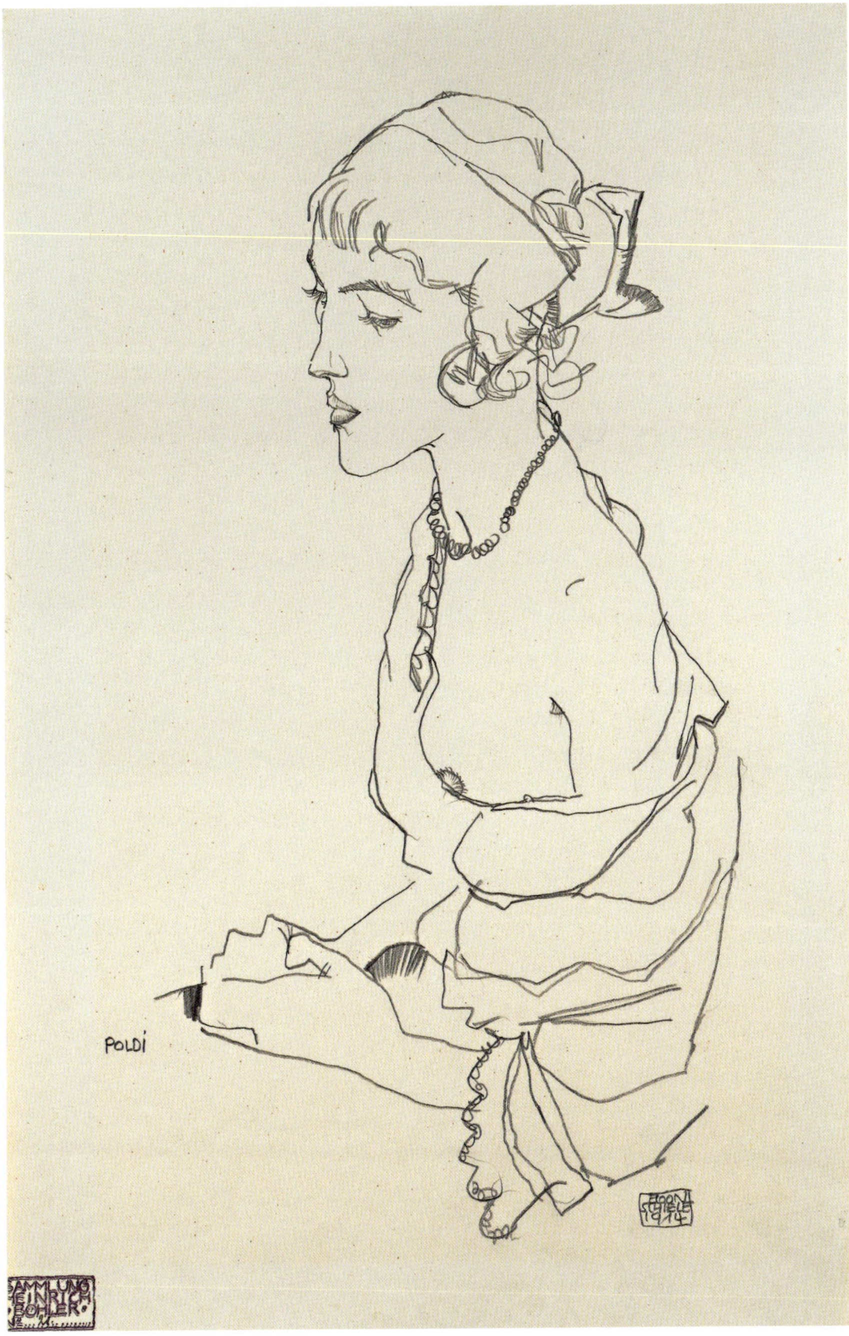
POLDI

1914

"ARTHUR ROESSLER"

This etching is a portrait of the influential Viennese art writer and critic Arthur Roessler, which Schiele prepared with two preliminary drawings (K D.1630, 1631). What is remarkable about the etching is the expressive execution of the hands, a characteristic also encountered in Schiele's drawings and paintings.

Roessler, who promoted Schiele all his life and collected many of his works, had encouraged the young artist in 1914 to produce graphic works, as there was "more of a market for them than for paintings, especially in Germany, where, with the help of an art dealer, such as Gurlitt in Berlin, he would certainly find buyers for his graphic works, etchings and woodcuts". Roessler offered to pay for the expensive printing plates and the necessary materials, while Schiele was instructed in the use of the etching needle by the painter and graphic artist Robert Philippi. However, Schiele soon lost interest in printed graphic works, as he found them too dull and time-consuming.

In 1922, only four years after Egon Schiele's death, a portfolio of the artist's complete prints was published by Rikola publishers. Roessler wrote the preface, in which he described the creation of these works and posthumously reminded Schiele of the advantages of printed graphic works. (BS)

Etching in black on paper
32.2 × 39.8 cm
Leopold Museum, Vienna, Inv. 3653
K G.8a

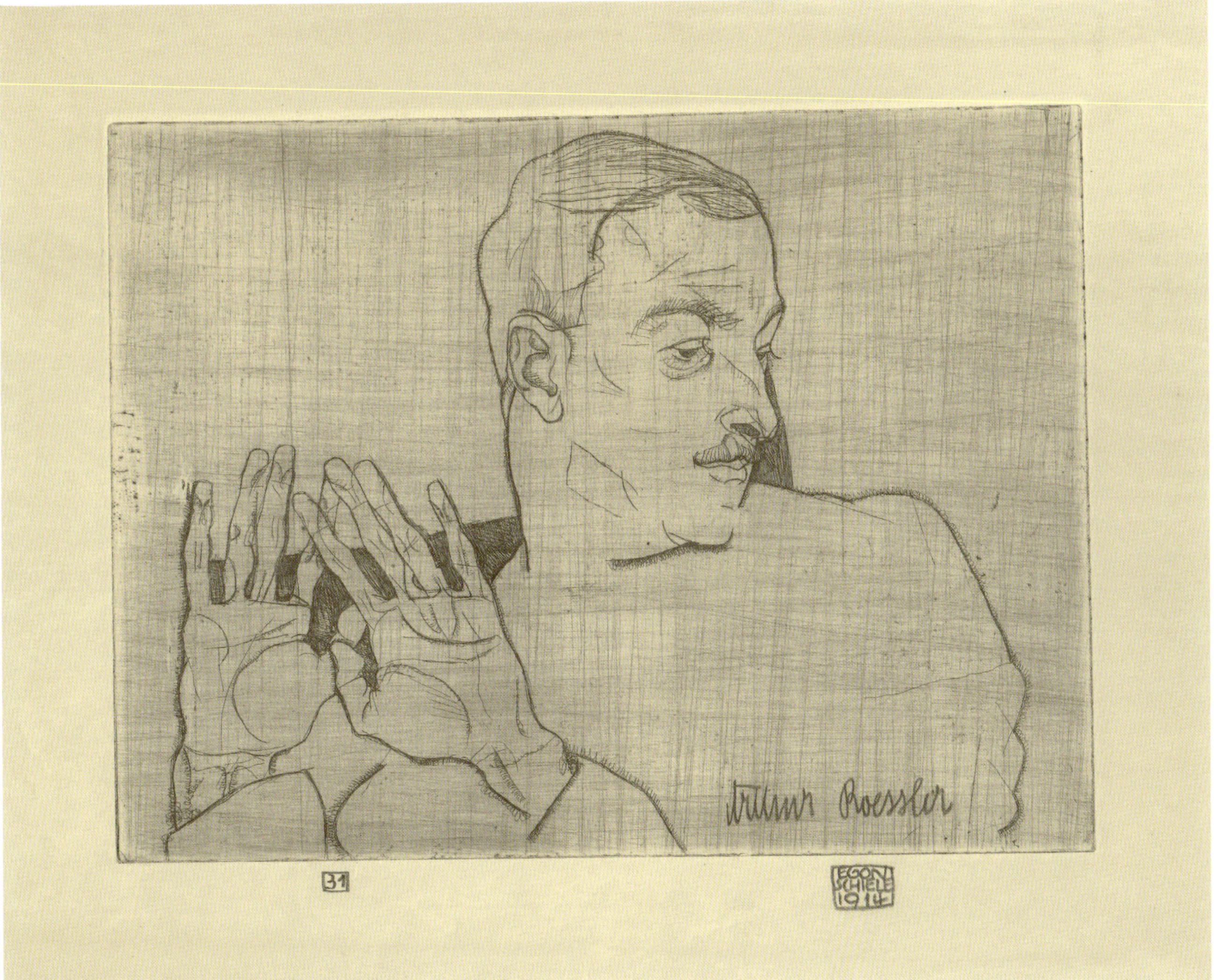
Arthur Roessler
31
EGON SCHIELE 1914

1914

PORTRAIT OF FRANZ HAUER

In 1914 Schiele was instructed in the techniques of woodcut and etching by the painter and graphic artist Robert Philippi. Arthur Roessler, who was one of the most important figures in Schiele's life and, through his excellent contacts, played a major part in the artist's advancement, had encouraged the artist to try these techniques and had provided him with the costly printing plates and materials.

Between May and August of that year, Schiele created two lithographs and six etchings, including the portrait of the art collector and Schiele promoter Franz Hauer, whom the artist had met through Roessler. In July 1912 Schiele had addressed his future collector in a letter: "Dear Mr. Hauer! I have heard that you are one of the few to purchase works by the most junior artists. Would you like to come and see me, or visit the Hagenbund exhibition, where some of my works are on display?" (ESAD, ID: 493). Franz Hauer ran a flourishing restaurant in Vienna's city center and started collecting art in 1908/09. He was particularly interested in contemporary art, collecting works by Albin Egger-Lienz and Oskar Kokoschka, among others, and from 1912 also by Egon Schiele. Only a year later, Hauer had Schiele grant him the right to view all of his works created until the autumn of that year before any other prospective buyers, and acquired six paintings. Hauer's unexpected death in 1914 at the age of only 48, however, shattered Schiele's prospects of more such lucrative sales. (BS)

Drypoint etching on paper
19.4 × 17.8 cm
Leopold Museum, Vienna, Inv. 5951
K G.5a

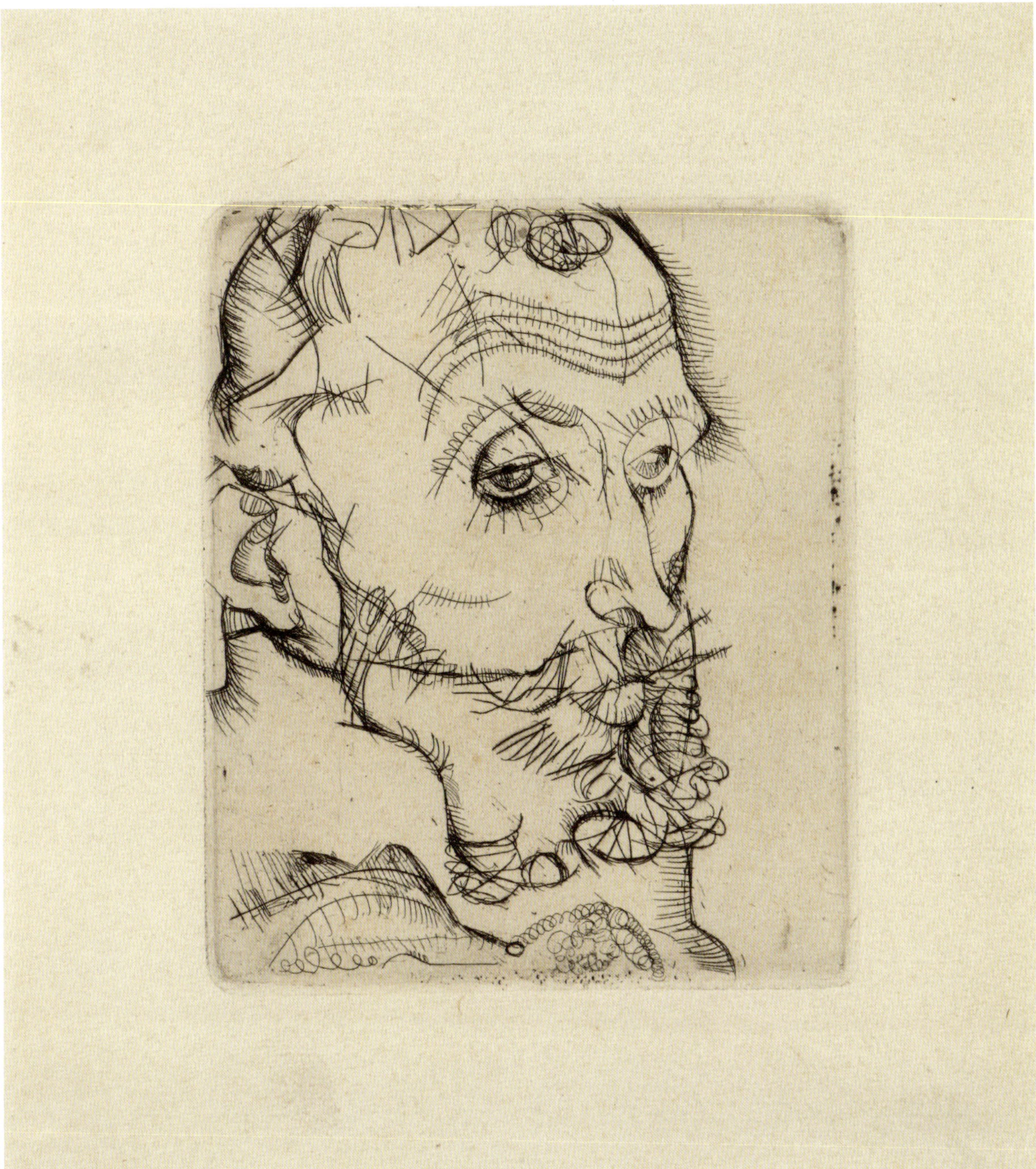

1915

LOVEMAKING (SKETCH)

Schiele did this drawing in preparation for his depiction of the sexual act as seen on p. 227. His paper obviously turned out to be too narrow. The woman's calf and shoe, especially, appear to have been later additions. Though fascinating in itself, the drawing reveals that the artist was still searching for formal clarification, as in the woman's left arm. (RL)

Pencil on paper
32 × 49.2 cm
Leopold Museum, Vienna, Inv. 1406
K D.1785

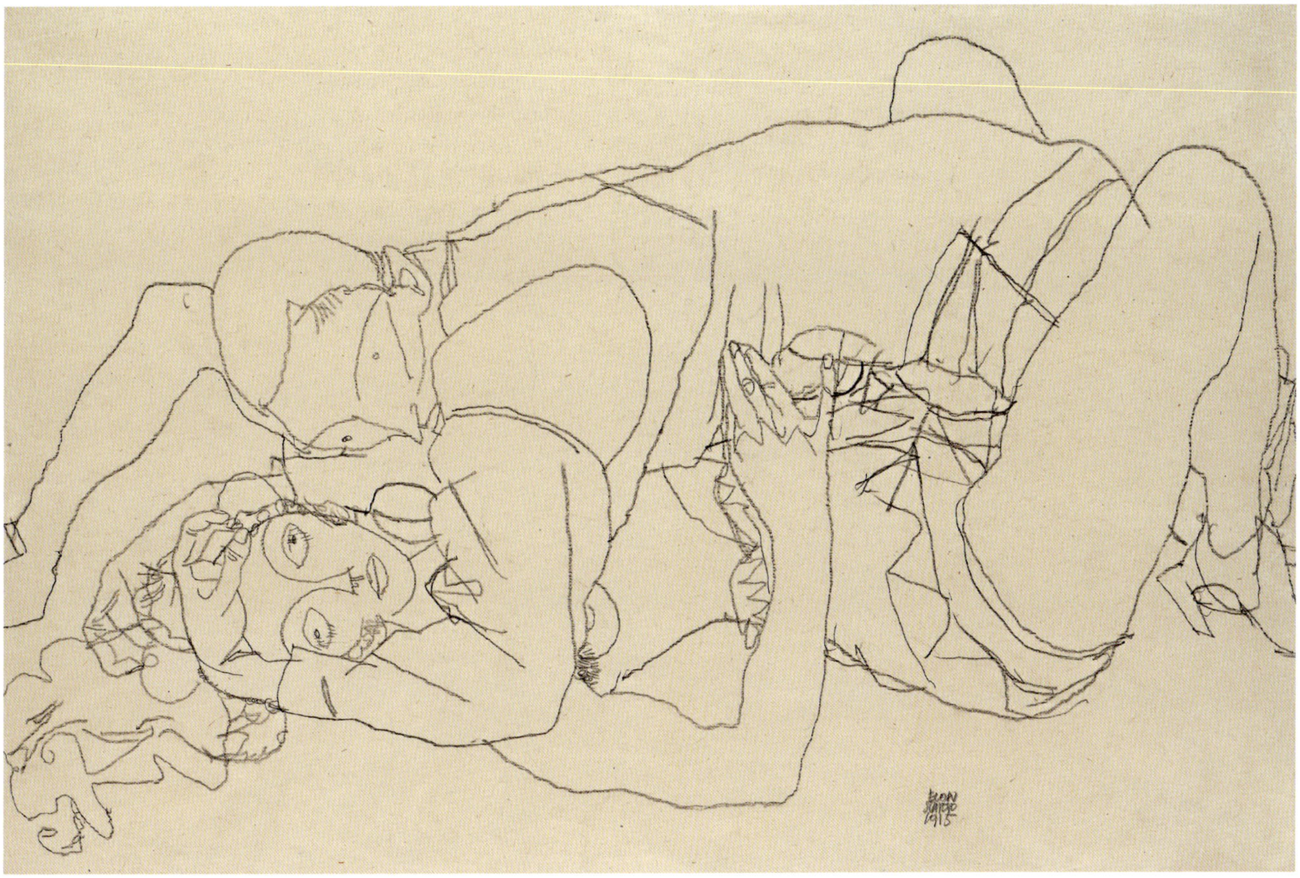

1915

LOVEMAKING

In this more finished version of the same motif as that on p. 225, Schiele changed a number of details. The woman's legs now project only slightly beyond the contour of the man's back. They appear to grip him tightly, as do her arms and hands. The splayed fingers of the man's left hand are placed over her hair, and his right hand clutches a portion of it. The heads are juxtaposed not only formally but also in their differing expressions. There is a certain fatefulness about the whole procedure. The man – clearly a self-portrait – embraces a doll-like creature. Sexuality, eroticism and world-weariness have become somehow blurred. (RL)

Pencil, gouache on paper
49.6 × 31.7 cm
Leopold Museum, Vienna, Inv. 1419
K D.1786

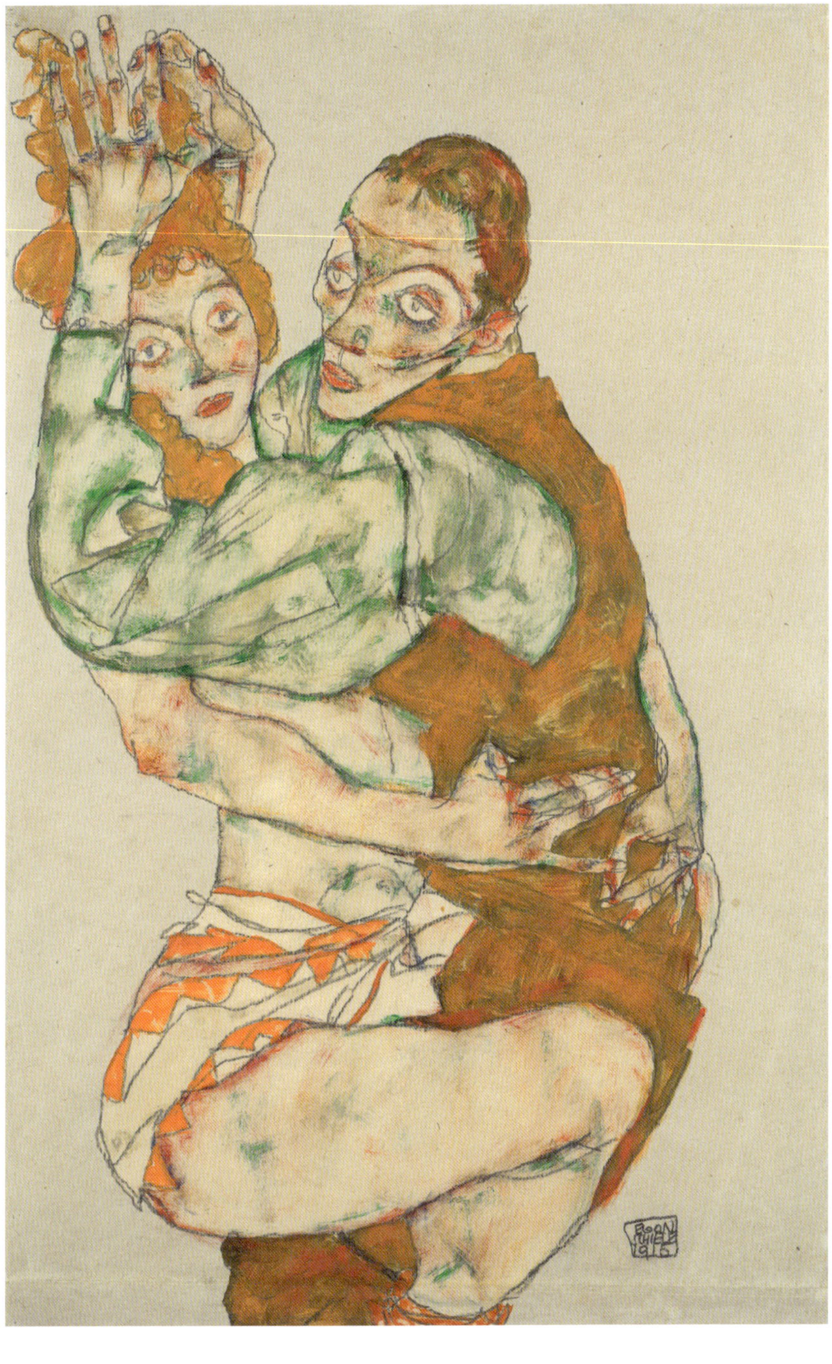

1915

SITTING WOMAN CLASPING HER FEET

Schiele drew this seated figure with strong pencil strokes. As in the following work, the board on which he placed his paper was not very smooth, and as a result the broad lines of his soft graphite pencil took on an interesting texture. He frequently used such a technique in his drawings from the years 1913 to 1916.

The center of the composition is the woman's genitals, visible below folds in her slip and surrounded by a web of shorter and longer lines. The angle of the slip's edge as it stretches between her knees is opposed to that of its lower edge and the roughly parallel line of the right heel. The supporting knee, the summarily sketched hair, and the fingers of the right hand constitute essential, asymmetrical elements in the composition. The contours of the left arm and calf descend steeply from the head. They are echoed by the angle of the right knee. That angle is balanced, in turn, by the head and the hand grasping the left foot – an especially beautiful demonstration of draftsmanship. Overall, this clear composition combines tremendous dynamism and great self-containment. (RL)

Pencil on paper
48 × 31.5 cm
Leopold Museum, Vienna, Inv. 2318
K D.1747

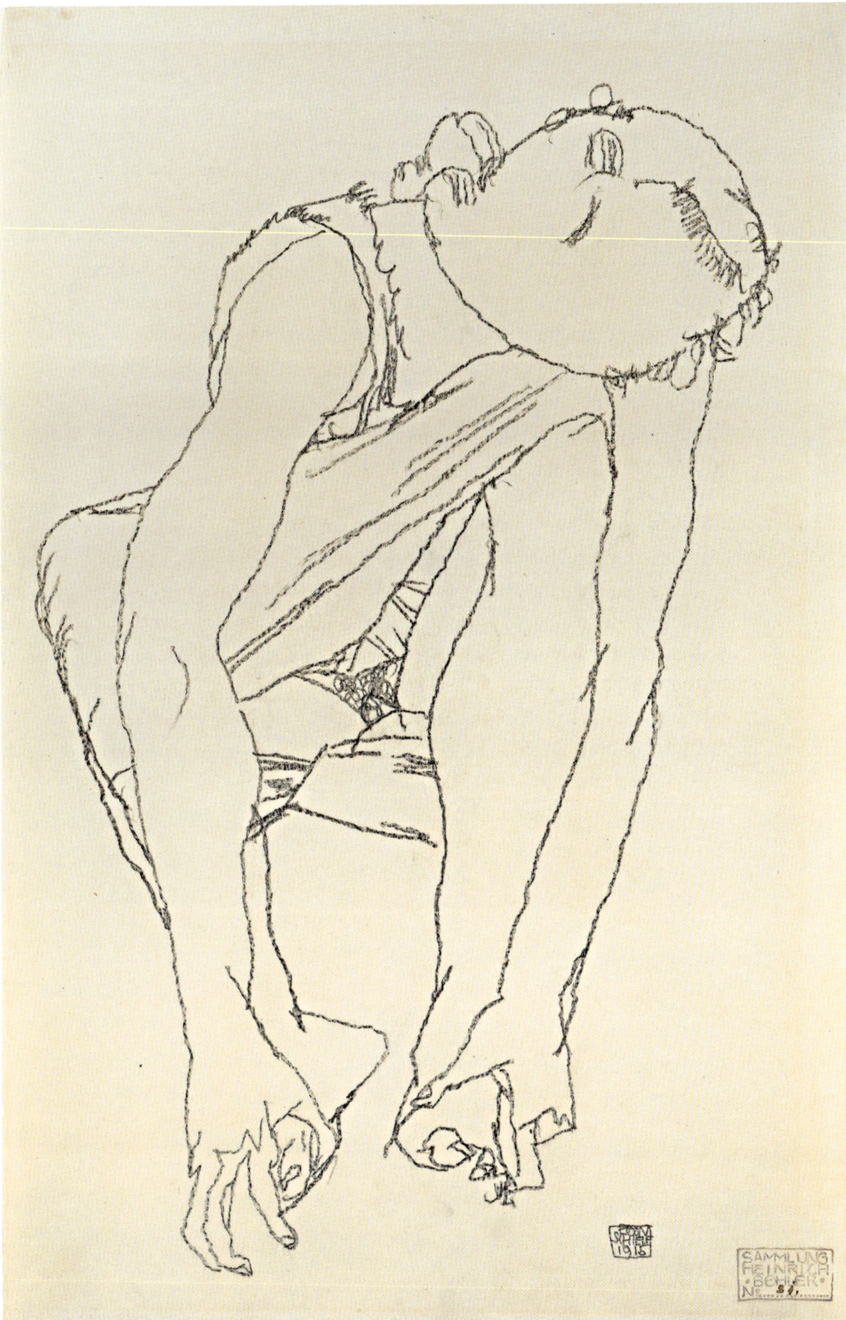
EGON SCHIELE 1916
SAMMLUNG HEINRICH BÖHLER
No. 21

1915

KNEELING WOMAN WITH BENT HEAD

This woman appears to have suddenly bent forward from a kneeling position. Her violet-colored slip billows outward as she moves. Her feet and calves lift up from the floor. The different manner of handling paint on the legs suggests their distance in space. The color in the right stocking is graphically structured, and therefore it appears more detailed and closer to us; in the left one the colors are blurred, so that it appears to be farther away. The stockinged legs with their high-top shoes are formally balanced by the shock of hair, which appears higher on the page than it would actually have been, right next to the shoulder. The head and neck appear to be missing, which only intensifies the sense of delirium suggested by her pose. Because of the position of the hand between her legs – the left foot hides most of it – and the visible labia beneath the slip, one gets an impression of almost compulsive abandon. Such a combination of delirium and sexuality is nothing new in Schiele's art.

Capturing motion in an artistic way was one of Schiele's major concerns in this period. Here the flowing curves that outline the exposed parts of the body and the billowing slip above them enhance the sense of movement. The drawing and painting of the latter are equally magnificent. (RL)

Pencil, gouache on paper
32.5 × 47.9 cm
Leopold Museum, Vienna, Inv. 2371
K D.1750

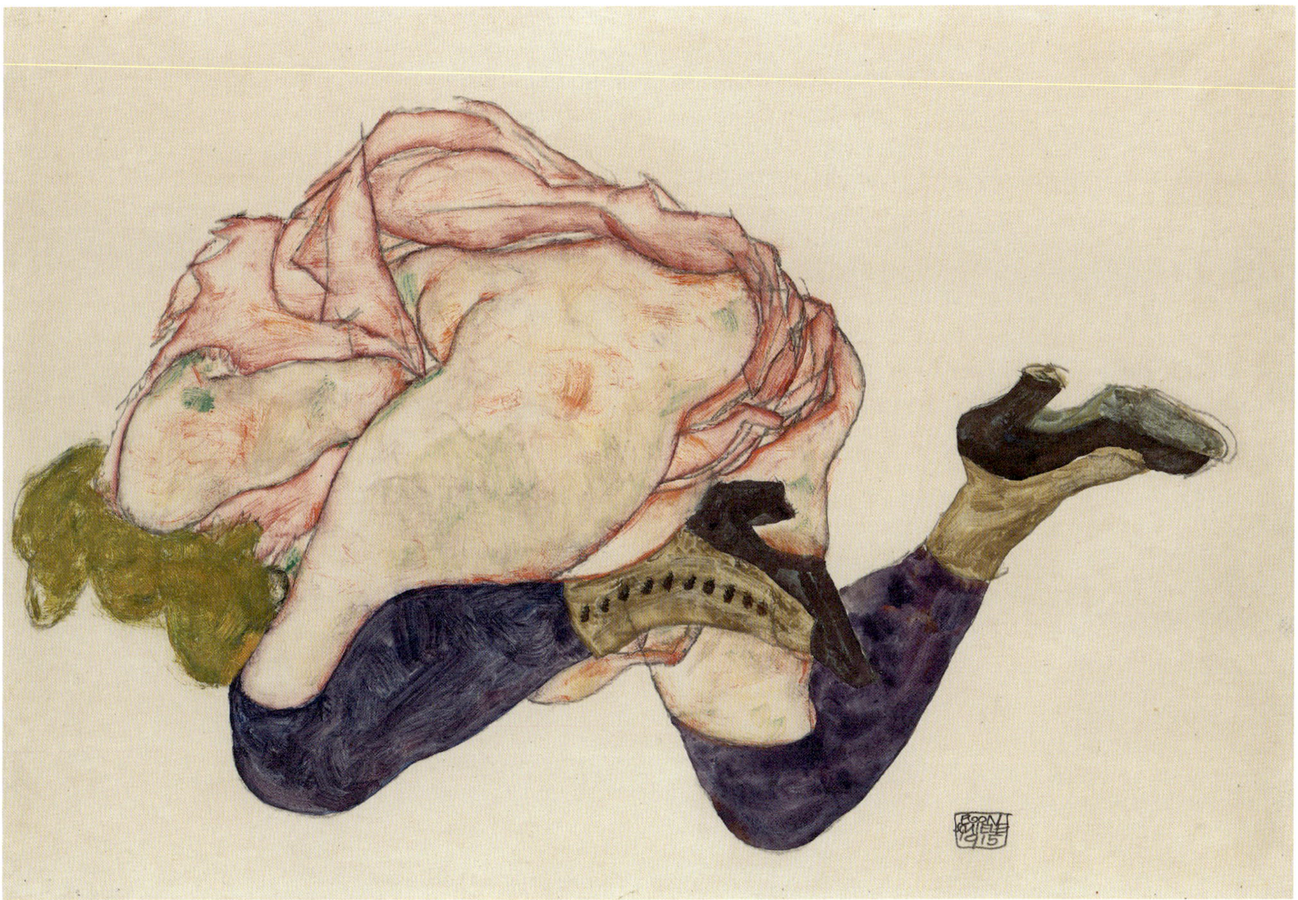

1915

CRESCENT OF HOUSES II (ISLAND TOWN)

This second version of the *Crescent of Houses* was likewise done in the first half of 1915. Here the houses have been entirely divorced from their topographical setting. The courtyard with whitish walls and two green-framed windows, an essential feature in the first version (L 258, K P.291), has grown smaller here and been rendered in broken gradations that diminish its significance. The courtyard no longer functions as a static center. Otherwise it would have "stopped the movement" which Schiele aimed to evoke at this period, even in certain townscapes.

The houses in this painting give the impression of flowing viscously into the background, a movement that seems even to communicate itself to the light band of ground behind the orange-yellow building complex at the top. This impression of gradual motion is underscored by the way the house facades diverge from the vertical to various extents and in various directions. The first two appear to lean forwards; the walls adjacent to the little white house set like a capstone tip backwards; the following, in this version overlapping walls tend to lean forwards, while the larger part of the tall houses appears to turn in the opposite direction as if leaning into a curve. The sense of motion is even clearer in the row of trees, whose middle portion seems to be pushed left as if by centrifugal force.

While in the first version the idea of a town crescent was subordinated to a more complete depiction of the district, the second is treated in a more focusing and symbolically evocative way. Here the arc configuration is surrounded by dark waters and set on a spit of land resembling an island. This is likely the source of Schiele's title, *Island Town*.

In part these houses with their bays, roofs and chimneys have the appearance of geometric solids. The facades are accompanied by green and purple bands which relate to them and to each other like the parts of a fugue. In order to emphasize the arc configuration, Schiele omitted the decorative laundry lines of the first version and replaced them by the row of autumnal trees mentioned, which is continued on the right by a few smaller trees in the background. Like borderlines between land and water, all of the trees and the numerous textures in the terrain are arranged in the form of an arc to underscore the direction of the massed buildings. (RL)

Oil on canvas
110.5 × 140.5 cm
Leopold Museum, Vienna, Inv. 456
L 260; K P.293

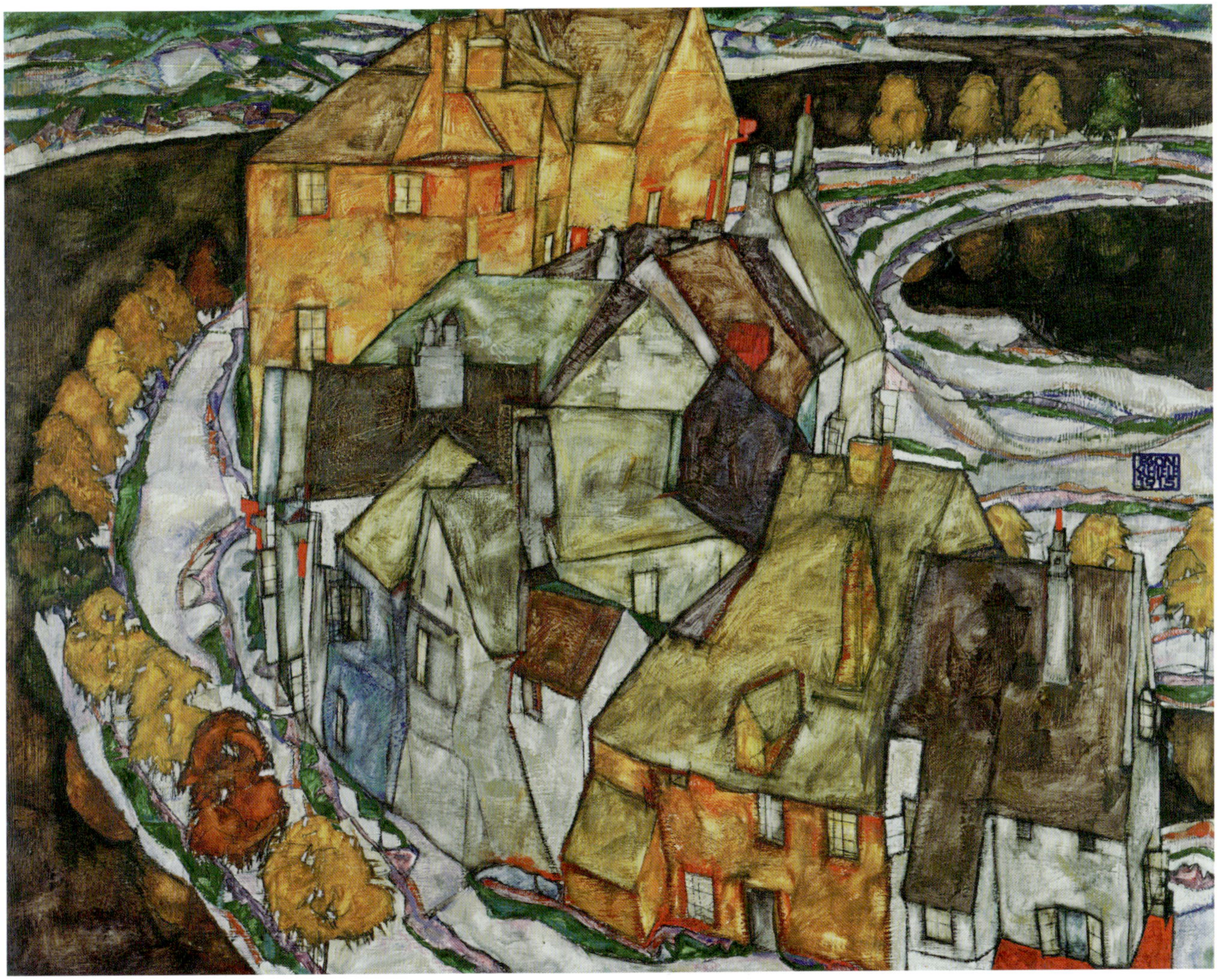

1915

MOTHER WITH TWO CHILDREN II

In 1915 Schiele worked on two paintings depicting a mother with infants; this one and another one that is in the Belvedere in Vienna (L 273; K P.303), which he completed only in 1917. In his 1966 catalogue raisonné, Otto Kallir erroneously presented the work reproduced here as an unfinished preparatory study for the other painting. It could hardly have been a study, for Schiele never painted one in such a large format. A small sketchbook that Kallir himself published in a facsimile edition proves that this picture cannot have served as any kind of preparation for the other painting. In the sketchbook one discovers numerous designs – including detail studies of children – for both paintings side by side. Moreover, two different full-page designs for the child on the right in each of the two works are known.

This large composition was left unfinished for various reasons, but Schiele's intentions in the work are fully realized nonetheless. Once again he sought to create a pictorial metaphor for a borderline situation between life and death. The mother's head resembles a skull, and the child lying in her lap looks as though it has died. These two figures constitute a kind of pietà. The colors of the background and the mother's garments enhance this impression: in contrast to the warm oranges of the surrounding space, her robe is rendered in a cooler, yellowish olive, her face in gray and blue-gray. The garment of the child held upright is unusually colorful. Schiele worked out its cretin-like, whitish mask of a face in a study, but there its head, unlike the one in the painting, rests quite naturally in its wrappings, which have been abstracted into a complex of brightly colored stripes. (RL)

Oil on canvas
149.5 × 160 cm
Leopold Museum, Vienna, Inv. 457
L 261; K P.287

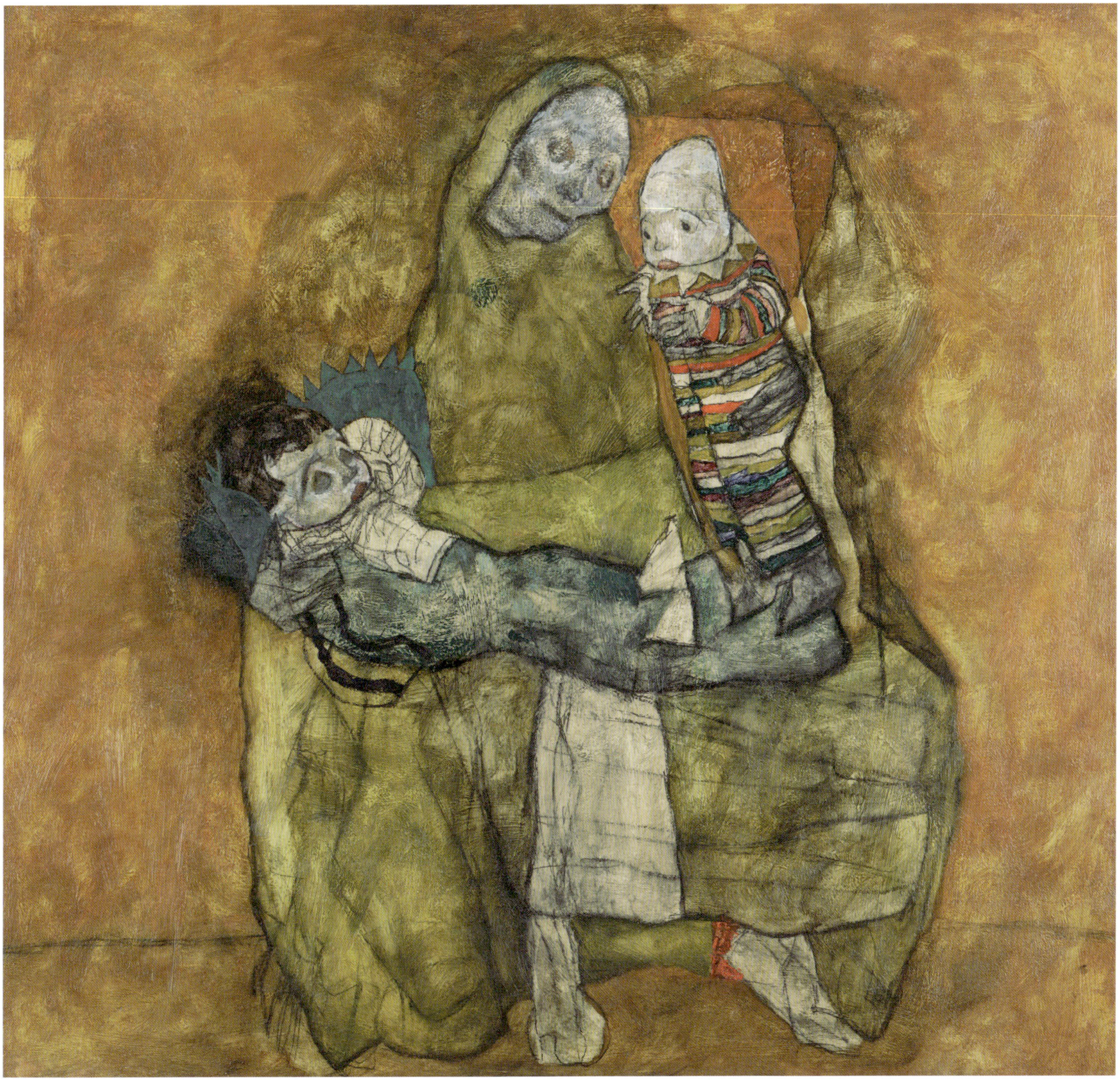

1915

HOUSE WITH SHINGLE ROOF (OLD HOUSE II)

The rendering has the effect of a penetrating portrait of a house that, so to speak, has succumbed to senility. Each of its sections reflects a unique fate: the decaying fence and the crumbling wall by the pillars, the warped windows, the weathered boards and the many shingles. Never before or after did the artist depict shingles with such eloquence. In reality, the color of the shingles would cause them to recede with respect to the foliage of the trees. Here it is just the opposite. The shingles (and, analogously, the laundry hung outside the upper story and the boards behind it) are rendered in a variety of enigmatically luminous tones. This reflects an Expressionist penchant to amplify essentials and subordinate everything else to them. The row of trees, for instance, serves merely to provide a pedestal for the "house monument". Its steep gable rises into a sky – painted entirely differently from the rest of the composition – which leaves no room for hope. The image becomes an allegory of loneliness and decay. (RL)

Oil on canvas
110 × 140 cm
Leopold Museum, Vienna, Inv. 469
L 262; K P.295

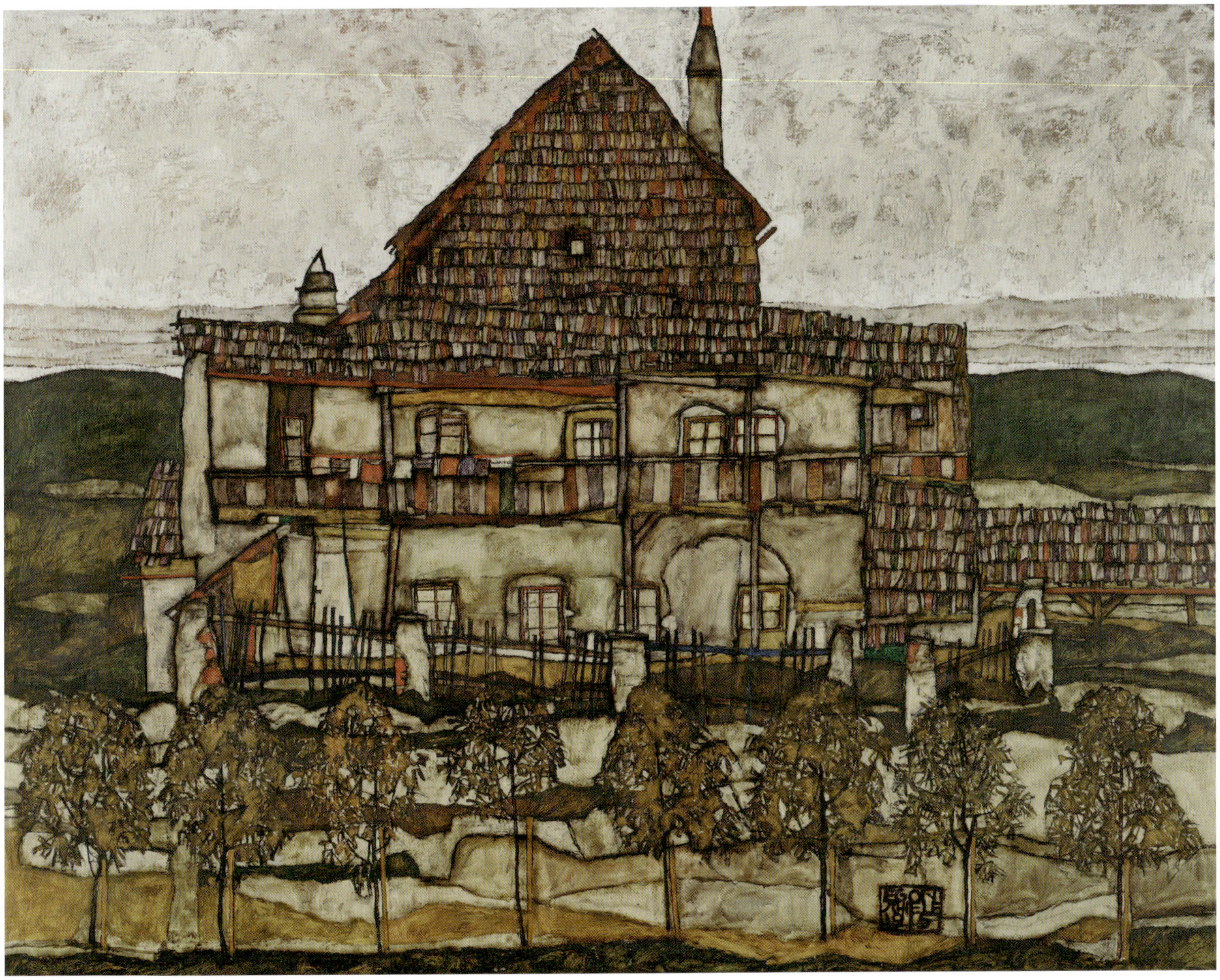

1915

HOUSE WALL ON THE RIVER

In this painting a house wall is the sole subject – augmented here by a river in which door and windows are reflected. The motif was provided by the façade of the former St. Jost's or St. Jodocus' Church on the left bank of the Vltava, a section of the adjacent house upriver and the river itself. The church, first mentioned in the records in 1347, was converted in 1596. The tower with onion dome was added in the Baroque period. After the Jesuit Order was abolished, the church was closed in 1788 and converted in 1791/92 to a residential building with annexes on the Vltava. These annexes and the connecting wooden veranda were once roofed with shingles. In 1964 the Vltava-side facades and all annexes were repainted. In the course of work, numerous windows, a door and the three round-arched windows of the former church were given an incongruous colored framing.

In the 1915 painting, Schiele reproduced the earlier view quite faithfully, including the chimney on the terrace, which had since been torn down. Since he wished to concentrate on the wall, Schiele purposely omitted the roof that begins above the round-arched windows.

The composition, basically horizontally arranged, is enriched by passages that diverge from left to right: first, the veranda with a row of windows and the light-gray strip under the hanging laundry; and second, the river-house borderline, which in the final quarter of the painting runs convergently to the opposite section of roof. Much more significant, however, is the composition of the facades with their windows and reflections in the river. This has such a picturesque appearance that one is reminded of old house walls in 19th-century pictures. Yet here no romantic or sentimental mood arises. Rather, the sight of these closed windows and crumbling facades, growing moldy near the water, makes one wonder how people could live here at all. The thin, irregular lines of the bars in the unglazed windows over the river suggests the dubiousness of the protection they offer, yet at the same time recall finespun spider webs. The multiple light reflections in the windows, too, bring a touch of eeriness into the scene of decay. The three upper arched windows of St. Jost's do not so much suggest church windows as the windows of old factories, with panes divided into small squares. Unlike the glaze technique used in passages of the river and the mostly thin color layers of the house walls, the items of laundry are rendered with heavily applied paint – an intentional contrast. Still, neither the light, variegated colors of the laundry nor the whitish hue of the wall behind awaken positive associations, but rather associations with proletarian life in the suburbs. (RL)

Oil on canvas
109.5 × 140 cm
Leopold Museum, Vienna, Inv. 468
L 263; K P.294

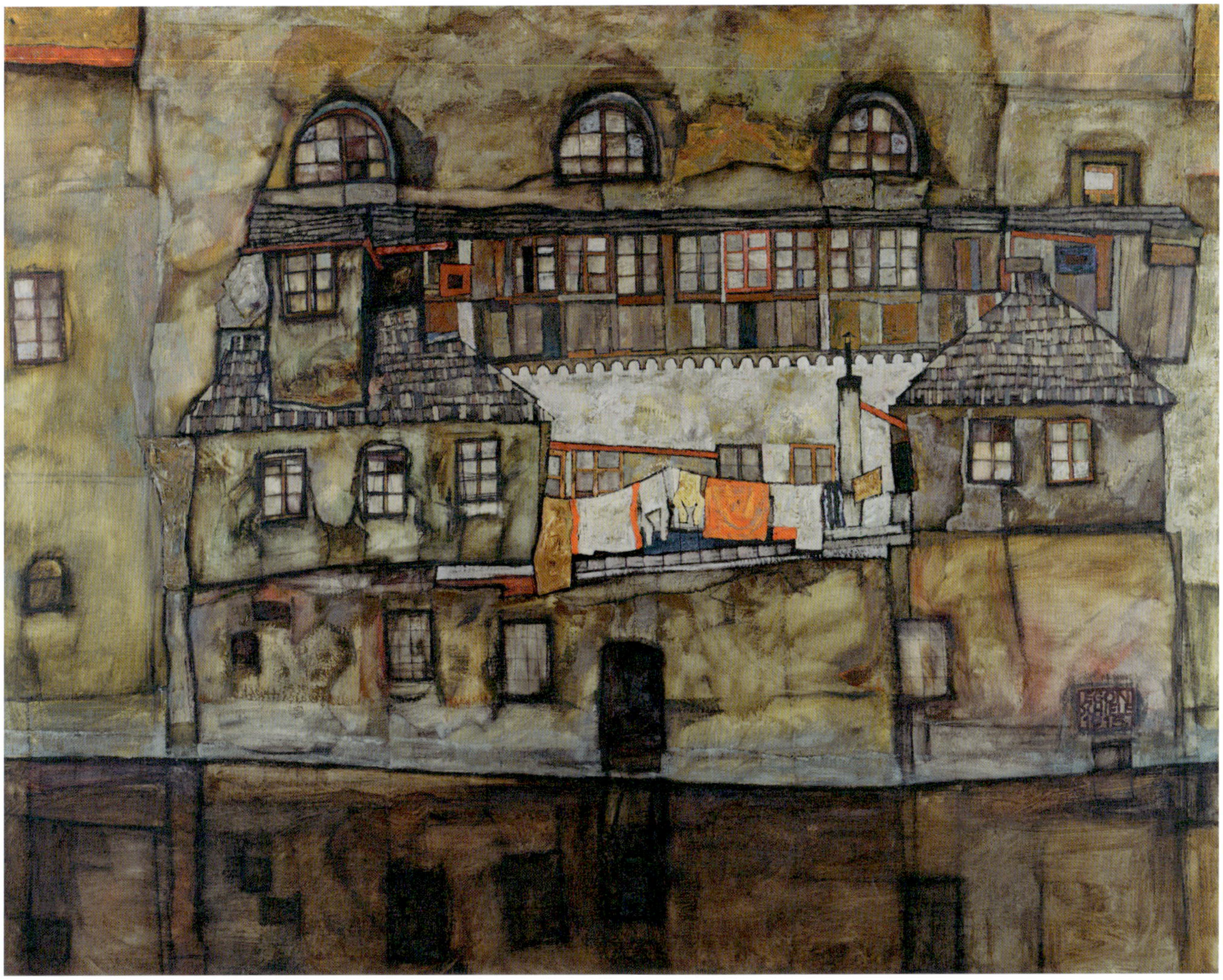

1915

LEVITATION (THE BLIND II)

This is one of the two large-scale paintings created in 1915 based on numerous design sketches (Sketchbook [1913]–1916) and several full sheet studies (see e.g. K D.1783).

Against the backdrop of a partly withered meadow meant to symbolize the world, two people are depicted in the act of dying. The lower figure still has its feet on the ground, but is already buckling. The upper figure is already dead, already levitating; its feet seem to have just left the ground, the skin has taken on a greenish hue.

Both figures have been composed in strict relation to one another. Since the artist's point of sight lies a little above the right knee of the levitating figure, the two forms are inevitably viewed from different perspectives. Their three-dimensionality represents a contrast to the more planar meadow. The tufts and strips of grass as well as the flowers have been developed to form various structures and areas of concentration which clearly correlate to the figures. The curvature of the upper figure's back, for instance, is echoed in the convex bend of a very slim strip of grass above the head, which, in turn, corresponds to a concave structure on the other end of the depiction.

In order to highlight individual body parts particularly clearly, Schiele either painted over the immediately adjoining area with a bright paint or scraped off the existing color to reveal the white base – in the case of the levitating figure this applies to the area around the right knee, the small patch between the curvature of the calf and the shirt-like dress, an area between the feet as well as a small strip to the left of the heel. The white of the eyes of the lower figure has also been highlighted using the same technique. Its gaze seems to be asking: What is coming next? The eyes and indeed the entire face of the levitating figure, by contrast, are marked by profound suffering. For from the point of view the artist – who depicted himself in both figures – man remains unredeemed even beyond death. (RL)

Oil, opaque color on canvas
200 × 172 cm
Leopold Museum, Vienna, Inv. 467
L 265; K P.288

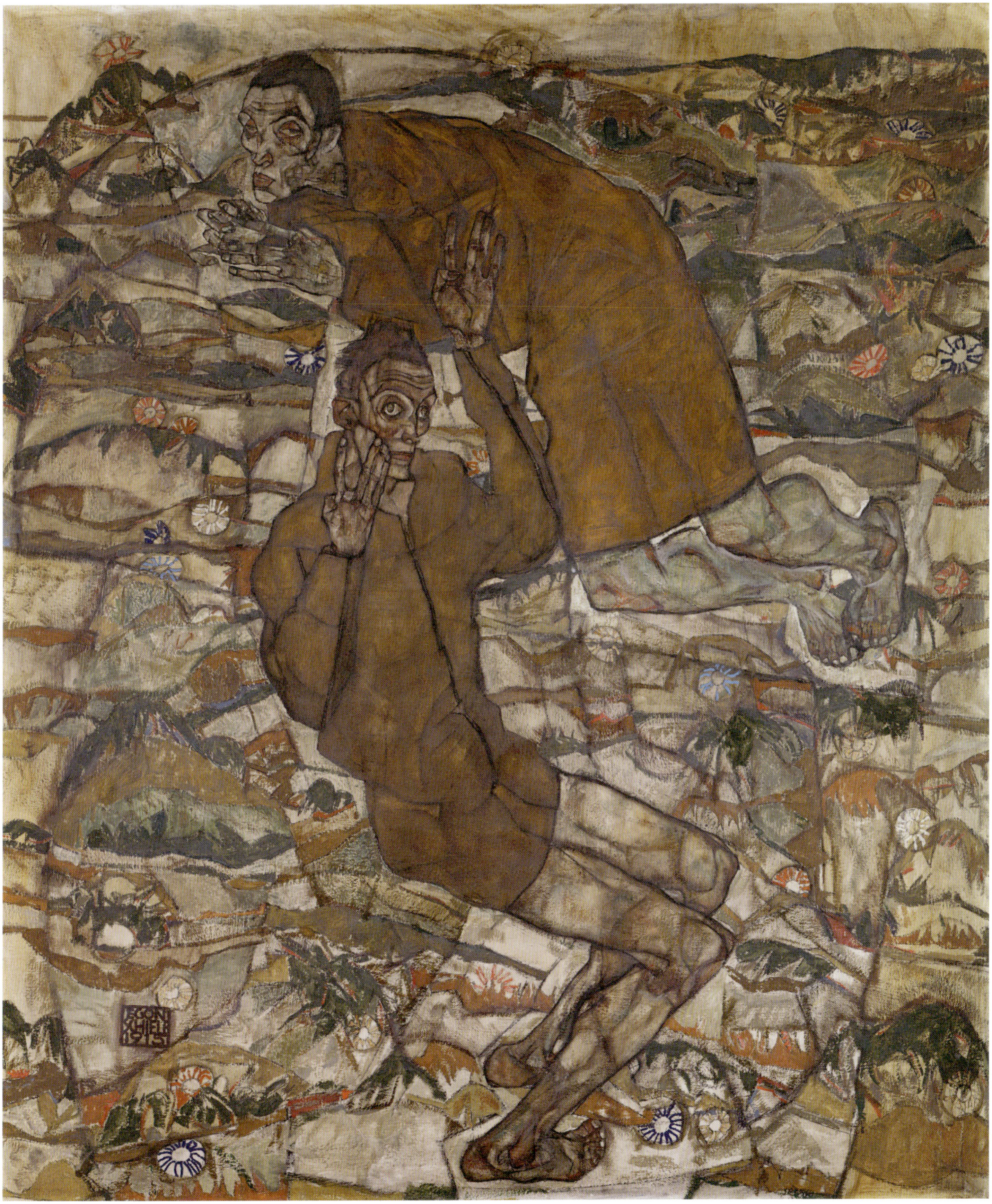

1915

WOMAN RUNNING

Although an interest in motion is apparent in numerous works from this period, sometimes even in depictions of stationary objects – the painting *Crescent of Houses II (Island Town)* (see p. 233), for example – Schiele rarely attempted movement as dramatic as this. It is quite wonderful how he captured the woman's speed formally and by the unusual rhythm in the contours of her legs. Although her movement threatens to burst through the boundaries of the sheet, his carefully plotted composition manages to contain it. One sees how far Schiele was willing to deviate from natural forms, when the subject matter demanded it, in order to achieve the desired expression.

Equally unnatural is the coloring: the flesh tones rendered mainly in bluish pink and greens, the dress she holds up out of her way in cinnabar-red with touches of blue-green and blue. The way the artist applied his strokes and spots of color with an only slightly moistened brush reveals the distinctly Fauvist quality of this painting. (RL)

Pencil, gouache on paper
47.1 × 31.4 cm
Leopold Museum, Vienna, Inv. 1424
K D.1735

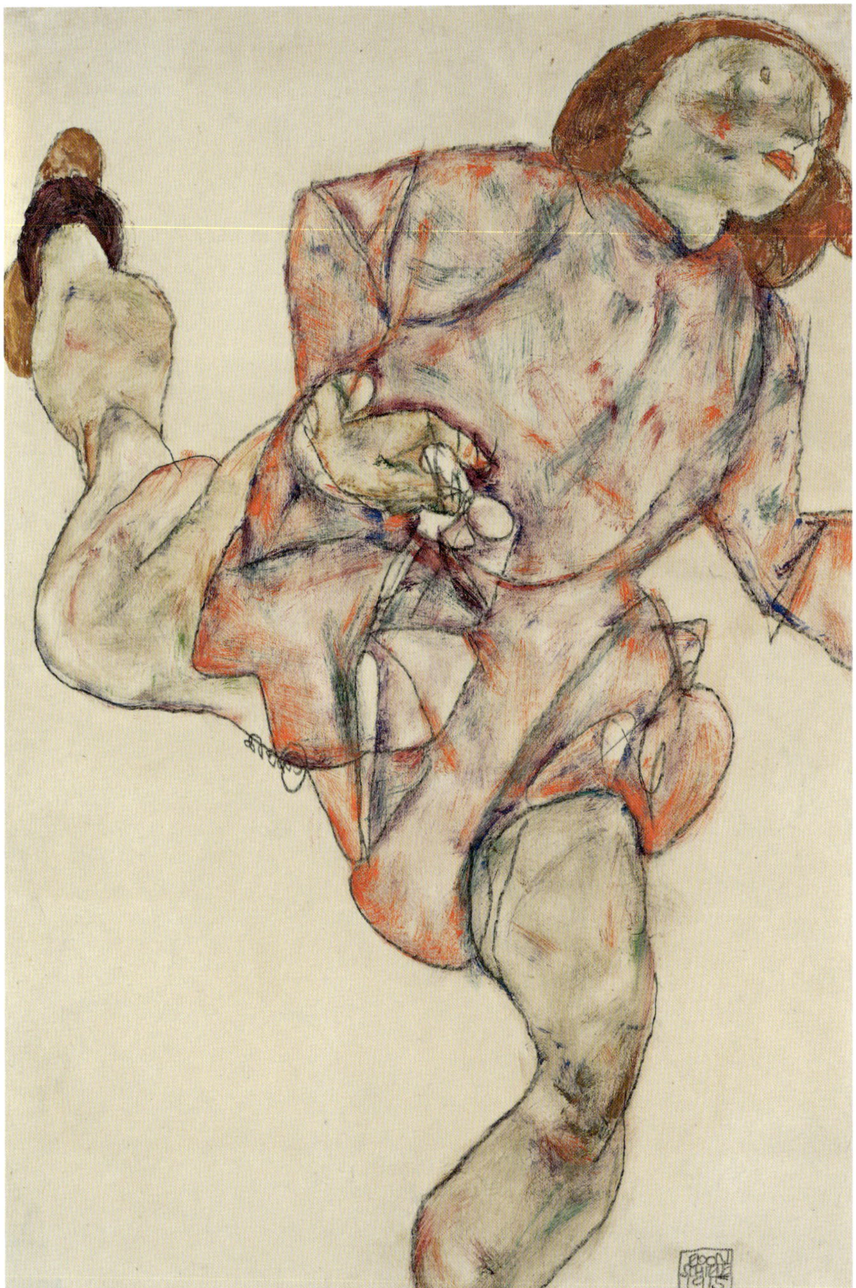

1915

NAKED GIRL WITH RAISED RIGHT LEG

Schiele was fond of exploiting unusual foreshortenings to give tension to his compositions. One can see them occasionally even in 1908, but beginning in 1910 they became more common. They were best captured by the harder lines of his drawing style from the years 1913 to 1915. In the present drawing, as in many other works from this period (see, for example, p. 193), sharply intersecting lines become dividing edges between planes.

This contorted figure with its astonishing perspective has been placed on the sheet at an angle. Her skin appears to be almost transparent, for the coloring, while suggesting the volume of her limbs, serves mainly to accentuate their contours. In this way Schiele emphasized their complex arrangement still further.

The few orange accents of the mouth, the nipple, the shoe and the stockings contrast with the mainly ocher tones of the flesh and hair. Even her labia have been toned down, an unusual touch for Schiele. The coloring thus becomes subordinate to the work's masterful draftsmanship. (RL)

Pencil, gouache on paper
48.3 × 32.8 cm
Leopold Museum, Vienna, Inv. 1421
K D.1741

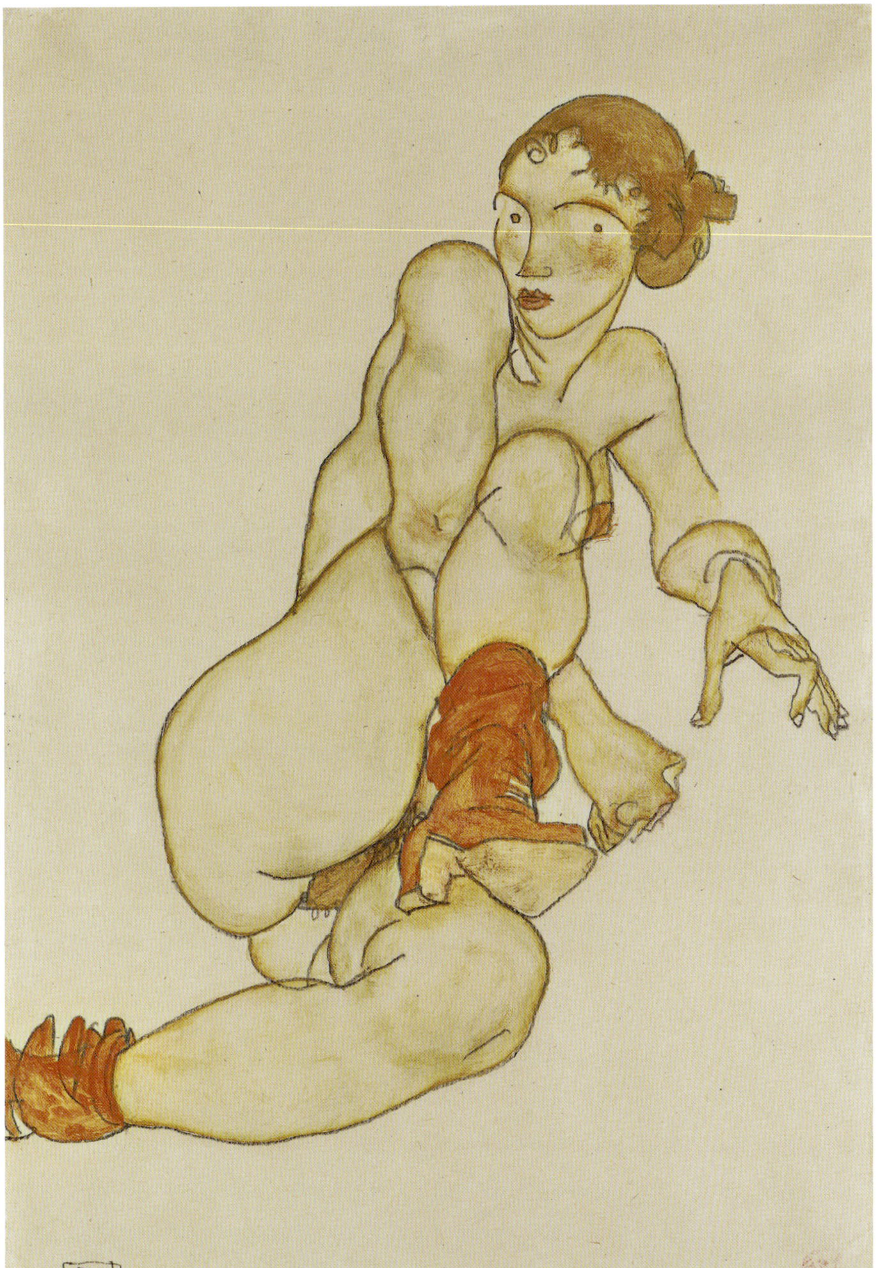
EGON
SCHIELE
1915

1915

EDITH SCHIELE WITH STRIPED DRESS, SITTING

In the 1960s, the model's sister, Adele Harms, wrote to me that in 1915, because good fabric was hard to come by during the war, she and her sister made dresses for themselves out of the striped curtain hanging in Schiele's studio. In the oil painting of his wife executed a short time after this drawing (L 267; K P.205), Schiele changed the stripes into different colors, but in his works in pencil and gouache he rendered them in their true black and white. He did not do this slavishly, of course; he added nuances of blue or brown to the black. But what is most impressive is Schiele's disposition of them, essentially drawing them with his brush. The result is a wonderful structure of lines that accurately reflects the three-dimensional form of the skirt and at the same time creates a delightful surface pattern. The hair and the jacket are rendered in subdued colors so that the black stripes and the various reds in the face and hands and on the collar dominate the drawing. To these he added only the dark blue-green of the ring and necklace and a lighter tint of the same color in the eyes and the skin. Edith Schiele's eyes were not this color, but the blue-green in combination with the red of her cheeks and especially of the lips seems perfectly natural. The slight sideways gaze of these light blue-green eyes causes her to look both questioning and withdrawn. (RL)

Pencil, gouache on paper
50.8 × 40.2 cm
Leopold Museum, Vienna, Inv. 4147
K D.1717

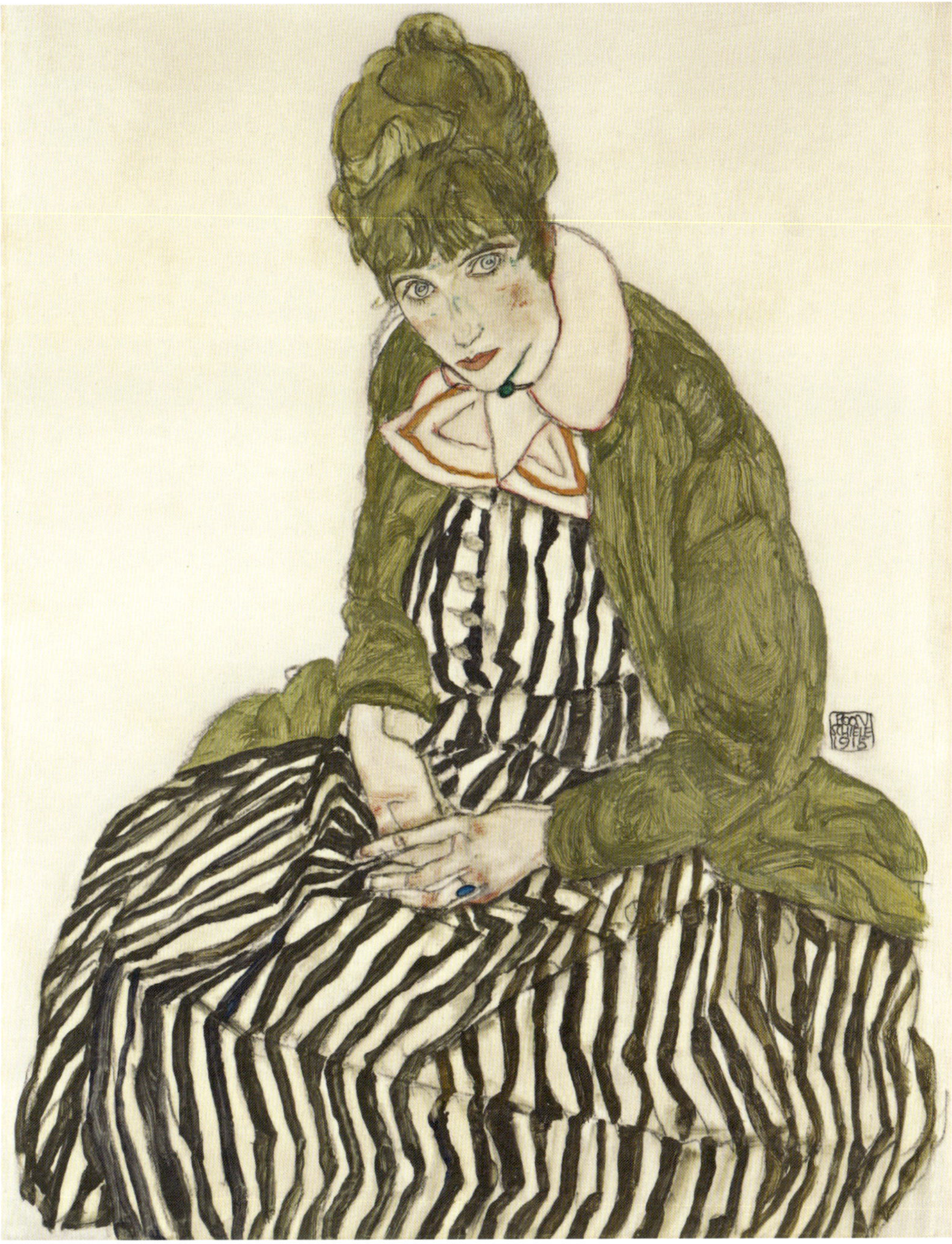

1915

PUTTO (ANTON PESCHKA JUN.)

Schiele produced two drawings of his little nephew, the first-born son of his younger sister. In this highly successful depiction he looks like a putto.

The outlines have been emphasized by the coloring. The almost straight vertical contour of the left side of the body, which continues without interruption in the left leg, is opposed on the right by a much more complex line – one that is even broken at the hip where the color has been omitted. This charming linear structure, in places suggestive of drawn bows, perfectly captures the naked body of a small child. Even its fatty wrinkles are precisely described. The slightly angled long axis of the cloth on which the child is standing runs parallel to an imaginary line drawn through his arms. The slight backward tilt of the head stabilizes the arrangement.

Despite its complicated pose, the child, wearing an expression of delightful innocence, seems perfectly natural. (RL)

Pencil, gouache on paper
51.8 × 31.9 cm
Leopold Museum, Vienna, Inv. 1423
K D.1705

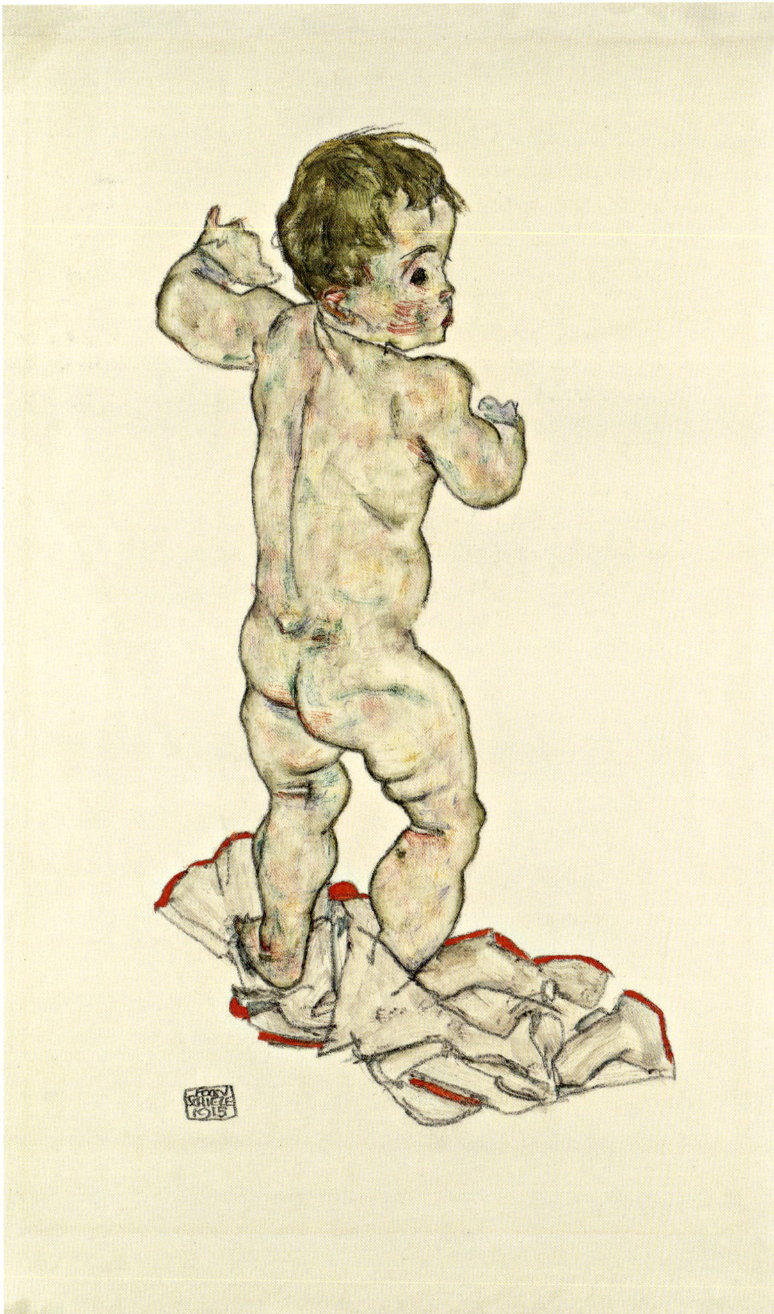

1916

NAKED WOMAN RECLINING. STUDY FOR *RECLINING WOMAN*

Schiele's wife served as the model for this semi-nude with her lower body exposed. In this same year, 1916, the artist depicted her in a seated pose with one leg raised and her genitals emphasized in a similar way (K D.1834). Both works were intended for a portfolio of five reproductions of erotic drawings. From the faces in the two drawings it would be difficult to determine that this woman is, in fact, Edith. More telling is the way she wears her hair, but Schiele usually depicted the character of his wife in a different way. Edith Schiele's sister, Adele Harms, assured me that in these particular works Schiele changed the face out of consideration for his wife.

What I have said in my text for the work on p. 54 about Schiele's habitual placement of his signature may not be entirely relevant in this case. Here he may have changed the horizontal format of the work into a vertical one deliberately so as to make it more explicit – it was to appear, after all, in a portfolio of erotic drawings.

What is much more important is that a year later Schiele incorporated the naked thighs and legs from this drawing almost unchanged into his painting *Reclining Woman* (see p. 265). There they are balanced by the similarly positioned arms, but here it is the bulk of the hairdo that echoes the angle of the right thigh and knee. One could point out a number of such formal relationships. This juxtaposition of forms is supported by the coloring. Schiele used the same unnatural ocher to highlight the contours of the thighs and those of the jacket and the raised skirt, also some of the internal structures of the two garments. For a contrasting color he chose blue-green. The highly expressive drawing and the sensitive coloring complement each other, and the combination is altogether satisfying. Schiele allows a portion of the raised skirt to reappear below the woman's spread thighs, thereby virtually framing and further emphasizing her nakedness (see also p. 76). (RL)

Pencil, gouache on paper
30.9 × 44.4 cm
Leopold Museum, Vienna, Inv. 2359
K D.1833

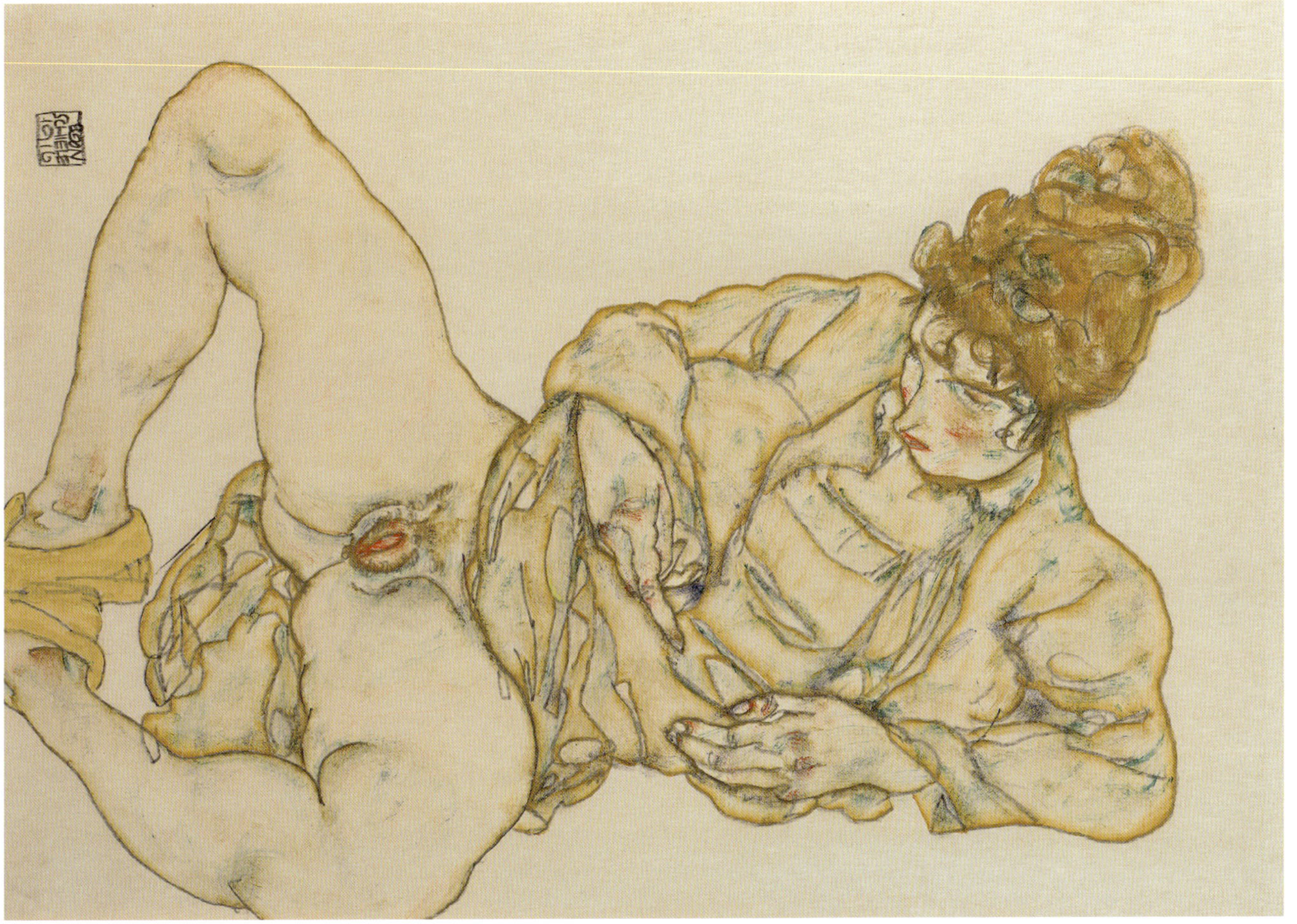

1916

LESBIAN COUPLE

This is one of the masterful drawings from 1916 – both in its composition and in its deft use of line. The main axis of this towering arrangement is a gentle curve that extends downward from the two women's heads along the right side of the body of the one in front and into her right thigh. Her raised garment billows still farther to the right. This is balanced on the left by an approximately straight contour. The clear lines of the drapery folds extend upward at a slight angle from the concave left side of the woman's body, and an opposing angle is described by the raised hem of her slip.

Schiele was never put off by ugliness in a motif. Not only did he include it, but he also exaggerated it – even in his later development – so as to present a specific type. In this drawing he communicated the corpulence of the figure in front by showing us not only her massive figure and naked buttocks, but even more tellingly by suggesting the wrinkles of fat on her right thigh beneath her underclothes. The woman behind, by contrast, seems almost emaciated, and the foreshortening of her face makes her appear even less attractive than she may have been. She has a long nose and her lips, indicated by only two parallel lines, seem to be pressed together. There is a certain rigidity in her upward gaze; perhaps it expresses indifference. (RL)

Pencil on paper
49 × 32.5 cm
Leopold Museum, Vienna, Inv. 2362
K D.1824

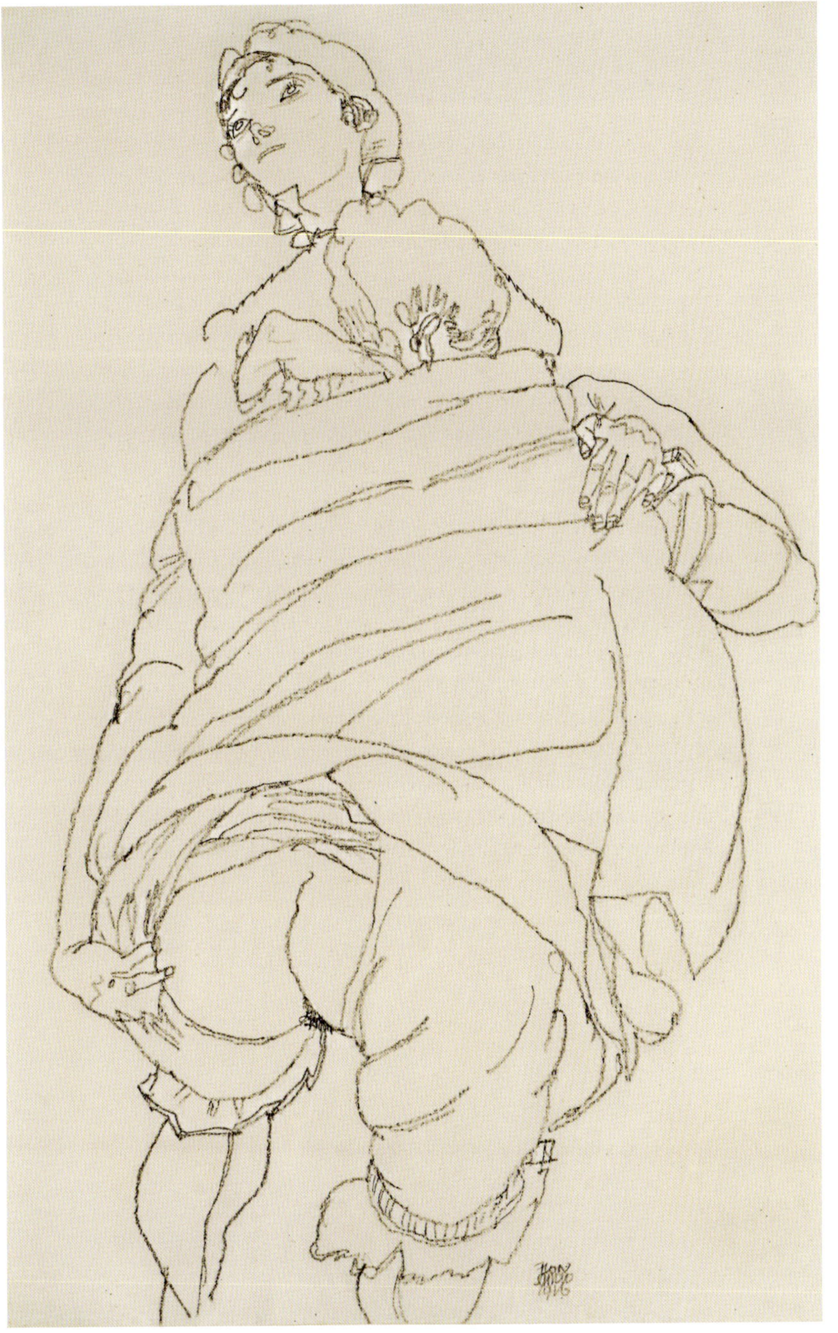

1916

RUSSIAN PRISONER OF WAR

There is a simple explanation for the fact that the right hand is missing in this depiction. When Schiele worked on paintings, he would divide up the painting surface beforehand. When working on paper (or on smaller oil sketches), however, he often neglected this. Thus he would sometimes run out of paper, like he did in this instance with the right hand of the man, which would have gone beyond the edge of the sheet. Leaving it out was the right decision in terms of formal considerations, even though it is noticeably missing from the portrayed person.
If we compare this portrait of a Russian officer with works from 1914, such as the *Sitting Semi-Nude with Blue Hairband* (K D.1594) or the male figure (K D.1644) on the reverse side of the present work on paper, it is unmissable that this depiction is closer to nature. This becomes even more apparent with the portrait of the *One-Year Volunteer* (see p. 259) and in the works of the following years. Schiele increasingly dispensed with geometrical shapes in his drawings – in the case of the Russian prisoner of war such geometrical elements can be discerned only in details like the right cheek, for instance.
Schiele aptly portrayed the prisoner's dull brooding expression, accomplishing a painterly master stroke with the three-dimensional rendering of this uniformed Russian. (RL)

Pencil, gouache on paper
46.5 × 30.5 cm
Leopold Museum, Vienna, Inv. 1417
K D.1838

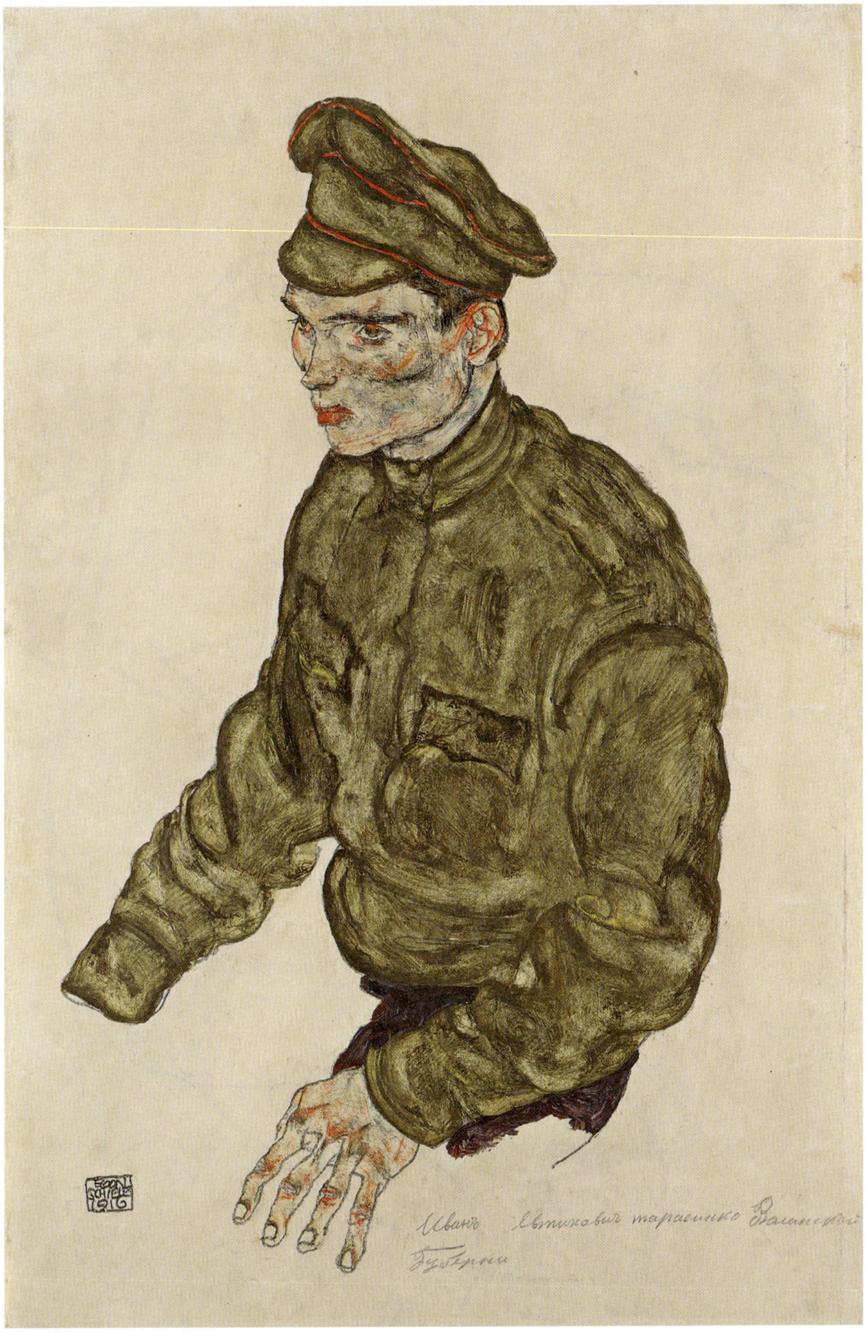

1916

WRITING DESK IN PRISONER-OF-WAR CAMP MÜHLING

In the prisoner-of-war camp at Mühling, Schiele not only did portraits of his superiors and a number of Russians, but he also drew the offices and his own workplace, as can be seen here. This drawing, with its wonderfully clean lines, is perhaps the most beautiful of these interiors.

Depth is suggested by the wall seen in perspective, with its notices and the bookshelf, and the view from above across two desks placed next to each other. In addition, Schiele leads the eye back into space with an almost zigzag movement of lines at a slight angle from the horizontal. His depictions of individual objects reveal draftsmanship of an extraordinary delicacy. Their volumes are suggested not only by perspective but also by alternating stronger and thinner lines and the occasional use of shading. The candle – to point out only one example – is clearly set apart from the wooden slat to the left of it and the match holder behind. (RL)

Pencil, gouache, colored ink, colored chalk on paper
46.1 × 29.9 cm
Leopold Museum, Vienna, Inv. 2360
K D.1871

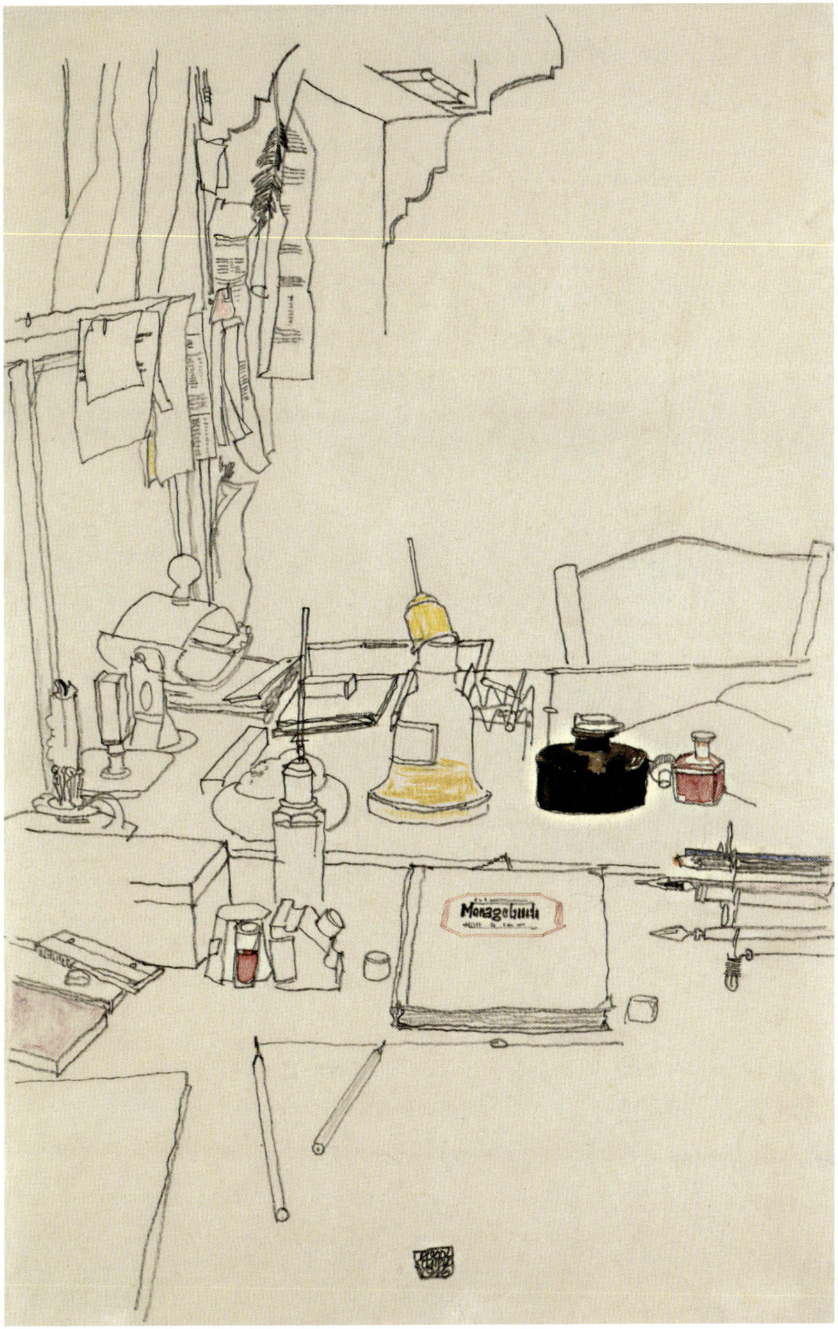
Monagsbuch

1916

ONE-YEAR VOLUNTEER

This is a portrait of one of Schiele's superiors. The figure ends indistinctly below the soldier's left shoulder, at the bottom of his shirt – a counterweight to the contour of the head – and along a roughly diagonal line leading down to the cuff of his right sleeve. The line of the hand, only partially sketched, points in the opposite direction, paralleling the less-pronounced axis of the slightly bent head.

The work is a fine example of Schiele's much more realistic approach at this time. He has even noted the distortion of the face's outline through the glasses. Although he presented only a portion of the figure, he managed to make this fragment a full psychological portrait. In photographs the young man appears to have been more lighthearted and cheerful; Schiele – as was his habit – transformed him into an earnest person with an intense, inquisitive gaze. The artist probably emphasized the academic, intellectual look of this volunteer so as to indicate how basically unsuited such men were for military life.

The light face, painted mainly in reddish tones, is effectively set off by a darker blue uniform. Schiele freely invented the faint traces of red in the jacket and its varying shades of blue, and the same applies to the yellow-olive of the shirt – a color he particularly favored. Here he placed it against the blue of the uniform and also related it to the man's blond hair. His rendering of the uniform is masterful. The lovely brushstrokes in various shades of blue are topped in a number of areas by highlights in opaque-white, gray-white, and reddish white. Although his painting is uncommonly free, it precisely describes the garment in question.

Schiele chose this work for inclusion in a portfolio of twelve full-size reproductions. It was published in 1917 by the Richard Lányi bookshop in Vienna in an edition of 400, and was the only such portfolio to appear during Schiele's lifetime. (RL)

Pencil, gouache on paper
48.2 × 31.4 cm
Leopold Museum, Vienna, Inv. 1418
K D.1849

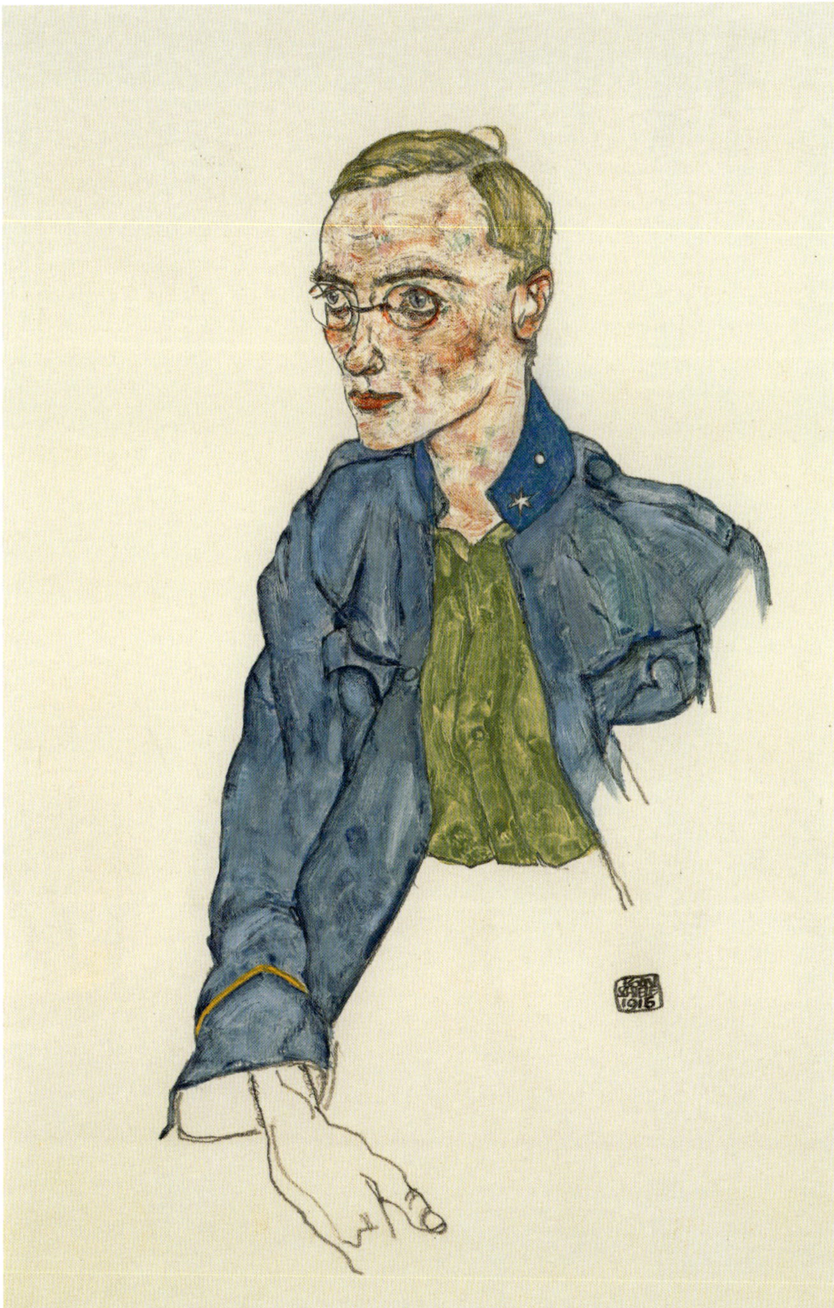

1917

PACKING ROOM

Schiele's former superior in the military, Dr. Hans Rosé, commissioned the artist to draw the most important rooms of the "Imperial Royal Supply Depot for Officers on active service" in Vienna and of its 28 branches all over the Habsburg Empire.
In keeping with the last period of Schiele's oeuvre, the artist's renderings were much closer to nature than before. While this is apparent in several details in this depiction, such as the broom hanging in the foreground or the bottles on the table, it is less obvious in the small strokes next to them – for it is not immediately clear that these casually drawn strokes are meant to represent bottle wrappings. Schiele beautifully rendered the representationality of the wicker basket in front as well as its three-dimensionality, both in itself and in relation to the table behind it, with nearly horizontal strokes, without lapsing into pedantic naturalism. (RL)

Black chalk on paper
43.8 × 30.1 cm
Leopold Museum, Vienna, Inv. 1416
K D.2161

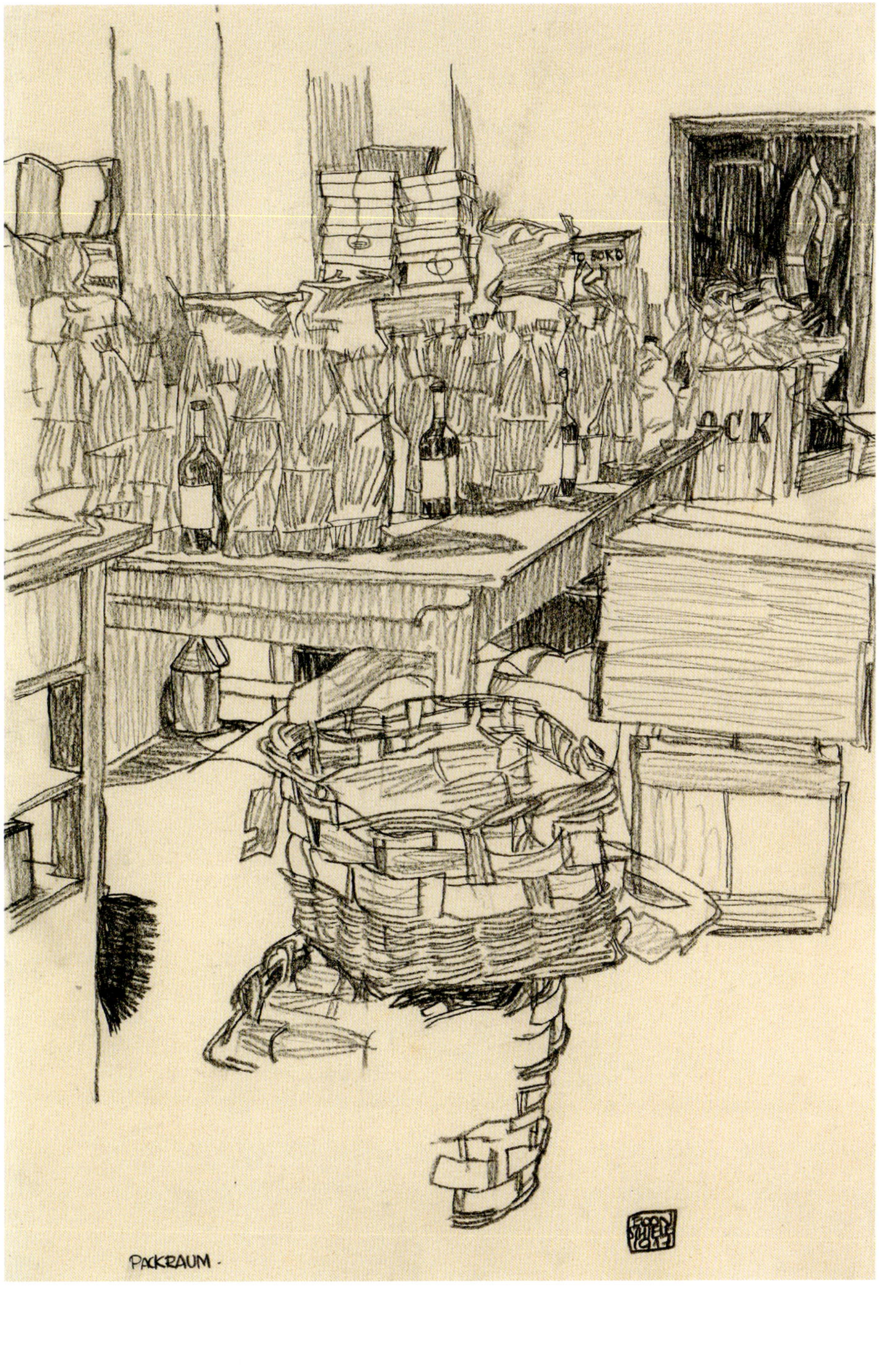
PACKRAUM -

1917

LEANING WOMAN IN UNDERWEAR

This woman sits casually, propping herself up with her left arm. The result is a composition filled with contrary movement – in the legs, for example, or in the head and the arm below it. Yet the line of the arm parallels that of the right calf, and an imaginary line drawn from the peak of the kerchief through the nose roughly continues the axis of the left calf. Correspondences such as these give the composition its solidity.

A degree of mannerism enters into Schiele's art in this period. Here it is evident only in minor details, such as the lacy hem of the woman's undergarments and the internal lines on her back. In other respects the drawing is altogether clear and sensitive. By varying the pressure on his crayon, Schiele managed to create lines of different thicknesses shading from black to gray. His brilliant draftsmanship is particularly apparent in his rendering of the face. In terms of composition, the way the sharply turned head presses against the shoulder and the arm extending downward from it is most impressive. (RL)

Black chalk on paper
29.1 × 45.3 cm
Leopold Museum, Vienna, Inv. 1399
K D.1922

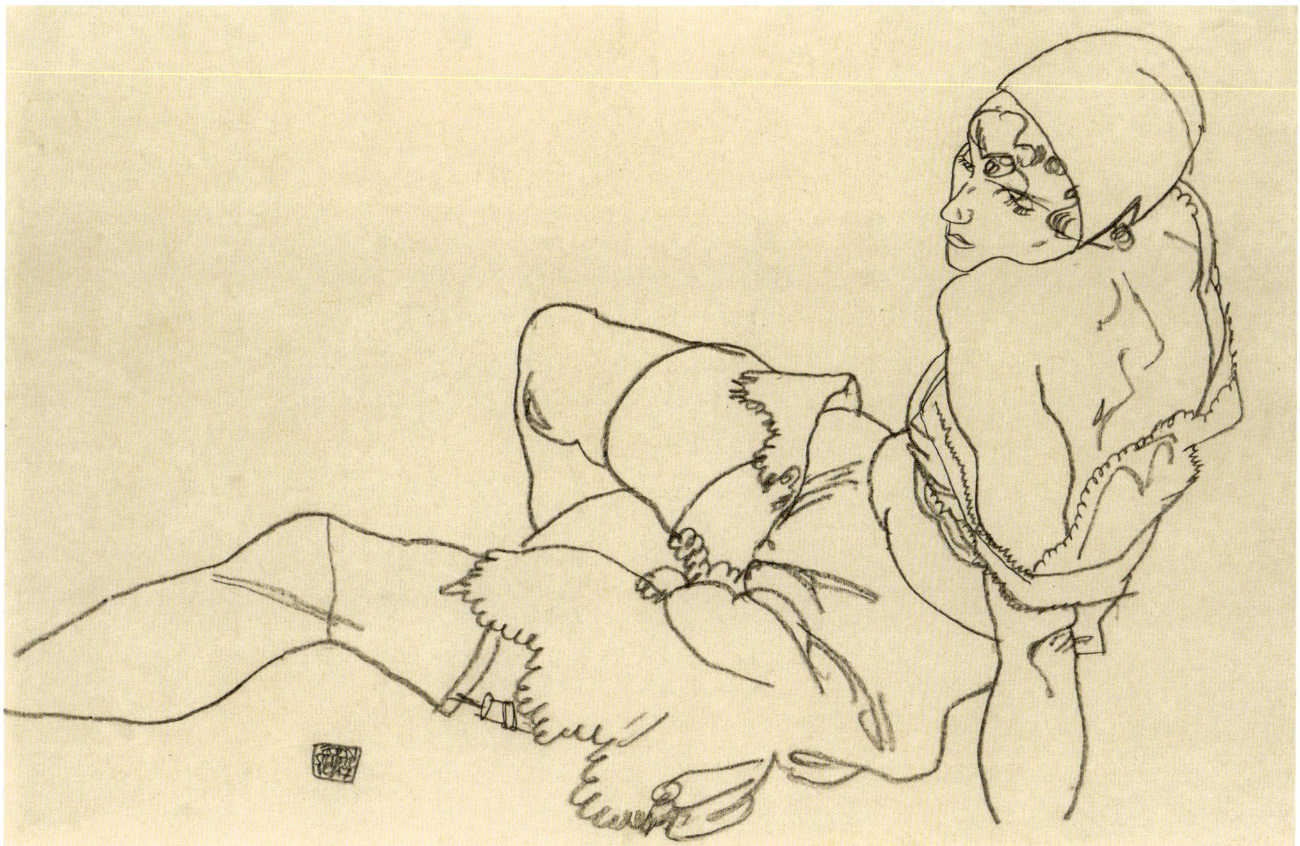

1917

RECLINING WOMAN

The undulating white cloth with its agitated folds appears to have been spread out on a sheet of gold foil. On it lies a nude woman with dark reddish brown wavy hair, masterfully drawn and painted with the brush. Her somewhat melancholy, severe expression is convincingly rendered. This is the loveliest head in all of Schiele's paintings from 1917 and 1918.

The bent arms and legs correspond to one another, as do the one hand and one foot. To emphasize this, some of the white cloth has been draped across the woman's waist, effectively dividing her body in two. In his painting *Embrace (Lovers II)* (L 276; K P.304), also from 1913, he did not set off the fabric convincingly from either the bodies or the background, but here the delicate drawing of the cloth and the contours of the body are successfully combined; the figure is as though interwoven into the fabric. But so as not to push the symmetry too far, Schiele created small deviations. The axis of the figure, unlike that of the cloth, is not horizontal but slightly angled. This brings the left knee much closer to the edge of the cloth than the right one, and the right elbow even reaches beyond it.

It was to emphasize this shape that Schiele chose to use a darker color for the legs than for the upper body. The discrepancy was intended; it has nothing to do with the fact that the painting was based on studies drawn from different models. The spread legs come from a drawing of Schiele's wife (see p. 251), while the head is borrowed from a study made with a professional model.[5] Schiele's ability to combine different motifs into a wholly convincing single image was remarkable. One sees it in a number of his cityscapes.

This work is unquestionably one of the most important achievements of the artist's final years. (RL)

5 | There is also a separate drawing of the left hand and arm (K D.1924) and two designs on a sketchbook page (Sketchbook 1916/17).

Oil on canvas
96 × 171 cm
Leopold Museum, Vienna, Inv. 626
L 278; K P.306

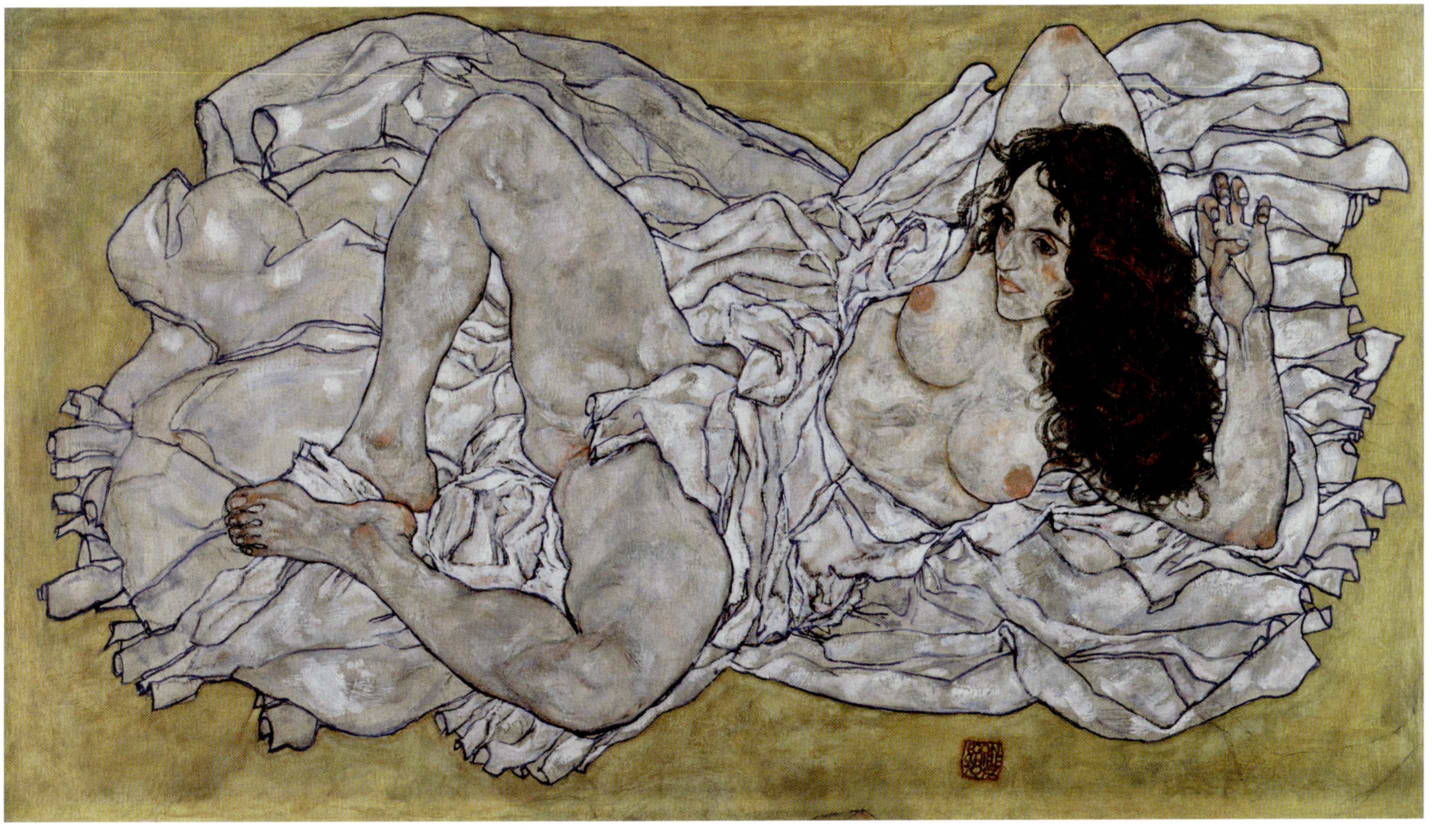

1917

KNEELING GIRL, RESTING ON BOTH ELBOWS

This is another of the drawings that Schiele later signed in such a way that it would appear he had executed it in vertical format. The girl, however, is clearly kneeling on the floor, braced on her elbows.

The sculptural effect of this figure is already assured by her placement on the page, at an angle running from the left foreground back and to the right. Her elevated buttocks dominate the image. They clearly inspired Schiele to create this erotic drawing, for his lines seem to caress their fleshy contours.

The colors are restrained and applied with a relatively dry brush. With them each area is given its appropriate volume. The cooler greens and blues of the bunched-up slip are exquisitely contrasted to the warm tones of the skin and the dark red-brown of the hair.

This drawing is one of the relatively few drawings from his late period in which Schiele achieved the same level of artistry that one finds in so many of his earlier ones. With this much more realistic style, he managed to imbue his figure with a wonderful vitality. (RL)

Black chalk, gouache on paper
28.8 × 44.4 cm
Leopold Museum, Vienna, Inv. 1397
K D.1952

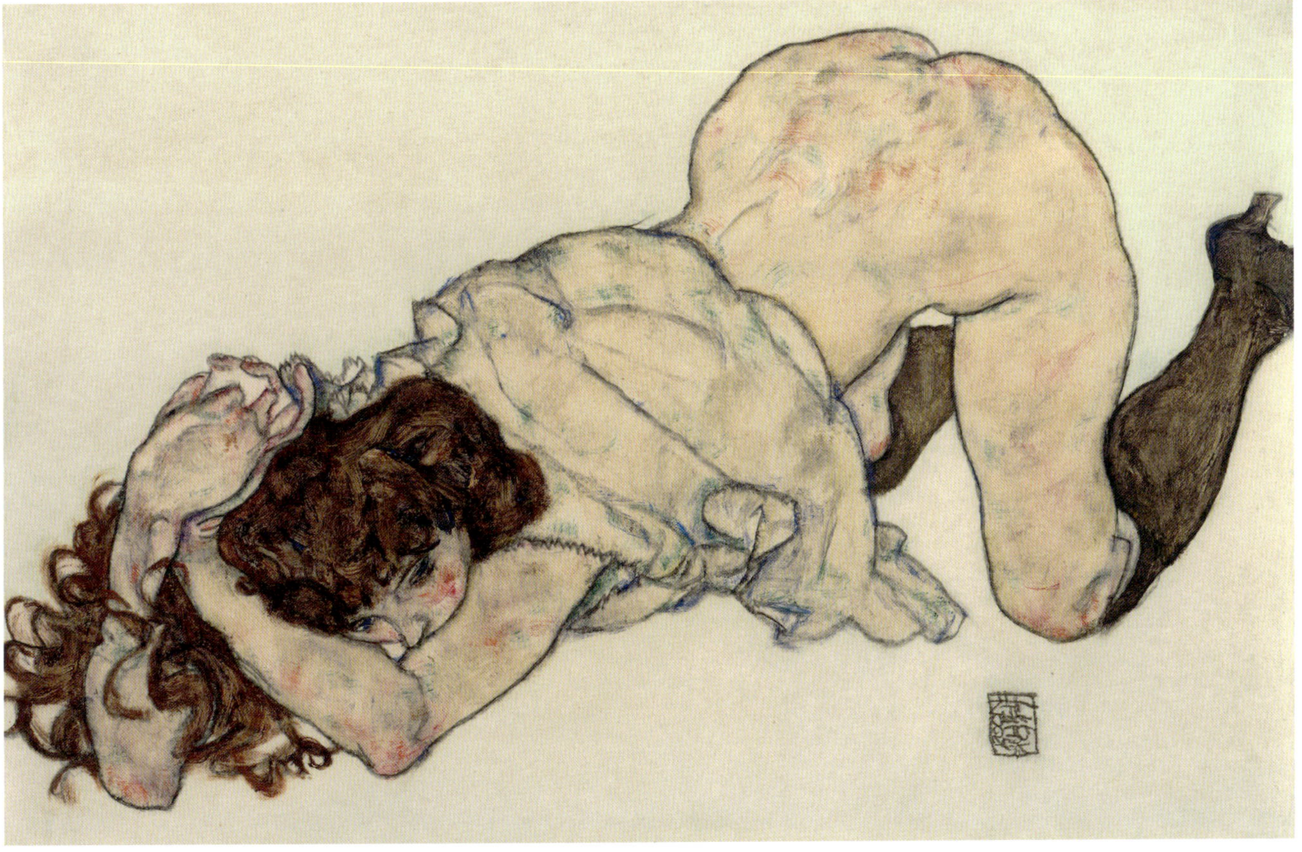

1918

PORTRAIT OF THE DEAD KLIMT ("GUSTAV KLIMT")

Gustav Klimt died on February 6, 1918. The next day Schiele made three drawings of him in the morgue of the Vienna General Hospital, where he had been shaved. He indicated the date on this drawing.

Schiele presumably did this drawing in a horizontal format, but then inscribed, signed, and dated it as though it were to be viewed vertically. The facial expression becomes more believable and more powerful if one simply turns the drawing back to the horizontal position. What makes it so successful is Schiele's masterful internal drawing.

Schiele never erased. If he corrected a line, as he did here with the contour of the nose, he left the original as well, for he felt that any line he had drawn had a value of its own. Comparing this portrait with the two others, I share the opinion of the Schiele expert Erwin Mitsch that this is Schiele's most impressive rendering of the dead Klimt, despite the twice-drawn nose area. (RL)

Black chalk on paper
46.9 × 30.1 cm
Leopold Museum, Vienna, Inv. 1415
K D.2443

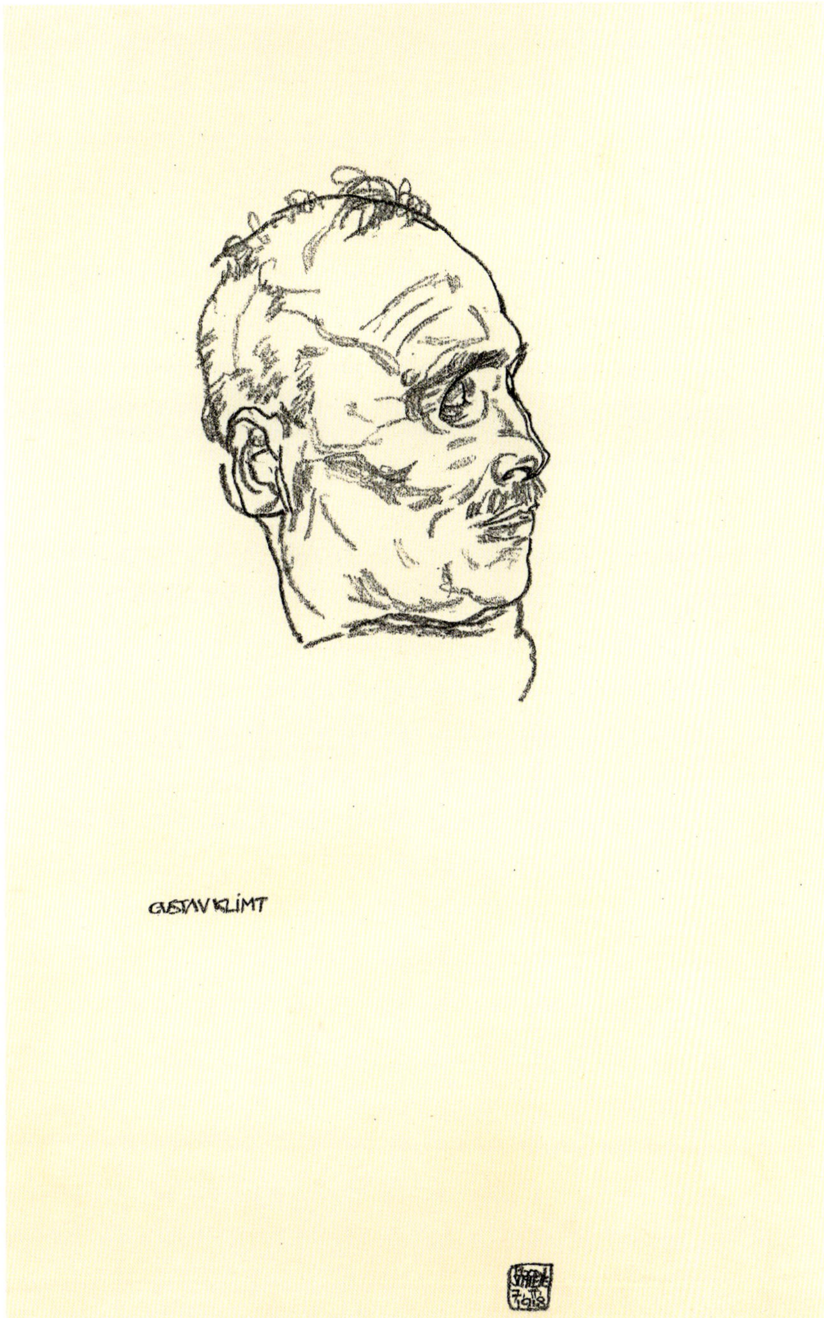
GUSTAV KLIMT

1918

ROUND TABLE. POSTER FOR THE 49TH VIENNA SECESSION EXHIBITION

This work is doubtlessly among the most congenial achievements of Schiele's late oeuvre. The composition may at first glance appear simple, but this is only on account of its completely natural solutions. The table rising moderately towards the right provides the basis on which the main part of the composition, which pulls steeply upwards, is built. The upper end of the table is more inclined to the left. The figure seated at the head (it is believed that Schiele depicted himself here) is also inclined towards that side, as are indeed the majority of chairs and figures. This results in a formal preponderance to the left, which is just about balanced in an exciting manner by means of several elements tending towards the opposite direction – such as the two men sitting close together on the left side of the table as well as the one figure above them. In between them even the table appears to be leaning towards the right. While this is unnatural, it is perfectly justifiable for formal reasons. What is more, the lettering drops slightly in its progression from left to right. This is one of the reasons why this lettering constitutes a compositional necessity. Therefore it is wrong to reproduce this poster or its sketch without the letters, which has been done in the past – all the more as lettering and representational depiction were brought together into a unity of rare beauty in this work, both in terms of shape and color. The lemon yellow, the different shades of red, ocher and reddish brown enter into a glorious chord with the delicate gray of the table, the parts that have been left blank, as well as with the black of the drawing, the background and lettering. Following a series of dull or at least less felicitous color combinations found in many paintings from the preceding years, Schiele once again achieved great success, the work's coloring being equally as compelling as its formal structure. (RL)

Lithograph on paper
68.5 × 53 cm
Leopold Museum, Vienna, Inv. 224
K G.15b

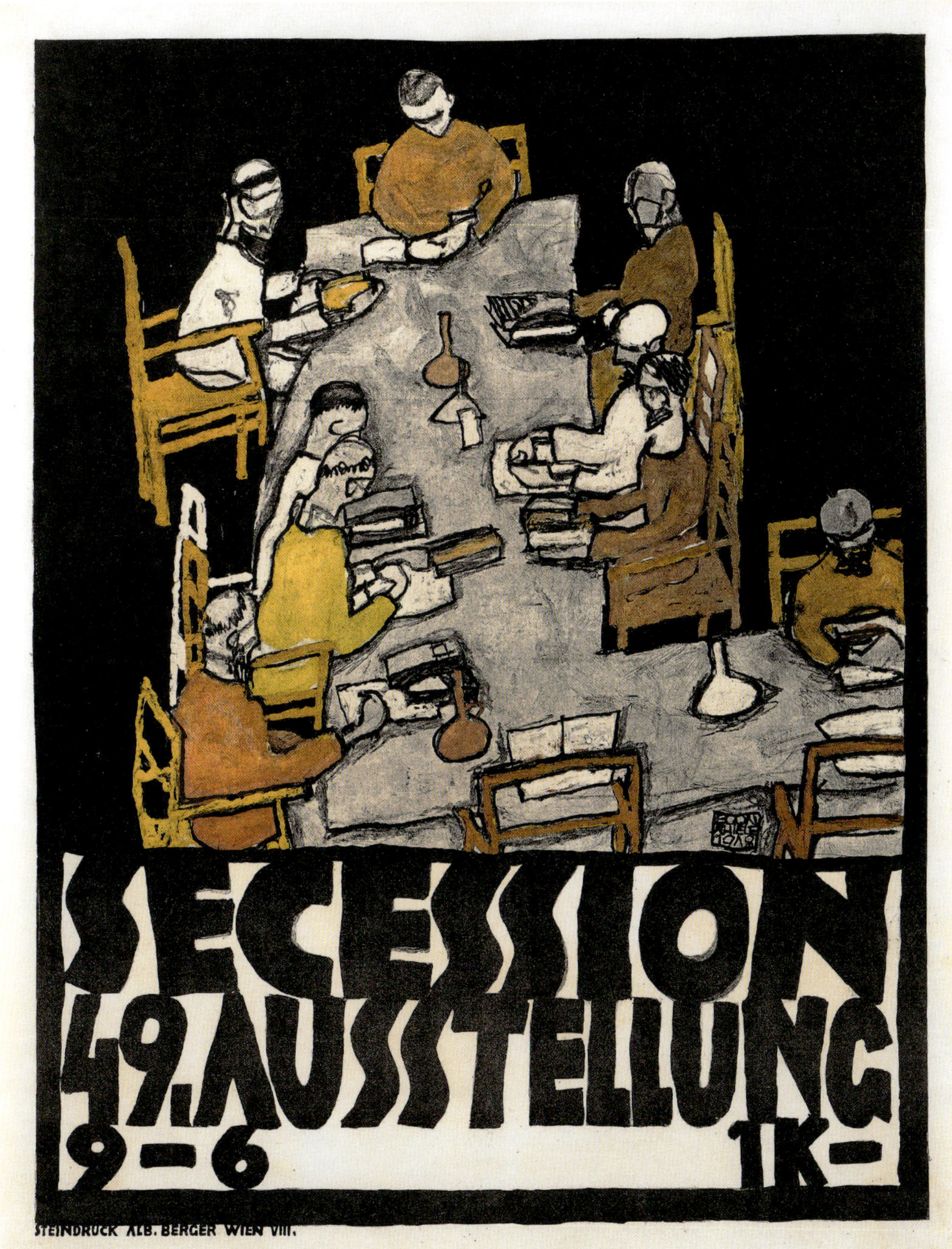
SECESSION
49. AUSSTELLUNG
9-6
1K-
STEINDRUCK ALB. BERGER WIEN VIII.

1918

RECLINING FEMALE NUDE WITH LONG HAIR

The drawing style of Schiele's late oeuvre, with his preference for convex contours, was well suited to the ample rotundness of this woman. In a number of these curves one notes a certain mannerism – those describing the inside of the arm, for example, or the one tracing the body on the left, which was drawn in a single stroke from the top and repeats a portion of the outline of the breast. This is also true of the line that cuts into the right knee from below. It is difficult to see, but this is actually the contour line of the left calf. In this area the artist was less interested in describing the reality before him than in providing his composition with an ornamental termination. One frequently sees a certain detachment from the actual forms of his motif in Schiele's early works as well, but there he tended to transform them into more exciting ornamental shapes.

It is true that those earlier compositions, brilliant as they are, do not always display the degree of technical mastery that he demonstrates so fully in his last year. And it would be unfair to suggest that the greater movement and especially the heightened realism of his final works are somehow less than positive developments. In contrast to the above-mentioned curve of the calf on the left side of the present composition, the contour of the thigh and pelvis, drawn in a single stroke, is not only elegant, but it also perfectly describes the woman's form. The imposing realism in this rendering of a female nude is in no way lessened by the fact that Schiele shows us the left thigh only where it lies next to the right one and omits the left arm altogether.

The arrangement of the composition is extremely clear. The arm descending at an angle forms its center axis, virtually dividing the image in two. The "step-like" sequence of the head, shoulder, and pelvis creates added interest.

Internal painting was hardly necessary here: the soft shading executed with the side of the crayon fully supplants it. One has the impression that light is playing over the naked skin. The shading in the face and the subtle drawing of its contours create an expression that's amazingly full of life. (RL)

Black chalk on paper
28.5 × 45.7 cm
Leopold Museum, Vienna, Inv. 2384
K D.2406

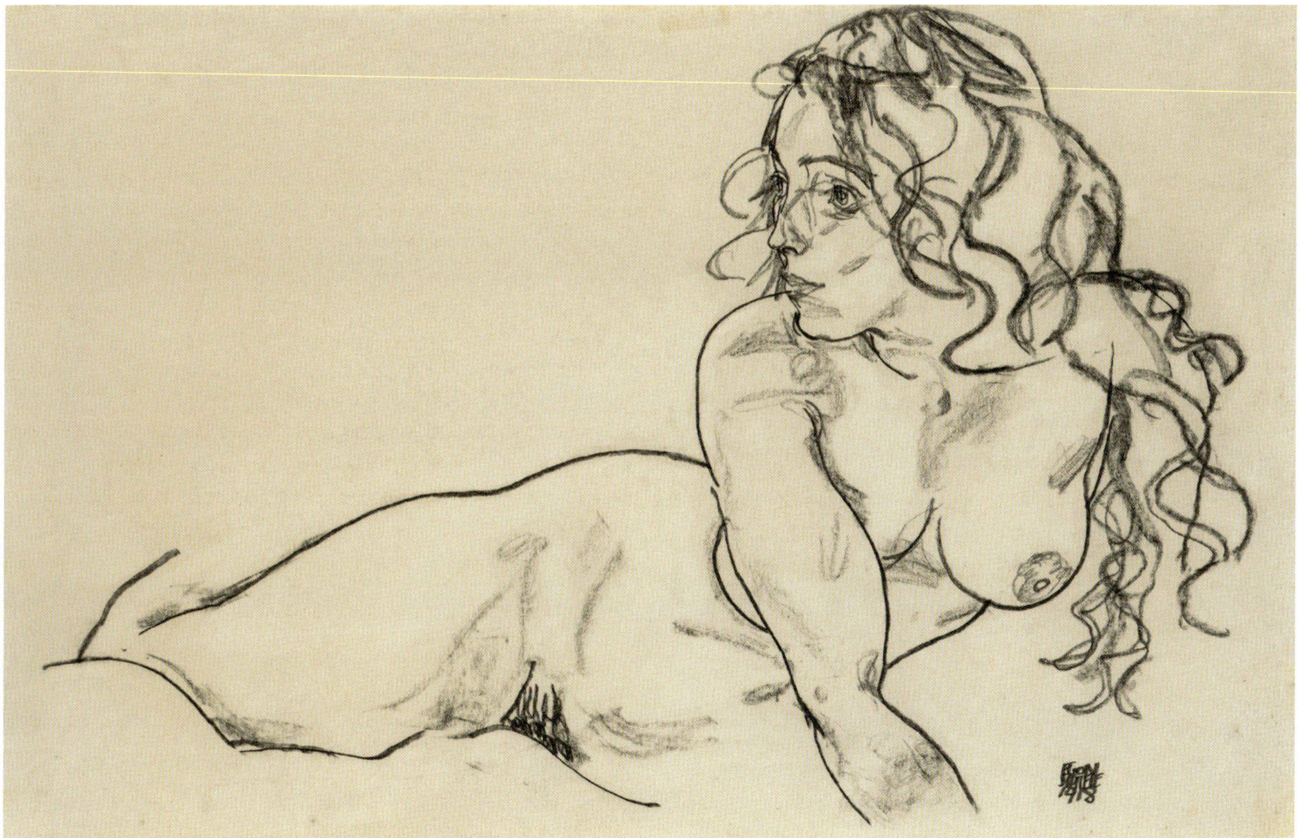

1918 (UNFINISHED)

TWO SQUATTING WOMEN

Schiele made several sketches (Sktechbook 1918) incorporating two crouching nudes side by side before settling on this well-balanced composition in which its inherent spirituality gives it a symbolic quality. The proportions of the crouching figures, the slight space that separates them, and the larger spaces between them and the four edges of the painting are precisely calculated. Their bodies and poses are very similar, and they have been placed symmetrically in the picture space, both gazing forward. Their faces are deliberately generic, apparently only representing types. All of these features contribute to the monumentality of the image.

Despite their great similarity, there are a number of subtle differences between the women's poses and expressions. The gaze of the one on the left, the way her head is turned slightly to the side, and the way she holds her legs slightly closer together suggest a trace of shyness, one that seems confirmed by the bit of cloth covering her genitals. The woman on the right, by contrast, gazes fixedly at the viewer, her legs spread farther apart and her genitals fully exposed. Still, there is no hint of the erotic. She appears to be the quintessential female. It was only in the last year of his life that Schiele created nudes such as this.

The V-shaped openings created by the spread legs and accented by the inner contours of the thighs are harmoniously closed off by the configurations of the arms, shoulders, and heads. The overall outer contour of each figure, much like that of the crouching woman in *The Family* (L 289; K P.326), takes the form of an oval. The formation of this shape is facilitated here by the absence of the child in the lower part of the figures. Important and immediately apparent, is the treatment of the background, which is quite similar to that of the Gütersloh portrait (L 294; K P.322).

Both of these figures – more obviously the one on the left, as she is more finished – are extraordinarily three-dimensional, as is to be expected in Schiele's late style. He commented that in this work he meant to enhance the sculptural quality of the figures by contrasting them to the brightly colored background, and in this he was wholly successful. (RL)

Oil, opaque color on canvas
110 × 140.5 cm
Leopold Museum, Vienna, Inv. 464
L 296; K P.327

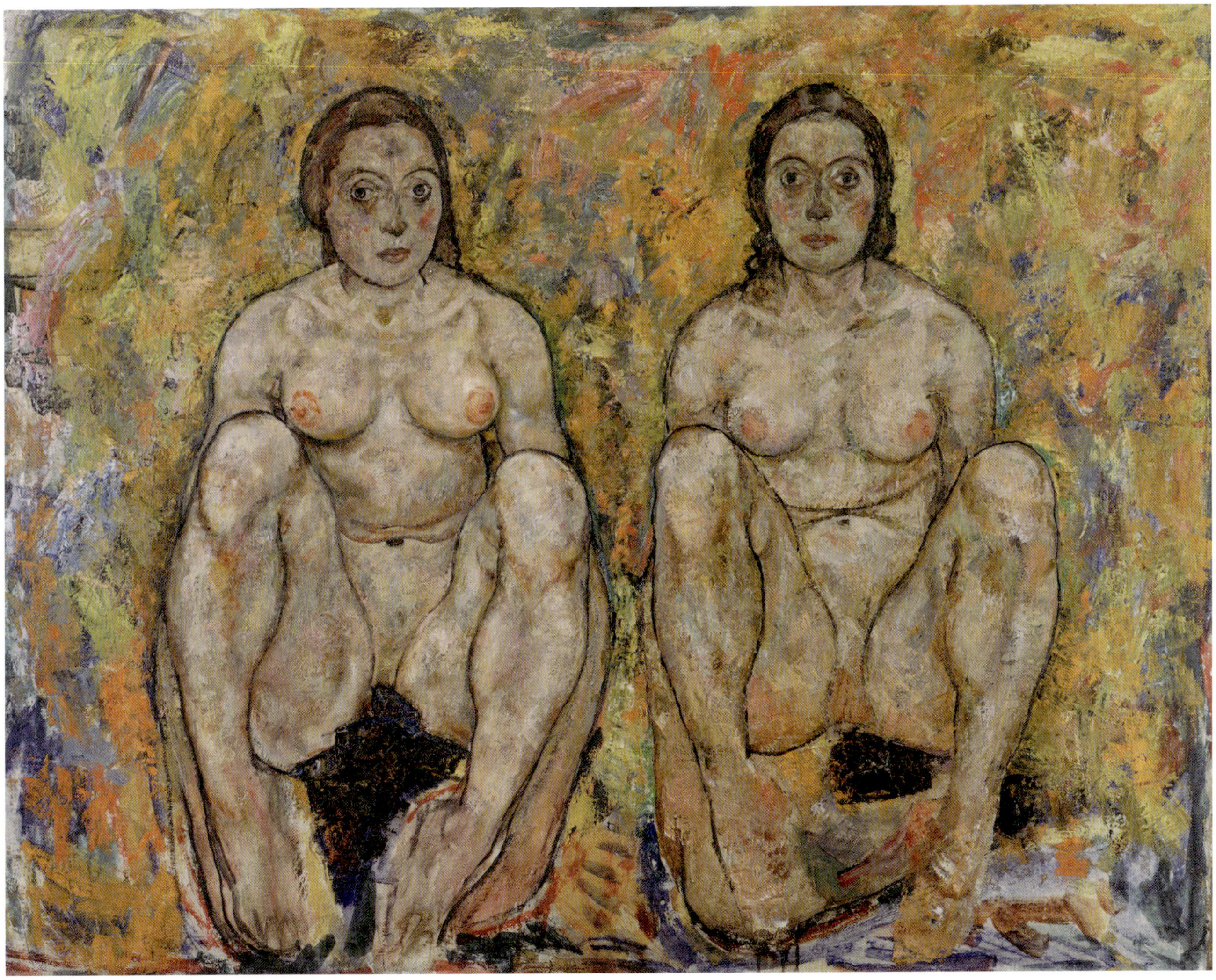

1918

SITTING GIRL WITH SPREAD THIGHS

This woman's gaze appears to devour us, and her revealing pose and unruly hair are all in character with it.
Her expression is as fascinating as the bravura drawing of her hair or the assured lines describing her face and the rest of her body. Although there are again traces of mannerism, Schiele has varied his lines with great delicacy, from incisive hardness to broad smudges, from deepest black to a warmer gray. (RL)

Black chalk on paper
46 × 30.6 cm
Leopold Museum, Vienna, Inv. 2341
K D.2417

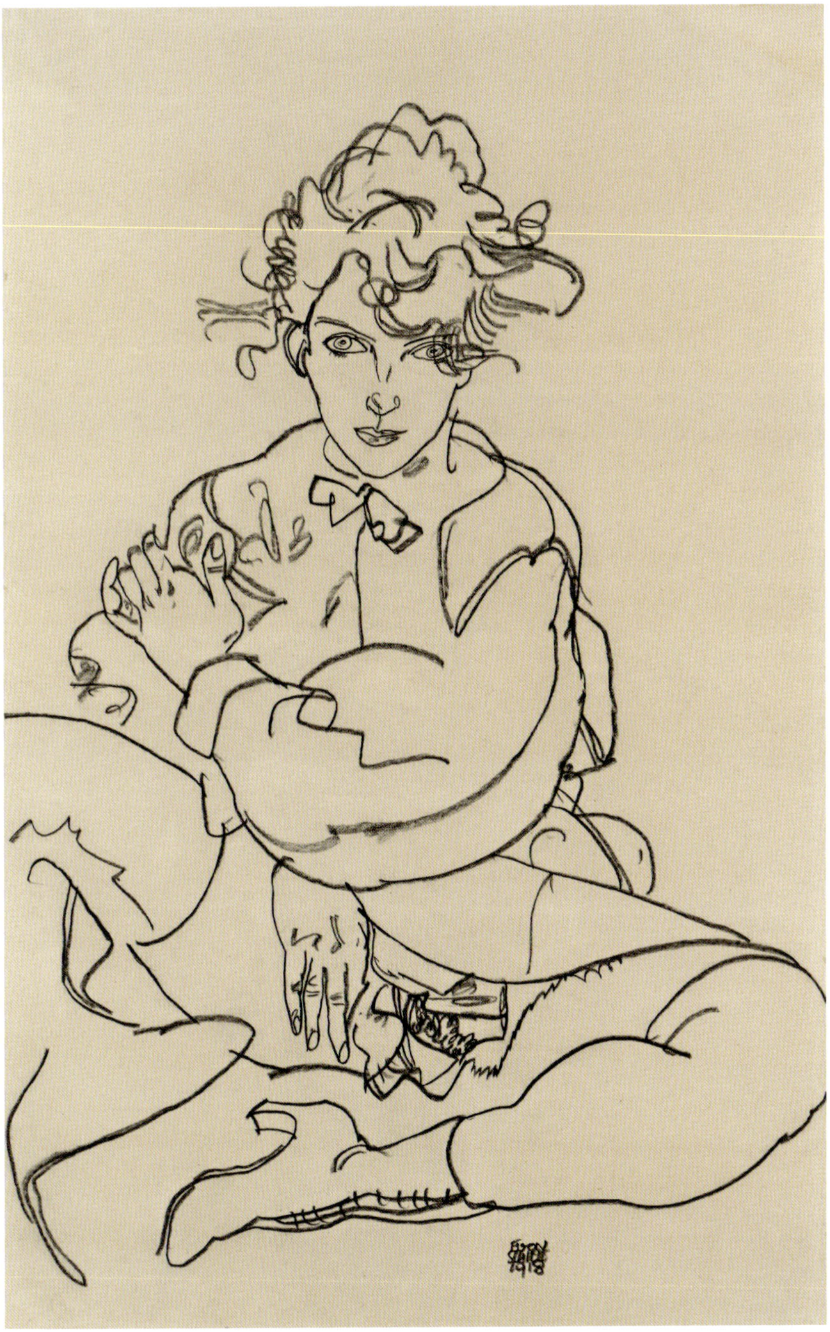

1918 (UNFINISHED)

THREE STANDING WOMEN (FRAGMENT)

Schiele made a number of sketches in preparation for this painting (Sketchbooks 1918). In some of them the grouping of female nudes stands alone, and in others they are placed next to a male figure. In one of the latter, the arrangement of the three women is very similar to what we see here, but in this painting Schiele decided to leave out the man.

The woman in the middle serves as the calm center of the composition and to that end is presented in a frontal pose. The one on the right embraces her; the one on the left has turned her face to the side and protects herself with her raised arms and hands. (The painting of her fingers is unfinished, but their arrangement is highly intriguing.) The expressions of the three women, like their poses, are very different. The one on the left, turned to the side, seems resigned. As is only appropriate, given the central figure's almost ceremonial pose, the outline of her face and its internal drawing are altogether harmonious, and she gazes calmly at the viewer with wide eyes. The woman on the right pressing against her seems much more relaxed, and her eyes are closed. The harsher brushwork in her face – like that of some of the outlines of the three bodies and their arms – is a clear indication that the work is unfinished (see p. 275). Even so, the painting of this face seems just as inspired as that of the completely finished figure on the left. The somewhat darker tone of the latter, with occasional impasto highlights, is appropriate to her melancholy expression – just as the more vivid coloring of the face and body of the woman on the right accords with her more voluptuous figure.

The painting of the bodies of these three women is astonishingly spontaneous and vivid. Note especially the back and rib cage of the one on the right and the area between the bent arms and neck of the one on the left – or, in the middle figure, the belly between the pubic hair and the navel, which was essentially finished and in which Schiele achieves a highly three-dimensional effect. Schiele sets off the hair of the right- and left-hand figures against the adjacent background, in the one case making it darker, in the other lighter. The hair of the woman on the right is painted in browns in contrast to the surrounding black; that of the one on the left a darker brown against a slightly lighter one mixed with green.

The painting is unfinished, to be sure, and is only a fragment. However, like *Lovers III (Man and Woman II)* (L 299; K P.329), also uncompleted owing to the painter's early death, it is a superb example of the new painting style characteristic of Schiele's work from the last year of his life. (RL)

Oil on canvas
101.5 × 108.7 cm
Leopold Museum, Vienna, Inv. 463
L 300; K P.330

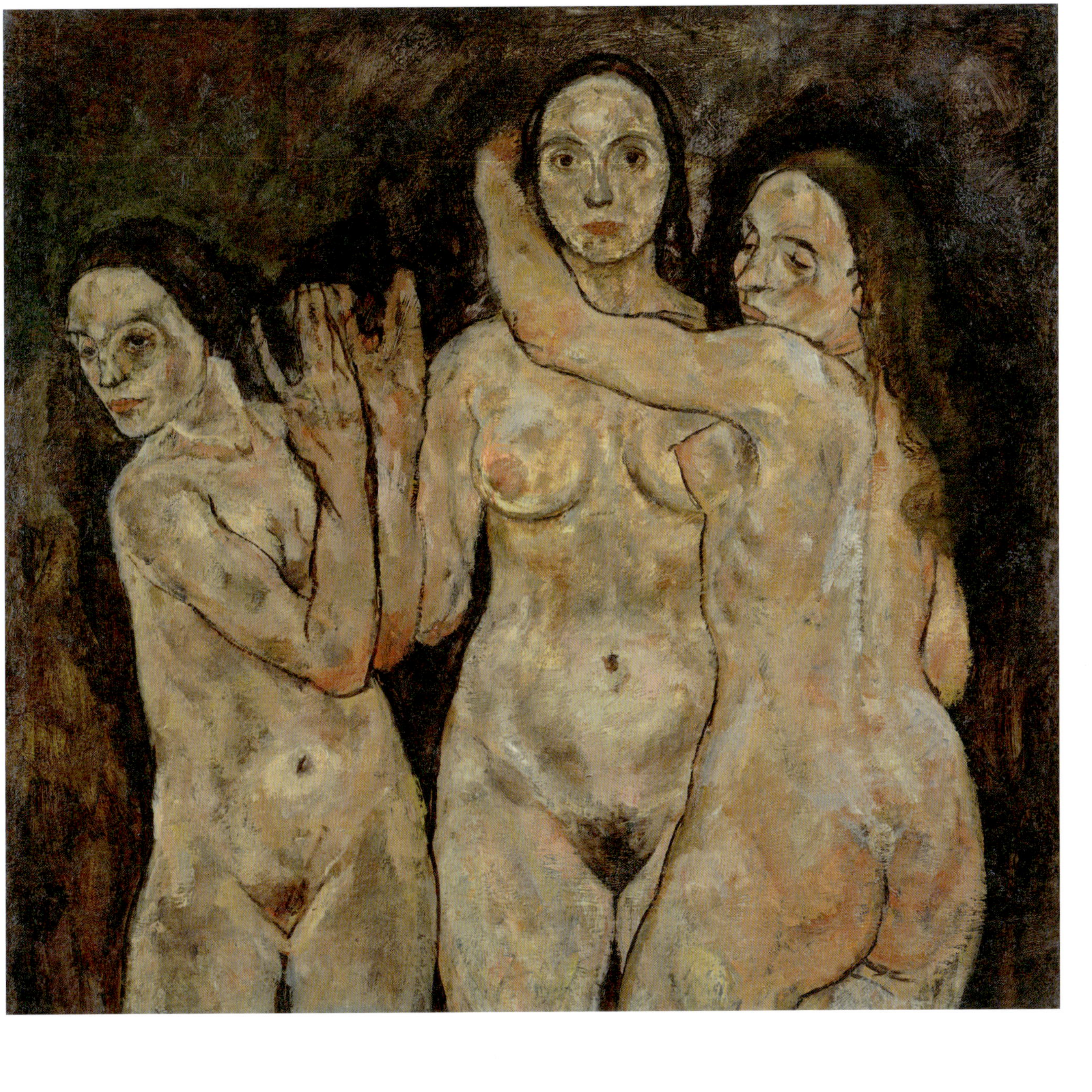

1918

NUDE SELF-PORTRAIT, SQUATTING

Stylistically, this squatting nude is closely related to the preparatory drawing (K D.2480) for the self-portrait in *The Family* (L 289; K. P.326). In contrast to it (and to another full sheet study, K D.2481, for the unfinished painting *Two Squatting Men (Double Self-Portrait)*, L 297; K. P.328), the inner surfaces of the drawing are shaded, which increases the darkness of the head and pubic hair as well as that of the eyes. More importantly, however, the two works have a number of common features that set them apart from most of Schiele's drawings: as opposed to a great number of earlier works on paper, there is no remarkable stylistic intent recognizable in the lineament, nor can we discern the same elegant lines found in many drawings created around the same time. Instead, an immediate preoccupation with natural forms and their graphic realization can be felt particularly clearly in these two works, but not at the expense of purely compositional elements, either in the work as a whole or in corresponding details. (RL)

Black chalk on paper
29.8 × 40.5 cm
Leopold Museum, Vienna, Inv. 2363
K D.2482

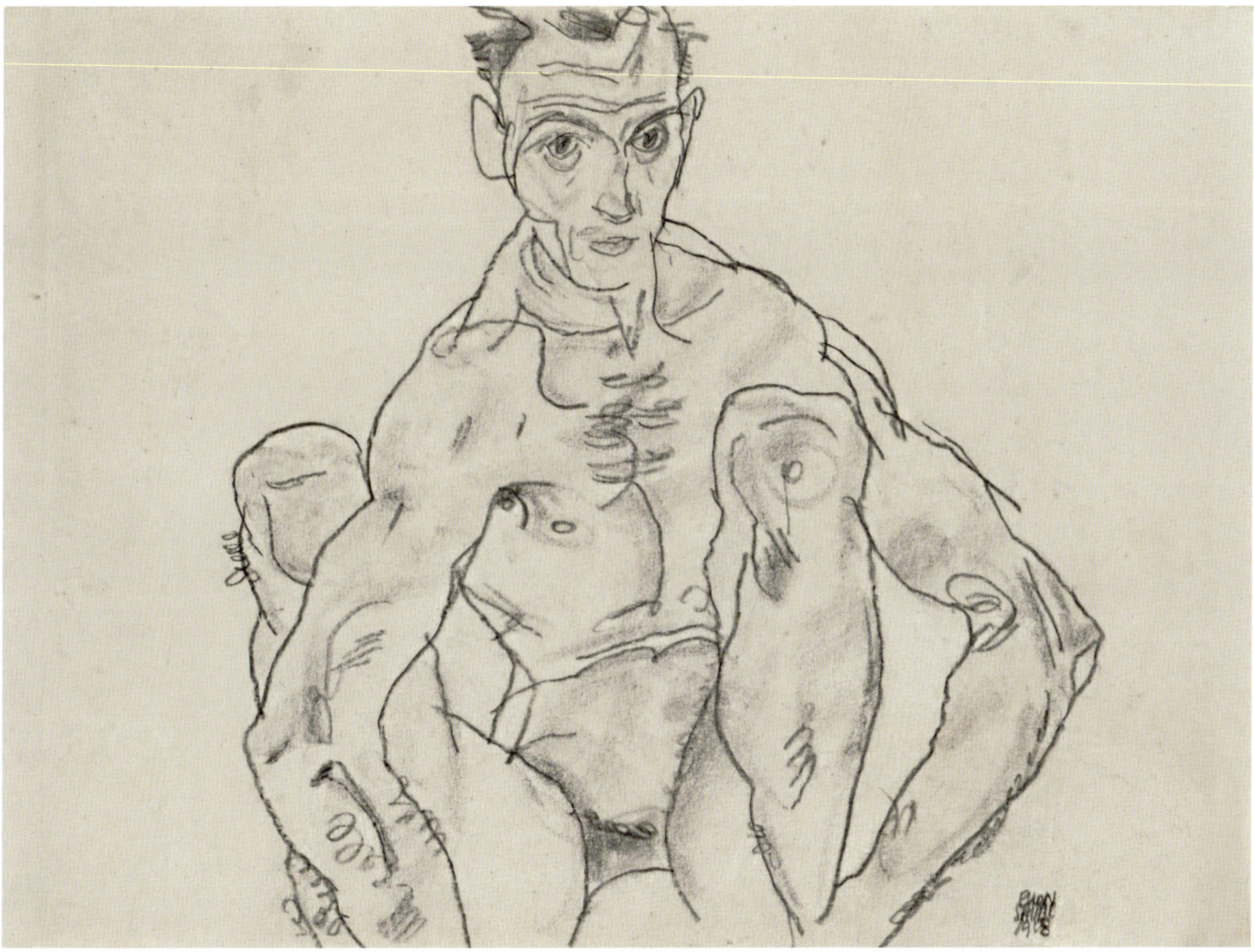

1918

EDITH SCHIELE, DYING

Schiele made two drawings of his wife on the evening of October 27, 1918. She died at about 8 o'clock the following morning. Just as he had in the case of the dead Klimt (see p. 269), Schiele more than likely drew this likeness in horizontal format (somewhat at an angle on the page), but then turned it into a vertical one with the placement of his signature and the inscription. He had begun doing this very early in his career. The beginnings and endings of some of the lines make it clear that his wife was lying down, and he was seated next to her bed. The same applies to the style of the drawing. Note, for example, the curls in her hair (she is lying on an invisible pillow), the bridge of her nose and the inner margins of the lower lip. All of these fall into their proper position as part of an organic whole only when one turns the sheet to the side. The eyes take on their proper perspective, the right one clearly closer to the viewer than the left.

Schiele's rendering of these eyes is profoundly moving. One senses the exhaustion of this woman who, deathly ill, gazes somewhat fearfully at her husband. In this, his last drawing, Schiele produced an unforgettable document. (RL)

Black chalk on brown paper
43.8 × 29.5 cm
Leopold Museum, Vienna, Inv. 2382
K D.2233

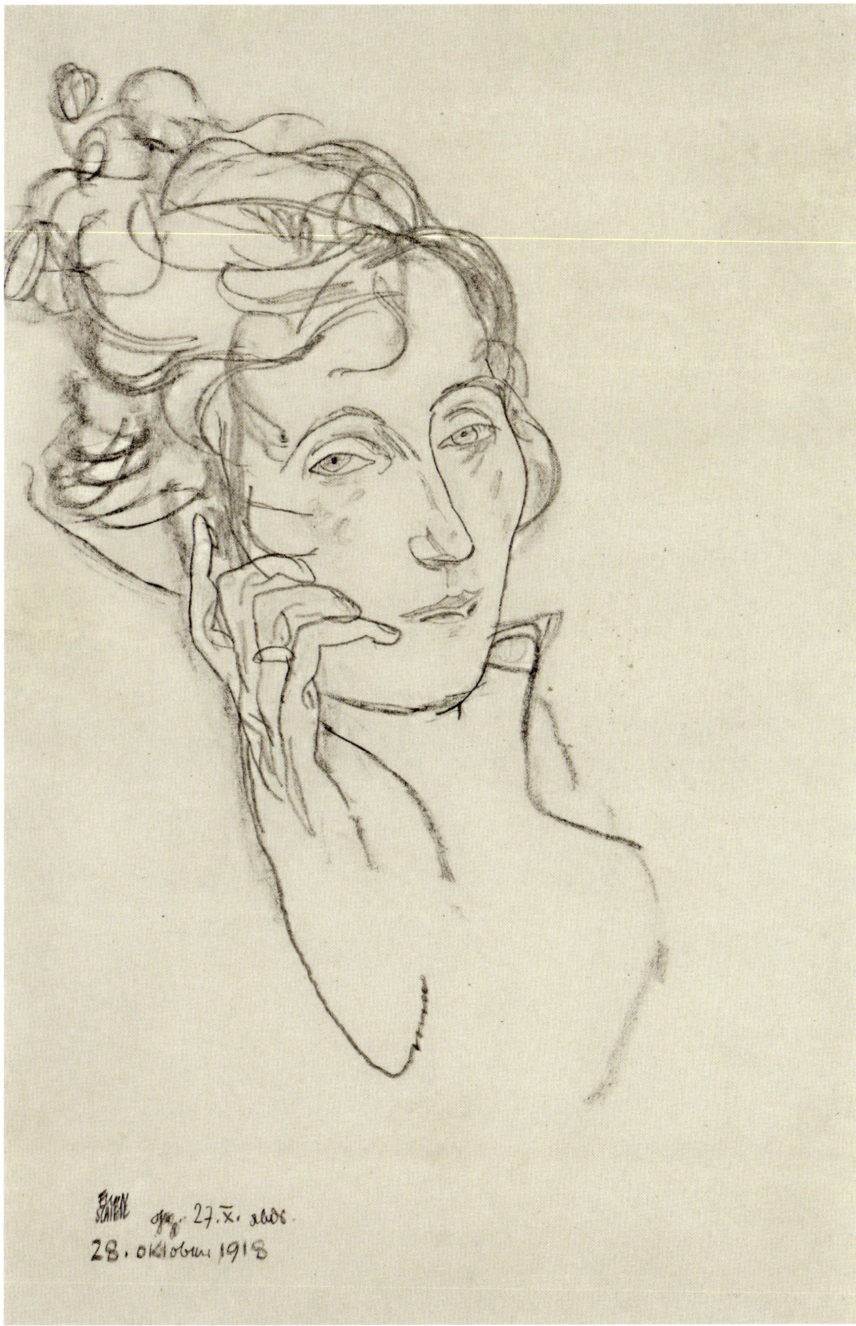
28. Oktober 1918

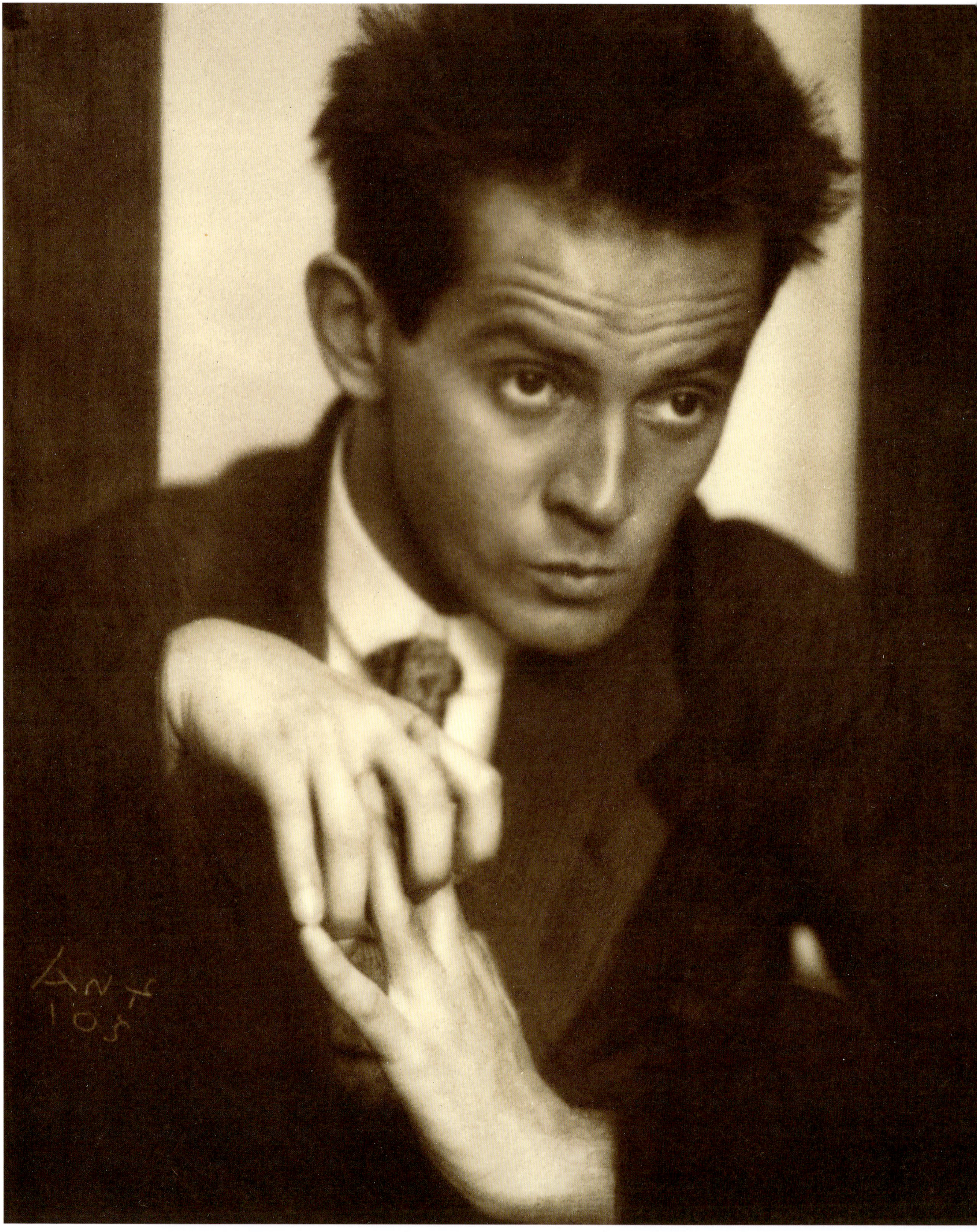

APPENDIX

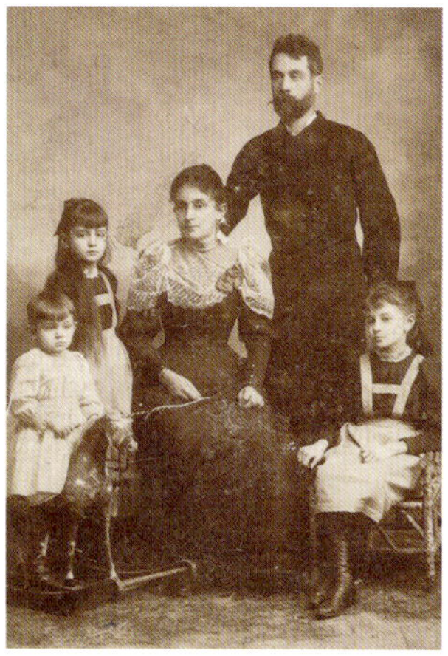

1

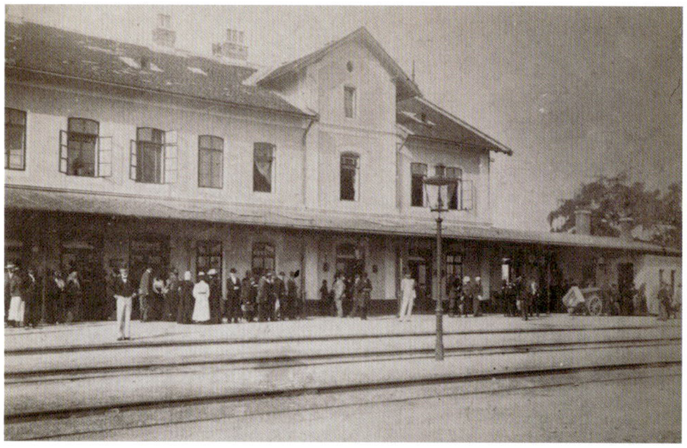

2

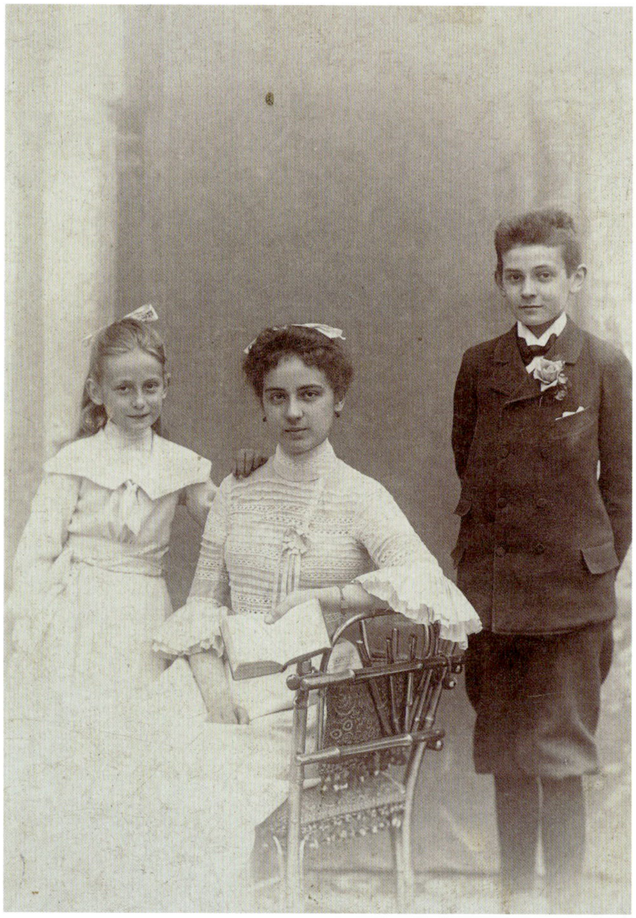

3

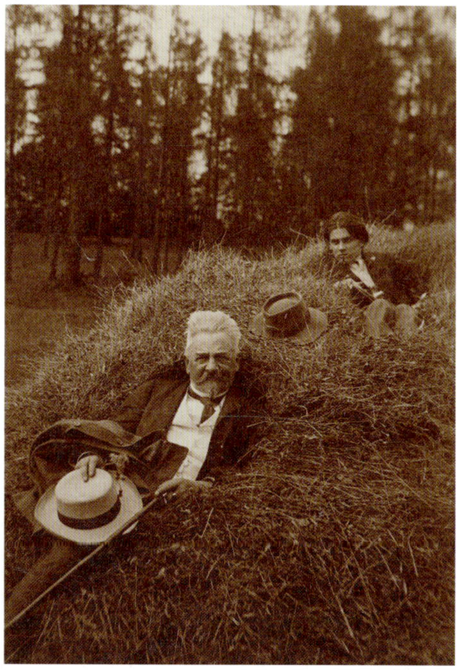

4

1 | Adolf and Marie Schiele with Egon, Melanie and Elvira | c. 1892 | Leopold, Private Collection

2 | Train station at Tulln | Leopold, Private Collection

3 | Arthur Josef Bett | Egon Schiele at his First Communion, with Melanie and Gertrude | c. 1903 | Leopold, Private Collection

4 | Egon Schiele with his uncle Leopold Czihaczek in Neulengbach, sitting in the hay | July 1908 | Leopold, Private Collection

BIOGRAPHY OF EGON SCHIELE

Rudolf Leopold

I am human,
I love death and
I love life.

Like so many of Vienna's creative giants, Schiele's forebears were not proper Austrians, but had found their way to the capital from the farther reaches of the Habsburg empire and even from abroad, so that he was a mix of nationalities. His father (1850–1904), though born in Vienna, was of north German ancestry. He came from a line of respectable and solidly bourgeois pastors, military officers and government officials of whom Schiele was rightly proud. In a sketch for an autobiography, he once wrote (ESAD, ID:291): "Old German blood flows in me, and I often feel within me the presence of my ancestors. A great-grandson of Friedrich Karl Schiele, the privy councillor […] I was born to a Viennese father and a mother from Krumau." The son of the privy councillor, Schiele's grandfather Karl Ludwig Wilhelm (Ballenstedt), was by profession an architect and in 1844 became the engineer of the Kaiser Ferdinand North Railway in Moravia. He then went on to build the Bohemian West Railway and served as its first inspector general, by which time he was a definite subject of the Austro-Hungarian monarchy. Schiele's mother (1862–1935) was born Marie Soukop in the Bohemian town of Krumau (Český Krumlov). Her people had been farmers, craftsmen and tradesmen in southern Bohemia, some of them Czech. In contrast to the family tree on Schiele's father's side, hers represented a whole spectrum of society.

1890

Egon Schiele, the third child of Adolf Eugen Schiele, a superintendant of the imperial railway, and Marie Schiele, is born on June 12 in the Lower Austrian town of Tulln and baptized Egon Leo Adolf. There are two older sisters: Elvira, born in 1883, who dies at the age of ten, and Melanie born in 1886. A final child, Gertrude is born in 1894. This sister will often pose for Schiele early in his career, even nude. She later marries the painter Anton Peschka (1885–1940).

1890–1905

Schiele's father, having previously served as a railway official in Lannsdorf, in Carinthia, is now an overseer at the train station in Tulln. The family lives in the manager's apartment in the station. By the time Schiele enters primary school, he is already producing drawings, mainly of Tulln's train station and the trains either passing through or standing on the siding. At ten Schiele begins secondary school in Krems. His performance is poor, however, and in 1902 his father transfers him to the larger provincial Gymnasium in Klosterneuburg. There his teachers soon complain that Schiele is disrupting their classes with his drawing. In a letter Schiele writes to Fritz Karpfen he confirms his early interest in art, reporting that he is busy producing "works" for their planned *Union-Kunstausstellung* [Union Exhibition], a collaborate effort (ESAD, ID: 202). Since his father's health has declined to the point that he can no longer keep his job, the family moves to Klosterneuburg as well. On New Year's Eve in 1904 Adolf Schiele dies from progressive paralysis. Just how great the 14-year-old Schiele's sense of loss must have been can be inferred from a letter written by the artist many years later to Anton Peschka (ESAD, ID: 133).

1906

Schiele's uncle and godfather, the engineer Leopold Czihaczek – his father's sister's husband – is named his guardian. It had been his father's wish that Schiele attends the local polytechnical school and Leopold Czihaczek concurs. Schiele's progress is poor, however – it appears that he will again have to repeat a grade – and his mother therefore appeals to one of her sisters, Olga Angerer, whose husband owns a chemigraphic plant, hoping that Schiele might be given work there as a draftsman. The sister's reply, dated June 9, dashes any such hope (ESAD, ID:204): "It strikes my husband as a serious fault that a boy should cause his mother such

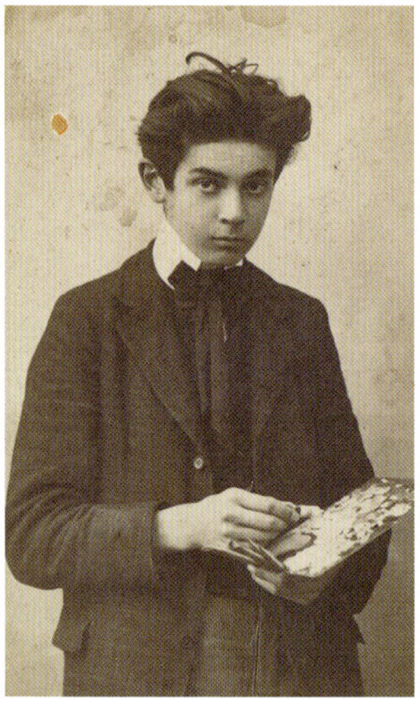

5

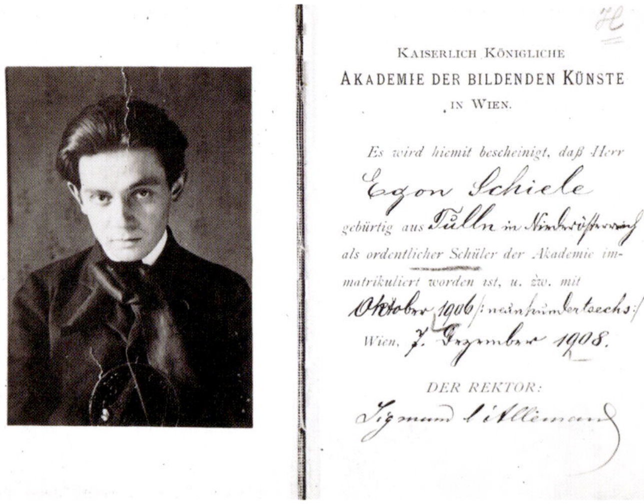

KAISERLICH KÖNIGLICHE
AKADEMIE DER BILDENDEN KÜNSTE
IN WIEN.

Es wird hiemit bescheinigt, daß Herr
Egon Schiele
gebürtig aus Tulln in Niederösterreich
als ordentlicher Schüler der Akademie immatrikuliert worden ist, u. zw. mit
Oktober 1906 (neunzehnhundertsechs)
Wien, 7. Dezember 1908.
DER REKTOR:
Sigmund l'Allemand

6

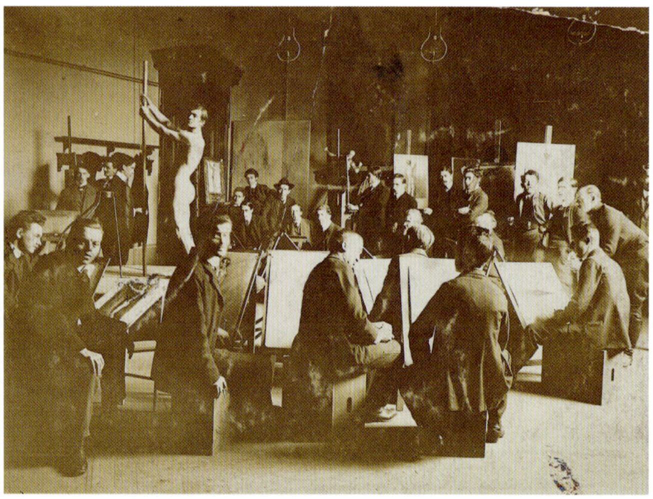

7

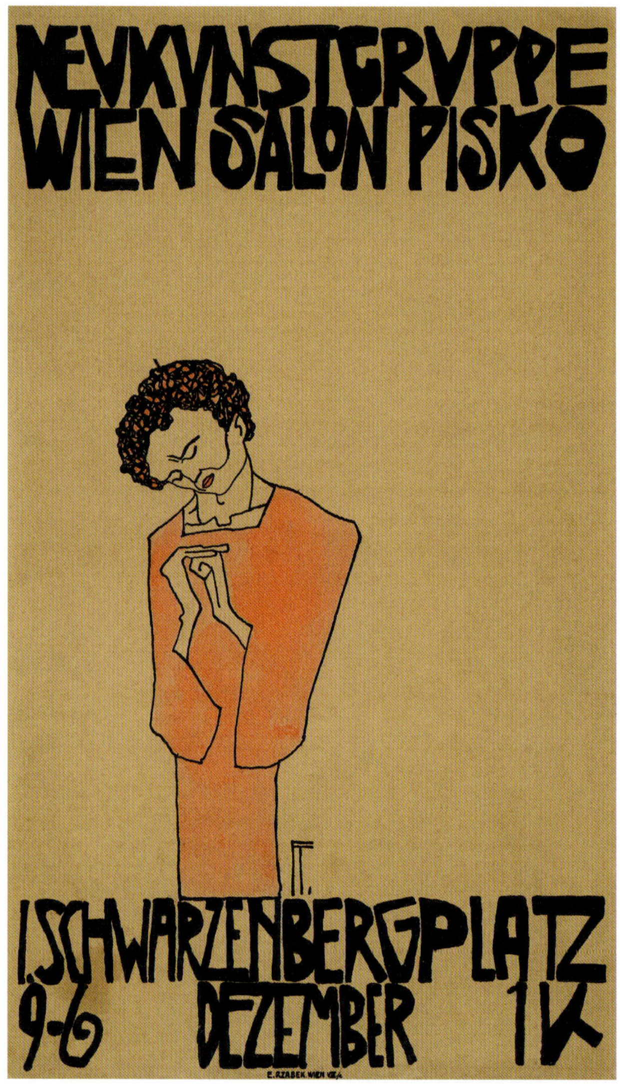

8

5 | Egon Schiele with palette | September 1906 | Leopold, Private Collection

6 | Egon Schiele's identity card from the Academy of Fine Arts | 1908 | Leopold, Private Collection

7 | Nude life class at the Academy, Egon Schiele visible in left background | c. 1907 | Leopold, Private Collection

8 | Anton Faistauer | Poster for the first exhibition of the Neukunstgruppe at the art salon Pisko in Vienna | 1909 | Kunsthaus Zug, Stiftung Sammlung Kamm

worry [...] I would have no sympathy for such a rascal. A boy must study and behave [...] Only dependable people manage to make something of themselves."
There is thought of sending Schiele to the School of Applied Arts in Vienna. Czihaczek opposes the idea. However, two of Schiele's instructors, his drawing teacher Ludwig Karl Strauch (1875–1959) and the Augustinian choirmaster Dr. Wolfgang Pauker, as well as the Klosterneuburg painter Max Kahrer (1878–1937) recommend that the boy be given artistic training. The drawings Schiele submits to the School of Applied Arts are so impressive that he is advised to think of the Academy of Fine Arts instead. His guardian relents after Schiele passes the entrance examination. On October 13 he joyously telegraphs his wife: "Egon passed splendidly" (ESAD, ID: 205).

1907

Schiele brings great enthusiasm to the new challenge, but in no time his relations with his hopelessly reactionary teacher Christian Griepenkerl (1839–1916), who is still deeply mired in the "Ringstrasse style", turns sour. Already that year, the young artist tries to befriend Gustav Klimt (1862–1918). With his younger sister, Gertrude, he goes on holiday to Trieste, where he produces a number of drawings of the harbor quarter. On his return, he moves into his first studio in Vienna's 2nd district on Kurzbauergasse 6.

1908

Schiele takes part in his first exhibition, a show in the Kaisersaal of the Augustinian monastery in Klosterneuburg that runs from May 16 to the end of June. He is represented by ten works.

1909

The committee for the art exhibition *Internationale Kunstschau* 1909, headed by Gustav Klimt, selects four works by the young Schiele for inclusion. On this occasion Schiele gets to know the architect Josef Hoffmann (1870–1956) as well, and through him becomes affiliated with the *Wiener Werkstätte,* also known as the Vienna Workshop. His teachers at the Academy, however, give him poor marks in all his subjects. He has an especially violent falling out with a Professor Griepenkerl. Finally, Schiele – now in his third year – withdraws from the Academy in April. With a number of like-minded artists he establishes the *Neukunstgruppe*. Among its members are Anton Faistauer (1887–1930), Rudolf Kalvach (1883–1932), Franz Wiegele (1887–1944), as well as the composer Arthur Löwenstein and the painter of theater sets Erwin Dominik Osen (1891–1970), who is a major influence on Schiele for a time. Hans Böhler (1884–1961) and Albert Paris Gütersloh (1887–1973) eventually join the group as well. Schiele serves as both president and secretary.
The *Neukunstgruppe* holds its first exhibition in December, at the Salon Pisko in Vienna. Schiele provides a manifesto for the show, which he publishes with various changes in 1914 in the weekly literary and political journal *Die Aktion* and at his behest Faistauer designs a poster. During this exhibition Schiele becomes acquainted with a number of Vienna's cultural elite, including the collectors Carl Reininghaus and Dr. Oskar Reichel, the publisher Eduard Kosmack and the art critic for the Austrian newspaper *Arbeiterzeitung* Arthur Roessler.

1910

The opening of the *Neukunstgruppe*'s second exhibition is held on February 1 at the Club of German Women Artists in Prague. Alongside Schiele's works, the presentation features contributions by Böhler, Faistauer, Gütersloh, Kalvach, Anton Kolig (1886–1950), Peschka and Wiegele. The exhibition's poster is designed by Kolig.
The *Wiener Werkstätte* publishes three Schiele fashion designs as postcards (K D.468, 486, 488). Its director, Josef Hoffmann, also arranges for Schiele's participation in the *Internationale Jagd-Ausstellung,* an international exhibition on hunting, presented from May to September. There Schiele shows a life-size seated female nude (L 143a; K P.170), the preliminary study for which – presently in the Wien Museum – is bought from the artist himself by the architect Otto Wagner (1841–1918). At the show's opening, however, Emperor Franz Josef expresses his displeasure with the painting, which is unfortunately now lost.
On May 12 Schiele travels with his friend Erwin Dominik Osen to Krumau, where he stays until June l. On June 6, his uncle, offended by Schiele's request for 40 crowns, gives up his guardianship, which he has exercised for five years.
Back in Vienna, Schiele lives in a studio in Vienna's 9th district, on Alserbachstrasse 39, until October, then moves to Grünbergstrasse 31 in the 12th district.
According to Arthur Roessler, Otto Wagner advises Schiele to paint life-size portraits of noted Viennese personalities, volunteering to pose for one himself. After only a few sittings, however, he runs out of patience, so only the head is finished. The most important of the six large portraits Schiele does complete are those of Roessler (L 153; K P.163), the painter Zakovsek (L 148; K P.160) and especially that of the publisher Kosmack (L 152; K P.165).
Schiele once more exhibits in the Augustinian monastery at Klosterneuburg in the fall. Heinrich Benesch, a high railway official, is so taken by a painting of a *Sunflower* (L 139; K P.159) that he decides to make the young artist's acquaintance. He becomes the most assiduous collector of Schiele's drawings and watercolors (his purchases now form a major part of the Schiele collection of the Albertina in Vienna).

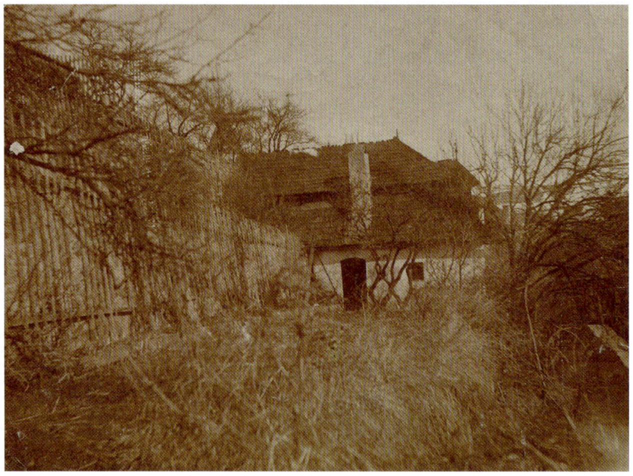

9

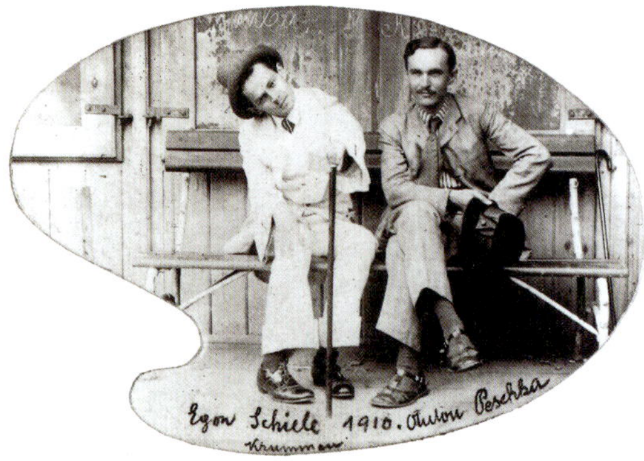

10

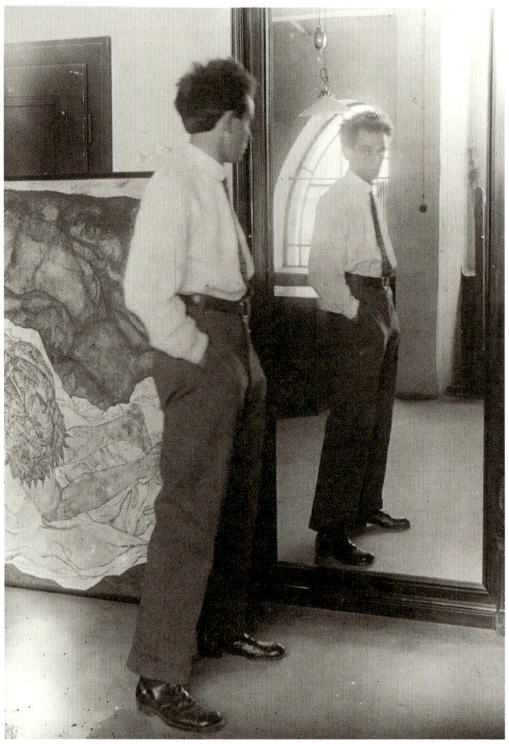

11

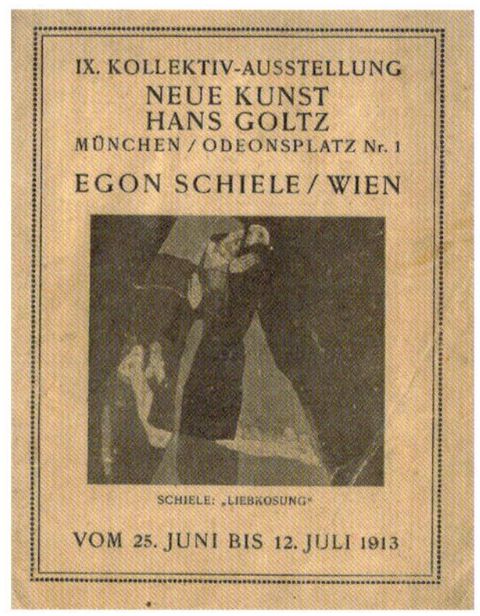
IX. KOLLEKTIV-AUSSTELLUNG
NEUE KUNST
HANS GOLTZ
MÜNCHEN / ODEONSPLATZ Nr. 1
EGON SCHIELE / WIEN

SCHIELE: „LIEBKOSUNG"

VOM 25. JUNI BIS 12. JULI 1913

12

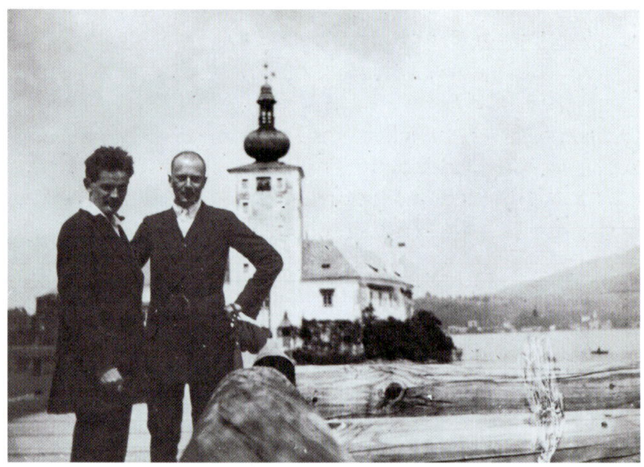

13

9 | Egon Schiele (?) | Egon Schiele's garden house in Krumau | 1911 | Leopold, Private Collection

10 | Egon Schiele and Anton Peschka in Krumau | 1910 | Leopold, Private Collection

11 | Johannes Fischer | Egon Schiele in front of the mirror in his Hietzing studio, in the background the painting *Death and the Maiden* | 1915 | Leopold, Private Collection

12 | Catalogue for Egon Schiele's solo exhibition at the Munich Galerie Goltz | 1913 | Leopold, Private Collection

13 | Egon Schiele with Arthur Roessler in front of Schloss Ort in Gmunden on the Traunsee | July 1913 | Leopold, Private Collection

1911

In the previous year – at the age of 20 – Schiele had achieved his independence as an artist, but not public recognition. Now this begins to come to him as well. Albert Paris Gütersloh's essay "Egon Schiele: Versuch einer Vorrede" [an attempt at an introduction] appears and Arthur Roessler publishes an article on him with illustrations in the monthly art journal *Bildende Künstler*. Vienna's Galerie Miethke also launches a first major showing of his work from April to May. In this same year, however, the Wiener Werkstätte rejects five lovely designs for postcards.

Schiele had already announced his intention to leave Vienna in 1910, in a letter to his future brother-in-law Anton Peschka (ESAD, ID: 33): "I'd like to get out of Vienna soon. It's so ugly here. Everyone's jealous of me and devious; my onetime fellow students raise their eyebrows at me. It's gloomy in Vienna, the city is black, everything has to be done by the rules. I want to be alone. I'd like to move to Bohemia." In early spring he does just that, settling in his mother's home town of Krumau. Presumably he has met the model Wally Neuzil a short time before and begun a relationship with her. He takes her along.

In Krumau, Schiele is extremely productive, creating among other things a number of imaginary, visionary cityscapes. He is soon forced to leave, however, as Krumau's small-town proprieties are offended at his having young local girls pose for him in the nude and at his keeping Wally as his "concubine." After a brief stopover at his mother's in Vienna, he settles in Neulengbach, a small town just outside the city.

Through Roessler, Schiele meets the Munich art dealer Hans Goltz, Ulrich Putze's successor, in September. In November he becomes a member of the Munich *Sema* group, an artists' association which includes members such as Alfred Kubin (1877–1959) and Paul Klee (1879–1940).

1912

The *Neukunstgruppe* exhibits in the Künstlerhaus in Budapest at the beginning of the year. From February 15 to March 15, Hans Goltz shows paintings and drawings by Schiele along with works of the artists' association *Der Blaue Reiter* in Munich. He then forwards Schiele's pieces, along with graphics by the now completely forgotten Frenchman Emile Zoire, to the Museum Folkwang, where Karl Ernst Osthaus presents an imposing exhibition from April to May. Schiele had also been represented in the exhibition by Munich's Secession in March and April. Schiele's lithograph *Nude Self* (K G.1b) is published in the *Sema Portfolio*.

This delightful upswing in the artist's career is brought to a sudden halt when, on April 13, Schiele is arrested in Neulengbach, accused of having seduced a minor. He is held pending an appearance before the district court in Sankt Pölten, where he is transferred on April 30. In early May the court acquits him of the main charge against him, but finds him guilty of "distributing obscene drawings" in as much as minors had been exposed to studies of nudes in his studio. Schiele is sentenced to three days in jail, which are added to the 21 days he spent in pre-trial detention.

The entire episode is shattering to Schiele. His stay in Neulengbach, one of his most productive periods, is thus brought to a close. On May 18 he writes to Arthur Roessler, who was not in Vienna at the time of his arrest (ESAD, ID: 474): "I am still completely shaken. During the trial a drawing of mine, the one I had hanging on the wall here, was burned. Klimt is hoping to do something. He assured me that the same thing could happen to one of us one day, another the next, that we're none of us free to do as we will." (In 1922, four years after Schiele's death, Arthur Roessler publishes what he claims are Schiele's "notes" from prison – a forgery, for they were written by Roessler himself.)

In part so as to take his mind off his troubles, Schiele travels to Klagenfurt and Trieste, then to Lindau and finally Bregenz, where he stays for some time. He stops over in Munich for only two days. For a short time he then rents what he claims is the cheapest studio in Vienna, the one belonging to his fellow-painter Osen, who is spending the summer in Krumau.

The important *Internationale Kunstausstellung des Sonderbundes* [International Sonderbund Exhibition] takes place in Cologne from May 25 to September 30. Three works by Schiele are included. He also participates in an exhibition at the Arnold Gallery in Dresden. In July, Schiele is well represented in an exhibition of the *Hagenbund*, with seven paintings, including his important large-scale rendering *The Hermits* (see p. 125). Through this exhibition Schiele becomes acquainted with a new collector, the hotelier Franz Hauer.

In November he finds a suitable studio (Vienna's 13th district, Hietzinger Hauptstrasse 101) that he then continues to use until his death.

Since Schiele is one of the very few Austrian artists to genuinely admire him, Gustav Klimt introduces him to one of his wealthiest collectors, the industrialist August Lederer. Lederer invites Schiele to visit him in Győr (Raab), where he spends Christmas and New Year's. Lederer's son Erich, whom Schiele portrays (L 223; K P.235), becomes his pupil.

1913

On January 17 the *Bund Österreichischer Künstler* [League of Austrian Artists] votes to name Schiele a member. Schiele exhibits four paintings and 20 drawings with that group in Budapest in March. As in the previous year, he is represented in the *Frühjahrsausstellung* [Spring Exhibition] of the Munich Secession. The Galerie Goltz in Munich presents a major Schiele retrospective from June 26 to July 15. His paintings

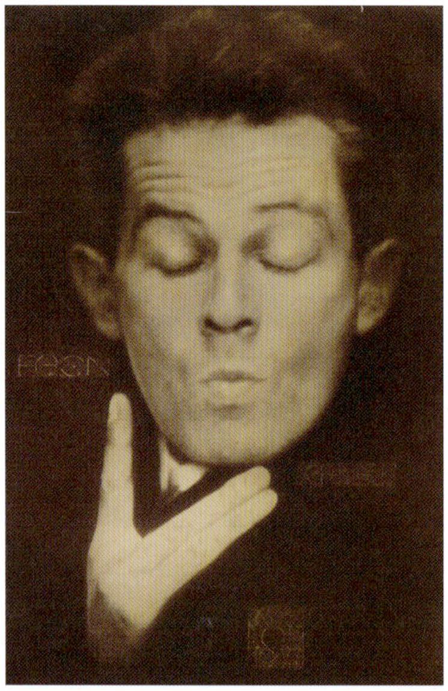

14

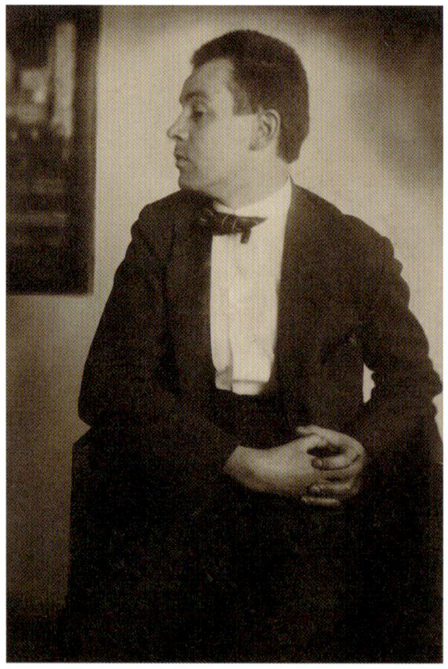

15

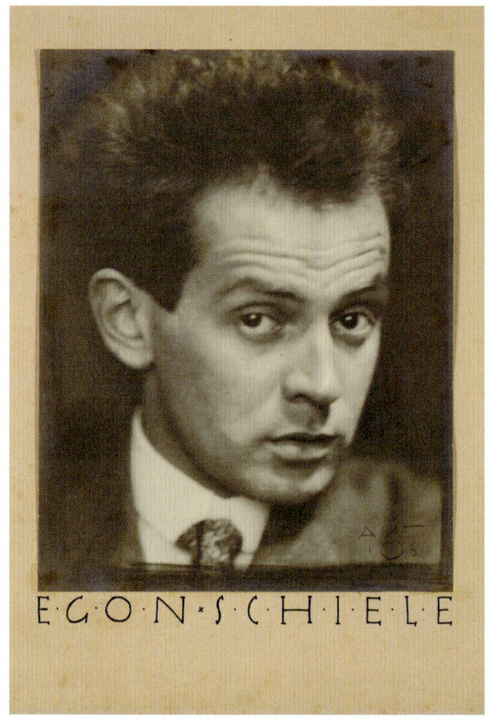

16

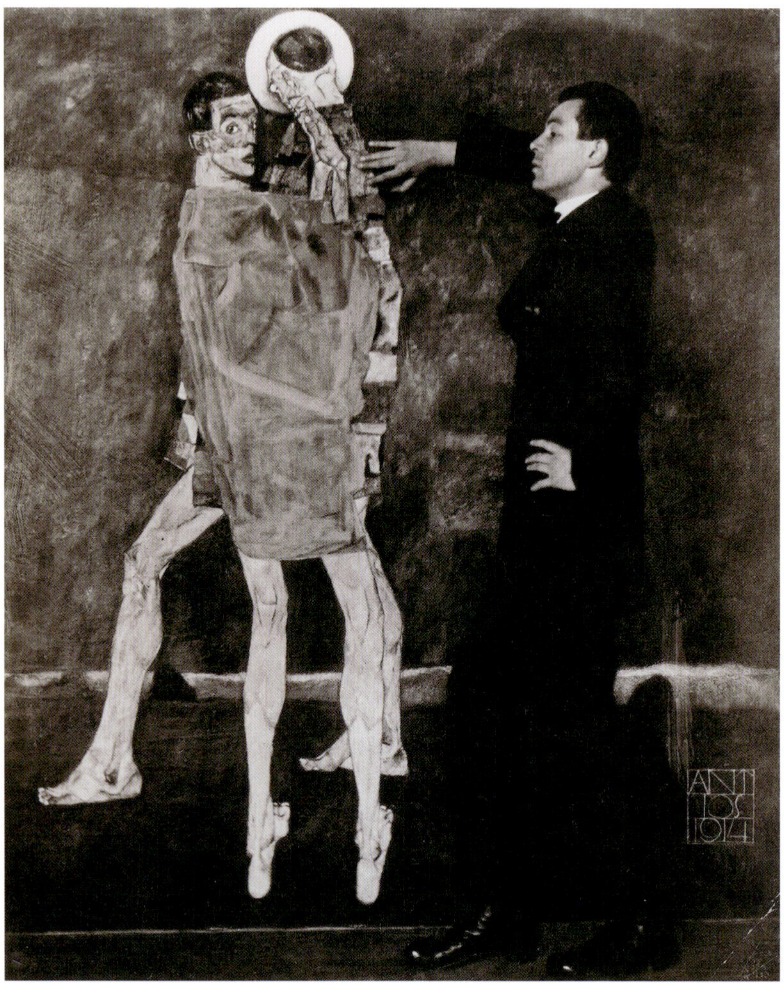

17

14 | Anton Josef Trčka | Egon Schiele with pursed lips | 1914 | Leopold, Private Collection

15 | Anton Josef Trčka | Egon Schiele in profile with the painting *Houses by the Sea (Row of Houses)* in the background | 1914 | Leopold, Private Collection

16 | Anton Josef Trčka | Egon Schiele | 1914 | Leopold, Private Collection

17 | Anton Josef Trčka | Egon Schiele with the now lost painting *Encounter* in the background | 1914 | Leopold, Private Collection

are also shown in the same year in Berlin and in Düsseldorf's *Grosse deutsche Kunstausstellung*, a major exhibition of German art. In Vienna, Schiele takes part in the *Internationale Schwarzweiss-Ausstellung* [International Black and White Exhibition] and the *XLIII Ausstellung der Wiener Secession* [Exhibition of the Vienna Secession].
Schiele also travels a great deal, often up into the Wachau, where he produces paintings of the town of Stein (L 232, 233, 239, 240; K P.266–269), and also to Krumau, Villach and Tarvis. He spends the first part of the summer with Wally at Roessler's at Lake Traun and the later part with his mother and Wally at Lake Ossiach, in Carinthia. Schiele becomes a contributor to the Berlin journal *Die Aktion*, a "weekly on politics, literature and art" published by Franz Pfemfert, in which he publishes both drawings and prose poems.

1914

Schiele takes part for the first time in exhibitions in non-German-speaking countries, first in Rome – at the International Secession – then in Brussels and Paris. In Germany his works are shown at two galleries in Dresden, in the Hamburg Kunstverein, in the Munich Secession and in the Cologne *Werkbund Exhibition*.
In the spring, Schiele has Robert Philippi (1877–1959) teach him how to make woodcuts and engravings, and by the summer he has produced six of the latter. Experimenting with the photographer Anton Josef Trčka (1893–1940), he produces some highly unusual portraits. In Heinrich Böhler (1881–1940), a cousin of the painter Hans Böhler, the artist acquires not only a wealthy new collector but also a pupil.
The house just across from Schiele's studio belongs at this time to the machinist Johann Harms, who lives there with his wife and his daughters Adele and Edith. It is possible that Schiele may have tried to introduce himself to the family in January, but he only gets to know the two sisters toward the end of the year. His letters to them frequently begin with wordplay on their names: "Liebes Fräulein Ed. [Edith] & Ad. [Adele]," or "Ad. & Ed.," or even "Liebes Fräulein EDADEDAD" (ESAD, ID: 818, 838).
At first the outbreak of war in July has little effect on his creative work, for on two occasions he is found to be unfit for military service and is allowed to continue his career.

1915

An impressive Schiele retrospective is presented at the Viennese gallery Guido Arnot in January. On May 31 Schiele is again required to report to his draft board and this time he is declared fit for active service. In the meantime, he has decided to wed Edith Harms. On June 17, four days before he is to report for duty in Prague, they are married. Edith follows him to Prague a short time later. A month later Schiele is transferred to Vienna, where he can fulfill his military duties in the city and its immediate environs. In December the Berlin Secession invites Schiele to participate in the *Wiener Kunstschau* [Vienna Art Show] with three large paintings and a number of drawings. Among the former is his *Levitation (The Blind II)* (see p. 241), which, according to a letter of Schiele's (ESAD, ID: 951), is hung in the foyer opposite Klimt's *Death and Life* (N 193).

1916

Die Aktion publishes a special Egon Schiele issue (nos. 35–36) containing, in addition to a number of reproductions of his drawings, the woodcut *Male Bathers* (K G.13b) and his poem *Abendland*. Issue nos. 39–40 includes his woodcut *Male Head* (K G.14) as well.
Schiele keeps a war diary from March 8 to September 30, which is now housed at the Albertina. In his free time he is permitted to work in his Hietzing studio. At the beginning of May he is assigned to a camp for captured Russian officers at Mühling. His wife joins him two days after he reports to his new posting. His hours of office work leave him little time for his art. He produces drawings of prisoners of war, as he had already done in Vienna, and also portraits of his superiors. He manages to finish only a single larger painting, *The Decaying Mill* (L 271; K P.301).

1917

In January Schiele is permitted to return to Vienna, where he is detailed to the Imperial and Royal Supply Depot for Officers on active service, under the command of First Lieutenant Dr. Hans Rosé. Rosé commissions Schiele to make drawings of the depot's quarters in Vienna as well as of those of its 28 branches throughout the country.
Schiele is asked, together with Albert Paris Gütersloh, to organize the *Kriegsausstellung*, a wartime exhibition held in 1917 in the Prater. On May 30 Schiele informs his brother-in-law Anton Peschka that he has been given the job of making selections for the *Bund Österreichischer Künstler*, the League of Austrian Artists and describes the trouble he is having with paintings by Gütersloh, Faistauer, Kolig, Ludwig Heinrich Jungnickel (1881–1965) and others, since none of them are war painters and yet everything is supposed to have at least some connection to the war. As for his own work, he changes the title of his picture *Resurrection* (L 236; K P.251) to *Resurrection from the Heroes' Graves*.
In the fall Schiele is granted his long-standing wish and is transferred to the K. u. K. Heeresmuseum [Imperial Army Museum]. There he is able to fulfill his military obligations and still have considerably more time for his art. Although exhibiting Austrian art outside the country is technically impossible because of the war, Schiele, however, is in fact invited to take part in exhibitions in Amsterdam, Stockholm and Copenhagen in this year and the following one. Schiele plans to establish a committee made up of representatives from the fields of literature, the visual arts and music to aid

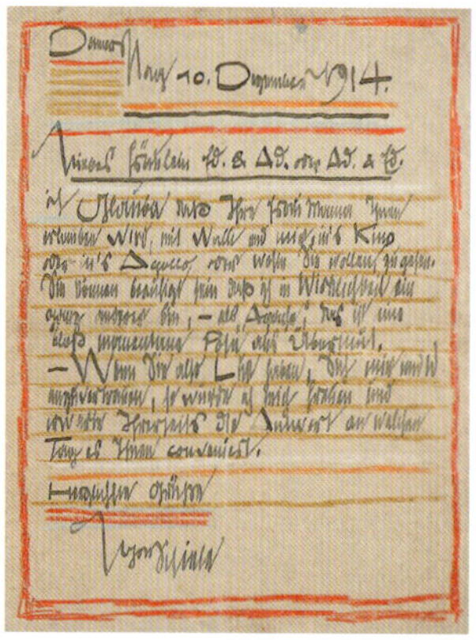

18

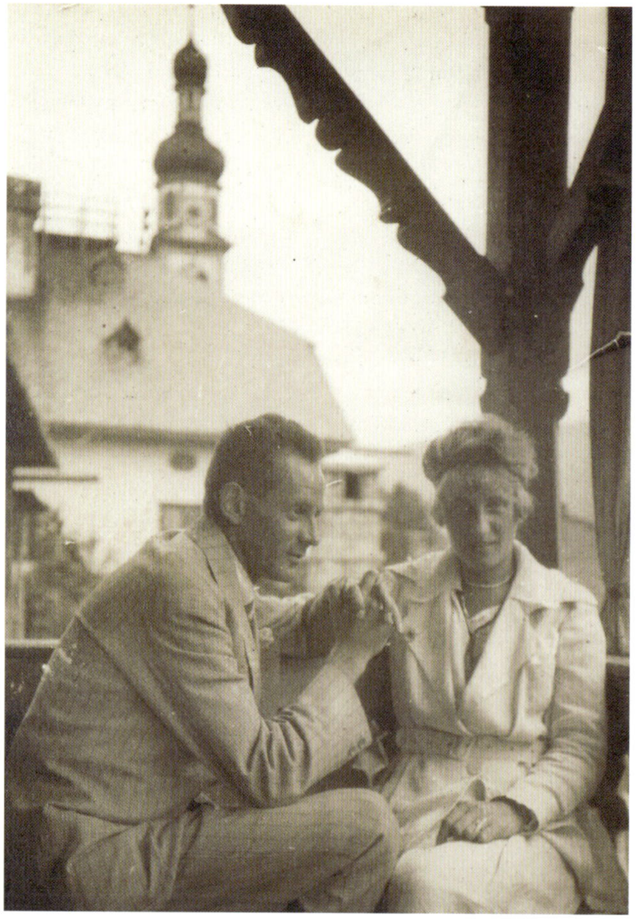

19

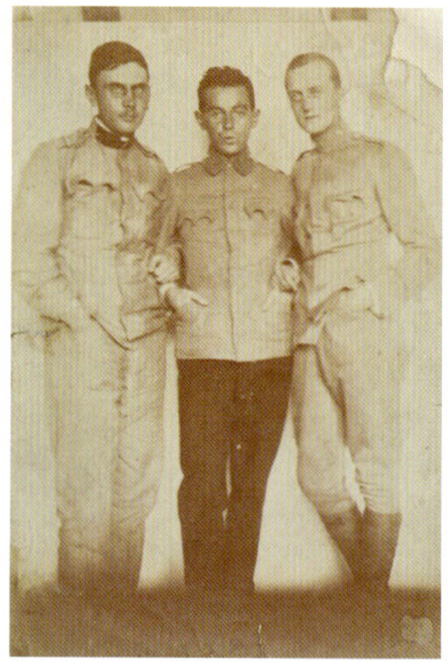

20

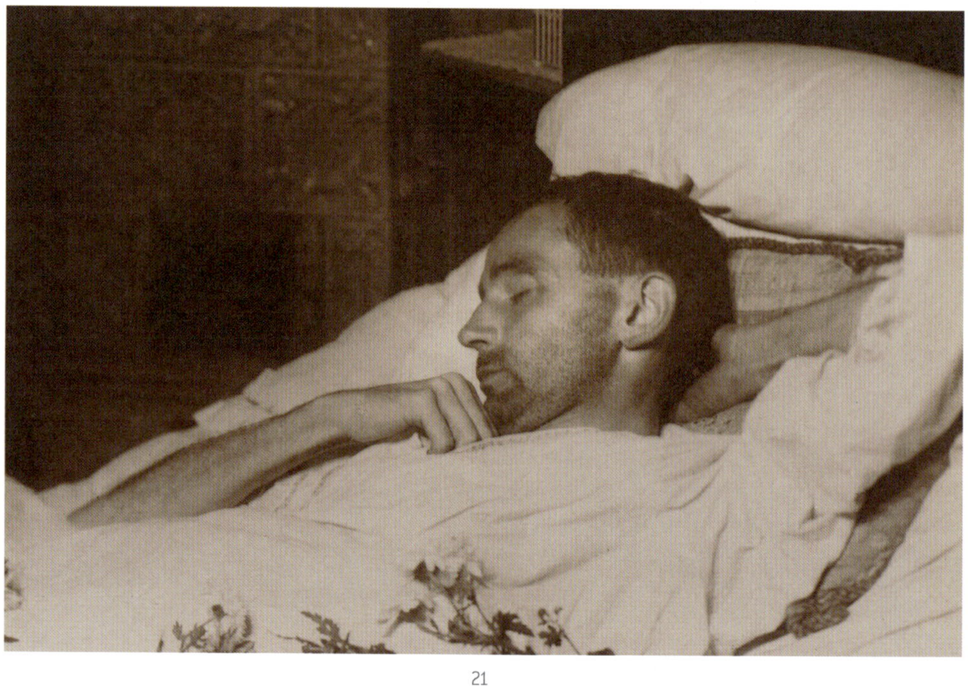

21

18 | Letter from Egon Schiele to Edith and Adele Harms | 10th December 1914 (handwritten) | Albertina, Vienna, Egon Schiele Archive

19 | Egon and Edith Schiele in Fulpmes, Tyrol | 1918 | Leopold, Private Collection

20 | Egon Schiele with two military comrades | 1916 | Leopold, Private Collection

21 | Martha Fein | Egon Schiele on his deathbed | 1918 | Leopold Museum, Vienna, Inv. 5389

with the cultural reconstruction after the war, intending to build an art space. While his plan is supported by Peter Altenberg, Anton Hanak (1875–1934), Arnold Schönberg, Josef Hoffmann and others, the project is not realized due to a lack of funds.

1918

Gustav Klimt dies on February 6. The next day Schiele captures the artist, whose beard has been shaved off, in three drawings at Vienna's General Hospital. He publishes a memorial tribute to Klimt in the journal *Der Anbruch*. The first two issues of this series of "broadsheets from our time" carry reproductions of Schiele drawings.
The Vienna Secession places its building at the disposal of Schiele and his group in March, reserving its main gallery for Schiele himself. He contributes 19 large paintings and 29 drawings to the exhibition, some of them with added watercolor. Artistically and financially, this is his first triumph.
In the exhibition *Ein Jahrhundert Wiener Malerei* [a century of Viennese painting] presented in the Kunsthaus in Zurich from May 12 to June 16, Schiele is represented by four paintings and numerous drawings. Following the success of the exhibition at the Secession Schiele founds the artists' association *Neue Secession Wien* [New Secession Vienna] together with Johannes Fischer (1888–1955) and Albert Paris Gütersloh. The only exhibition of this association, which lasts only a few months, is held in Prague. The *Art Union of Bohemia and Prague* exhibits 200 graphic works by Schiele and members of the *Neue Secession Wien* at the Künstlerhaus Rudolphinum in Prague, and the same show is then presented in Dresden at the Arnold Gallery. Richard Harlfinger, the president of the Vienna Secession, asks Schiele if he would like to take part in the portrait exhibition scheduled for the fall.
On July 5 Schiele moves into a new studio on Wattmanngasse 6 in Hietzing, although he also keeps his former one on Hietzinger Hauptstrasse.
In July and August Schiele negotiates for a suitable exhibition space for his group, which maintains an office at the gallery belonging to Gustav Nebehay in Vienna's 1st district.
On August 21 Carl Moll invites Schiele, at Nebehay's behest, to "put together a small collection" of his works for an exhibition at the art society *Nassauischer Kunstverein* in Wiesbaden (ESAD, ID: 1749).
Owing to quarrels with Johannes Fischer and Albert Paris Gütersloh, Schiele founds the association *Sonderbund* on September 2 1918 together with the former members of the *Neue Secession Wien*. The art dealer Gustav Nebehay acts as the association's president. Schiele hopes to win Oskar Kokoschka (1886–1980), Alfred Kubin and Johannes Itten (1888–1967) as further members.
However, all this was not to be. On September 20 Schiele writes to Broncia Koller-Pinell (1863–1934) that much as he likes his new studio, it is becoming increasingly unpleasant because of its dampness and he hopes it will not be bad for his health.
From one of Schiele's letters we learn that his wife, then six months pregnant, comes down with Spanish influenza on October 19 (ESAD, ID: 1835). She dies nine days later, on October 28, at eight o'clock in the morning. The previous evening Schiele made two drawings of her (K D.2232, 2233). These are his last works. He too has the flu, and at one o'clock in the morning on October 31 he succumbs at the age of 28. Martha Fein photographs him on his deathbed and Gustinus Ambrosi takes a death mask. Schiele is buried on November 3 in the cemetery at Ober St. Veit.

1 | For all catalogue raisonné numbers cited in this essay, see the index of abbreviations on p. 17.

REFERENCE WORKS

Selection

MONOGRAPHS

Arnold 1984
Matthias Arnold: *Egon Schiele: Leben und Werk*, Stuttgart 1984.

Bauer 2013
Christian Bauer (ed.): *Egon Schiele. Der Anfang/The Beginning*, Munich 2013.

Bauer 2015
Christian Bauer (ed.): *Egon Schiele. Almost a Lifetime*, Munich 2015.

Benesch 1965
Heinrich Benesch: *Mein Weg mit Egon Schiele*, New York 1965.

Benesch 1951
Otto Benesch: *Egon Schiele als Zeichner. Portfolio*, Vienna 1951.

Bornscheuer 2015
Marion Bornscheuer: *Wilhelm Lehmbruck und Egon Schiele. Die Rekonstruktion der Ausstellung im Hagener Folkwang Museum 1912 und weiterführende Überlegungen*, Norderstedt 2015.

Breicha/Fritsch 1964
Otto Breicha/Gerhard Fritsch: *Finale und Auftakt: Wien 1898–1914. Literatur, Bildende Kunst, Musik*, Salzburg 1964.

Clegg 2015
Elizabeth Clegg: *Egon Schiele (1890–1918). Works on Paper (1908–1918)*, Vienna 2015.

Comini 1966
Alessandra Comini: "Egon Schieles Kriegs-tagebuch 1916", in: *Albertina Studien*, vol. 4, issue 2, Vienna 1966, pp. 86–102.

Comini 1974 (1)
Alessandra Comini: *Egon Schiele's Portraits*, Berkeley 1974.

Comini 1974 (2)
Alessandra Comini: *Schiele in Prison*, London 1974.

Comini 1976
Alessandra Comini: *Egon Schiele*, New York 1976.

Comini 1978
Alessandra Comini: *The Fantastic Art of Vienna*, New York 1978.

Dichand 1986
Hans Dichand: *Die Künstler der klassischen Moderne in Österreich*, Graz 1986.

Fischel 1918
Hartwig Fischel: "Egon Schiele", in: *Kunst und Kunsthandwerk*, issue 21, Vienna 1918, pp. 152–153.

Fischer 1994
Wolfgang G. Fischer: *Egon Schiele 1890–1918: Pantomimen der Lust, Visionen der Sterblichkeit*, Cologne 1994.

Gütersloh 1911
Albert Paris Gütersloh: *Egon Schiele. Versuch einer Vorrede*, Vienna 1911.

Hofmann 1968
Werner Hofmann: *Egon Schiele: "Die Familie"*, Stuttgart 1968.

Kallir 1930
Otto Kallir (Nirenstein): *Egon Schiele. Oeuvre Catalogue of the Paintings*, New York/Vienna 1930.

Kallir 1966
Otto Kallir: *Egon Schiele. Oeuvre-Katalog der Gemälde*, Vienna 1966.

Kallir 1970
Otto Kallir (Nirenstein): *Egon Schiele. The Graphic Work*, New York/Vienna 1970.

Kallir 1980
Jane Kallir: *Austria's Expressionism*, New York 1980.

Kallir 1990
Jane Kallir: *Egon Schiele. The Complete Works*, New York 1990.

Kallir 1998
Jane Kallir: *Egon Schiele. The Complete Works*, New York 1998.

Kallir 2003
Jane Kallir: *Egon Schiele. Aquarelle und Zeichnungen*, Vienna 2003.

Kallir 2012
Jane Kallir: *Schiele's Women*, Munich/London/New York 2012.

Karpfen 1921
Fritz Karpfen: *Das Egon Schiele Buch*, Vienna 1921.

Karpfen 1923
Fritz Karpfen: *Österreichische Kunst*, Vienna 1923.

Koschatzky 1968
Walter Koschatzky (ed.): *Egon Schiele: Aquarelle und Zeichnungen*, Salzburg 1968.

Kuchling 1982
Heimo Kuchling: *Egon Schiele und sein Kreis*, Ramerding 1982.

Künstler 1946
Gustav Künstler: *Egon Schiele als Graphiker*, Vienna 1946.

Lampert 1975
Wolfgang Lampert: "Egon Schieles Wiener Zeit: Seine Ateliers und seine Begegnungen", in: *Alte und moderne Kunst*, year 20, no. 140, Vienna 1975, pp. 33–35.

Leopold 1959
Rudolf Leopold: "Egon Schiele. Ein Genie aus Österreich", in: *BP Querschnitt*, issue 1, Vienna 1959.

Leopold 1972
Rudolf Leopold: *Egon Schiele. Gemälde, Aquarelle, Zeichnungen*, Salzburg 1972.

Leopold 2010
Rudolf Leopold: *Egon Schiele. Landscapes*, Munich and other places 2010.

Leopold Museum 2008
Leopold Museum (ed.): *Egon Schiele. Poems and Letters 1910–1912 from the Leopold Collection*, Munich 2008.

Markowitz 1921
Alfred Markowitz: "An der Wende zweier Weltanschauungen. Zur neuesten Egon Schiele Literatur", in: *Arbeiterzeitung*, 30th June 1921, pp. 5–6.

Mitsch 1961
Erwin Mitsch: *Egon Schiele: Zeichnungen und Aquarelle*, Salzburg 1961.

Mitsch 1974
Erwin Mitsch: *Egon Schiele 1890–1918*, Salzburg 1974.

Müller-Tamm 1995
Pia Müller-Tamm (ed.): *Egon Schiele. Inszenierung und Identität*, Cologne 1995.

Nagy/Kallir 2011
Richard Nagy/Jane Kallir et al. *Egon Schiele. Women*, London 2011.

Natter 2003
Tobias G. Natter: *Die Welt von Klimt, Schiele und Kokoschka. Sammler und Mäzene*, Cologne 2003.

Nebehay 1968
Christian M. Nebehay: *Egon Schiele. Frühe Werke und Dokumentation,* Vienna 1968.

Nebehay 1977
Christian M. Nebehay (ed.): *Egon Schiele (1890–1918): Die Gedichte,* Vienna 1977.

Nebehay 1979
Christian M. Nebehay: *Egon Schiele 1890–1918. Leben, Briefe, Gedichte,* Salzburg 1979.

Nebehay 1980
Christian M. Nebehay: *Egon Schiele: Leben und Werk,* Salzburg 1980.

Nebehay 1983
Christian M. Nebehay: *Egon Schiele. Leben und Werk in Dokumenten und Bildern,* Vienna 1983.

Nebehay 1987
Christian M. Nebehay: *Gustav Klimt, Egon Schiele und die Familie Lederer,* Bern 1987.

Nebehay 1989
Christian M. Nebehay: *Egon Schiele. Von der Skizze zum Bild. Die Skizzenbücher,* Vienna 1989.

Nebehay/Krug 1974
Christian M. Nebehay/Hansjörg Krug (eds.): *Remigius Geyling. Künstler und Literaten gezeichnet in Wien um 1900,* Vienna 1974.

Price 2005
Renée Price: *Egon Schiele. The Ronald S. Lauder and Serge Sabarsky Collections,* Munich 2005.

Roessler 1918
Arthur Roessler: *Kritische Fragmente: Aufsätze über österreichische Neukünstler,* Vienna 1918.

Roessler 1921
Arthur Roessler: *Briefe und Prosa von Egon Schiele,* Vienna 1921.

Roessler 1922 (1)
Arthur Roessler: *Egon Schiele im Gefängnis. Aufzeichnungen und Zeichnungen,* Vienna 1922.

Roessler 1922 (2)
Arthur Roessler: *Erinnerungen an Egon Schiele,* Vienna 1922.

Roessler 1928 (1)
Arthur Roessler: "Egon Schiele", in: *Der neue Pflug,* year 2, no. 11, November 1928, pp. 3–8.

Roessler 1928 (2)
Arthur Roessler: "Egon Schiele: Zu den Gedächtnisausstellungen im Hagenbund und in der Neuen Galerie", in: *Bühne, Welt und Mode,* issue 158, November 1928, pp. 546–550.

Roessler 1929
Arthur Roessler: "Egon Schiele zum Gedächtnis", in: *Österreichische Monatshefte,* year 5, June 1929, pp. 283–292.

Samsonow 2010
Elisabeth von Samsonow: *Egon Schiele: Ich bin die Vielen,* with an epilogue by Peter Sloterdijk, Vienna 2010.

Samsonow 2012
Elisabeth von Samsonow: *Egon Schiele. Sanctus Franciscus Hystericus,* Vienna 2012.

Smith 2004
Kimberly A. Smith: *Between Ruin and Renewal: Egon Schiele's Landscapes,* New Haven 2004.

Smola 2003
Franz Smola: "Neukunst und Klimtgruppe. Wiens Avantgarde in Budapest 1912/13", in: exh. cat. Vienna, Kunsthistorisches Museum 2003, pp. 525–535.

Vergo 1975
Peter Vergo: *Art in Vienna 1898–1918,* London 1975.

Weiermair 1968
Peter Weiermair: *Egon Schiele,* Innsbruck 1968.

Werkner 1986
Patrick Werkner: *Physis und Psyche: Der österreichische Frühexpressionismus,* Vienna/Munich 1986.

Werkner 1994
Patrick Werkner (ed.): *Egon Schiele: Art, Sexuality and Viennese Modernism,* Palo Alto 1994.

Whitford 1981
Frank Whitford: *Egon Schiele,* London 1981.

Wilson 1980
Simon Wilson: *Egon Schiele,* Ithaca/New York 1980.

Wischin 1994
Franz Wischin: *Egon Schiele und Krumau,* Vienna 1994.

EXHIBITION CATALOGUES

Exh. cat. Vienna, Historisches Museum der Stadt Wien 1990
Egon Schiele. Ewige Kindheit, reife Jugend, ed. by Historisches Museum der Stadt Wien, Vienna 1990 (exh. cat. Historisches Museum der Stadt Wien, Vienna, 10th May 1990–2nd September 1990).

Exh. cat. Innsbruck, Landesmuseum Ferdinandeum 1998/99
MenschenBilder. Egon Schiele und seine Zeit. Meisterwerke aus der Sammlung Leopold, ed. by Rudolf Leopold/Gert Ammann, Cologne 1998 (exh. cat. Landesmuseum Ferdinandeum, Innsbruck, 17th September 1998–17th January 1999).

Exh. cat. Vienna, Kunsthistorisches Museum 2003
Zeit des Aufbruchs. Budapest und Wien zwischen Historismus und Avantgarde, ed. by Wilfried Seipel, Vienna 2003 (exh. cat. Kunsthistorisches Museum, Vienna, 10th February 2003–22nd April 2003).

Exh. cat. Vienna, Wien Museum 2004
Schiele & Roessler. Der Künstler und sein Förderer. Kunst und Networking im frühen 20. Jahrhundert, ed. by Tobias G. Natter, Vienna 2004 (exh. cat. Wien Museum, Vienna, 8th July 2004–10th October 2004).

Exh. cat. Vienna, Leopold Museum 2004/05
Egon Schiele. Landschaften, ed. by Rudolf Leopold, Munich 2004 (exh. cat. Leopold Museum, Vienna, 17th September 2004–31st January 2005).

Exh. cat. Amsterdam, Van Gogh Museum 2005
Egon Schiele. Love and Death, ed. by Jane Kallir/Edwin Becker/Suzanne Bogman, Ostfildern-Ruit 2005 (exh. cat. Van Gogh Museum, Amsterdam, 25th March 2005–19th June 2005).

Exh. cat. Frankfurt, Schirn Kunsthalle 2005
The Naked Truth. Klimt, Schiele, Kokoschka and other Scandals, ed. by Tobias G. Natter, Munich and other places 2005 (exh. cat. Schirn Kunsthalle, Frankfurt, 28th January 2005–24th April 2005; Leopold Museum, Vienna, 13th May 2005–22nd August 2005).

Exh. cat. Vienna, Albertina 2005/06
Egon Schiele, ed. by Klaus Albrecht Schröder, Munich 2005 (exh. cat. Albertina, Vienna, 6th December 2005–19th March 2006).

Exh. cat. Vienna, Belvedere 2006
Die Tafelrunde. Egon Schiele und sein Kreis, ed. by Tobias G. Natter, Cologne 2006 (exh. cat. Belvedere, Vienna, 14th June 2006–24th September 2006).

Exh. cat. Liverpool, Tate Liverpool 2008
Gustav Klimt. Painting, Design and Modern Life, ed. by Tobias G. Natter/Christoph Grunenberg, London 2008 (exh. cat. Tate Liverpool, Liverpool, 30th May 2008–31st August 2008).

Exh. cat. Milan, Palazzo Reale 2010
Schiele e il suo tempo, ed. by Rudolf Leopold/Franz Smola, Milan 2010 (exh. cat. Palazzo Reale, Milan, 24th February 2010–6th June 2010).

Exh. cat. Basel, Fondation Beyeler 2010/11
Wien 1900. Klimt, Schiele und ihre Zeit. Ein Gesamtkunstwerk, ed. by Barbara Steffen, Ostfildern 2010 (exh. cat. Fondation Beyeler, Basel, 26th September 2010–16th January 2011).

Exh. cat. Wien, Belvedere 2011
Egon Schiele. Selbstporträts und Porträts, ed. by Agnes Husslein-Arco/Jane Kallir, Munich 2011 (exh. cat. Belvedere, Vienna, 17th February 2011–13th June 2011).

Exh. cat. Wien, Albertina 2011
Egon Schiele: "Das unrettbare Ich". Werke aus der Albertina, ed. by Helmut Friedel/Helena Pereña, Cologne 2011 (exh. cat. Städtische Galerie im Lenbachhaus und Kunstbau, Munich, 3rd December 2011–4th March 2011).

Exh. cat. Melbourne, National Gallery of Victoria 2011
Vienna. Art and Design. Klimt, Schiele, Hoffmann, Loos, ed. by Christian Witt-Dörring, Melbourne 2011 (exh. cat. National Gallery of Victoria, Melbourne, 18th June 2011–9th October 2011).

Exh. cat. Vienna, Leopold Museum 2011/12
Egon Schiele. Melancholy and Provocation. With Dialogues by Rudolf Schwarzkogler, Günter Brus, Elke Krystufek, Franz Graf, Claudia Bosse, Philipp Gehmacher, ed. by Elisabeth Leopold/Diethard Leopold, Vienna 2011 (exh. cat. Leopold Museum, Vienna, 23rd September 2011–30th January 2012).

Exh. cat. Budapest, Szépművészeti Múzeum 2013
Egon Schiele and his Age. Masterpieces from the Leopold Museum, Vienna, ed. by László Baán, Budapest 2013 (exh. cat. Szépművészeti Múzeum, Budapest, 26th June 2013–29th September 2013).

Exh. cat. New York, Neue Galerie New York 2014/15
Egon Schiele. Portraits, ed. by Alessandra Comini, Munich 2014 (exh. cat. Neue Galerie New York, New York, 9th October 2014–20th April 2015).

Exh. cat. Zurich, Kunsthaus Zürich 2014/15
Egon Schiele – Jenny Saville, ed. by Zürcher Kunstgesellschaft, Ostfildern 2014 (exh. cat. Kunsthaus Zürich, Zurich, 10th October 2014–25th January 2015).

Exh. cat. London, The Courtauld Gallery 2014/15
Egon Schiele. The Radical Nude, ed. by Peter Vergo/Barnaby Wright, London 2014 (exh. cat. The Courtauld Gallery, London, 23rd October 2014–18th January 2015).

Exh. cat. Vienna, Leopold Museum 2015
Wally Neuzil. Ihr Leben mit Egon Schiele, ed. by Diethard Leopold/Stephan Pumberger/Birgit Summerauer, Vienna 2015 (exh. cat. Leopold Museum, Vienna, 27th February 2015–1st June 2015).

Exh. cat. Frankfurt, Schirn Kunsthalle 2015
Künstler und Propheten. Eine geheime Geschichte der Moderne 1872–1972, ed. by Pamela Kort/Max Hollein (exh. cat. Schirn Kunsthalle, Frankfurt, 6th March 2015–14th June 2015).

Exh. cat. Vienna, Belvedere 2015/16
Klimt, Schiele, Kokoschka und die Frauen, ed. by Agnes Husslein-Arco/Jane Kallir/Alfred Weidinger, Munich and other places 2015 (exh. cat. Belvedere, Vienna, 23rd October 2015–28th February 2016).

EXHIBITIONS

List of exhibitions held between 1912 and 2016 which featured works selected for this publication.

1912
Munich, Neue Kunst Hans Goltz: *Second Editorial Exhibition: Der Blaue Reiter/Black and White.* 15th February–15th March 1912.
Munich, Secession: *Spring Exhibition,* spring 1912.
Vienna, Hagenbund: *Spring Exhibition,* spring 1912.
Cologne, Städtische Ausstellungshalle: *International Art Exhibition of the Sonderbund westdeutscher Kunstfreunde und Künstler,* 25th May–30th September 1912.

1913
Budapest, Müveszhäz: *Bund Österreichischer Künstler és Gustav Klimt/Gyüjteményes Kiällitäsara,* March 1913.
Munich, Secession: *Spring Exhibition,* spring 1913.

1914
Munich, Secession: *Spring Exhibition,* 3rd March–19th April 1914.
Berlin, Kunsthandlung Feldmann: *Summer Exhibition,* July 1914.
Vienna, Galerie Arnot: *Collective Exhibition Egon Schiele,* 31st December 1914–31st January 1915.

1917
Amsterdam, Stedelijk Museum: *Tentoonstelling van Werken van Oostenrijksche en Hongaarsche Schilders en Beeldhouwers,* 14th October–November 1917.
Stockholm, Liljevalchs Konsthall: *Österrikiska Konstutställningen,* 1st September–late September 1917.
Copenhagen: *Østrigsk Kunststudstillin,* December 1917–January 1918.

1918
Vienna, Secession: *49th Exhibition of the Vienna Secession,* March 1918.

1919
Vienna, art dealers Gustav Nebehay: *The Drawings: Egon Schiele,* April 1919.

1920
Vienna, Österreichisches Museum für Kunst und Industrie: *Kunstschau,* June–September 1920.

1923
Vienna, Neue Galerie: *Egon Schiele,* 20th November–December 1923.

1924
Vienna, Künstlerhaus: *Portraits and Self-Portraits of Austrian Artists of the Past 100 Years,* December 1924.

1925
Vienna, Kunsthandlung Würthle: *Egon Schiele,* December 1925–January 1926.

1926
Frankfurt on the Main, M. Goldschmidt & Co.: *Egon Schiele,* 1926.
Berlin, Kunsthandlung Fritz Gurlitt: *Tsugouharu Foujita, Egon Schiele,* April 1926.
Dresden, Städtischer Ausstellungspalast: *International Art Exhibition,* June–September 1926.

1927
Vienna, Österreichisches Museum für Kunst und Industrie: *The Creation of an Artwork,* October–November 1927.

1928
Prague, Národní Galerie: *Moderní umění Rakouské,* 8th September–7th October 1928.
Vienna, Hagenbund and Neue Galerie: *Memorial Exhibition Egon Schiele,* October–November 1928.

1930
Zurich, Kunsthaus: *Exhibition,* 23rd March–21st April 1930.
Vienna, Neue Galerie: *Unknown Works by Egon Schiele,* October 1930.

1932
Vienna, Hagenbund: *Collection Carl von Reininghaus,* 24th January–7th February 1932.
Vienna, Neue Galerie: *Spring Exhibition,* April 1932.

1933
Vienna, Neue Galerie: *Anton Faistauer, Gustav Klimt, Oskar Kokoschka and Egon Schiele,* June 1933.

1937
Paris, Musée du Jeu de Paume: *Exposition d'Art Autrichien,* May–June 1937.
Bern, Kunsthalle: *20th Century Austrian Art,* 20th August–20th September 1937.

1939
Paris, Galerie St. Etienne: *L'Art Autrichien,* 10th February–1st March 1939.

1941
New York, Galerie St. Etienne: *Egon Schiele,* 7th November–5th December 1941.

1948
Vienna, Academy of Fine Arts: *The Development of Austrian Art from 1897 to 1938: Paintings, Sculptures, Drawings,* March–April 1948.
New York, Galerie St. Etienne: *Egon Schiele: Paintings, Watercolors, Drawings,* April 1948.
Venice, Austrian pavilion: *XXIV Biennale di Venezia,* summer 1948.
Vienna, Grafische Sammlung Albertina: *Egon Schiele: Memorial Exhibition,* autumn 1948.
Vienna, Neue Galerie: *Egon Schiele: Memorial Exhibition on the 30th Anniversary of the Artist's Death,* October–November 1948.

1949
Linz, Neue Galerie der Stadt Linz: *Egon Schiele,* March 1949.
Zurich, Graphische Sammlung der Eidgenössischen Technischen Hochschule: *Gustav Klimt-Egon Schiele: Drawings and Watercolors,* 28th May–14th August 1949.

1950
Salzburg, Künstlerhaus: *Egon Schiele from the Collection of Wolfgang Gurlitt,* 1950.

1953
New York, Galerie St. Etienne: *Lovis Corinth, Oskar Kokoschka, Egon Schiele,* 27th May–26th June 1953.

1954
Vienna, Neue Galerie: *Egon Schiele,* February–March 1954.

1956
Basel, Kunstmuseum: *Collection Rudolf Staechelin,* May–June 1956.
Bern, Gutekunst & Klipstein: *Egon Schiele: Paintings, Watercolors, Drawings, Graphic Works,* 8th September–6th October 1956.
Amsterdam, Stedelijk Museum: *Kunst uit Oostenrijk,* 16th November–16th December 1956; Eindhoven, Stedelijk Van Abbemuseum, 22nd December–26th January 1957.

1957
New York, Galerie St. Etienne: *Egon Schiele: Watercolors and Drawings,* 21st January–23rd February 1957.
Munich, Galerie Wolfgang Gurlitt: *Egon Schiele,* 14th February–11th March 1957.
Bern, Kunsthalle: *Austrian Art,* 16th February–24th March 1957.
St. Gallen, Kunstmuseum: *Austrian Art,* 6th April–12th May 1957.
Salzburg, Residenz-Galerie: *Expressionism: Painting in Austria, Germany, Switzerland,* June–September 1957.
Stuttgart, Württembergischer Kunstverein: *The Classics of Austrian Modern Art from Klimt to Wotruba,* November 1957.

1958
Baden-Baden, Staatliche Kunsthalle: *Gustav Klimt and Egon Schiele,* January–February 1958.

1959
Düsseldorf, Städtische Kunsthalle: *Masterpieces of Austrian Painting 1800–1930,* 16th May–28th June 1959.
Recklinghausen, Städtische Kunsthalle: *The Artist's Handwriting,* 23rd May–5th July 1959.
New York, Galerie St. Etienne: *European and American Expressionists,* 22nd September–17th October 1959.

1960
Berlin, Hochschule für bildende Künste: *Exhibition of Graphic Works from the Vienna Secession,* 1960.
New York, Bayer Gallery: *Egon Schiele, 1960. London, Arts Council Gallery: Austrian Painting and Sculpture 1900 to 1960,* 4th May–4th June 1960.
Boston, Institute of Contemporary Art: *Egon Schiele,* 6th October–6th November 1960; New York, Galerie St. Etienne, 15th November–15th December 1960; Louisville, Kentucky, J. B. Speed Art Museum, 3rd January–31st January 1961; Pittsburgh, Carnegie Institute, 2nd March–2nd April 1961; Minneapolis, Minneapolis Institute of Arts, 19th April–21st May 1961.

1961
Brussels, Palais des Beaux-Arts: *Art Autrichien au vingti me siècle,* April–May 1961.
Vienna, Galerie im Griechenbeisl: *Egon Schiele,* 20th June–15th July 1961.

1962
Heidelberg, Heidelberger Kunstverein: *Gustav Klimt, Egon Schiele,* 18th February–18th March 1962.
Cologne, Wallraf-Richartz-Museum: *European Art 1912,* 12th September–9th December 1962.

1963
Berkeley, University Art Gallery of the University of California: *Viennese Expressionism 1910–1924,* 5th February–10th March 1963; Pasadena, Pasadena Art Museum, 19th March–21st April 1963.
Innsbruck, Tiroler Landesmuseum Ferdinandeum: *Egon Schiele,* May–June 1963.
Turin, Galleria Galatea d'Arte Contemporanea: *Schiele,* 8th June–15th July 1963.

1964
Bern, Kornfeld & Klipstein: *Exhibition 1864–1964: Drawings – Watercolors,* 1964.
Munich, Haus der Kunst: *Secession: Fin-de-Siècle European Art,* 14th March–10th May 1964.
Florence, Palazzo Strozzi: *L'espressionismo: pittura, scultura, architettura,* May–June 1964.
Vienna, Historisches Museum der Stadt Wien: *Vienna around 1900,* 5th June–30th August 1964.
London, Marlborough Fine Art: *Egon Schiele: Paintings, Watercolors and Drawings,* October 1964.

1965
New York, Solomon R. Guggenheim Museum: *Gustav Klimt and Egon Schiele,* February–March 1965.
Götzis, Galerie Hämmerle: *Egon Schiele: Watercolors, Drawings,* 20th February–20th March 1965.
New York, Galerie St. Etienne: *Egon Schiele (1890–1918): Watercolors and Drawings from American Collections,* March–April 1965.

1967
Darmstadt, Mathildenhöhe: *2nd International Drawing Exhibition,* 16th July–9th September 1967.

1968
Vienna, Grafische Sammlung Albertina: *Gustav Klimt – Egon Schiele: Commemorating their Deaths 50 Years Ago,* 5th April–16th June 1968.
Vienna, Österreichische Galerie: *Egon Schiele Paintings,* 5th April–15th September 1968.
Salzburg, Museum Carolino Augusteum: *Egon Schiele (1890–1918),* July–August 1968.
New York, Galerie St. Etienne: *Egon Schiele (1890–1918),* 31st October–14th December 1968.

1969
London, Marlborough Fine Art: *Egon Schiele: Drawings and Watercolors, 1909–1918,* February–March 1969.

1970
Vienna, Künstlerhaus: *Motifs: City- and Townscapes by Austrian Artists since 1910,* 10th June–30th August 1970.

1971
London, Royal Academy of Arts: *Vienna Secession: Art Nouveau to 1970,* 9th January–7th March 1971.
Bregenz, Künstlerhaus Palais Thurn und Taxis: *Jugendstil – Vienna Secession,* 23rd July–30th September 1971.
Iowa, Des Moines Art Center: *Egon Schiele and the Human Form: Drawings and Watercolors,* 20th September–31st October 1971; Ohio, Columbus Gallery of Fine Arts, 15th November–15th December 1971; Chicago, Art Institute of Chicago, 3rd January–13th February 1972.

1972
London, Fischer Fine Art: *Egon Schiele: Oils, Watercolors, Drawings and Graphic Works,* November–December 1972.

1973
Innsbruck, Galerie im Taxispalais: *Gustav Klimt, Egon Schiele: Drawings and Watercolors,* July–August 1973; Graz, Kulturhaus, September–October 1973.
Zurich, Kunsthaus: *50th Anniversary of the Kunsthandelsverbund der Schweiz,* 15th September–11th November 1973.

1974
Lucerne, Kunstmuseum: *Austrian Art 1900–1930,* 14th July–8th September 1974.

1975
Munich, Haus der Kunst: *Egon Schiele,* 22nd February–11th March 1975.
London, Fischer Fine Art: *Egon Schiele: Watercolors, Drawings, Graphics,* June–July 1975.

1977
Wörgl, Bundes-Realgymnasium: *Egon Schiele: Works Owned by the Neue Galerie Graz,* March 1977.
Innsbruck, Galerie Annasäule: *Egon Schiele,* June–July 1977.

1978
New York, Cooper-Hewitt Museum: *Vienna Modernism: 1898–1918,* 27th November 1978–4th February 1979; Houston, The Sarah Campbell Blaffer Gallery, University of Houston, 2nd March–29th April 1979; Maine, Portland Museum of Art, June–July 1979; Chicago, Art Institute of Chicago, September–November 1979.

1979
Tokyo, Seibu Museum of Art: *Egon Schiele,* 27th April–6th June 1979.
London, Marlborough Fine Art: *Egon Schiele: An Exhibition of Watercolors and Drawings,* June–August 1979.
Vienna, Niederösterreichisches Landesmuseum: *Egon Schiele: Family-Owned Works,* 19th October–30th December 1979.

1980
Tulln, town hall: *Egon Schiele 1890–1918: Return to Tulln 1980,* March 1980.
Vienna, Galerie Würthle: *60 Years of Modern Art in Austria,* 6th May–7th June 1980.

1981
Brussels, Palais des Beaux-Arts: *Klimt, Schiele, Kokoschka,* 3rd April–17th May 1981.
Hamburg, Hamburger Kunsthalle: *The Armageddon Experiment: Vienna around 1900,* 10th April–31st May 1981.
Vienna, Historisches Museum der Stadt Wien: *Egon Schiele: Drawings and Watercolors,* 24th September–1st November 1981;

Linz, Neue Galerie der Stadt Linz, 19th November 1981–16th January 1982; Munich, Museum Villa Stuck, March–April 1982; Hannover, Kestner-Gesellschaft, 23rd April–13th June 1982.

1982
Kirchheim unter Teck, Kulturring: *Egon Schiele: The Artist's Legacy,* 23rd May–13th June 1982.

1983
New York, Bellmann Gallery: *German Expressionists,* January–February 1983.
Edinburgh, National Museum of Antiquities of Scotland: *Vienna 1900,* summer 1983.

1984
Vienna, Academy of Fine Arts: *Egon Schiele, from Student to Master: Drawings and Watercolors 1906–1918,* January–March 1984; Milan, Accademia di Belle Arti di Brera, 16th March–10th May 1985; Palermo, Villa Zito, 28th February–14th April 1985; Tel Aviv, Tel Aviv Museum of Art, 20th April–23rd May 1985; Hamburg, Hamburger Kunsthalle, 31st May–14th July 1985; Salzburg, Rupertinum, 27th July–19th September 1985; Graz, Schloss Plankenwirth, October–November 1985; Innsbruck, Tiroler Landesmuseum Ferdinandeum, 7th January–7th February 1986; Bottrop, Josef Albers Museum, 16th February–15th April 1986; Nuremberg, Nürnberger Kunsthalle, 23rd April–22nd June 1986.
Venice, Palazzo Grassi: *XLI Biennale di Venezia: Le Arti a Vienna, dalla Sezessione alla caduta dell'imperio asburgico,* 20th May–16th September 1984.
Rome, Pinacoteca Capitolina: *Egon Schiele,* 21st June–5th August 1984; Venice, Galleria Internazionale d'Arte Moderna, 25th August 1984–12th January 1985; Martigny, Fondation Pierre Gianadda, 26th November 1986–25th January 1987.

1985
Vienna, Künstlerhaus: *Dream and Reality: Vienna 1870–1930,* 28th March–6th October 1985.

1986
Tokyo, Isetan Museum: *Egon Schiele and Fin-de-Siècle Vienna,* 1st March–1st April 1986; Nagoya, Aichi Prefectural Museum of Art, 9th April–24th April 1986; Nara, Nara Prefectural Museum of Art, 17th May–29th June 1986; Fuefuki, Yamanashi Prefectural Museum of Art, 18th July–17th August 1986; Kamakura, Kamakura Museum of Modern Art, 20th September–3rd November 1986.

1987
Charleroi, Palais des Beaux-Arts: *Egon Schiele,* 18th September–16th December 1987.

1988
Zurich, Kunsthaus: *Egon Schiele and His Time: Austrian Painting and Drawing from 1900 to 1930 from the Leopold Collection,* 25th November 1988–9th February 1989; Vienna, Kunstforum, 16th March–23rd June 1989; Munich, Kunsthalle der Hypobank-Kulturstiftung, 28th September 1989–8th January 1990; Wuppertal, Von der Heydt-Museum, 21st January–31st March 1990; London, Royal Academy of Arts, 23rd November 1990–17th February 1991.

1991
Tokyo, Bunkamura Museum: *Egon Schiele from the Leopold Collection, Vienna,* 12th October–8th December 1991; Nagoya, Nagoya City Art Museum, 11th January–23rd February 1992; Osaka, Daimaru Museum, 4th March–16th March 1992; Fuefuki, Yamanashi Prefectural Museum of Art, 4th April–12th May 992.

1994
Tobu, Japan, Museum of Art: *Japonism in Vienna,* 20th December 1994–12th February 1995; Yamaguchi, Yamaguchi Prefectural Museum of Art, 21st February–26th March 1995; Nagoya, Aichi Prefectural Museum of Art, 11th April–14th May 1995; Takamatsu, Takamatsu City Art Museum, 23rd May–25th June 1995; Kamakura, Museum of Modern Art, 1st July–6th August 1995.

1995
Munich, Städtische Galerie im Lenbachhaus: *The Battle of the Sexes,* 8th March–7th May 1995.
Tübingen, Kunsthalle: *Egon Schiele: The Leopold Collection, Vienna,* 2nd September–3rd December 1995; Düsseldorf, Kunstsammlung Nordrhein-Westfalen, 21st December 1995–3rd March 1996; Hamburg, Hamburger Kunsthalle, 13th March–16th June 1996; Graz, Neue Galerie am Landesmuseum Joanneum, 18th June–14th September 1997; New York, Museum of Modern Art, 8th October 1997–4th January 1998; Barcelona, Museo Picasso, 16th February 1998–31st May 1998; Tulln, Stadtgemeinde Tulln, 19th June–13th September 1998.

1997
Tokyo, Seiji Togo Memorial Yasuda Kasai Museum of Art: *Egon Schiele: The Leopold Collection, Vienna,* 18th January–13th April 1997; Tsu, Mie Prefectural Art Museum, 19th April–25th May 1997; Yokohama, Sogo Museum, 15th March–5th May 1997.

1998
Brussels, Musée d'Ixelles: *L'Expressionisme en Autriche. De Schiele et Kokoschka aux années vingt. Painters of Austrian Expressionism 1905–1925,* 10th June–20th September 1998.
Innsbruck, Tiroler Landesmuseum Ferdinandeum: *Images of Humanity. Egon Schiele and His Time,* 17th September 1998–17th January 1999.

2000
Hannover, Kestner Gesellschaft: *Departure into Modernism. Vienna 1900–1930. Masterpieces from the Leopold Collection,* 17th June–13th August 2000.
Holte, Gl. Holtegaard-Breda Fonden: *Egon Schiele. Drawings,* 15th September–15th November 2000.
Aosta, Archäologisches Museum: *Schiele e Klimt e i maestri dell'arte moderna austriaca dalla Fondazione Leopold di Wien,* 7th December 2000–18th March 2001.

2001
London, Tate Gallery: *Century City: Art and Culture in the 20th Century Metropolis,* 10th January–30th April 2001.
Berlin, Nationalgalerie Berlin: *The Potsdamer Platz. Ernst Ludwig Kirchner and the Fall of Prussia,* 26th April–12th August 2001.
Rome, Complesso del Vittoriano: *Klimt – Kokoschka – Schiele. From Art Nouveau to Expressionism,* 6th October 2001–3rd February 2002.
Warsaw, Galeria Zacheta: *Bound – Unbound,* 18th October 2001–3rd January 2002.

2002
Trieste, Museo Revoltella: *Klimt, Schiele, Kokoschka: L'etá d'oro di Vienna con i suoi maestri,* 8th February–21st April 2002.
Emden, Kunsthalle Emden: *The Nude in 20th Century Art,* 26th October 2002–26th January 2003.

2003
Lugano, Museo d'Arte Moderna: *Egon Schiele,* 16th March–29th May 2003.
Verona, Galleria d'Arte Moderna, Palazzo Forti: *La Creazione Ansiosa,* 12th September 2003–11th January 2004.
Frankfurt on the Main, Städelsches Kunstinstitut: *Naked! Female Images. Artists' Intentions. Departure into Modernism,* 25th September 2003–11th January 2004.
Vienna, Kunsthistorisches Museum: *Francis Bacon and the Tradition of Art,* 15th October 2003–19th January 2004; Basel, Fondation Beyeler, 8th February–29th June 2004.

2004
Bologna, Galleria d'Arte Moderna: *Ideale e realità. Una storia del nudo dal Neoclassicismo ad oggi,* 1st January–9th May 2004.

Vienna, Leopold Museum: *Egon Schiele – Horst Janssen. Self-Dramatization, Eros and Death*, 4th March–4th July 2004; Oldenburg, Horst Janssen Museum, 29th October 2004–20th February 2005.
Palermo, Civica Galleria d'Arte Moderna: *Egon Schiele from the Leopold Collection*, 28th May–1st August 2004.
Vienna, Wien Museum: *Schiele & Roessler. The Artist and His Patron. Art and Networking in the Early 20th Century*, 8th July–10th October 2004.
Vienna, Leopold Museum: *Schiele Landscapes*, 16th September 2004–31st January 2005.
Tulln, Egon Schiele-Museum: *Egon Schiele*, 4th October–22nd November 2004.

2005
Frankfurt on the Main, Schirn Kunsthalle: *The Naked Truth. Klimt, Schiele, Kokoschka and other Scandals*, 28th January–24th April 2004; Vienna, Leopold Museum, 13th May 2005–22nd August 2005.
Vienna, Österreichisches Theatermuseum: *Fritz Grünbaum*, 10th February–8th May 2005.
Amsterdam, Van Gogh Museum: *Egon Schiele Retrospective*, 25th March–19th June 2005.
Dorf Tirol, Schloss Tirol: *The Dark Eagles. World War I in Art, Literature and Everyday Life – Illusion and Reality*, 28th June–31st November 2005.
Paris, Grand Palais: *Klimt, Kokoschka, Schiele, Moser*, 3rd October 2005–23rd January 2006.

2006
Vienna, Österreichische Galerie Belvedere: *The Round Table. Egon Schiele and His Circle*, 14th June–24th September 2006.
Vienna, Leopold Museum: *Body, Face, Soul. The Female Image from the 16th to the 21st Century*, 9th June–2nd October 2006.
London, The National Gallery: *Rebels and Martyrs: The Artist in the 19th Century*, 28th June–28th August 2006.

2007
Madrid, Museo Thyssen: *The Mirror and the Mask. The Portrait in the Age of Picasso*, 6th February–20th May 2007.
Krems, Kunsthalle Krems: *Japan. Meiji-Art and Japonism from van Gogh to Schiele*, 25th February–3rd June 2007.
Rome, Palazzo Quirinale: *Capolavori dell'Arte Europea*, 23rd March–20th May 2007.
Oslo, Munch Museum: *Egon Schiele*, 18th April–17th June 2007.
Edinburgh, Scottish National Portrait Gallery: *The Naked Portrait*, 6th June–9th September 2007.
Athens Megaron – The Athens Concert Hall: *Klimt, Schiele, Kokoschka and Their Time. Masterpieces from the Leopold Museum, Vienna*, 20th October 2007–1st January 2008.

2008
Linz, Lentos: Troublemakers: *Enfants Terribles of the Avant-Garde from Makart to Nitsch*, 31st January–18th May 2008.
Liverpool, Tate Liverpool: *Gustav Klimt. Painting, Design and Modern Life in Vienna 1900*, 30th May–31st August 2008.
Madrid, Museo Thyssen: *1914! The Avant-Garde and the War*, 7th October 2008–11th January 2009.

2009
Linz, Lentos: *Best of Austria*, 2nd January–10th May 2009.
Linz, Oberösterreichisches Landesmuseum: *Henri de Toulouse-Lautrec – The Intimate Look*, 1st March–21st June 2009.
Bleiburg, Werner Berg Museum: *European Exhibition 2009: The Power of Words – The Power of Images*, 26th April–8th November 2009.
Vienna, Leopold Museum: *Edvard Munch and the Uncanny*, 16th October 2009–18th January 2010.

2010
Milan, Palazzo Reale: *Schiele e il suo tempo*, 24th February–6th June 2010.
Vienna, Leopold Museum: *Hidden Treasures of Austrian Watercolor Painting*, 5th March–24th May 2010.
Krumau, Egon Schiele Art Centrum: *Egon Schiele. On His 120th Birthday*, 16th April–31st October 2010.
Basel, Fondation Beyeler: *Vienna 1900. Klimt, Schiele and Their Times. A Total Work of Art*, 26th September 2010–6th February 2011.
Darmstadt, Darmstädter Sezession: *The Total Work of Art in Expressionism. Art, Film, Literature, Theater, Dance and Architecture 1905–1925*, 24th October 2010–13th February 2011.

2011
Vienna, Belvedere: *Egon Schiele. Self-Portraits and Portraits*, 17th February 2011–13th June 2011.
Barcelona, CaixaForum: *Portraits of the Belle Époque*, 19th July–9th October 2011.
Vienna, Leopold Museum: *Egon Schiele. Melancholy and Provocation. With Dialogues by Rudolf Schwarzkogler, Günter Brus, Elke Krystufek, Franz Graf, Claudia Bosse, Philipp Gehmacher*, 23rd September 2011–19th April 2012.
Ghent, Museum voor Schone Kunsten Gent: *The World of George Minne and Maurice Maeterlinck*, 22nd October 2011–19th February 2012.

2012
Neulengbach, Museum Region Neulengbach: *100 Years Egon Schiele in Neulengbach*, 14th April–9th September 2012.
Vienna, Leopold Museum: *Fantastic! Rudolf Kalvach. Vienna and Trieste around 1900*, 7th June–10th September 2012.
Vienna, Leopold Museum: *Klimt: Up Close and Personal. Images – Letters – Insights*, 24th February–27th August 2012.
Vienna, Leopold Museum: *naked men. from 1800 to the present*, 19th October 2012–28th January 2013.
Linz, Lentos: *The Naked Man*, 26th October 2012–17th February 2013.

2013
Vienna, Leopold Museum: *Clouds. Fleeting Worlds*, 22nd March–1st July 2013.
Kitzbühel, Museum Kitzbühel: *Roofs and Landscapes*, 8th May–31st October 2013.
Budapest, Szépművészeti Múzeum: *Egon Schiele and His Age. Masterpieces from the Leopold Museum Vienna*, 26th June–29th September 2013.
Paris, Musée d'Orsay: *Masculin / Masculin. L'homme nu dans l'art de 1800 à nos jours*, 23rd September 2013–20th January 2014.
London, The National Gallery: *The Portrait in Vienna 1900*, 9th October 2013–12th January 2014.

2014
Vienna, mumok: *The Present of Modernism*, 14th March 2014–15th February 2015.
Vienna, Leopold Museum: *And Yet There Was Art! Austria 1914–1918*, 9th May–15th September 2014.
Vienna, Leopold Museum: *Line and Shape. 100 Master Drawings from the Leopold Collection*, 23rd May–27th October 2014.
Zurich, Kunsthaus Zürich: *Egon Schiele – Jenny Saville*, 10th October 2014–25th January 2015.
London, The Courtauld Gallery: *Egon Schiele: The Radical Nude*, 23rd October 2014–18th January 2015.

2015
Vienna, Leopold Museum: *Wally Neuzil. Her Life with Egon Schiele*, 27th February–7th September 2015.
Vienna, Leopold Museum: *Tracey Emin – Egon Schiele. Where I want to go*, 24th April–14th September 2015.
Frankfurt on the Main, Schirn Kunsthalle: *Artists and Prophets. A Secret History of Modern Art 1872–1972*, 6th March–14th June 2015.

2016
Vienna, Leopold Museum: *Wilhelm Lehmbruck. Retrospective*, 8th April–4th July 2016.
Vienna, mumok: *Body, Psyche, and Taboo – Vienna Actionism & Early Vienna Modernism*, 4th March–16th May 2016.
Toronto, Art Gallery of Ontario: *Mystical Landscapes: Masterpieces from Monet, Van Gogh and more*, 22nd October 2016–29th January 2017.

PHOTO CREDITS

Albertina, Vienna: pp. 2, 294 (18)

Leopold Museum, Vienna/Manfred Thumberger: Front cover (detail), pp. 6 (detail), 9, 10 (detail), 16 (detail), 19, 21, 23, 25, 27, 29, 31, 33, 35, 37, 39, 41, 43, 45, 47, 49, 51, 53, 55, 57, 59, 61, 63, 65, 67, 69, 71, 73, 75, 77, 79, 81, 83, 85, 87, 89, 91, 93, 95, 97, 99, 101, 103, 105, 107, 109, 111, 113, 115, 117, 119, 121, 123, 125, 127, 129, 131, 133, 135, 137, 139, 141, 143, 145, 147, 149, 151, 153, 155, 157, 159, 161, 163, 165, 167, 169, 171, 173, 175, 177, 179, 181, 183, 185, 187, 189, 191, 193, 195, 197, 199, 201, 203, 205, 207, 209, 211, 213, 215, 217, 219, 221, 223, 225, 227, 229, 231, 233, 235, 237, 239, 241, 243, 245, 247, 249, 251, 253, 255, 257, 259, 261, 263, 265, 267, 269, 271, 273, 275, 277, 279, 281, 283, 294 (21)

Leopold Museum, Vienna/picture archives: p. 5

Leopold, Private Collection, photo Leopold Museum, Vienna/Manfred Thumberger: pp. 8, 12, 13, 284, 286 (1, 2, 3, 4), 288 (5, 6, 7), 290 (9, 10, 11, 12, 13), 292 (14, 15, 16, 17), 294 (19, 20)

Kunsthaus Zug: p. 288 (8)

FRONT COVER (DETAIL):

Egon Schiele | Portrait of Wally Neuzil | 1912 | Leopold Museum, Vienna, Inv. 453

DECORATIVE PAGES (DETAILS):

P. 2 | Johannes Fischer | Egon Schiele with the painting *Shrines in the Forest II* in the background | c. 1915 | Albertina, Vienna

P. 6 | Egon Schiele | Cardinal and Nun (Caress) | 1912 | Leopold Museum, Vienna, Inv. 455

P. 10 | Egon Schiele | Setting Sun | 1913 | Leopold Museum, Vienna, Inv. 625

P. 16 | Egon Schiele | Small Tree in Late Autumn | 1911 | Leopold Museum, Vienna, Inv. 459

P. 284 | Anton Josef Trčka | Egon Schiele | 1914

QUOTES

P. 7 | Egon Schiele | Art cannot be modern; art is eternal | 1912 | Albertina, Vienna

P. 11 | Letter card from Egon Schiele to Oskar Reichel | 31st January 1911 (postmark) | Private collection

P. 287 | Egon Schiele | Poem *A Self-Portrait* | 1910 | Leopold Museum, Vienna, Inv. 4495

PUBLISHER'S NOTES

Editor
Leopold Museum Private Foundation
Museumsplatz 1, 1070 Vienna
Tel.: +43.1.525 70 | Fax: +43.1.525 70-1500
office@leopoldmuseum.org | www.leopoldmuseum.org

Artistic Director Hans-Peter Wipplinger
Managing Director Gabriele Langer

Texts Elisabeth Leopold, Rudolf Leopold, Franz Smola, Birgit Summerauer, Hans-Peter Wipplinger
Editing Birgit Summerauer
Graphic design Nina Haider
Image rights Daniela Kumhala
Translated from the German by Agnes Vukovich, with the exception of: "A Sketch of the Era" by Christopher Barber; "An Introduction to Egon Schiele's Work", "Biography of Egon Schiele" and texts in the plates and catalogue by Rudolf Leopold by Russel Stockman.
Proof reading Agnes Vukovich
Print, binding, image editing Grasl FairPrint

First edition

Published by
Verlag der Buchhandlung Walther König
Ehrenstraße 4, 50672 Cologne

Bibliographic information published by the Deutsche Nationalbibliothek
The Deutsche Nationalbibliothek lists this publication in the Deutsche Nationalbibliografie; detailed bibliographic data is available on the Internet at http://dnb.d-nb.de.

Printed in Austria

Distribution
Germany and Europe by
Buchhandlung Walther König
Ehrenstraße 4
D – 50672 Cologne
Tel. +49 (0) 221 / 20 59 6-53
Fax +49 (0) 221 / 20 59 6-60
verlag@buchhandlung-walther-koenig.de

Outside the United States and Canada, Germany, Austria and Switzerland by
Thames & Hudson Ltd., London
www.thamesandhudson.com

Distribution in the United States and Canada by
D.A.P. / Distributed Art Publishers, Inc.
155 6th Avenue, 2nd Floor
USA – New York, NY 10013
Tel. +1 (0) 212 627 1999
Fax +1 (0) 212 627 9484
eleshowitz@dapinc.com

ISBN: 978-3-96098-081-0

Partner of the Leopold Museum

BUNDESKANZLERAMT ÖSTERREICH
KUNST UND KULTUR